Diary of a Shipping Clerk
VOLUME 3

Diary of a Shipping Clerk
VOLUME 3

David Miles-Hanschell

DIARY OF A SHIPPING CLERK ~ Volume 3
by David Miles-Hanschell

First published 2025

Copyright © David Miles-Hanschell 2025

The right of David Miles-Hanschell to be identified as
the author of this work has been asserted by him
in accordance with the Copyright, Designs
and Patents Act 1988.

All rights reserved.
No part of this book may be reproduced in any form
or by any electronic or mechanical means, including information
storage and retrieval systems, without written permission from
the author, except for the use of brief quotations in a book review.

Copyedited by Northern Editorial
Cover design by Red Axe Design
Book interior by Eleanor Abraham

Typeset in Adobe Garamond Pro and Proxima Nova

Diary of a Shipping Clerk Vol 3 Print: 978-1-7391426-4-3

Diary of a Shipping Clerk Vol 3 ebook: 978-1-7391426-5-0

Contents

Dedication	6
Introduction to Volume 3	7
Chapter Thirteen – I am Confronted with Problems of My Own Making	9
Chapter Fourteen – The Shipping Clerk Settles into New Quarters	120
Chapter Fifteen – Will There Be Some Light at the End of This Tunnel?	216
Chapter Sixteen – The Shipping Clerk Opens the Book Store	298
Appendix	397
Charity Work in Detail	401
Pro Bono Assistance	410
Administrative Help	416
Press Articles	417

Dedication

I dedicate this edition to Tom Walker, container surveyor; Allan Galt, road haulier; and Ioannis Kottorris, freight forwarder, who all made the shipments possible.

Introduction to Volume 3

The events recorded in this diary continue on from Volumes 1 and 2, and are about the 'shipping clerk' attempting to continue to salvage fit-for-purpose, surplus to requirements, educational resources from schools and colleges during the period 2009–2012. These institutions were being demolished as part of the Private Finance Initiative Scheme.

Why did I think it necessary to self-publish yet another volume if Volumes 1 and 2 give an account of the beginning and successful development of the Surplus Educational Supplies Foundation initiative from 2005 to 2009? Vast amounts of educational resources continued to be crushed and trucked to landfill at the taxpayer's expense, and this unsustainable waste continued to upset me greatly. I wanted to demonstrate that it was possible to continue to put some of these salvaged resources to further use.

The increasing difficulties that the shipping clerk encountered in pursuing the objectives of the Surplus Educational Supplies Foundation deserved some comment. In preparing this introduction I have been able to reflect on the entire project, which only came to an end in 2017.

This project was a success and a failure. The project was a team effort from start to finish. The shipping clerk lined up the key players and, with their collaboration and goodwill, the shipments were made to happen, while I took full responsibility and bore the consequences: the pressure, the financial cost of a self-funded project, coping with ill health and not having sufficient business expertise to manage a self-funded social enterprise business.

Greenock Ocean Terminal, 2012. 'Please David, don't buy any more containers.'

Chapter Thirteen
I am Confronted with Problems of My Own Making

Tuesday 22/12/2009

11:45 a.m. Home. I call Barry the executive coach, who is keen with words, and who returned my call to support my initiative. *'You have a great story to tell. What did you establish from your visit to Nicaragua?'* he asks. He does not wish to hear how I got on or read my report.

2:35 p.m. I call Peter Kilfoyle MP. *'I'm in Brussels and I'm driving. I'll take it up at ministerial level'.* He sounded supportive.

Wednesday 23/12/2009

10:10 a.m. Home. I call John Murray at WH Malcolm Transport Ltd to make arrangements to transfer educational resources from GATU4072944 into two ISO-plated 20-footers to ship to Bluefields City, Costa Caribena, Nicaragua, Central America. *'That will not be a problem,'* he said. He is always helpful. David and Johanna are holding the fort; there is a dusting of snow on the hills of the Cowal Peninsula.

First stop into the town was to wish the folk at The Bike Shed a Happy Christmas. I paid the electricity disconnection bill at Buckeridge, then over to the post office to purchase stamps for Marion's Christmas cards and then back along to Bute Naturally to purchase Surplus Educational Supplies Foundation (SESF) calendars. I then went along to Michael Swift the horologist in the Gallowgate to get another battery for my watch, and around to the Victoria Hotel to have a bowl of soup, pot of tea and chat with Emilio, who tells me he is quitting and returning to Slovakia. I then headed up the road to Rothesay Health Centre for my appointment with Dr Lewis-Smith, who prescribed an antibiotic after giving an unintelligible name to the sharp pain I experience on my left side.

It was then back down Castle Street, or is it the High Street? Back across Victoria Road to Winter Gardens Tourist Board Shop and I bought shortbread and ginger biscuits for Royal Bank of Scotland (RBS) staff, Ross & Co Accountants and the health centre, along with a potted plant. I headed home and here I am.

5:32 p.m. Home. For the last while I have been acquiring more information about the municipality of Bluefields, a city on the Republic of Nicaragua's Caribbean coast, which I had the privilege of being able to visit; the words of the Wikipedia article resonate with the little of what I saw and heard during that short visit a week ago.

Today I set off in the freezing fog on David's bike, the thick wheels of which easily negotiated the sludge, to head into Rothesay. It cleared up later, when the sun shone through. I had to post the calendar's views of the Isle of Bute and SESF flyers: Peter, Transport Manager of Russell, Coatbridge, who have one SESF 40-foot ocean freight container; John, general manager Russell Hillington, who have given me two scrap containers with pinholes; Andrew, Operations Manager, Clydeport Container Base, Greenock, where I have stored a 40-foot ocean freight container; Fraser, Accounts Manager Freightliner Ltd, Coatbridge; Jim O'Donnell, at John G Russell Transport Ltd, Coatbridge; Hugh at Clydeport Ocean Terminal, Port of Greenock; John, Logistics Manager, WH Malcolm Transport Ltd, Newhouse, where I have one 40-foot ocean freight container in temporary storage; Eric, Operations Manager Duncan Adams Transport Ltd, Grange Dock where I have three 40-foot ocean freight containers in temporary storage; and SeaFreight Agencies Lines Team, Miami, Florida, USA. I stopped off at The Bike Shed to wish David and Liam a Happy Christmas. I met John the plumber, who was telling me that his wife is seriously ill with the effects of a heart attack and had received poor attention. I was back on my bike to the post office and I met Tam Boag coming out the door, who said to me, *'Lang may yer lum reek with someone else's coal.'* He told me that he was off for a bevvy.

6:13 p.m. I am looking at a Shuttle view of Florida. *'Dad that's dinner,'* he said.

Wednesday 30/12/2009

3:15 p.m. Home. I have called Allan, Galt Transport Ltd, Broadmeadow Industrial Estate, Dumbarton and they gave me the time of day. I am to call them tomorrow. I was speaking with Gregor at Action Aid in Bristol, who tells me that he is not long back from a trip to Colombia, South America. I speak to Liz Rougvie, the journalist, who is supportive. Don't forget the pallets at Community Services, Elizafield Industrial Estate, Edinburgh.

Monday 04/01/2010

This week, contact: Food for the Poor, Florida, USA, to speak with Art Gold, Nora is the gatekeeper; and Morningside Library Edinburgh. It's now Sam Green in charge. Sandra Wright is now at the MacDonald Library Leith Walk.

Thursday 07/01/2010

3:49 p.m. Home. David, who is studying at the Nautical College in Glasgow, has just told me that he got 85% in his stability/balancing cargo exam. I haven't got this far being faint-hearted.

I woke with aching bones and needle-like pain behind my right eyeball.

Friday 15/01/2010

12:16 p.m. Home. A New Year beckons. I have not long returned from giving Amy a lift up to the Flexi Tech car park – she's on her way to collect two children to take them up to Glasgow as part of her Achievement Bute remit. I am now going to push myself through the rain up and over Canada Hill and collect my prescription and a few messages. It's the least I can do.

2:25 p.m. Home. I made it along the Mount Stuart Road, up and around and up to Eastlands Farm, down Minister's Brae and stopped off at Cowal Builders Ltd to order two pine toilet seats, collect a cup of soup from the machine, and wish Ronnie, Chris, Alan and David a Happy New Year. I went along to the pharmacy to collect my prescription and wished Peter Campbell the same, and stopped off at the Co-op for messages and wished Katie, a former pupil now employed there, a Happy New Year, then back up the road and I feel better already. I am now going to fix myself a sandwich and a mug of tea.

Tuesday 19/01/2010

Home. *'I'm not at my desk now,'* he said – I have just called John, who is at Aspire to Enterprise, Edinburgh Chamber of Commerce. I left a message. He hasn't called me back.

For Wednesday 20 January: call Helen or Alex to book a stand for the Surplus Educational Supplies Foundation at the Gathering Exhibition in Edinburgh; contact Bruce for visuals. I need contracts. A contract. Just one from COSLA would be great.

Wednesday 27/01/2010

Social Enterprise Academy, 3rd Floor, 5 Rose Street, Edinburgh. **11:30 a.m.** I have a meeting with the executive coach, Barry. *'You are a fringe player, David. You will not survive unless you become businesslike; you typically make things happen, but people like you the system spits out. Quantifying every appeal ends up saying for £10 you can do this. Whatever it is, you need a concrete story. What you are doing is too vague. Look. There are 15x schools in a desperate state in Bluefields. You get what they need from A to B. You need people to help you to become more businesslike. You need an advisory board who will help you.'* He said that he will make a pitch on my behalf at the SCVO Gathering Conference on the 19th. *'You'd better be there, well, whether you are there or not, I am going to talk about you: this is what he is doing. What can you do help him?'* he said. He is going to address his ten-minute talk to the business people in the audience. *'Is there anybody out there who will assist DMH to move up a gear. Here is someone who needs business support,'* he said. That's decent of him and I leave this coaching session encouraged.

The second meeting also went well with Sanjay, but with no tangible result. He is pleased, however, that SESF has a set of accounts and said that fundraising could begin on the basis of these figures, but I have to prepare a budget of projected costs.

I am walking into the setting sun. I bought myself a cup of peppermint tea and swapped a cheese and onion sandwich for a large bag of McVities baked mini biscuits. I am going to chill for the next few minutes as the train hurries on its way back to Home City.

Thursday 28/01/2010

11:12 a.m. Home. I was speaking to the Grenada High Commission and to Her Excellency. I am trying to determine whether or not there is still a need for educational resources in Grenadian government schools.

2:15 p.m. I was chatting to John the stove engineer, who has travelled and worked all over the African continent. He tells me that his daughter is going to Mongolia to teach English and that he has links with North and South Lanarkshire Councils, and says that he will tell his friends about what I am doing.

That is kind of him. I intend to add value to the educational resources that have been salvaged from the waste stream: trying to make it better, refurbish if necessary to increase the shelf life once they have been graded and refurbished. *'Our rubbish is their treasure.'*

I left a message for Stephen, partner at Burness Solicitors, Glasgow.

3:15 p.m. Home. I am going to walk around the block and over Canada Hill and back into Rothesay town to collect the bicycle being repaired at The Bike Shed.

5:02 p.m. Home. The bicycle is running like a charm. *'You had worn it out,'* he said to me as I was coming out of the big Co-op later with comestibles: 4 kg of sugar, brown and white, apricots, five lemons, three limes and olive oil. I am now going to cook up some supper.

Monday 01/02/2010

12:30 p.m. Home. I have just called Barry. He has received my portfolio. *'It will be very helpful,'* he said. He is giving the talk on 19 February. I have been writing letters to Helen, Facilities Manager, City of Edinburgh, Pat at Angus Council Education Department, and Colin, Director of School Services, Dumfries and Galloway Council, which I am off to post and get some fresh air.

3:13 p.m. Home. I cycled back from Rothesay in the rain.

Wednesday 03/02/2010

1:22 p.m. Home. I received a call from Anne, classroom assistant, Southwood Primary School, Macedonia, Glenrothes, Fife, to tell me that she had seen an article dated 23 December 2009 by Liz Rougvie in the *Fife Herald,* their local newspaper, and she is offering me a complete set of the Ginn Reading Scheme. I said, 'yes, please'. I gave her Graham at Community Services contact number: they might be able to collect these resources and possibly store them for me, and if not she can get back to me. 'We may have some other stuff.'

Thursday 04/02/2010

9:09 a.m. Home. Argyll College have sent me some information and an application for a place on a new business incubation project 'Enterprise Experience'. I have a dentist appointment at 10:20 a.m. Call Patrick Kilfoyle at Warrant Freight Ltd, Port of Liverpool. What is your tariff for shipping a 20-foot ocean freight container to Florida?

11:37 a.m. I am back from Harry the dentist. One crown-rescue restoration of a stump.

Okay, get to work. I was interrupted by someone knocking at the kitchen door – that was Joy, who lives in the top-floor rented flat of the small Edwardian apartment block along the road, who had come by with a gift of card. She told me that her grandad had a rose garden in Southall, that was before it became a mini upmarket suburb of Lahore.

I have to source two 20-foot ocean freight containers. I call Eldapoint Ltd: that will be £850 plus VAT. I have arranged to purchase one 20-foot for the time being. I will have to see whether WH Malcolm Transport Ltd at Fouldubs depot, Grangemouth, will allow me to deliver another container into their yard and

I AM CONFRONTED WITH PROBLEMS OF MY OWN MAKING

*Fould Dubs Container Base, Grangemouth, Saturday 06/02/2010.
Mark shifts a 40-foot ocean freight container with a forklift designed for that purpose. This Scottish Road Haulage company and their operatives gave SESF pro bono assistance with logistics and advice which contributed to the successful delivery of educational resources worldwide.*

*Fould Dubs Container Base, Grangemouth, Saturday 06/02/2010.
SESF 20' Ocean freight containers.
'You only want to move it once!'*

Friday 05/02/2010

transfer resources from the 40-foot container that is already in their depot. She tells me, '*They are just across the road from us.*'

Friday 05/02/2010

4:49 a.m. I am up, shaved and washed. All that lies before me is to bring about what is at the back of my head. Here is what beckons: cycle to Rothesay; park the bicycle; purchase return ferry ticket and on arrival at Wemyss Bay purchase a return train ticket to Glasgow Central Station; walk up to Queen Street Station and purchase a ticket to Falkirk Central Station; find my way to Eldapoint Ltd, Laurieston Road, Thornbridge, Grangemouth; pay for the 20-foot ocean freight container and see if it has been moved across to WH Malcolm Transport Ltd depot at Fouldubs up the road. I can't do it all on my own, but I am going to try. What else am I supposed to do? I have created this complex state of affairs, I cannot stop midstream and walk away from all that I have set in place! I've got a 20-foot container, which I can begin to load with good quality school furniture for schools in Bluefields City, Costa Caribena, Nicaragua, Central America. If I want to eat a bowl of porridge before I leave the house, I had better stop this scribble.

8:50 a.m. I am en route for Falkirk High Station. Pressing forward with determination. I must continue to make the most of what has been achieved since 1 July 2005.

I can make a start on the next shipment by transferring educational resources from 40-foot ocean freight container GATU4033193 into 20-foot ocean freight container TRLU2519369. I am heavy of spirit. I did not skip up Buchanan Street earlier. I know that I am not everyone's cup of tea, but I am back in the ring and in forward motion.

See Sam the digital expert's video on YouTube, SESF two 20-foot and one 40-foot containers at WH Malcolm Ltd, Fouldubs yard in Grangemouth, and the website he built for www.haitirelief. org.uk.

Saturday 06/02/2010

5:56 p.m. Home. I experience a sense of achievement and I press on regardless. I managed this morning and most of the afternoon to load a 20-foot ocean freight container TRLU2519369 with desks, chairs, tables, both wooden and metal of excellent quality, bookcases and a medical bed. Awaiting a donation of football strips and donations of stationery to fill the gaps between the furniture.

2:50 p.m. *'Next stop, Glasgow Queen Street,'* he said. I have not long been let off the bus at the foot of the steep hill which leads up to Falkirk High Station. I walked out from WH Malcolm Transport depot to the now familiar busy main road to catch a bus, which took me into the Falkirk Bus Station and back out again.

From 6 a.m. to 8 a.m. I cooled my heels at the Rothesay ferry terminal: there is only the early ferry on a Saturday morning. I walked up from Glasgow Central and took a train to Falkirk High Station and a taxi to the WH Malcolm Ltd, Grangemouth, Fouldubs depot. I checked in with security at the gate and got a warm greeting from Mark, who is the big 40-foot ocean freight container forklift driver, who told me that he had just come back from spending his honeymoon in Barbados, West Indies.

I put on my boiler suit and balked momentarily at the task that lay before me. There was nothing else for it, so I got stuck into shifting stuff out of one ocean freight container into another, with Eric Adams' words ringing in my ears: *'David, you only want to move it once.'* The 20-foot ocean freight container is now almost full and I am unable to close the doors of either of my two containers, and will have to see Eldapoint about the 20-footer. Call Eldapoint Ltd on Monday.

Saturday 06/02/2010

I did all that I was able to do and stopped at 1:45 p.m., having worked without a break. A fair day's work with no pay. I am going to swallow a swig of cold Sprite, which I have not long purchased from the kiosk at Falkirk High Station. I call John Murray, WH Malcom Transport Ltd, who is now based at their Linwood head office.

4 p.m. I was speaking to Richard in Señor Oscar's office. I am pressing hard but getting nowhere.

7:15 p.m. Home. I have washed the supper dishes and I am now back at the desk drafting a letter to Señor Oscar, Delegade de la Ministerio de Educacion de Bluefields, Costa Caribena, Meso America.

10 p.m. I send an email to Roland Malins-Smith to determine whether Bernuth Lines will still deliver my 20-foot ocean freight container to El Rama; the Nicaraguan Blue Fielders will have to demonstrate their commitment to receiving a shipment from the Surplus Educational Supplies Foundation. First, they must let me know what they have done with the one-cubic-metre pallet of 40 boxes of library books which was shipped out last year to Bluefields at my own expense before I ship TRLU2519369, assuming it will pass an ISO inspection. Eldapoint had assured me that it would.

I call Alison, the accountant at Ross & Co, and ask if they can let me have a copy of accounts for OSCR (Office of Charity Regulator) and for Companies House. See Eldapoint Ltd about the unsatisfactory condition of the two containers, which I had purchased from them on trust. I was unable to close the doors of either of the two containers. I trusted their word and I am disappointed. *Caveat emptor.*

Monday 08/02/2010

9:30 a.m. Home. I call John at WH Malcolm Transport Ltd HQ, Linwood, to let him know that the two containers can be moved. I told him that the doors will not shut properly and he said, *'Nae bother, we'll use a forklift to shut the doors.'*

11:15 a.m. It is a beautiful day of spring sunshine. I call the Nicaraguan consulate and write a letter to Linda, Principal of Forth Valley College of Further Education, Grangemouth Road, Falkirk. Posted 8 February.

Tuesday 09/02/2010

Home. Beautiful morning. Bright sunshine. Back to winter cold. No complaints about the weather. I call Eldapoint Ltd to tell them that the doors of the two containers that I bought from them won't shut properly and a forklift had to be used to close the doors.

I left a message for Alison the Accountant at Ross & Co regarding the letter about Companies Act.

12:22 p.m. I am back from Rothesay town. I paid Phil of Bute Naturally for the SESF flyers. I paid Karen at Print Point and bought a *Herald* and four pies, bird nuts and bird seed.

'Live as if you will die tomorrow. Learn as if you, will live forever.' Mahatma Ghandi.

Wednesday 10/02/2010

12:48 p.m. *'This train is for Glasgow,'* she said. I have just left Haymarket railway station. I got the bus earlier from Edinburgh Airport, where I had been attending a Sandler Seminar – '10 Reasons Why Sales People Fail.' Iain and Joan, whose firm runs these seminars, let me take away the five remaining croissants from the break for coffee. *'They will just be thrown out,'* she said.

It was, I thought, a worthwhile two-hour session, from someone who knows what he is talking about: 'Selling as a Profession'. Are we not all engaged in selling of one kind or another? What have you learned Davey Boy? To talk less, ask questions and listen! Are we wasting each other's precious time? At the close of the session, I asked the seminar leader if I could make a short pitch about the SESF initiative. He said fine. I gave my spiel. I gobbed off, which afterwards led only one of the participants, rather annoyed at my effrontery, to say, *'You have hijacked the meeting'.* I did not win any friends: there I go, being presumptuous – why should anyone be interested in what I have to say or be wholeheartedly committed to attempting to further the objectives of a circular economy? So much for the sales talk.

Thursday 11/02/2010

10:30 a.m. Home. I called Eldapoint Ltd, Grangemouth. *Could they please repair the doors on my/SESF 20-foot containers TRLU2519369 and GATU4033193, which were supposed to be in seaworthy condition?* I asked politely. I am not happy with what I have bought. I should have asked Tom Walker, the container surveyor, to check them over prior to purchase. It is always the wisdom of hindsight: *act in haste, David and you will repent at leisure.* It is now too late, and all I can do is complain and hope Eldapoint Ltd will make them good for ISO inspection; so much for 'one-way shippers'.

The dealers and sellers have me over a barrel unless I take their word.

10:52 a.m. I have left a message for Sam, the unofficial High Commissioner at the Grenada High Commission. I have had no response from the Government of Grenada Ministry of Education and Human Development. Do I send more educational resources, or has the time come for me now to draw the line? I am going to call Grenada, West Indies.

Raymond, President Parent-Teacher Association, St Paul's Government School, St Paul's, St George's, Grenada. *'How are you, man?'* I ask. *'I quiet, man,'* replies Raymond. I ask him if Principal Peterkin, could she, or he, send me some photographs or an assessment of the SESF 40-foot ocean freight shipment of educational resources that I had delivered to their school in 2007; I never heard from them again.

Call Business on Board. SCVO seminar, 'Profit vs Loss. Can you afford to transform someone's bottom line?': location Edinburgh, February 19 meeting, at which executive coach Barry says he will say a few words on behalf of the Surplus Educational Supplies Foundation Scottish (Registered Charity SCO39331 and Company registered in Scotland No. 337348).

Friday 12/02/2010

11:30 a.m. Home. It is a beautiful day of spring sunshine. I am going to get on my bicycle and head into the little town of Rothesay to collect my suit from the dry cleaners and launderette and get some messages. I am not feeling too great. I call the Inverclyde Council movers and shakers: Provost McCormick; Tom Read; Andrew Gerrard; Councillor Stephen McCabe. Write to Señor Oscar, Delegate of the Ministry of Education, Bluefields, Nicaragua.

Friday 19/02/2010

11 p.m. Home. It has been a long day. I attended the SCVO Gathering EEIC in Edinburgh. It was a day for me of enabling grace and journeying mercies.

Thursday 25/02/2010

2:30 p.m. Home. I received a call from Elspeth to tell me that they have 17 boxes of educational resources stored in a bedroom, collected from school closures in the Borders. Was I interested? Yes please. I will make arrangements to collect as soon as possible. How? Problem to solve. (*I did not call her again until 3 March.*)

SEAU4272551, GATU4033193, TRIU5079422 at Duncan Adams Transport Ltd, Grange Dock depot; TRLU2519369 at WH Malcolm Transport Ltd, Fouldubs, Grangemouth; INBU4923875 Galt Transport Ltd, Broadmeadow Industrial Estate, Dumbarton; GATU4072944 and OCLU1354487 are at Babcock, Rosyth Business Park; MSKU6311690 Carson Transport Ltd, Cumbernauld.

5:01 p.m. Marion home from school. David and Johanna are studying. It has been a day of wet, cold, snowy and sleety weather. Tomorrow I am heading up to Glasgow for an appointment with Andrew, one of the 'Syndicate' who own Point Faulds Park in Gourock at the Millennium Hotel, George's Square. I am raising my hopes; I am thinking of selling on my seven ocean freight containers plus contents and release some funds, and concentrate on shipping the one 20-foot ocean freighter to the schools in El Bluff, Costa Caribena. I am awaiting word from the Nicaraguan Ministry of Education regarding my shipment of 40 boxes, one cubic metre, of library books which were sent out in September 2009. What is the hold up? I am not feeling 100%. I will just have to keep plodding forward.

Friday 26/02/2010

10:45 a.m. Millennium Hotel Glasgow. I am here to meet with Andrew of Stony, Stratford. I have two questions for him:
1. What is the likely fee for clearing the Foulds Point premises?

2. Debit side, what are the likely costs of collecting surplus-to-requirements educational resources from schools and transportation?

Range of figures will vary. Broad range of figures, haulage fee? Contact Eric for costs of collection. I am well and truly out of my depth.

11:50 a.m. Glasgow Central Station, Platform 14. I just made the Wemyss Bay train. The meeting went well; Ray, one of the Gourock warehouse owners, is thorough and astute. He wanted the numbers from me for their business plan.

He said he would contact my contacts in the Scottish road haulage industry to find out what their tariff would be to collect and deliver containers of salvaged educational resources to their Gourock warehouse. He said he would try and get information from English local education authorities about their disposal costs. He wanted to hear how the Surplus Educational Supplies Foundation had evolved and said he was now glad that he had met me and knows my story, contrary to what he had learned from Lora about me. He will now report back to his colleagues and see whether the numbers add up. He emphasised the fact that the owners of Faulds Point warehouse in Gourock will need to convince their bankers that they and SESF have a credible business plan, and in order to put this plan together they and SESF will have to see if councils across Scotland will pay to remove surplus educational resources, minus costs of collection, labour, transport, fuel and storage. He looks like the actor who plays the part of Mr Bean, he is softly spoken, a process thinker. I gave him transport details and costs.

3:26 p.m. Home. I wrote to Andrew and cycled back into the town to post the letter same-day recorded delivery; the ball is back in their court. I received an email from Simon, estates manager Erskine Stewart's Melville Schools, offering SESF surplus educational supplies and school furniture, which will become available in the summer. I have nowhere to put that donation but I shall cross that bridge when I come to it.

5:30 p.m. I received a call from Bill, who used to be the Port and Property Manager at the former Rosyth Naval Dockyard, now Babcock Ltd. They have a big warehouse available; the current general manager, Alan, will be expecting my call next week. All thanks for this lead must go to Paul Fisher who joined these dots to make a desired result happen; this positive development has cheered me up no end.

Monday 01/03/2010

10:45 a.m. I have spoken to Alan, who will see me on Wednesday. I am to meet him at the Babcock Marine main gate to the dockyard, Rosyth Business Park at 11 a.m.

2:53 p.m. Home. It is a beautiful sunlight-filled day. I set off early to walk up Ardencraig Road and over Canada Hill round past the golf course. The 'tops' of the Isle of Arran were covered with snow. I walk down the Minister's Brae past the cheery snowdrops, which are now in full bloom growing beside the drive way up to what was once the minister's manse.

I crossed the High Street into Cowal Builders to pay a bill. I collected some coppers, chatted with Brian at the desk and further down the High Street I stepped into the Musicker for a coffee, bought a CD of Woody Guthrie and listened to it. I walked back up Castle Street and down Bishop Street and into the Co-op for cereal, vegetable stir-fry mixture, washing-up liquid and a *Scotsman. I hoofed it along the corniche and home.*

3:01 p.m. I call Glasgow Caledonian University, Glasgow Environmental Centre to speak to John. '*He doesnae work here* *anymore,'* she said. I had seen an article about his work in relation to the disposal of waste in *The Herald* newspaper. I am given his telephone number and give him a call, and left a message.

3:21 p.m. I call Patrick at Warrant Freight Ltd, Port of Liverpool, who tells me that he has given the strips he promised to SESF to Oxfam.

Tuesday 02/03/2010

Midday Home. I have just received a call from Dorothy, the Argyll and Bute Library Services Children's Librarian, offering SESF two boxes of children's books. Yes, please. She will drop them off at the boatyard and I will collect them on Thursday.

Wednesday 03/03/2010

8:35 a.m. I got a taxi from Central Station to Buchanan Street Bus Station, Glasgow. I have just boarded the bus for St Andrews and I am heading for Dunfermline, and from there another bus to Rosyth. On the way up the taxi driver asked me, *'Is that you going to work?'* I am wearing my fluorescent high-viz jacket, which gives me a certain superficial credibility among the real workers. I tell him where I am going and why. He wishes me good luck.

A smoky sun is shining through wispy grey cloud. I am sitting above the choked traffic on Cathedral Street. On the way over from Rothesay, on the MV Bute, I met Lennie, who kindly bought me a hot chocolate and told me that he was off to Perth to attend a board meeting. Here I am once again. Yes, I am off to work, under my own steam and direction. I have an appointment at 11 a.m. with Alan, general manager of Port and Property Services, Rosyth Naval Dockyard.

I am hoping that this firm will loan me some space in which to store, inventory sort, refurbish and prepare educational resources that I am able to salvage from the waste stream, and somewhere nearby to park SESF containers temporarily and later load my containers for shipment. I went out this morning forgetting to put on my belt, which I cannot recall ever having done before. I am now a bit loose round the waste. *'Davie, waurs yur troosers?'* I am on the road again, as always journeying hopefully.

9:30 a.m. I am now on a No. 18 bus in Dunfermline bus station, up from Marks & Spencer, heading over the hill to Rosyth Dockyard.

12:09 p.m. Alan has not long dropped me off at the bus station. Earlier, he took me on a brief tour of the yard and showed me where I could store my containers. He will let me know in due course when. He would like to see if Babcock International will sponsor the work of the Surplus Educational Supplies Foundation. He took me into his office and asked someone at reception to bring me a coffee.

    I am now sitting in the bus for Edinburgh and we are about to cross the Firth of Forth Bridge, which I walked across as dawn was breaking in early July 1974 on my way to Blairgowrie to pick berries. I only got as far, later that day, as Gairneybridge, a village outside the town of Kinross, where I found work at Classlochie Farm beside Loch Leven for the next two months, picking strawberries, raspberries and lifting potatoes, supervising families of pickers from Dundee, and other chores. I would be ever grateful to farmer Donald McLaren and his hospitable family, who gave me temporary employment, a place to lodge in an empty bothy, and enabled me, a wandering visitor (who had arrived at Prestwick on 18 May 1973 with an Air Canada return ticket from Halifax, Nova Scotia, Canada), with a six-month visitor visa and afforded me the opportunity to apply to the Moray House College of Education in Edinburgh for a course in postgraduate primary education. I recall the day, 30 July 1974, when the McLaren family invited me into their kitchen to celebrate my birthday with a freshly baked cake. I continue to travel as I did then, one step and one day at a time.

1:10 p.m. I arrived in Saint Andrew Bus Station and the bus is leaving for Glasgow. I am about to enjoy a wee snack, a late breakfast of a bottle of Tropicora multivitamin squash, a cheese and onion roll and a packet of McCoy's cheddar cheese and onion crisps; the sun continues to shine through an overcast sky.

I am glad I went to the trouble to make the arrangements and keep this appointment; personal effort is the leitmotif of this initiative from the beginning. I left my banner, folder and calling card with the general manager, who was supportive from the outset of this initiative. (See *The Herald* article by journalist Simon Bain. *The Herald Business,* Monday, 13 July 2009, 'Call for surplus school supplies to be donated. Waste not: David Hanschell wants his school materials scheme to get more official recognition'.)

The sun is breaking through as the bus moves slowly down Princes Street.

2:45 p.m. I am on the train for Wemyss Bay.

4:30 p.m. On the ferry MV *Argyle*, returning to Rothesay.

5:15 p.m. Home. Marion has called to tell me that Mum has fallen and broken a bone in her leg, and is now in the Royal Alexandra Hospital in Paisley. Amy and herself will be staying in Kilbarchan; there is always someone for whom things are going right and someone for whom things have gone completely wrong.

Thursday 04/03/2010

11:34 a.m. Home. The sun is shining brightly through the windows at the end of the corridor. I am sitting here at a desk and

Saturday 06/03/2010

I would rather be out of doors. I am preparing what I am going to say to a group of Tom and Betty Walker's friends tomorrow evening in Chryston. The phone goes. It is the Argyll and Bute Council Library Services librarian going to drop off library books at SESF depot at the boatyard.

1:20 p.m. I am heading out to Port Bannatyne on the bike to put the boxes of library books into the Caribbean Relief Depot.

3:42 p.m. It is Phil, a consultant, of Virtual Jigsaw, representing the Gourock Point Faulds Syndicate, who said *'We want to help you make the lease work for SESF.'* I know that, but my occupancy, however desirable, is still going to cost me money.

Saturday 06/03/2010

11:am MV Argyle is moving smoothly across the Firth of Clyde. I am on my way home to Rothesay. I have not long scoffed a sausage roll and downed a hot chocolate. The sun is shining brightly on the almost, flat calm water. Tom Walker dropped me off at Central Station. I then had to run as fast as I could to get to Platform 15 to board the train for Wemyss Bay. I was not much out of puff.

Yesterday afternoon I arrived in Chryston, Muirhead by bus from Buchanan Street Bus Station, passing through Stepps, where I lodged with John and Nan when I taught at Sunnyside Primary School, Craigend in 1975 to 1982. Betty gave me a bowl of chicken soup on my arrival and later her neighbours Iain, a retired assistant head teacher, and his wife Christine came by and took us along to the 17th Chryston Girl Guides Hut, where I was to give my talk. I said to myself more than once on the way over, *'all you have to do is stand up, speak up, sit down and shut up'*. I answered questions from the audience and that was it.

This morning the Walkers collected their son Peter from his

flat and drove on to Anderston Church of Scotland in Anderston, where Betty is one of the workers. Tom comes from the Gorbals. He is a time-served engineer and trained at Harland & Wolff. He now inspects whisky tanks and ocean freight containers, and I count him a friend; they are the salt of the earth.

5:49 p.m. Home. I had a brief chat with Phil, consultant for the Point Faulds Park Syndicate, Gourock, who is going to contact me next week. I have questions for them: what are the rates, insurance, holding costs, the licence to occupy? I knew all along that we were wasting each other's time.

Tuesday 09/03/2010

11:05 a.m. Home. I have called Derek, Port Manager, Forth Ports, Port of Grangemouth, who is in a meeting. I left messages also for the Point Faulds Syndicate and their consultant. I am now going to make some toast and coffee and sit in the sun.

1:09 p.m. I called Sam at Shanks Waste Management, who is now based in the Lake District. He said he would make some calls on my behalf regarding storage space. I called Derek again, who is still in a meeting. I am going to go for a walk up and over Canada Hill.

12:29 p.m. I was speaking with Martin the facilities manager at Balfron High School, who has told me that they have 50 art tables, which can be reassembled. I sent an email to Sanjay regarding this offer.

12:46 p.m. I called Eldapoint Ltd who can let me have, gratis, a 20-foot and 40-foot for storage. I called Tom Walker to see if he would check the two 'boxes' at WH Malcolm Transport Ltd, Fouldubs depot in Grangemouth.

Friday 12/03/2010

1:15 p.m. I am still here, going to make one more phone call.

I call the manager of the Mary's Meals charity and speak to Marie, who tells me to call their warehouse and speak to the warehouse manager, Charlotte. *'We are downsizing and we are very sorry we can't help you,'* she said.

Thursday 11/03/2010

9:57 a.m. Home. I called Russell Kincaid of Sweeney Kincaid Auctioneers in Hillington, while my cereal grew cold this grey morning, and later an email.

It is almost noon; there is a small patch of blue sky appearing above my head so I am going to push myself and my bicycle round the Isle of Bute.

5:45 p.m. I called Allan Galt about storage and he told me that *'derated'* transport warehouses can't be used. He also tells me that they do deliver to Babcock Marine at Rosyth. I spoke with Simon of the charity Education for All, based in Corby: they are the corporate social responsibility wing of the educational furnishing firm Thorpe Kilworth. He said he would send me an email next month as he is away travelling and expressed an interest in the work being done by the Surplus Educational Supplies Foundation, and said that Phil, the Point Faulds Syndicate consultant, was around to see him, checking on my bona fides.

Friday 12/03/2010

1:53 p.m. I am calling Derek, Port Manager, Forth Ports Plc, to confirm their generous offer to allow SESF to park its containers at the dockside prior to shipment, waiving all handling charges. What's the situation regarding the containers:
1. MSKU6311690 40-foot loaded with library shelving. Contact Fraser, Freightliner Ltd, Coatbridge.

2. OCLU1354487 is partially loaded 40-foot (see diary note for contents). Contact Peter, Russell, Coatbridge. The two scrap 40-foots at Hillington – contact John are they still at the depot?
3. Forty-foot ocean freight containers, SEAU4272551, TRIU5079422, GATU40729442 are loaded with educational resources. Contact Eric, Duncan Adams Transport Ltd, Grange Dock.
4. Forty-foot GATU4072944 contents? (see diary notes). Contact Allan, Galt Transport Ltd, Dumbarton. Make arrangements for them to move the container to Babcock Marine, Rosyth Business Park. I call Nina, Estates Manager, Waterfront Edinburgh Ltd, West Shore Business Centre.

I wish to express my appreciation for that contact given to me by Isabel at Lofthus Signs Ltd, who had suggested I call Nina about storage, which led later to my occupancy pro bono of Unit 12, West Shore Business Centre, Granton between 2010 and 2017.

I have arranged a meeting with Waterfront Edinburgh Ltd on Monday, 16 March at 11 a.m. at the West Business Centre, Granton. I called Louise at Knight Swanson, Freight Forwarders, Grangemouth. I speak to Gary. I enquire about the Mediterranean Shipping Company rates, he said, '*We don't do charity*'. I did not expect any.

2:28 p.m. I am calling round the town; hot-desking dude. I am working the phone. '*I'm in a meeting. I didn't know my mobile was switched on. I'm delighted with that, thanks for the call,*' said Barry, who I had told that SESF had at long last sourced a storage facility.

I call and speak briefly to the current High Commissioner for Grenada '*They are not obligated to you in any way to acknowledge your shipments of educational resources,*' she said. True, but a little acknowledgement from the government of Grenada for all that we have done in Scotland for the Isle of Spices in their time of need post Hurricane Ivan 2004 would be appreciated.

Friday 12/03/2010

Rothesay Library. Shelving and boxes of books.
Too good to crush and dump into landfill, these resources went to the National Education Trust, Jamaica W.I. in 2014; kudos to the supportive librarians.

I am not looking for a medal or recognition at all, what I would like is a commitment from your Government of Grenada, Petit Martinique and Carriacou to facilitate the objectives of the Surplus Educational Supplies Foundation – something I have sought from your government.

4:27 p.m. Calling ZIM Port of Liverpool enquiring: what is the tariff ex Grangemouth, Southampton to Miami and Bluefields? Carriage? Freight? I was speaking to Birke now at ACL Atlantic Container Lines, Port of Liverpool. *'Can I just stop you there,'* she said. *'Sure, go ahead,'* I said. I must not forget that there are two pallets of library books sitting over at Community Services on Newhaven Road.

4:58 p.m. Call Eric about the possibility of exchanging two 20-foot ocean freight containers for one forty-foot ocean freight container *'Doesnae work that way, a 20-footer is almost as much as a 40-footer,'* he said. It's back to the drawing board.

Saturday 13/03/2010

9:01 a.m. Home. That was Ivor, my learned friend from the Isle of Bute Museum, who has just called to tell me that he will meet me at the Russell Street Church Hall in Rothesay town, where he has a donation of Church of Scotland Women's Guild crockery that is going into a skip and that I should bring some boxes with me. *'Marion, may I borrow your car?'*

Monday 15/03/2010

3:49 p.m. Home. I have spoken to Alan the general manager of Babcock Marine Rosyth, who has just told me that the Surplus Educational Supplies Foundation can park its containers at the Rosyth Business Park for free – and that they will inventory contents and smarten up the exteriors with a lick of paint and repair 'pinholes'. What can I say except thank you. *'What my team and I discussed is a goer,'* he said.

4:02 p.m. I called Derek, Port Manager Forth Ports Plc, Port of Grangemouth, who told me that they will handle the SESF containers prior to loading on the vessel free of charge. And they can stay at Duncan Adams Transport Ltd Grange Dock depot up the road until ready to be shipped. That is another big step forward. *The costs of haulage and storage have been kept to a minimum, thanks to the pro bono help of these two major corporates.*

I am to meet Ivor at 6:30 p.m. Russel Street Hall to collect the remaining donation of crockery – all of the crockery was heading for the skip, which was on the street outside the hall door.

Mary and her husband Iain lent a hand and then they drove me out to the boatyard at Port Bannatyne. Fortunately the gates were open and we shifted the boxes of good quality crockery and kitchen utensils into the Caribbean Hurricane Relief Depot, which has been inside the main gate since April 2005. I pray that someday some where people will appreciate this crockery and kitchen utensils. David is home and having his supper in front of the telly and Johanna is attending an interview at the Rotary meeting at the Kingarth Hotel. Marion and Amy are visiting Mum who is in hospital. We are holding the fort. I have been low all day. No energy. It is cold and overcast and I have barely seen the sun; I am on with my skates for Edinburgh tomorrow.

(This marvellous one-off collection of Church of Scotland kitchenware and crockery, which went after seven years in storage in the final shipment from Surplus Educational Supplies Foundation, Unit 12 in Granton, Edinburgh, was shipped to Ecole Solidarite Dame Marie, South West Region, Republic of Haiti on 14 April 2017.)

I AM CONFRONTED WITH PROBLEMS OF MY OWN MAKING

Tuesday 16/03/2010

6:46 a.m. The engines of the ferry MV *Bute* are vibrating and humming through the hull. I am perched on this swivel stool at the Coffee Cabin Café on my way to Edinburgh. It doesn't seem that long ago that I was still half-awake lying in bed. I am now back in gear. It is a mild spring morning. The blackbirds were singing away as I cycled into Rothesay. I am giving this project another try after the wonderful encouragement I have received recently from Forth Ports, Babcock International, and the unequivocal support from Peel Ports at Clydeport Ocean Terminal.

1:18 p.m. The present moment, Saint Andrew Bus Station, Edinburgh. I have just got on the Glasgow bus. I purchased, two minutes ago, some luncheon purvey prior to its departure. This morning I got the No. 16 Silverknowes to Princes Street bus back from Granton Square, West Harbour Road.

What's new? Waterfront Edinburgh Ltd are going to let me have Unit 12, West Shore Trading Estate, Granton. I met Alasdair, the security and site manager, and his colleague Gumon, an ex-Gurkha from Nepal, at 10:45 a.m. on site. They opened up Unit 12 for me. I looked at the premises: there is no electricity, water or toilet, there is an unfinished rubble floor with a large pool of water, which I can cover with pallets; the water presumably has come from a leak in the roof. I recoiled at first, but I can't be too choosy. I said that the Surplus Educational Supplies Foundation would be glad to take occupancy, provided that given its unsatisfactory condition the premises were rent-free. Alasdair, there and then, got on his mobile phone to Anna at Waterfront Edinburgh Ltd. The landlord told him to tell me to come up to Granton House on the way up. I passed the sites of demolition and the new high flats. I walked up and waited at the door, and then the Stamper Land Fruit delivery driver came by and got me access to the headquarters, where I was met by David and Anna who made me a coffee and I signed the lease. I am heading home with a set of new keys. I feel really good.

2:30 p.m. I am now on the train for Wemyss Bay. I had walked past the concert hall, and retraced my steps back up to the Buchanan Street Bus Station to ask staff at the lost property office if my spectacles had been handed in from the bus that had taken me over to Edinburgh this morning. No joy! I win some and I lose some. I'm blind for reading without them.

7:40 p.m. Home. It has been a long day and there is still more to do.

I have returned from the Russell Street Church of Scotland Hall where my friend, who I had met at the Ardbeg Baptist Church some months ago, met me at 6:10 p.m. to assist me in collecting the remaining donation of crockery

10:25 p.m. Mary and her husband, Iain, have come here to deliver some more boxes salvaged from the Russell Street Hall. The unmerited kindness that I have received from so many of you here on this island of Bute and over on the mainland, without it, this initiative would have folded long ago.

Thursday 18/03/2010

3:11 p.m. Home. Calling Allan, Galt Transport Ltd, Dumbarton, to see if they could lift a 40-foot ocean freight container to Rosyth. I spoke to Simon. *'No problem,'* he said. They will shift the box from Clydeport Ocean Terminal Container Base in Port of Greenock to Rosyth. I then called Hugh at Clydeport to let him know GATU4072944 is to be picked up. I send Nina an email about the possibility of flooring Unit 12 with cement.

3:57 p.m. I spoke to Alasdair, the head of security and estates supervisor at Waterfront Edinburgh Ltd. I discussed with him whether it was possible to have a floor laid in the unit and he said he would have to clear it with the engineer; the roof leaks and a large pool of water collects at the far end of the unit. I am now undecided as to whether I really want to move over there. Is it more trouble than it is worth? But this is the best offer so far.

Tuesday 23/03/2010

6:40 p.m. Home. I spent the morning at Starbucks Café, Glasgow Airport with Phil of Virtual Jigsaw discussing his SESF proposal for the FPDS Syndicate. He arrived at 8:55 a.m. on flight 785 easyJet from Gatwick. I stressed the downside. I can spend no more money. Whatever the outcome, it has to be a viable risk, yes, but the onus of that risk has to be on the landlords and not me; the risk of occupancy falls on my shoulders. They are keen to see muggins carry the can. It was a positive and constructive meeting up to a point. I had the feeling, a vibration, that their representative would have me agree to their terms. Well, no way. Send an email to the general manager of Port and Property Services, Babcock International Group Marine Division to inform him of the transfer of containers from Clydeport and Coatbridge to Rosyth Industrial Park.

6:45 p.m. Davina called with an offer of knitting machines, which I gratefully accepted and said I would collect them as soon as possible.

Thursday 25/03/2010

8:40 p.m. Home. I am in better heart than yesterday. I was way down in the hole and at least I am out of it, thanks to a brief word from Alan, general manager, Port and Property Services, Marine Division, Babcock International Group, Rosyth Business

Park, who told me that they will indeed accommodate a couple of Surplus Educational Supplies Foundation ocean freight containers, inventory the contents and refurbish if necessary – this is a fantastic offer! As you can imagine reader, this news has cheered me up no end. Thanks must go also to Paul Fisher, who put me in touch with Bill, the former general manager at Rosyth, who made the final connection to Alan.

Friday 26/03/2010

3:57 p.m. Home with Marion. Raindrops splattering the skylight window all day yesterday and today. I spoke to Kim at First Port about the upgrade of the SESF website. I called Knight Watson Ltd, Grangemouth, and spoke to the principal, Louise.

Monday 05/04/2010

10:48 a.m. Home. It is a wet morning. Marion and I saw David Alexander off at Glasgow Airport in the early part of yesterday morning. He was en route for Houston via Schiphol, Amsterdam, where he is joining his next ship, the *Saxonia Express,* as part of his course at Glasgow Nautical College.

Tuesday 06/04/2010

8:32 a.m. Home. It is raining and there is a strong wind blowing up the Firth of Clyde. Marion and Johanna have left for the mainland to attend a hospital appointment and shopping. Later they will be visiting Mum who is in the Royal Alexandra Hospital.

I am here, and Amy is here on the island: she is working today for Achievement Bute. David Alexander, apprentice watch officer, has signed on the *Saxonia Express*, out of Houston, Texas.

5 p.m. It is still wet and grey. I have been at the computer and working the telephone all day; it is not for want of trying and sustained effort that I have made such slow progress with my initiative. I have been attempting to get some idea from the local authorities across Scotland about the amount and kind of surplus-to-requirements educational resources that are likely to become available as a result of replacement, the number of school closures, information about the Private Finance Scheme and the number of new schools and colleges being built. See the 16 emails I sent recently to the chief executives of the Scottish local authorities requesting this information. I have another 20 to send, which I will try and contact tomorrow. I am unable to do anything else at the moment.

Wednesday 07/04/2010

10:28 a.m. Home. It is just Amy, the SESF company secretary, and me holding the fort. I am going to give it another ago. I will try to get the numbers from the 32 Scottish local authorities: the number of school buildings that have been demolished, or are going to be demolished or refurbished, and new schools and colleges contracted out to be built. They are reluctant to divulge this information. I wonder if the amount of this profligate wastage is of any concern to anyone except this blagging idjit? Eric Adams, when asked by Louise Swanson who I was replied, '*He's a nutter from the West Coast.*'

I will go for a stroll up and over Canada Hill later.

2:05 p.m. I have just returned from my walk. The sun is shining, it's back to spring. Amy is fixing us some lunch and I am listening to Radio 4.

5:30 p.m. It is time to call it a day. Knock off. Clock off. I sent 17 emails to the remaining Scottish local authorities and made countless telephone calls today.

Thursday 08/04/2010

11:30 a.m. Home. I received a call from Norman at First Port offering to contact a housing association in Edinburgh, which is a social enterprise, to see if they would like to collaborate with the Surplus Educational Supplies Foundation. He continues to give me all these leads, but they lead nowhere, the most recent being the massive warehouse in Gourock. His leads just serve to raise my expectations and they take me further and further out of my depth.

I received an email from Tommy, environmental health officer, North Lanarkshire Council, Coatbridge. I am going to call Fettes School. I have been told they have recently built a new primary school wing and may have fit-for-purpose, surplus to their requirements, educational resources.

12:49 p.m. I am going to wash the dishes. It is still wet, windy and grey outside. I must keep struggling and moving forward, if for no other reason than to keep faith with all those individuals and their organisations that have helped me get this far and are willing to continue to support the work of the Surplus Educational Supplies Foundation.

Friday 09/04/2010

11:25 a.m. Home. It is dry but hazy and overcast. The sunshine is beginning to break through slowly and so does my spirit break free; there are now sunbeams at the end of the corridor. The house is quiet. Johanna is studying in David's room. Amy and Marion have driven into the town to collect Vera, Elaine and her colleagues from her school. I am in the doldrums. In the dumps again. I will be hanging around to welcome them and then I will bicycle out to the Caribbean Hurricane Relief Depot, Port Bannatyne, to box the rest of the crockery, cutlery and kitchen utensil donation, to either sell and shift it somewhere suitable on the mainland, or better still, ship to a deserving beneficiary. These still fit-for-purpose kitchen resources were to form part of a shipment to Ecole Solidarite, Dame Marie, South West Region, Republic of Haiti post Hurricane Matthew in 2017.

Monday 12/04/2010

8:30 a.m. Home. I receive this message from Simon at Galt Transport Ltd, Broadmeadow Industrial Estate, Dumbarton, which has encouraged me greatly: *'I have spoken to both ends and its fine with them. I'll let them know when they can pick up your containers; everything is fine, don't worry,'* said Simon. I am going to call Carson Transport Ltd, Cumbernauld.

7:15 p.m. Home. Johanna and I are holding the fort. It has been a beautiful day of sunshine and clear blue skies. I boxed crockery at the Caribbean Hurricane Relief Depot, Port Bannatyne, North Bute; Martin was as good as his word, and came over this morning with a cheque for £700. It was not what I had paid for the 20-foot Gray Adams reefer nearly five years ago, but considering that Martin has never invoiced me for keeping the storage facility in his boatyard all that time, plus all the help and encouragement he, John and many others gave to me, it was far more than I had a right to expect. I shall miss working from it and the many good people I met over the past five years in Port Bannatyne. It has been a while now, and the time has come to ship out from the comfort zone of the port – and the painful memories of 1992–2008, for me, that lay under the surface of Kames Bay: the time has come for me to leave it all well and truly behind me.

    I hope to move the good stuff out of the Caribbean Hurricane Relief Depot by next week and have it transported across the Central Belt of Scotland to Unit 12, West Shore Business Centre, Granton. I have an appointment with Nina the estates manager,

Waterfront Edinburgh Ltd, on 14 April to confirm arrangements. The unit is not ideal, nor the location, but I will do my utmost to make the most of this generous offer, initially rent-free for six months.

(I was to be there for the next seven years, rent and rates free, and terminated my lease in April 2017.)

Tuesday 13/04/2010

11:31 a.m. Home. Called TNT transport. I wish to speak to their transport manager. I am asking a favour, begging as usual. Called DFID in East Kilbride, sent email.

1:44 p.m. Breakthrough contact Special Services TNT and spoke to Holly.

Wednesday 14/04/2010

6:42 a.m. I have boarded the bus for Edinburgh at Buchanan Street Bus Station. I left Marion, Amy and Johanna asleep in Kilbarchan, Renfrewshire. I got the 6:15 a.m. in to Glasgow. I am getting the good out of my bus pass. The sky is beginning to brighten up. I have an appointment with the estates manager of Waterfront Estates Ltd. I am now on another stage of the journey which began when I heard of the devastation wrought on the island of Grenada in the West Indies by Hurricane Ivan in 2004 and decided I would do something to help. I am going to confirm my occupancy of Unit 12, West Shore Business Centre, Granton.

I can only keep on trying.

9:55 a.m. I got a taxi from George Street to here, Madelvic House, Park Avenue, Granton.

10:15 a.m. I am on the top deck of a No. 16 bus.

Gumon, Waterfront Ltd security, ex-Gurkha, *'I am from Nepal,'* he told me. He has not long dropped me off at the bus stop. Nina made me a coffee and Gumon came and collected me and took me along to Unit 12. I opened up the unit. I salvaged some pallets that Mitie Ltd, in a unit across the car park, said I could have. The unit is not as bad as I thought, but for the huge puddle of water at the far end. It will have to do the Surplus Educational Supplies Foundation for the time being.

I am now on my way over to Lofthus Signs Ltd, Corn Exchange. I get off at Princes Street and then get a No. 44 bus. The bus is now moving along Star Bank Road;. I am in the village of Newhaven where just up the road, in one of my many previous lives, spring of 1975, I did my final teaching practice at Victoria Primary School. The Firth of Forth is on my left as I sit here on the top deck of the bus, the master of all I survey.

10:30 a.m. I am now riding on the top deck of another Edinburgh bus, having alighted a few moments ago. *'If I remember, I'll tell you when to get off,'* said the helpful driver. I am on my way to the Corn Exchange to visit Lofthus Signs Ltd, to thank Gillian and Isabel and company who suggested I contact Waterfront Edinburgh Ltd.

12:10 p.m. I am now on another bus from Slateford Corn Exchange bound for the city. Lofthus Signs Ltd have offered to do the Unit 12 Surplus Educational Supplies Foundation signage pro bono at the entrance to West Shore Business Centre. I am heading back to Haymarket Station and back to Glasgow.

12:30 p.m. I am waiting in the queue to purchase a ticket to Glasgow Queen Street. I saw there was no train, so I hurried back out onto the narrow busy St John's Road out of Auld Reekie and I am now on the bus for Glasgow. I have learned to change plans, directions and agendas quickly when necessary. I have accomplished today what I visualised to achieve, by faith, in the small hours of this morning from my bed on the Isle of Bute. I have reconnected with Waterfront Edinburgh Ltd and Unit 12, West Shore Business Centre, and the team at Lofthus Signs Ltd; it was great to open the doors of the SESF new premises. I found Gumon the security operative helpful, and Nina likewise.

Thursday 15/04/2010

1:46 p.m. Home. I have been speaking to the special services department at TNT transport, Bellshill. They have kindly agreed to collect the resources pro bono from the Caribbean Hurricane Relief Depot in Port Bannatyne and deliver to Unit 12, West Shore Business Centre, Edinburgh.

Monday 19/04/2010

9:31 a.m. Home. I have before me the lease, witnessed and to sign, for Unit 12, West Shore Business Centre.

'What's next?' Eric asked me that afternoon on Saturday, 16 December 2006. Uncertainty and contingencies have overruled my best-laid plans from the moment I conceived and began to implement this initiative to salvage, store, inventory, refurbish and deliver fit-for-purpose, surplus to requirements, educational resources to deserving beneficiaries, so I continue to take faltering steps forward – there is no other choice for me if I don't wish to throw away five years' struggle against the odds. I must make a fresh start and thereby I will continue to create more shipments of educational resources that have inestimable value for the materially less fortunate in Blue Planet Village. Call it my legacy if you will. Quit now? No way! I have no other choice but to press on; I could not have kept the Caribbean Hurricane Relief Depot at the boatyard at Port Bannatyne indefinitely, so I was able to sell it. Decision taken. Now I must move the boxes of resources

accumulated in it, over many months, across to Granton. Having a base over there in the City of Edinburgh may enable me to further the objectives of the Surplus Educational Supplies Foundation.

1:37 p.m. I am back from the town. I signed the lease. I met Ailsa, the Argyll and Bute Council dog warden, a friend from way back. I am glad to be home again, where I have made myself a fried egg sandwich and a pot of tea. The sun is shining at long last on the back step and you know where I am going with the purvey, indeed you do.

Tuesday 20/04/2010

9:18 a.m. Home. I am going to call TNT Bellshill. *'Holly is in a meeting,'* she said.

9:36 a.m. I have munched my way through two pieces of toast and marmalade and I'm enjoying a mug of coffee. I shall now fold SESF flyers. I must remind Phil at Bute Naturally to make additions that were left out in the last printing. Nothing is perfect, so make the most of it.

11:22 a.m. I call Holly at TNT Bellshill. I let her know that there are three dozen boxes, so she is going to speak to the general manager and call me back.

Thursday 22/04/2010

9 a.m. Home. I am going to call TNT for the third or fourth time. Will they, or won't they, assist me in the uplift of boxes from the depot? *'You'll be dealing with me from now on,'* said Lorraine.

9:20 a.m. I called Alan of A&M Transport, Ardbeg, to see if they will take boxes to the TNT depot in Hillington and he said that they could do that. I then called Lorraine at TNT who told me

Friday 23/04/2010

that as soon as the arrangements had been made to uplift the boxes from Port Bannatyne to Mundell's warehouse in Hillington, so TNT could collect them from that depot, which would save them the trouble of having to come across to the Isle of Bute. TNT Special Services, Rigghead Industrial Estate, Bellshill, Brian general manager; it was Alastair, who I had met in the Musicker Café, Rothesay, who had suggested I contact him. I am to meet the TNT driver, Phil, on Monday 26 April.

1:55 p.m. Grey and damp. I am going out to the boatyard to meet A&M Transport Ltd to load boxes.

3:56 p.m. Alan met me at the depot at 2:30 p.m. and we loaded the boxes into his van. He will drop them off at Ben Mundell's depot in Hillington where they will be collected by TNT and delivered to Unit 12 in due course. Collect knitting machines from Davina on 4 May.

There still remains some boxing and tidying up to do in the depot; shelving and tables remain in the Caribbean Hurricane Relief Depot, which Alan will take over to Edinburgh for me, for a fee of course. Most transport nationwide and the shipments abroad 2005–2017 were funded by the prime mover (see financial statements).

Friday 23/04/2010

5:31 p.m. Home. This morning I went out to the boatyard with the car to make another attempt at tidying up the depot, where there remain enough useful resources to fill another dozen or so boxes. I returned to have lunch with Amy and then I went back out again. I stopped off at Bute Naturally to collect a few more boxes from Phil – he is always the same, helpful and encouraging to me, like so many in this island community since our arrival in the autumn of 1990.

I am Confronted with Problems of My Own Making

Monday 26/04/2010

8:30 a.m. I have got on the train for Edinburgh. I walked up from Central Station to Queen Street Station dragging the barrow with the roll of Visqueen tied on to it. It must weigh at least 50 kg. I cannot bend my right arm easily for some reason; my elbow is quite painful and has been for some time. Amy brought the barrow and the roll of plastic sheeting down to the Co-op car park, while I managed to cycle in. There is a heavy humid grey mist sitting low on top of the island and on the surrounding hills of the Cowal Peninsula. I met Jean from Paisley walking her dog at the Albert pier, who kindly held the roll while I tied it on to the barrow. She is always cheerful and interested in learning what I am currently up to and attends the Baptist Church meeting, which is now held at King Street Hall.

I hope to be at Unit 12 later this morning to receive the delivery of the boxes from the Port Bannatyne boatyard thanks to TNT Transport Ltd. The train is approaching Waverley Station. I did not fancy lifting the barrow and roll of plastic up Haymarket Station steps so I am alighting here. The sun is shining on the page as I scratch these lines. *'Go for it!'* as I heard someone say on Radio 4 one morning. I think it was one of the original jazz folk musicians from the deep southern states of the USA who said, *'If you wanna keep flyin, don't look down.'*

4:03 p.m. I am on the bus for Glasgow. I arrived at Waverley Station and went out the side entrance and got a taxi. We drove out past Fettes and around to Granton, along Shore Road. I had to tell the driver where to go. The sunbeams are pouring through the sunroof of this bus as it rumbles along the M8. I arrived at Unit 12 and opened up, feeling proprietorial and daunted by the responsibility of what I had taken on.

I am glad now that I had taken the trouble to bring the barrow and roll of plastic, both of which will prove useful. It is a

Monday 26/04/2010

Unit 12, West Shore Business Centre, Granton, Edinburgh. Monday 26/04/2010. Pat the TNT driver has just delivered three pallets from their depot in Bellshill.

bright light-filled morning. I found a large Viridor skip parked, overflowing with builder's rubbish and all sorts from Mitie Ltd, the property services refurbishment people; that skip is too close for comfort. I thought that before I changed into my boiler suit I would visit the other units surrounding the car park and introduce myself to my fellow tenants. First off, I met John nearby where they make bespoke garden furniture using a form work and a mix of concrete. The next three units were vacant. I went round to Unit 5 and met Bahram from Iran, who invited me into his office for coffee and explained his new business, which was manufacturing crisps for vegetarians using different vegetables and which he distributes nationally and to the USA. Bahram has been in situ for a number of years perfecting his unique vegetable-based product. He heard my patter and he was impressed by my altruistic commitment to the objectives of the Surplus Educational Supplies Foundation. We exchanged business cards.

The next unit was Forth Engineering Ltd, a firm that manufactures ball bearings I think, and I met personable Alan. Then to Stamper Fruit and Vegetables, a wholesaler and distributor with almost a dozen vans in and out of the centre, obviously doing very well, and there met the young lad who was helpful and who came by with his firm's forklift truck to take the pallets out of the TNT van.

I had a long chat with Pat, the TNT driver, who had driven all the way from Bellshill via Hillington and then back up the M8 to Granton. I was grateful. I then changed into my boiler suit and later I helped the Mitie Ltd operatives pick up the scattered rubbish from the overflowing skip, and Murray, a Mitie Ltd employee, said I could use their toilet in Unit 7. I then called Isabel at Lofthus Signs Ltd, who said they would have SESF signage on Unit 12's roller-shutter doors and on the business centre noticeboard at the entrance off West Harbour Road Business Centre next time.

The sun is shining. I hoofed it up the road to get the No. 16

bus back to the St James Centre where I bought myself a coffee, a cheese and egg sandwich, bottle of Orangina, bottle of water and a packet of cheese and onion crisps: a well-earned treat, I reckon. I did today what I had planned on doing. The challenge is to make these 'new' SESF premises work effectively. *The goal is to collect, inventory and shift fit-for-purpose, surplus to requirements, educational resources to wherever they are most needed and appreciated.*

I have made face-to-face contact with some of the tenants in the West Shore Business Centre, who appeared welcoming – Alan at Forth Engineering Ltd in particular, who loaned me a ladder so I could tie up the SESF small banner above the Unit 12 'office'.

Tuesday 27/04/2010

10:13 a.m. Home. It is grey and damp. I am not feeling up to it and going nowhere; I have eight ocean freight containers parked at five different locations across Scotland. It is weighing heavily on me. I have had no word from Carson Transport and Lifting Solutions Ltd or Galt Transport Ltd as to whether they have moved the containers to Rosyth or not. What am I going to do with the nine container loads of educational resources that I collected? Distribute or sell to worthy recipients, wherever they might be, is a possibility.

10:29 a.m. Contact A Call to Business, who have links to Sierra Leone, and who I last heard were building a school.

5 p.m. I received a call from Eric to say that they will buy my containers back from me: that's great, but where do I store the contents of the 40-foot container at WH Malcolm Transport Ltd, Fouldubs depot? For tomorrow call John now based at Linwood to see if they will let me have some space to store the resources in GATU4072944.

Wednesday 28/04/2010

8:26 a.m. I receive an email from Roland, SeaFreight Agencies Lines Inc., Miami, USA, suggesting I should stick with the islands. He said he was going to Grenada and he would speak to his former school friend Alexis, who is now the current Minister of Education, about further donations of surplus-to-requirements educational resources. I was glad to get a word from him. After this message I am off the floor and having another go.

9:37 a.m. I am going to call John Murray at WH Malcolm Transport Ltd to see if they will move GATU4033193, which has been partially emptied – the rest of the contents can go into SEAU4272551, which is over at Duncan Adams Transport Ltd, Grange Dock depot. This self-directed project is now no longer any fun, having to presume on the goodwill of individuals, who I respect and like, in order to get me out of difficulty.

'We will do that for you,' he said. I felt greatly privileged to hear those words from John Murray on behalf of WH Malcolm Transport Ltd. I then picked up the phone and called Duncan Adams Transport Ltd to let them know WH Malcolm Transport Ltd will be bringing an SESF container across from Fouldubs depot. I asked him if it could it be set down beside SEAU4272551. I spoke to Shirley and then with Margaret who always give me the time of day.

11:11 a.m. I called Alan who tells me that they will shift the rest of the stuff from the Caribbean Hurricane Relief Depot at the boatyard next week.

12:21 p.m. I have just called Galt Transport Ltd, Dumbarton. They have delivered 40-foot container GATU4072944 to Rosyth. *'That will be £250 please.'* I called Carson Transport Ltd, Cumbernauld, to see if the other container has been moved to Rosyth.

12:21 p.m. I spoke to John, who said ominously *'As long as you know what you are doing, otherwise, you, or we, are in trouble.'*

12:57 p.m. I am still here at the desk. I have been sitting here long enough, the time has come to move, having tried to work out what to do with a problem of my own creation. I will keep the container up at Russell, Coatbridge, where it is for the time being, since it is only partially loaded. The container at Clydeport Ocean Terminal, Greenock, is now at Babcock Marine in Rosyth, where it can be temporarily stored and contents inventoried – a problem solved, having relied on the goodwill offer of Alan Nicoll. I called Alasdair, Head of Security and Estates Supervisor, Waterfront Edinburgh Ltd, to see if it would be possible for SESF to temporarily park one of its containers on their property at Granton. He said, *'You can't have it on a trailer, it could be stolen.'* He said he would call me tomorrow. That was a marathon session on the phone. I am going to head into Rothesay on the bike to get some fresh air and a few messages. *'Struggling man got to move on,'* sang Jimmy Cliff.

Thursday 29/04/2010

Home. Grey and damp. Bill the IT Technician came round to repair the computer. I spoke with Shirley at Grange Dock, who told me that my container has been brought over and parked beside SEAU4272551.

4:30 p.m. I received a return call from Alastair of Len Lothian Self Storage Ltd, Granton Square, who said that they will store my 40-foot container-load of library shelving at a price.

I am Confronted with Problems of My Own Making

Saturday 01/05/2010

8:50 a.m. I am on the train for Central Station, Glasgow, which has just left Wemyss Bay. I am journeying over to Grange Dock once more. I hope to see if I can have container GATU4033193 set down beside container SEAU4272551 so that I can empty one of the containers into the other. Eric has told me that he will buy them back from me. When? I am not feeling too good, but I will press on, because as the say in this part of Blue Planet Village, *'There's nothing else fur it. Jimmy.'*

11 a.m. Duncan Adams Transport Ltd, Grange Dock, Port of Grangemouth depot. I walked in from the Forth Ports Plc security gate. I had got a taxi down from Falkirk High Station, showed my passport at Forth Ports Grangemouth security, and arrived at Duncan Adams Transport Ltd reception to meet Eric, in running gear, who took me out into the yard after I had put on my high-viz jacket (which he had kindly given me some time ago). He introduced me to Alan the box lift driver, who greets me with *'Here comes trouble, sorry ah cannae move it today.'* I take in a deep breath, smile, and say, *'No problem.'* There is no point in complaining, Duncan Adams Transport Ltd have been doing me big favours since the day I stepped down into the yard from the cab of one of their artics that Saturday afternoon 16 November 2006. I bid them all a cheery goodbye and trudge my way out of the dock and over to Grangemouth town centre to get a bus up to Falkirk High Station.

Home, home, at last. I wrote a thank you letter to TNT Transport Ltd.

Monday 03/05/2010

8:29 a.m. *'We are now approaching Springburn, this train is for Falkirk Grahamston,'* he said. There is bright sunshine on my face

Monday 03/05/2010

and not a cloud in the sky. I walked up from Glasgow Central Station. On the ferry coming over from Rothesay I met Keiron, former pupil at North Bute Primary Port School, who tells me he is working for Scottish Widows Insurance in Edinburgh; I pinned his ears back with my story when he asked me what I was doing and where I was going. He gave me his news and news about his young brother, Romilly, who was in one of my classes at the Port School and is now working as a money broker in Switzerland. Keiron asks me, *'Did you see that coming from him?'*

I told him that I was returning to Grange Dock, where I hoped to be able to empty one of my containers of educational resources and transfer the contents into one that was only half full. It is not a satisfactory arrangement, but it is the best I can do for the time being. Eric had said to me some time ago, on more than one occasion, you only want to move it once in an ideal world if it is possible to do so.

At this moment the train is passing through Stepps, which always brings back memories of my time there, 1975–1980, when I boarded in the home of John and Nan, Alexandra Avenue, and the summers of 1976 and 1977 that I spent visiting patients in Gartloch Hospital and shut-in elderly folk in the housing schemes of Ruchazie and Garthamlock. The patients and residents in these schemes names had been given to me by the district health nurse who visited the Sunnyside Primary School, Craigend, where I was teaching. *'The next stop is Gartcosh.'*

10:05 a.m. The road transport yard, Grange Dock. I arrived here by taxi from Falkirk Graham Street Station about three-quarters of an hour ago. I was met by Richard at reception and taken out into the yard to find Alan, who was up in the cab of the forklift, who told me that my boxes were behind the warehouse. I opened up the containers: there is some job before me of shifting educational resources from one container, GATU4033193, loaded with classroom furniture from Fife Council schools and into SEAU4272551, which had been loaded way back when? (See diary entry with educational resources: almost new infant classroom chairs and chalkboards from Penicuik Primary School, Midlothian Council.) I am going to have my play piece, swallow my orange juice and get stuck in.

3:36 p.m. I have boarded the train for Wemyss Bay and have with me a Cornish pasty and a cup of tea. I did manage to tidy the two boxes; there were more resources in GATU4033193 than I had anticipated. I had shown up and worked away stacking wooden chairs, which came originally from the former Bell Baxter High School in Cupar. It is all good kit. Well, I would say that, wouldn't I? Here's my inventory for the day:

- SEAU4272551 – 78 wooden chairs; 70 plastic-seated metal-legged chairs; 2 small chalkboards; 5 large chalkboards; 5 round Formica-topped tables.
- GATU4033193 – 5 tall, metal filing cabinets; 3 half-size metal filing cabinets; 2 normal-size filing cabinets; 80 Formica-topped secondary school tables; 100 wooden secondary school chairs; 50 plastic-seated metal-legged secondary school chairs.

After recording all that data I am now going to enjoy a railway journey treat, which is now stone cold. The taxi driver who drove up the road from Grangemouth town centre told me that he is an avid reader and had, on the dashboard, a novel by Robert Goddard, who he told me is a conspiracy theorist. He asked me, '*Where were you in November 1963?*' I told him that I was a student, in my first year at Dalhousie University, and I was staying in a King's College University Hall of residence, in Halifax, Nova Scotia, Canada. He told me, '*I was six years old.*'

Thursday 06/05/2010

10:35 a.m. Home. I am back on the phone. I called the following individuals: Gary at Greenock Chamber of Commerce;

Friday 07/05/2010

Nieves at the Foreign and Commonwealth Office, who is helpful; United Kingdom Trade and Investment; British Library; The City Business Library.

I am trying to find out which companies trade with Nicaragua on a regular basis.

12:41 p.m. I was speaking to Ben at Containerlift Ltd in Essex. For 7 May, phone health centre to make an appointment to see Dr McGhie before 8:30 a.m.

3:21 p.m. I am back on the phone. I called the British Council, Sierra Leone, and spoke to British Director June Rollinson; Venezuela, British Director Cherry Goth.

3:58 p.m. I am trying once more to liaise with the Sierra Leone High Commission in London. I managed this time to speak to the Head of Chancery. She says that she never received my email sent ages ago.

5:52 p.m. I am researching the list of companies sent to me by the very helpful Maureen, who I had spoken to this morning at the Scottish Business Information Services Libraries and Archives.

Friday 07/05/2010

1:47 p.m. Home. The sun is shining once more on the back door. I have called Len Lothian Ltd, to determine whether I can temporarily store the library shelving, salvaged from the Jubilee Gardens Library in 2008, at their warehouse on West Harbour Road in Granton. I spoke to Steve who said he would call me back. I will return to my chair and resume sitting in the sun – when it when it shines through the banks of cloud.

I have been working outside tidying the garden up the back, sweeping the steps, cleaning windows and squaring things away, from which I gain much satisfaction. Light is shimmering off the flat-calm Firth of Clyde. I stay at my desk. I'll have to hang around the back till I get the call from Len Lothian Ltd.

Later I received a call from Steve, to whom I am to give 48 hours' notice and they are going to charge me £26 per man hour to unload the container. No way. Forget it!

1:59 p.m. I will have to waive arrangements to move container MSKU6311690 from Freightliner Ltd, Coatbridge, to Len Lothian Ltd.

2:01 p.m. I am calling Fraser the finance manager at Freightliner Ltd. He is always helpful, but this time there is no chance of a 'free haul'. The price of diesel has gone way up and this firm have gone more than the second mile for me since our first ocean freight container shipment of educational resources to Grenada, West Indies, was collected by that company Friday 1 July 2005. (Reader you can check entry in *Volume One, Diary of a Shipping Clerk*, published 25 September 2022.)

4:01 p.m. I called Containerlift Ltd in Essex. Stewart tells me he had seen my email yesterday and he will get back to me on Monday. Is there the possibility of this firm picking up the container from Coatbridge and shifting it to Edinburgh? I am trying to spread the net for one-off favours: executive coach Barry said to me recently, '*David, you don't want to run out of favours.*'

Monday 10/05/2010

8:28 a.m. Home. Overcast and cool. I am calling Rothesay Health Centre to make an appointment. '*The number you called is busy.*'

12:18 p.m. I had appointment with the doctor, who is going to reduce my prescription of Avodart to one a day and I am to have a blood test on Wednesday. I stopped off at the Mill Garden Centre, then along to the Musicker Café for a coffee and a chat with Gordon. I am now going to get stuck into working in Le Jardin. *Il faut cultive mon jardin.*

5:46 p.m. I have cooked supper of smoked fish pie and rice. I prepared another garden bed where the water runs off the cliff and collects into a pool and trickles its way into the backyard. I have renewed my General Teaching Council for Scotland membership fee by direct debit, just in case, you never know I might pick up a piece of chalk and strut my stuff, if not here perhaps far away from here: dream on dude.

Thursday 13/05/2010

11:39 a.m. Home. Johanna is getting some lunch ready. I cycled into the metropolis, paid a bill at the builder's merchant and got some groceries. It is dry with a cool wind blowing heavy clouds up from the south. Calling Containerlift Ltd.

2:30 p.m. Davina is delivering the knitting machines and printers, which will be much appreciated by the recipients. *(They were part of a shipment of educational resources eventually sent from Surplus Educational Supplies Foundation, Unit 12, West Shore Business Centre to a school in Tanzania.)* I called Nieves at the Foreign and Commonwealth Office and left message.

4:15 p.m. I am calling the Sierra High Commission in London for the umpteenth time. Why do I persist in the face of such indifference? *'May I speak to the Head of Chancery, please?'* I asked. *'She's not on her seat,'* she replied. *'Oh in that case, when will she sit down? I shall call again tomorrow.'*

Friday 14/05/2010

12:19 p.m. Home. I have been packing away the donation of knitting machines, a large bag of wool, computers and a printer. Amy said she would run me across to Unit 12 in Granton provided I cleared the stuff from the end of the corridor. I am going to tidy the bicycle shed to make room.

I have arranged to meet university chaplain Nicholas at the Edinburgh University Chaplaincy Centre on 18 May, who Stewart had introduced me to. Stewart had also suggested I meet Owen Dudley Edwards. I called Fraser at Freightliner Ltd, Coatbridge. *'He's at a Freight Club meeting, they know about your container MSKU6311690,'* she said.

I call Barry, the social enterprise executive coach, to tell him that I have a meeting in Edinburgh with an Edinburgh University chaplain and I hope to enlist some students in the work of the Surplus Educational Supplies Foundation, and would he like to meet up afterwards. I called Duncan Adams Transport Ltd, Grange Dock, to speak to Michael and spoke to Linda. *'He's on a call at the moment,'* she said. I asked them if they would deliver the container of educational resources to Unit 12 in Granton, which they will purchase from me when empty. They will call me back. I am now calling Peter at John G Russell Transport Ltd, Coatbridge.

12:44 p.m. I was speaking to Jim about container OCLU1354487. I can only ask if they will give me a 'free haul' to Babcock Marine, Rosyth Business Park.

12:49 p.m. I spoke to Michael, now in the Russell office, Gartsherrie Road, Coatbridge.

1:03 p.m. I spoke to Alan at Babcock Marine, who will get back to me as soon as OCLU1354487 is shifted over there. He said they will refurbish the containers during the summer months and will get in touch with their business development department. I called Fraser at Edinburgh Chamber of Commerce.

1:13 p.m. It is time to get back outside and finish the work I had started, while the sun is still shining. I call Elspeth in Bishopbriggs about the collection of educational resources she had salvaged from skips outside primary schools in the Borders that she had been visiting as part of her work. I need to arrange transport: how and from whom? Another problem to solve. Remember to ask Nick the chaplain SJ if the Edinburgh Settlement could loan SESF some transport to collect boxes of educational resources from Bishopbriggs, or possibly ask Jimmy at Edinburgh Community Transport? I am floundering again. Serves me right!

Wednesday 19/05/2010

10:16 a.m. I am in the Edinburgh University Settlement Office having a meeting with the treasurer and Lynne. I had called Nick from the Dugald Stewart Building, he tells me he can't make the meeting as he had his toenails removed. OUCH!

The helpful receptionist showed me how to get here; Geet, the treasurer from India, is looking through my file. He has listened to my pitch and I have already said who I am and what I am after. He tells me that he used to run the Moray House Student Union. Lynne is responsive to the ideas and practice of REUSE, REDUCE, RECYCLE: the circular economy for Blue Planet and the sustainable survival of our fragile Global Village. She sat beside the deputed interviewer and showed some interest and said she would help SESF with unloading the container when it is brought to Unit 12 on Saturday 22 May. I am counting on their offer of support to assist me in unloading the 40-foot ocean freight container.

It is grey and overcast. I call the executive coach to let him know how the meeting went.

11:45 a.m. *'This is the 11:45 to Glasgow,'* he said.

12:50 p.m. I am on the train for Wemyss Bay: I just made it. Platform 13. I had to run as fast as I could, pump the Raleigh Spokes; one of my nicknames at Lodge School 1955–1961. The teasing and bullying in that benighted colonial establishment – the boys hall made me ashamed of my spindly shanks, but toughened the fabric for tougher days. Never, never give up, no matter how fast you are able to move in the direction you are heading.

What was this morning's meeting in the Edinburgh University Settlement Office all about? I set out what I expected and who I was looking for to come on board the Surplus Educational Supplies Foundation's bus; these privileged Edinburgh University students were individuals whose skill set in finance, marketing and fundraising would complement my skill set. *'You are a fixer.'* That's what Coach Barry called me. I hoped they would share my values of integrity, dedication and determination to overcome difficulty, and a willingness to achieve the objectives of the Surplus Educational Supplies Foundation, would want to have some fun in the achievement of its objectives, and furthermore appreciate the effort and personal investment of my track record and see that there is the potential, for them also, to build and extend on what's been accomplished. *'You have a fantastic project,'* said the executive coach.

There are already six ocean freight containers with fit-for-purpose, surplus to requirements, educational resources, collected from primary and secondary schools in the Scottish education system, delivered to schools in Grenada, West Indies, since 2005: two 20-foot containers and four 40-foot containers, which were delivered to Grenada government schools that had been devastated by Hurricane Ivan 7 September 2004. One 40-foot container was gifted to a charity in Huddersfield for its schools in Ghana, West Africa. The foundation still has eight 40-foot containers loaded with educational resources awaiting shipment to

Wednesday 19/05/2010

deserving beneficiaries worldwide. Recently 40 boxes (1 cubic metre) of library books salvaged from the Morningside Library, Edinburgh, were delivered to the anglophone student community in the city of Bluefields, Costa Caribena, Nicaragua, Central America.

The foundation has recently acquired, rent-free for six months, an industrial unit in a North Edinburgh business centre, so what is the next step? I now need to recruit, enlist, inspire and build a team, who together will move the Surplus Educational Supplies Foundation to another level. Can these individuals build on what has been accomplished since the Surplus Educational Supplies Foundation first shipment to Grenada, 1 July 2005? Are these Edinburgh University students able to assist me in turning this charitable foundation into a viable social enterprise? The ball is back in Nick and his Edinburgh University students' court. He mentioned in the course of our telephone conversation that I could use the Edinburgh Settlement Office: he said, *'You are now one of us.'* My hopes have been raised once more.

'Please mind the gap when alighting from this train,'

2:36 p.m. Home. I must now make arrangements to collect the boxes of educational resources from Bishopbriggs. I called Arnold Clark customer services, Greenock showroom. *'I'll put you through to somebody.'* She tells me to call this number. *'I'll speak to you soon,'* she said. Everyone I speak to is receptive and helpful; this firm will let me have the loan of a van. Wonderful!

2:56 p.m. I have just had a call from Graham of Lofthus Signs Ltd, who is trying to locate the West Shore Business Centre. I gave him directions. He is now on his way to do the signage on Unit 12. I then called Lee Ann, marketing, Arnold Clark. They are going to do me a favour; I get back on the phone and call Arnold Clark, Bishopbriggs rental desk. I am to collect a van from them tomorrow. BRILLIANT!

I am Confronted with Problems of My Own Making

Thursday 20/05/2010

7:10 a.m. I am sitting in a railway carriage in Wemyss Bay Station. I left home on the bike at 6 a.m. There was a thick, grey, wet mist hanging over the island's surrounding coastline.

7:13 a.m. I am en route for Glasgow Central Station. There goes the whistle peeping noise and the doors of the carriage shut. I am going to make the most of whatever this day has in store, all I can do is give it my best shot. As I was about to walk up the gang plank to the ferry earlier, Graeme from the port, who is now one of the pier men, says to me cheerily, *'Go easy'*. I'll need to go carefully, for this pensioner will need to: he who has never owned an automobile, and has seldom driven the car owned by Marion, and whose accustomed form of transport for many years back has been a bicycle, is about to put himself and others in serious jeopardy.

9:05 a.m. Arnold Clark showroom, on swish Kirkintilloch Road, Bishopbriggs. I am sitting here awaiting the collection of a van. I have called Elspeth to let her know that I hope to be along fairly soon. I have given my driving licence to the van rental desk, I got a taxi up from Glasgow Central Station; I told the friendly taxi driver from Central Station what I was trying to do, he thought it was *'Brill!'*

2 p.m. The sun is shining brightly on the front door of Unit 12, West Shore Business Centre, Granton, with Lofthus Signs Ltd's brilliant signage, and also on the big noticeboard on West Harbour Road entrance.

I collected the resources at long last from Elspeth and Helen in Bishopbriggs: I was introduced to her home help, who lives in Craigend, who tells me that her son goes to Beavers at Sunnyside Primary School where I was on the teaching staff from 1975 to 1982, and which was my focus for a new life in Scotland and a community where I was to build the foundation for the rest of my life. It is a small world.

Arnold Clark could not have been more helpful. Now I have to drive the van, a Transit Diesel Ford, which is bigger than I thought; it's good that I have had some practice driving Stirling Yacht Services Ltd's similar van. Here I go, onward and upward. *'No turning back, no turning back'*. One of the Mitie Ltd men drops by and asks me, *'Did you get the pallets ah left yuh?'* 'Yes, I did, thanks a lot,' I said.

3:50 p.m. Bishopbriggs Railway Station. I have walked up the Kirkintilloch Road from the Arnold Clark showroom. I returned the van keys to Patricia, who could not have been more pleasant to me. I am relieved there had been no messes. It is not something I do every day; now all I have got to do is find somewhere to spring a leak, and by the looks of it that will have to wait until the train gets into Queen Street Station. *Haud ye watta, Jimmy.*

4:26 p.m. I am sitting in the train for Wemyss Bay. As I got off the train at Queen Street, mutual looks of recognition – there was George, MEP for Argyll and Bute near the ticket barrier. I paused to shake his hand, wished him well and told him that I had cast my vote recently for his colleague Alan Reid's re-election to parliament.

I can hardly believe that I achieved what I had visualised to accomplish in the small hours of this morning. I managed – apart from breaking the wing mirror of the helpful motorcyclist that was beside me at the lights on the main road junction back to Edinburgh, who, when I asked him for directions, said simply *'Follow me'*. With that instruction, he took me up Corstorphine Hill and down to Murrayfield. I gave him one of the SESF flyers and told him to send me the bill. I was granted journeying mercies, another job of work done.

6:30 p.m. Home. I met Marion on the MV *Argyle* on her twice-daily commute.

Friday 21/05/2010

9:58 a.m. Home. I am setting off for the town to post a thank you letter to Arnold Clark and his smart team, collect dry cleaning and get something for our lunch, then along to Cowal Builders Ltd to pay for the rental of the power wash, of which Ronnie waived the fee. I stopped off at Bishops Street, Print Point, for a chat with Frank the music teacher over a hot chocolate. He is always interesting to talk with and encourages me.

12:25 p.m. I am calling Duncan Adams Transport Ltd to confirm it is okay for them, at 10 a.m., to deliver INBU4923875 to Unit 12 for me to unload. I spoke to Eric, who said he would buy it back from me.

1:11 p.m. Speaking to Barry, who said, *'The chairman of Project Scotland is a friend of mine.'* He has a lot of friends and he makes no introductions to any of them. We arrange to meet at Unit 12 on 25 May.

1:18 p.m. Speaking to Craig at Freightliner Ltd, Coatbridge, who tells me that Fraser will not be back until Monday.

Saturday 22/05/2010

8:29 a.m. I have walked up from Glasgow Central to Queen Street Station and am now on the train for Edinburgh Waverley. I said goodbye to Marion in Kilbarchan and waited at the bus stop from 6:15 a.m. to 7:30 a.m. for the bus to Johnstone Railway Station. I should have walked it. For the record, my new life really and truly began when Marion and I began our married life in the village

Saturday 22/05/2010

in top flat, 21 Easwald Bank, 1 January 1987. The sun is shining brightly.

10 a.m. Unit 12, West Shore Business Centre, Granton. I flagged a taxi on Princes Street, across from the Balmoral Hotel. Iain, the taxi driver who comes from Corstorphine and I shot the breeze on the way to Granton. He tells me that he went to Silverknowes Primary School in Pilton, where in September 1974 I did my first teaching practice.

I am here to begin another job of work. I met Alan who works for Forth Engineering Ltd, whose unit is across the square. He let me use their phone to call Grange Dock and I spoke to Richard, who told me that the container was on its way to Unit 12. Now prepare to work.

10:55 a.m. I have just met Stewart's HGV with the 40-foot ocean freight container INBU4923875.

4:10 p.m. I nearly killed myself unloading that container. Never, ever, again will I do that: the team of students from Edinburgh University had not bothered to show up. The sun continues to shine brightly with Stewart's unstinting help, for it was definitely not in his remit to lend a hand: together we have unloaded this 40-foot-high cube ocean freight container of primary and secondary classroom furniture. I know that you only want to move it once Eric, but there you are and here I am, and I'm now going to shut up shop and head for home. There was a lot more school furniture in the container than I had anticipated to unload and I had feared that we would never get it emptied; it was a job which I never, ever, wish to do again. I was knackered. Unit 12 is now chock-a-block with quality fit-for-purpose educational resources. I will now need to get it shifted, marketed and sold, if possible, or better still donated and ultimately delivered to where it will be put to good use.

4:45 p.m. Stewart dropped me off in front of the Balmoral Hotel. I walked down the steep steps and got the train for Glasgow Queen Street.

Monday 24/05/2010

8:30 a.m. Home. Johanna and I are holding the fort; the sun is shining out of a clear blue sky To do: follow up contact to the Nicaraguan Embassy, thanks to Nieves at the Foreign and Commonwealth Office; contact Nick, chaplain, Edinburgh Resettlement Centre (there has been no response to my pitch last week); contact Eric to tell him to make the cheque payable to me for the container, less the cost of delivering the container to Unit 12; shop for messages for supper; work in the garden.

9:18 a.m. Contact First Secretary at the Nicaraguan Embassy, Señora Giselle Morales Echaverry.

9:25 a.m. I called no answer. I called Eric.
 'Your daughter sounds like a nice person,' he said.
 'Eric, she's an absolutely brilliant person,' I said.
 'Where were all your student helpers on Saturday morning?' he kindly enquired.
 'I guess they could not be bothered, and there was nothing else for it but for me to tackle the removal of all that classroom school furniture myself. I am really grateful to Stewart for his help, for without it, I would have been stuck there,' I said.
 'Stewart said you were really tired,' he said.
 'I was Eric, totally whacked; it nearly killed me,' I said.

9:51 a.m. Called Nick, the Jesuit priest, Edinburgh Student Union and told him that the ball was back in their court. I am calling the Nicaraguan Embassy once more, no answer.

Wednesday 26/05/2010

9:53 a.m. I called Simon, Erskine Stewart's Melville Schools, about their offer of surplus school furniture. *'He's in a meeting,'* she said. I left a message for him. Rosetta from South Africa, who lives at the end of a cul-de-sac in Ardbeg, who called asked abruptly *'Are you making marmalade?'* I said I would drop by with a jar for her at 10:45 a.m.

I contact Leslie the undergraduate adviser, Strathclyde University Business School. I was passed on to Michelle and then on to Sandra at Careers and Marketing. (See email from the head of marketing.) Is there any possibility of engaging some of their students in my project? I contact the librarian, Sandra, at the MacDonald Library in Edinburgh. I call the charity A Call to Business with Sierra Leone.

4:45 p.m. I am speaking to Maria at the Nicaraguan Embassy, who sounds supportive and says she will pass my message on to Giselle tomorrow. This is another possible front from which to facilitate delivery of educational resources from Scotland to Bluefields. There has been no problem with the shipment of library books that arrived in Managua but, as yet, they have not been delivered to the beneficiaries in Bluefields City. I am trying to build links in the chain of supply. *'Logistics is just a big word,'* said Eric to me once, in the early days of this project.

Wednesday 26/05/2010

12:15 p.m. Home. I called Giselle at the Nicaraguan Embassy, who is sympathetic to my objective to deliver fit-for-purpose educational resources to schools in the city of Bluefields, and the Costa Caribena. She told me to contact her at the end of July.

12:44 p.m. I call Ricky, the City of Edinburgh councillor, to make an appointment to see him about the vandalism of the former Curriehill Primary School buildings. He tells me that he has put in a motion before the council to be debated regarding the unnecessary destruction of fit-for-purpose educational resources (see article in *Edinburgh Evening News*). Call Russell Transport Coatbridge and speak to Michael and Raymond.

3:52 p.m. Called Peter, the transport manager at Russell, about the removal of container OCLU1354487 to Babcock Marine, Rosyth Business Park. *'We will do it for you,'* he said. What more can I say, except thank you.

Thursday 27/05/2010

8:29 a.m. Buchanan Street Bus Station. I have just boarded the bus for Edinburgh. I walked up from Central Station under a grey sky and it was cool this morning – a change from yesterday. I am making the effort and taking the trouble to achieve something that is worthwhile; there will be another shipment of fit-for-purpose, surplus to requirements, educational resources to where it will be appreciated. I have arranged to meet Barry, executive coach from the Edinburgh Social Enterprise Academy, at Unit 12, West Shore Business Centre, Granton, this morning and Councillor Ricky at 3 p.m. I can only hope that each of these meetings will further my objective to deliver educational resources to the Costa Caribena and the city of Bluefields. What else is there for me to do?

2:15 p.m. I am on the train for Glasgow Queen Street. I walked down the steep steps from the High Street. I had come from the Edinburgh City Chambers. I had coffee in the Members' Room. I was met by Councillor Ricky at reception, who graciously carried my bag up three flights of stairs and poured me a coffee. He said, *'I am a realist, but I will see what I can do to assist you in your initiative.'* He is a man of his word. He writes a column in a local newspaper. He will try and drum up support.
1. Raise funds to ship a 20-foot ocean freight container of much

needed educational resources to the schools in El Bluff, Costa Caribena.
2. Raise funds to purchase containers to store educational resources at Currie Hill Pentlands, Councillor Henderson's ward.

We can only see what happens. I leave this meeting encouraged to persevere. He suggests I get in touch with Denis, the founder of Edinburgh Direct Aid. I make an appointment to see him on 7 June. Ricky told me that Denis is interested in 'High Value Aid'. What's that?

11:07 a.m. I spoke with Alastair, Edinburgh City Council surveyor, who will call me back about the educational resources that remain in the Curriehill Primary School, Pentlands.

Wednesday 02/06/2010

1:30 p.m. Home. I received a call from Graeme at the Edinburgh University Settlement, who tells me, *'My thing is organisation and what you need is a presence on the East Coast.'* Do I? Well Unit 12 is a foothold if nothing else. He said he would call me next week.

3:39 p.m. I call the Nicaraguan Embassy in London. Nica Solidarity Campaign.

3:48 p.m. Call BT Sponsorship support about their corporate assistance sector programme development. BT contact Julie.

4:07 p.m. *'Are you getting anywhere, Dad?'* asks Johanna.

Monday 07/06/2010

7:25 a.m. I am on the train for Glasgow Central Station. I walk up to Buchanan Street Bus Station and I am soon on the bus to

Edinburgh, where I hope to have a meeting later on this morning with Denis, who is the founder of Edinburgh Direct Aid. I call Joanne, Project Leader, West Dunbartonshire Schools Estates Division. Call Telford College.

Wednesday 09/06/2010.

4:50 p.m. I am on the bus for Glasgow, which has not long left Saint Andrew Square bus station, where I grabbed a quick bite and a coffee. The sun is shining brightly.

I left home for Rothesay town at 6 a.m. to board the ferry. I chatted with Alan of A&M Transport on the way over. Train up to Glasgow and I walked up to Buchanan Street Bus Station. I resisted the train option. I got the bus to Edinburgh, where I got some keys cut for Unit 12. Got a taxi on Leith Walk. Stewart the driver tells me that his mum runs a charity, but did not tell me for what.

I opened up Unit 12 and felt proprietorial and pleased with myself for all the effort; I have now forgotten all the hours of hassle and expense it took me to get here. The donation of chairs had been recently brought into the unit, thanks to Gumon and the Waterfront Edinburgh Ltd security team of ex-Gurkhas. I strolled across the car park to speak to Bahram at Unit 5 and the door was opened by James, who told me later that his brother lived in Barbados. Bahram made me a cup of tea and is full of praise for my efforts to salvage stuff. He has offered to form a board of management and will speak to his business associates about the work of the Surplus Educational Supplies Foundation. I can only take him at his word for this impromptu interest: it is still an encouragement from someone who is engaged in building a new business in organic vegetable-based snacks. I told him about my coaching sessions with Barry; he said he knew him personally and would make a pitch to him on my behalf for financial support. I then took Bahram over to show him Unit 12.

Monday 14/06/2010

He was not pleased that a donation of chairs had been left on my doorstep. I changed into my boiler suit and shifted the boxes of educational resources that had been collected by Elspeth from schools in the Borders: fortunately I had covered them with some of the plastic sheeting, otherwise they would have been ruined. Later, I met Iain the scrap dealer, who came by with his family to see what was in the skip outside Unit 12, and Gumon's colleague dropped in to see how I was getting on. It was he who had brought the chairs inside and I thanked him. Another step forward into sunlight; a day of self-directed work. It was Kevin at Unit 1, the artisan mason in concrete garden furniture, who had called to let me know that the chairs were getting wet.

Friday 11/06/2010

9:37 a.m. Home. I received a call from Ann from Southwood Primary School, Macedonia, West of Glenrothes, who is offering SESF a complete reading scheme. She told me that they will get the local Scout troop to help them move the reading scheme into one of my containers at Rosyth Business Park. I then call Mike, the journalist at the *Glenrothes Gazette*, to see if they will give the school, the Scouts and SESF a puff?

Monday 14/06/2010

9:22 p.m. Home. Marion and Amy are watching television. I have washed more dishes. Amy and I cycled round the island on this sunny day. Later in the Co-op I met Ian and his little son, Gregor. He asked me if I was still teaching at the Port School. He told me that he was unemployed with three little boys; he knew me, but I could not place him. My heart went out to them.

I AM CONFRONTED WITH PROBLEMS OF MY OWN MAKING

Tuesday 15/06/2010

1 p.m. Called Nicola, Muirhouse Community Social Work Centre, about recruiting interested helpers for work in Unit 12. I contact the young snappers, Alistair from Rothesay and his colleague Stephen. I call Councillor Henderson about Curriehill Primary School's surplus educational resources. What's happening on that front?

Wednesday 23/06/2010

8:39 a.m. Home. Why do I get these debilitating feelings of inadequacy? I am rested, fed, clothed and washed. What do I do in the here and now? I need to do meaningful work, here in the time that I have left. I want to finish my life still being useful. I can, this day, by doing what I can do: a Spanish lesson. Listen to the tapes, run through the dialogues and go for a walk along Craigmore Road and up Ardencraig Road, past the trailer park and the first tee of the golf course, down the steep hill past the Ascog water works, and up another steep hill. I'll go down to Mid Ascog farm, down the wee brae to the Mount Stuart Road, back up the road to Montford and home. And if I do that, I know that I shall feel and in better spirits than I do now.

9:25 a.m. No sooner do I settle to my Spanish lesson than the phone rings. It is Anne from Southwood Primary School, to tell me that they had not heard from Alan at Babcock International, Rosyth, or rather she had been unable to contact him. I had left a message for him last week. We don't want the janitors and Scouts showing up at Babcock Security with the reading scheme for my container and being turned away, so I called the Babcock Marine office and left another message for Alan. Nothing worthwhile is ever achieved without difficulties.

I then received another call from Joanne at West Dunbartonshire

Wednesday 23/06/2010

Council to tell me that Golden Hill Primary School, Hardgate, Clydebank, will be demolished on 3 July.

10:10 a.m. I spoke with Padraic, the council estates surveyor, who put me on to Gerry, who is now the site manager for Interserve Projects Ltd at Barnhill Primary School, Alexandria, whose firm will be building the new Golden Hill Primary School. He said he would speak to Joanne tomorrow. I contacted Aggreko Enquiries and spoke to Yvonne, who put me on to Chris, Dumbarton sales, who in turn put me on to Grant their general manager for the North. There is no turning back now.

11:45 a.m. I call Galt Transport Ltd, Dumbarton. *'I'll let you speak to either Simon or Alan,'* she said helpfully. So much for the Spanish lesson. The sun is shining and I will have to forgo my walk, but I will take a break and sit outside for a while.

12:02 p.m. I speak to Valerie, the head teacher of Golden Hill Primary School, and let her know that Joanne had been in contact and suggested I introduce myself and make an appointment to meet her.

1:42 p.m. I then called the *Clydebank Post* and spoke with Jamie and Linda the news editor, who have generously taken me on board and will publicise, at short notice, in next week's edition of their newspaper, the need for volunteers to assist SESF on Saturday 3 July in the uplift of educational resources from the classrooms into the container.

1:46 p.m. I sent an email via Angela to Jim McColl, chief executive of Clyde Blowers Ltd, seeking his firm's sponsorship of this collection.

2:42 p.m. I spoke with Stevie of Recycle Scotland. I told him about the 40-foot SESF container and donation of educational resources to the Christian African Relief Trust (CART) charity based in Huddersfield for their schools in Ghana, West Africa. He made no comment about my Herculean efforts since 2005 raking school bins and janitors' skips: the daft saga of a waste-stream miner.

2:44 p.m. For the third time today I have tried to speak to the head teacher of Golden Hill Primary School and left another message. Her school secretary said, *'She's very busy at the moment.'*

3:05 p.m. Contact! The head teacher tells me that all of the laptops at Saint Andrew's Secondary School in Clydebank were stolen the day that SESF was making a collection (see diary entry for that day). I told her I knew about the theft and resented her suggestion that my organisation had anything to do with it. I told her that there were other groups working away in the former Saint Andrew's Secondary School at the time. I am wondering whether I should call this collection from Golden Hill Primary School, Clydebank, off. I have been here at the desk since this morning almost without a break. The time has come to down tools and head to the kitchen and make tea for the troops in residence.

Thursday 24/06/2010

12:15 p.m. Home. I receive a call from Zak, who tells me that he works for SCVO as an IT technician, is associated with Recycle Scotland, and he wants to send educational resources to his village school in Ghana, where he is the hereditary chief. I arrange to meet him at Unit 12 on 1 July.

2:07 p.m. It has been drizzling and chilly all day. I am going to cycle into Rothesay to deliver a cheque to the garage for car repairs and let Alistair at D S Murray Ltd know that I am unable to collect their donation of a computer.

Monday 28/06/2010

4:07 p.m. I have just made Johanna and myself a pot of tea having got the preparations for supper: I peeled the potatoes from Israel, topped the strawberries from Elsinore, Scotland, got the fish from the North Sea ready to bake, and sorted tomatoes, the Big Reds from Thomson of New Covent Garden Market.

Friday 25/06/2010

9:11 a.m. Home. I have sent 200 words plus of my trip to Bluefields, Nicaragua, off to Bruce Callow at the British Embassy, San Jose, Costa Rica, as he requested. *(Which can be read in Diary of a Shipping Clerk, Volume Two, published 27 October 2023.)* I called Clyde Blowers Ltd about the possibility of sponsorship of the collection and shipment of educational resources to Bluefields, Costa Caribena, and left a message for Jim McColl.

9:17 a.m. Spoke to Allan, of Galt Transport Ltd, Dumbarton, who is helpful. *'I know a man who might have some spare containers, hang on a minute, I'll just find his telephone number,'* he said. I call and ask, *'Do you have any spare boxes? Allan suggested I give you a call.'* Call Stevie at Recycle Scotland. I call Zak from Ghana; possible Ghana links.

Monday 28/06/2010

5:59 a.m. Home. I have replied to an email from Bruce, British Embassy, San Juan, Costa Rica, who had received the digital photographs of my visit last year to Bluefields City, Costa Caribena, to say he is putting out a press release for the Foreign and Commonwealth Office website about our visit to Bluefields and Rama Cay in December last year. Today I need to make arrangements to visit Golden Hill Primary School, Hardgate, Clydebank.

I am meeting the Ghanaian chief tomorrow, who is coming over from Edinburgh, and I will be taking him up to the school so he can see for himself what educational resources are on offer. He is also going to visit Unit 12 in Granton on Thursday morning, to see what the Surplus Educational Supplies Foundation has to offer. I will meet later with Chris, website designer. I am going to shut my eyes for a bit.

9:05 a.m. I have climbed out of bed and it seems to take me a while to get going. I called West Dunbartonshire Council to speak to Joanne. *'She's stepped out of the office,'* she said. I sit and wait.

10:15 a.m. I called Alistair, the City of Edinburgh estates surveyor, corporate property and contingency planning, who sounded keen to help me. *'I agree with what you are you doing,'* he said. Earlier I had called Councillor Ricky for the ward of Currie Hill and Pentlands and left a message.

Tuesday 29/06/2010

8:45 a.m. To see Zak at Queen Street Station.

10:20 a.m. Sam, the master of most trades, calls to offer me some paid employment. I accepted gladly. I am always the willing horse. I am going to don my overalls and join him when he returns: three hours work refurbishing a top flat, Bloomfield House, Kilchattan Bay, Isle of Bute.

I contact Valerie, head teacher Golden Hill Primary School, Hardgate, Clydebank to arrange a visit to view resources. I speak to Lynne, public relations, West Dunbartonshire Council.

2:45 p.m. I am now on the train for Wemyss Bay. I said goodbye to Zak, the Ghanaian chief and IT technician with SCVO in Edinburgh, and who is connected to Recycle Scotland in some capacity. We had not long got off the No. 62 bus from Golden Hill, Hardgate, where we had visited Golden Hill Primary School.

Tuesday 29/06/2010

Earlier today, Zak and I got a No. 4 bus from Renfield Street having met at 9:15 a.m. in Queen Street Station when he came off the train from Edinburgh. We had got off the bus before we needed to, and spent a good three-quarters of an hour trudging up Great Western Road to the Hardgate roundabout, past the BAM Construction Ltd site of the almost finished St Peter the Apostle High School, and on up the Golden Hill Road to the primary school. We were trudging up Great Western Road to meet the head teacher, who asked us to wait outside her office, where we cooled our heels until 12:01 p.m. The school secretary brought us a tray with a pot of tea, two china cups and saucers, sugar, milk and a tray of biscuits, for which we were most grateful after our long walk in the sunshine. The head teacher, accompanied by the school janitor, took us on a tour of the school classrooms, and the latter marked those items of classroom furniture which Zak and the Surplus Educational Supplies Foundation could uplift on Saturday 3 July. We'll see what happens, as all arrangements are provisional and go awry.

I excused myself from the group, telling them I had a brief appointment with the site manager of Interserve Projects Ltd, the contractor for the new PPP/PFI school being built adjacent to the 'old school'. I then walked up to the Interserve site office, where the construction of the new school was in progress, to see if this firm might provide some volunteer help with the uplift of school furniture from the school's classrooms into container INBU4923875, the delivery of which had still to be arranged. The sun was shining brightly.

I return home. My work for today does not stop. I call Irene, who has left a message to say that she has books that she no longer wants and was I interested? I said yes. I call Brian, the site manager of Interserve Projects Ltd who was not in the site office earlier, to confirm if there will be some voluntary help from his team to lend a hand with the shifting of school furniture on Saturday 3 July. He, as always, cuts me some vital slack. I call Terry. No joy. He doesn't have any spare containers. I then call Galt Transport Ltd. *'I'll have Allan call you tomorrow,'* she said. I call Joanne at West Dunbartonshire Council to let her know the steps taken so far to make this collection of educational resources a reality.

Wednesday 30/06/2010

8:38 a.m. Home. I have not long dropped Marion off at the ferry. Johanna is watching TV and I have got work to do. I need to arrange for a 40-foot ocean freight container to be delivered to Galt Transport Ltd depot, Broad Meadow Industrial Estate, and then see if they will deliver the container to Golden Hill Primary School (opened 1955), Hardgate, Clydebank on or before Saturday 3 July. I call Linda, the news editor of the *Clydebank Post*, to let her know that the collection will take place this coming Saturday. She is always supportive and an encouragement to the efforts of SESF. I try Terry once more for a 'spare container'. As soon as he hears my voice he puts me on the answer machine. I call Brian, just to confirm that there will be some help with the uplift on Saturday: he assures me that there will be. I am encouraged to keep on plugging away at this 'removal'. I call Alan, who tells me *'If you can manage to get a container to us before Saturday, we will deliver it for you.'* I am extremely grateful, as always, for this assistance from him offered at such short notice.

10:22 a.m. Call Zak to assure him that there will be voluntary labour to help us with the uplift of educational resources on Saturday.

I am carrying the can once more, as always. What do I expect? I then take a deep breath, and call Duncan Adams Transport Ltd, Grange Dock, and make arrangements with them to deliver my container to Galt Transport Ltd depot in Dumbarton this coming Saturday. *(Which they did, along with their driver, Stewart, who we together had emptied the contents on Saturday 22 May!)* They will call me back. I have brought this pressure on myself by cutting things so fine. I call Norman of First Port in Edinburgh, who tells me that I will get public funding and asks me if I know Ross who sends computers to Ghana. Norman said, *'I am off to London'*.

12:17 p.m. Spoke to Joanne, the projects officer at West Dunbartonshire Council to let her know that 'the logistics' are in place for the Surplus Educational Supplies Foundation to uplift their council's surplus-to-requirements educational resources, which they have donated, and which the prime mover is salvaging, at his expense, and made possible by the goodwill of many great people who are in a hurry to salvage educational resources from Golden Hill Primary School on Saturday 3 July before the school buildings are due to be demolished; all being well, in the next 48 hours.

I call Duncan Adams Transport Ltd, Grange Dock, to confirm with Brian that they will have my container at Galt Transport Ltd, Dumbarton depot. Call Allan to let him know that my container is being brought across from Grange Dock by Duncan Adams Transport Ltd before Saturday. He has already told me that they will be able to trailer it to Golden Hill Primary School. I call Brian, site manager Interserve Projects Ltd, to let him know that the container will be brought to the school on Saturday morning, and confirm that they will, as arranged, lend a hand with the uplift of classroom furniture. Contact the press and media: the *Clydebank Post* will have a snapper on site at noon to record the collection of classroom furniture and so, yet again, I have joined the dots and lined up the actors. Is this what they call project management? Only, in my exceptional case, on the basis of some pro bono assistance and much goodwill and cooperation.

Councillor Ricky returned my call earlier. He was positive and told me that there were four other City of Edinburgh Council schools with educational resources that must be collected before the schools were demolished. I told him, *'That's great, I will take the lot,'* – and as I told him this I realised that my wholehearted commitment and enthusiasm to this initiative, and ego pride-driven hubris, had taken me over the top and it would take me a long time (in fact, it was to be another costly seven more years) before I climbed out from under the problems that I brought on myself by attempting the impossible project of attempting, on a shoestring, to single-handedly stem the avalanche of good quality fit-for-purpose educational resources from being crushed and dumped into landfill. I mentioned to Councillor Henderson that the Nicaraguan chargé d'affaires was coming to Scotland and could she be given a civic reception and receive official recognition from the City of Edinburgh? I called Alistair, the City of Edinburgh estates surveyor, who tells me that the Currie Hill Community were happy to see their primary school educational resources donated to SESF. Where will it go?

12:57 p.m. I am going to call Jemma, journalist with the *Edinburgh Evening News*. It was Jemma who had, out of the blue, called to tell me that the Curriehill Primary School buildings were being vandalised. My coffee has grown cold.

1:19 p.m. I received a call from Brian, the site manager of Interserve Projects Ltd, to tell me that he had met the head teacher, who was now concerned that the SESF container would get in the way of their removal firm. I told him that Galt Transport Ltd would let him know as soon as possible when their firm were ready to deliver the container to their site. Check with Galt Transport Ltd later this afternoon.

4 p.m. *'I told them the name of my company.'* That was Zak, the Ghanaian chief who called to tell me that he's a cherry picker, who only takes the best stuff (which I learned later).

4:19 p.m. *'I've loaded containers before,'* said Alec, the Clydebank volunteer, who had just called to tell me that he was coming on Saturday to lend a hand. He had seen the advertisement in the Clydebank Post asking for volunteers to help SESF with the uplift of resources. Good on him. *'I will be wearing a blue boiler suit,'* I said. For 1 July: call AGT Ltd to confirm arrival of the SESF container from Duncan Adams Transport Ltd, Grange Dock.

I call Interserve Projects Ltd so they can tell the Galt Transport Ltd artic driver where to park the trailer with the container when it arrives at Golden Hill Primary School. Meet with Zak to view resources in Unit 12. Meet with Chris to discuss the construction of the new SESF website. See if I can get a free haul to move MSKU6311690 with library shelving, currently parked at Freightliner Ltd Container Base, Coatbridge. See Kevin, Unit 1, to thank him for calling me about the chairs that had been left outside Unit 12 and were getting wet.

Thursday 01/07/2010

---

9 a.m. ScotRail service to Edinburgh. I got into Central Station, withdrew some funds and purchased a single ticket, and dashed aboard this train having forgotten that this was a slow train with stops along the way. Ah well, typical of me to either miss the boat, or get on board the wrong one.

It is a grey, humid and wet morning. The sunshine will come through. I came over on the MV *Bute,* Marion drove me to get the 6:30 a.m. ferry, which now departs at 6:25 a.m., so back we went to Delhi Cottage and she drove me in again to get the 7 a.m. boat. The lids of the three jars of marmalade, which I had placed in my haversack, had come off: fortunately, all was not spilt. Frank, the steward from England, bless him, got me a wet cloth and I cleaned up the mess.

On the boat I met Sam, master of all trades, who said he would collect me for another job on Sunday at 10 a.m. *'Have you got a spade?'* he asked. *'Yes,'* I said. *'Well bring it,'* he said. On the train

I met the Gatongi family, who were on their way to Kenya for a holiday. I wished them a safe journey and a safe return. Francis gave me a big wave when they got off the train at Paisley Gilmour Street. A young office worker came and sat down opposite me and put her umbrella down beside her bag, on which was printed the Burness, solicitors in Bothwell Street, logo. I introduced myself and asked her if she knew Stephen. She did and said he worked in the office opposite. I gave her an SESF flyer to pass on to him.

9:10 a.m. The train has stopped. On my left the city of Glasgow stretches west and east under a thick blanket of grey cloud. Premises of Network Rail, Babcock Rail, Alstom, Apex Generators, FedEx and Morrisons. The conductor has told me that I had boarded a train with insufficient fare and had to stump up £11.30. I had the coppers, so enjoy the journey. We are about to cross a shallow River Clyde.

Whizzed past Uddingston Station and have stopped at Bellshill – remember to thank TNT Transport Ltd for delivery of boxes to Unit 12. *'The next stop is Shotts,'* he said. Been there, as I remember it in the rain. I am journeying across the Central Belt: a Scottish pink rose is waving at me from a hedge. Holy Town: the Rowan trees growing on the other side of the station platform are laden with berries still to ripen.

9:45 a.m. Passed the three cone-shaped byngs of West Calder. It has started to rain and the next stop is Livingston South. I was here in 2008 en route from Edinburgh to collect educational resources from Inveralmond Community High School and had to get a taxi from that station to the school. That was another expensive ride. What's so creative about destruction? Demolition. Construction. Demolition. A 21st century civilisation leitmotif; for how much longer can 'creative destruction' continue on a planet of finite resources?

West African, Caribbean and Scottish links. I would like to

Thursday 01/07/2010

do some research some day in the National Library of Scotland about Mary Slessor of Calabar and Dundee. What is the connection? Looking at your dream home in West Lothian. The next stop is Haymarket, Kirkliston. Rosebay Willowherb brightens up the verge. Removal Services Scotland Ltd. Power lines strung overhead like spaghetti. We are travelling pretty quickly – too fast for me to read the station names. Got that one, Slateford, with graffiti. Corstorphine Hill, which I have been up and down in a Ford van. Allotments. Balfour Beatty Construction Ltd – would they sponsor me I wonder? ASDA. Wardlaw Terrace, Tynecastle High School, a huge new car park and Tesco Bank. Graham Construction Ltd.

10:05 a.m. Haymarket Station. *'We believe you can.'* Carnegie College.

3:15 p.m. I am now on the Stagecoach bus for Glasgow. I have bought myself a savoury cheese sandwich, a packet of crisps and a bottle of Fanta. Enjoy!

I had walked up Leith Walk in the sunshine from the Graphics Company Ltd, Annandale Lane, where I met Chris the web designer, who is going to give me quote. I would be still hoofing it along the road unless I had kept on asking passersby to confirm the directions that I had been given. On arrival in Edinburgh this morning I got a taxi to Unit 12, West Shore Business Centre, headquarters of www.haitirelief.org.uk. I have done what I had set out to do today. I met Zak at Unit 12 and he collected the resources that he wanted. I paid courtesy calls on Kevin, the artisan in cement in Unit 1, Alan at Forth Engineering Ltd, Unit 7. and the roofing company in Unit 3.

I AM CONFRONTED WITH PROBLEMS OF MY OWN MAKING

Golden Hill Primary School, Hardgate, Clydebank. Saturday 03/07/2010. Zak the Ghanaian chief has come all the way from Edinburgh to collect a van load of classroom furniture for his village school in Ghana, West Africa. He is being helped by Richard, a builder from Interserve Projects Ltd. This firm will build the new school when the old school is demolished.

Saturday 03/07/2010

9 a.m. Golden Hill Primary School, Hardgate, Clydebank. I arrived up here earlier by taxi from Central Station. *'It's £20 outside the city boundary,'* he said. I've got to be up there on time. *'Okay,'* I said.

On arrival I met Richard, the only Interserve Projects Ltd volunteer, along with Gary the boxer, David who drove their Inter Serve Manitou, and the team of volunteers: part of the collection uplift team who had already begun loading school furniture into container INBU4923874310. I met Festus from Nigeria, the security man, and Richard who lent me his mobile and I called Zak, who was on his way.

I am going to snap a few digitals, don my boiler suit and join the team of helpers: Jim, from Clydebank; Colin, a teacher from Balloch; Alec, who had called me a supporter of Mary's Meals; Stevie, the janitor; and Robert, from Galt Transport Ltd, who later that amazing day gave me a lift up to the depot at Broadmeadow Industrial Estate, Dunbarton. Zak was accompanied by his chum, a disc jockey, and his van who took away over 100 metal-legged conference chairs. By noon the container was almost fully loaded with Formica-topped classroom tables, chalkboards, wire-mesh shoe trolleys and lots more. I suggested to Galt Transport Ltd that they leave the container while we loaded it and they come back at midday to collect it, so they jacked it up. I gave Robert my SESF folder for him and Allan Galt to look at, should they care to do so, which he returned to me and said the boss had perused it over breakfast. They have about 15 of these high hab trailers; on arrival at the AGT Ltd depot Allan Galt invited me into the office for a mug of coffee and a biscuit; he is a gentleman, friendly and supportive of my initiative. I told him that I will have my container shifted to Babcock Marine, Rosyth Business Park, as soon as possible, where the resources loaded this morning can be properly inventoried and the container painted.

2:55 p.m. The sun is shining on the page as the train rumbles into the west. I have done what I set out in fear and trembling to accomplish today. I did not take what I had hoped to accomplish for granted. We got some media coverage from the *Clydebank Post,* the means by which I was able to acknowledge my gratitude to the Hardgate Community and my relationship to Interserve Projects Ltd, who generously provided a team to help shift the classroom furniture, and without whose help the uplift of educational resources to meet the West Dunbartonshire Council deadline within the time limit of a few days would not have been possible. I acknowledged crucial arrangements, made at the last minute, with haulage firms Galt Transport Ltd and Duncan Adams Transport Ltd, which went without a hitch, and not least the Bankies, who gave up a Saturday morning to rescue good quality classroom furniture.

Wednesday 07/07/2010

12:18 p.m. Home. I am sitting outside in the sunshine reading *Confessions of an Irish Rebel* by Brendan Behan. Zak has returned my call. He wants more.

Saturday 10/07/201

9 a.m. I am on a slow train for Edinburgh Waverley. Next stop is Bellshill.

1 p.m. Unit 12, West Shore Business Centre, Granton. Here I am looking out over the car park. Splat, splat, water dripping from the ceiling through the hole in the roof into the big puddle that has formed at the far end of the unit, which I will have repaired one day soon.

I am dry here at the main entrance. As I walked along West Harbour Road from Granton Square towards the West Shore

Business Centre I got within sight of the Granton Gasworks gasometer and I saw Denis drive out from Longcraig Rigg Road to come and collect me. Shortly after 11 a.m. Denis and I set to work, and then Iain, a professor colleague of his, appeared and took away with him a couple of books, one on St Patrick and another on marine life, which he thought he was entitled to do. Give him his due, however, he was very helpful and took a meticulous inventory of the stock and measurements of all the tables. Mark, driving a Jag, stacked the pallets and soon more helpers from Edinburgh Direct Aid appeared and I explained to them what was required: a general tidy up and an inventory taken of the educational resources that had accumulated over the last couple of months.

1:35 p.m. I have been chatting to Daryl, a cheerful lad who lent me his mobile phone and offered to help me; he works for Charles Stamper Wholesale Ltd, wholesale fruit and vegetable merchant suppliers to the catering trade. It is grey and cloudy.

I can now munch my corned beef sandwiches and crunch some Polish pickles. I am all alone here and it is very quiet and I am going to head home. Another job done.

Sunday 11/07/2010

11:54 a.m. Sam, who can build anything, is going to show me the next job he wants me to do. *'I'll meet you at half past one at the Boat Yard,'* he said. *(He did not tell me what he wanted me to do. I was soon to find out.)*

Tuesday 13/07/2010

Working for Sam. I spent two days working on his yacht at the Port Bannatyne boatyard, two days working on a kitchen in Largs, and one afternoon digging post holes for a pergola in a Crichton

Road back garden. *I'm tracking all these wee jobs. I'll settle with you at the weekend,'* he said.

Thursday 15/07/2010

3:09 p.m. Home. I have returned from the dentist in Greenock. I am going to call the following: Zak; Councillor Ricky; Alastair; Andrew Wishart & Sons Ltd, Rosyth; Jamie and Linda at the *Clydebank Post*.

10:29 a.m. Home. I spoke to Simon, who works for the charity Education for All, linked to the firm Thorpe Kilworth based in Corby. *'I will walk you through our process,'* he said. I am none the wiser after the walk.

Monday 19/07/2010

4:01 p.m. Home. David Alexander and the auld dad met Sam, master of all trades, at 8 a.m. and we set off to Battery Place to collect scaffolding and deliver to a house in the town. Then it was on to Kilchattan Bay, via the Boat Yard, to sandpaper and fill holes with Polyfilla, and we were back here by 3:30 p.m.

Tuesday 20/07/2010

7:16 a.m. I am on the train for Glasgow Central Station. I cycled into Rothesay, and on the boat I bought myself a mug of restorative hot chocolate and chatted to a lecturer at the Nautical College till we docked at Wemyss Bay. It is a very wet morning and there is nothing else for it but for me to push myself forward on this journey: my mission with the vision. I am heading for Edinburgh Haymarket Station and will get the bus from there out to Curriehill Primary School to meet Alistair, the City of Edinburgh Council estates surveyor, and Zak. *(See YouTube* *vandalism of the abandoned school in Curriehill – Abandoned School – Edinburgh, a film by TeEnZie, 16 May.)* Why? I am trying to raise my game. How? Creating links and collaboration with individuals and organisations with similar objectives. I know intuitively what I am trying to achieve, but until I've done it I won't be able, or seem unable at this moment, to put it into words. *'I don't see your logic,'* he said. *'Don't worry, I will continue to get on with what I have to do,'* I replied.

10:30 a.m. Curryhill Primary School. I am here to meet Alistair and Zak, who wants furniture for his village school in Ghana, where he is a chief.

1:41 p.m. *'Please have your tickets ready for inspection,'* he said. I arrived in Edinburgh and walked out of Haymarket Station, across to Dalry Road and asked directions, and within minutes hopped on a No. 44 Balerno bus. The sun is shining warm this morning; the bus climbing the hill into the upmarket environs of Auld Reekie. I got off at Curriehill Primary School, which was all boarded up. There is a small library in a Portakabin at the front of the main building which is still functioning. I was early as usual for the appointment. Soon borrowers appear in their cars.

    I cooled my heels, pacing up and down in what was once the school playground. Burly Zak the Ghanaian chief, brimming bonhomie, appeared. I told him that he would have to let me know soon what he intended to do with the educational resources that I enabled him to collect from Goldenhill Primary School, Clydebank on 3 July, because I will have to shift my container from the Galt Transport Ltd depot, Dumbarton, before much longer. He did not seem concerned, as he had already collected what he wanted. *'That's your problem.'*

    Soon Alistair appeared, greeting me with a firm handshake. He let us into the building. The YouTube amateur-made film does not show the full extent of the vandalism. I can see that insufficient resources remain to make a collection worthwhile, but Alistair seems keen to promote my charitable foundation's objectives. From up here in Curriehill, there are panoramic views of the City of Edinburgh from the rear of the school buildings. The surveyor was unable to gain access to where he said the resources had been stored and he was disappointed. I like him, he is keen and conscientious.

Alistair gave me a lift back to the Corn Exchange, where I dropped in at Lofthus Signs Ltd, New Mart Street, with a small minder of appreciation for Isabel, Graeme and team for the pro bono signage done at Unit 12 and at the entrance to the West Shore Business Centre. I got the No. 44 bus back to Haymarket Station. I'm heading home. It looks like I have left the sunshine behind.

No I did not, I found the sun shining brightly on the Costa Clyde.

Wednesday 21/07/2010

8:08 p.m. Home. Raindrops are pattering heavily off the skylight window. I cooked supper for Amy, David and Johanna. Marion is in Kilbarchan with Mum. I spent the day preparing information for Ross & Co, the accountants in Dunoon and drafting a letter for the City of Edinburgh councillors. I cycled into Rothesay in the rain to post the letter recorded delivery. Richard, the postmaster, is always cheerful and helpful: he gave me a towel to dry myself so I wouldn't smudge the letters. I went along to the Co-op to get some messages. I did what I set out to do this morning. I am tired.

Wednesday 28/07/2010

2:40 p.m. Home. I returned Zak's call and will meet him at 9:30 a.m., Unit 12, Tuesday 3 August. He will collect whatever he

Wednesday 04/08/2010

wants. It is all take and no give. It's not mine to keep and so long as it goes to where it is supposed to then it's no longer any of my concern.

I was speaking to the *Clydebank Post* newspaper. For the attention of Moira: cheque payable to *Clydebank Post*.

4:02 p.m. Called Royal Bank of Scotland in the town and spoke to Anne Marie, who is always cheerful and very efficient. *'Somebody is looking after you, your account is in credit,'* she said.

Monday 02/08/2010

8:55 a.m. Home. I called Bahram and left a message. I called Zak and cancelled the appointment for tomorrow. He said that he would send me some information about his charity.

I am going to walk into the town to post letters and get some exercise. We are looking forward to the visit over the weekend from our Nicaraguan English friends, Alistair, Naddy and Citlai. We are glad to offer hospitality to them. I have made an appointment to visit Jean and Ronnie in Edinburgh on 4 August. They had me to their home for supper in the autumn of 1975 when I was a student at the Moray House College of Education; Jean was my first Scottish teacher when I did my first teaching practice at Silverknowes Primary School. I call Andrew Wishart & Sons Ltd, Rosyth, to see if they will give me a 'free haul' and I left a message; call Sweeney Kincaid Auctioneers, Hillington – will they buy my containers?

Wednesday 04/08/2010

10:40 a.m. Unit 5 Apfelsnapz Ltd office, West Shore Business Centre, Granton. I am here to meet Bahram. Earlier I unloaded the car of four Brother brand sewing machines and some IT gifts from Davina of Rothesay. We get a welcome from Bahram, James, and Iain the accountant of Apfelsnapz Crisps Ltd. The former gave me and Marion the time of day. Bahram said he would help the Surplus Educational Supplies Foundation to get some funding. The first thing I have to do is prepare a credible business plan, and send him my accounts and the background to my initiative by tomorrow. Some notes – SESF needs more structure; possible funding from Bahram; in return I might be able to offer Apfelsnapz Ltd some publicity; a business plan; I need to be selective; what do the recipients require?; do the educational resources that SESF collects have a resale value?; what do I need to do to get funding?

He tells me, *'I don't think there is a sufficient income. Contact all companies to tell them this is what SESF does. Next, source of income is what you sell, of which there will be a small amount. You will need funding to cover your costs. How do you use the surplus which SESF acquires from schools? You must determine the costs of collection, storage and delivery prior to shipment; you will need a rolling fund because eventually the surplus educational resources will dry up. David, if you cannot meet these basic requirements, you are not a businessman.'*

This is a serious reality check, for I knew from the start I was not running a business. Why didn't I just stop there and accept the fact that I was, in Coach Barry's words, 'a dead duck'. I must send Bahram my records e.g., accounts, business plan, my spending, etc., and await a reply from him.

The meeting ended at 11:30 a.m. The next meeting will be to prepare a budget and advocate to schools that they become involved in the circular economy. Marion and I returned to Unit 12, I donned my boiler suit and unloaded the IT equipment: four Brother sewing machines; scanner and printer from the Hansons in Rothesay; and books from the Glass family of Wellpark Road. Zak appeared with a Rent-a-Van man and driver and I helped them load the SESF donation of the following resources: 70 metal-legged plastic-seated infant chairs; IT equipment; 10 leatherette-seated staffroom lounge chairs; and 2 Brother knitting machines. Zak wanted more, but I told him rather testily that would be all for the time being.

Marion and I then set off for Silverknowes Place, up the road, to visit Jean and Ronnie. Jean was my first Scottish teacher colleague, whose Primary 7 class I worked with on my first teaching practice assessment lesson when I was doing the Postgraduate Certificate in Primary Education course at Moray House College of Education in September 1974. They both gave us a warm welcome.

7:23 p.m. Home. I am not long in. I walked up the road from Rothesay; it is a beautiful afternoon. Amy and David are home. Marion dropped me off outside Paisley Gilmour Street Station and was on her way to visit Mum in Kilbarchan.

Thursday 05/08/2010

5:02 p.m. Home. Amy is in the kitchen cooking supper. Johanna is in Malawi, East Africa, working with two of her classmates from Rothesay Academy in a Malawian village. Marion is with Mum in Kilbarchan. I left in a hurry this morning to board the 8 a.m. ferry.

I got the bus up to Greenock and into the Oak Mall Shopping Centre to collect another spectacles case, and then back out and walked across to the Frederick Street Dental Practice where the dentist gave me four jags to pull a tooth and remove the roots. My mouth is very sore.

Back to Wemyss Bay on the Largs bus, into the Station Café to recuperate with a mug of sweet tea and was introduced to the landlord. On to the boat with lots of trippers, including me. The sun is shining brightly. A beautiful day. I had a cup of soothing chicken soup, courtesy of a kind steward. Bike back up the road.

I sat from midday until 2:15 p.m. preparing the information

Bahram requested. It is a beautiful day. I had another mug of gum-soothing homemade chicken soup. I got on the bike and back up the road to Print Point to photocopy Ross & Co Ltd accountant's pro bono accounts for 2008–2009, and then around the corner to the post office to post first-class, next-day delivery to Bahram. I am doing the best I can with what I have to work with: doing what I believe to be necessary and leaving as little as possible to chance. I then cycled up to RBS to deposit the gift of £50 from Jean and Ronnie into the SESF account, then around to the Musicker Café to shoot the breeze. I sat with Laurence, who I had met there a while back. He is receiving a lot of physiotherapy and acupuncture and is in a lot of pain. And I met Maureen who once worked for the prison service.

Saturday 07/08/2010

11 p.m. Home. I have made some marmalade. It has been a beautiful day. I walked along the Craigmore and around and over Canada Hill and down Minister's Brae into the town to the cashpoint, then into the Discovery Centre to get a selection of Scotland Tourist Board brochures to send to Felix in Grenada, West Indies. Then along to Print Point to purchase ink for the printer, where over a hot chocolate I wrote a line to my Grenadian supporter, and on to the post office to post the package of Scottish Tourist Board publicity. I then walked home and sat in the sunshine with Marion, David and Gran. Later I cycled in to purchase ingredients for David's barbecue. Whew! I am ready to hit the sack.

Monday 16/08/2010

7:20 a.m. I am in a rolling carriage on a train for Glasgow Central. I am en route for Bellshill to meet with TNT Transport Ltd, Rigghead Industrial Estate. It was Peter the TNT driver who brought the boxes of crockery from the Ben Mundell Hillington

Monday 16/08/2010

depot to Unit 12, West Shore Business Centre, Granton, on 26 July. It was Holly, in the TNT Corporate Social Responsibility Department, who oversaw this collection and it was Lorraine in that department who I spoke to on 22 April, and who tied this wonderful pro bono collection and delivery together.

8:04 a.m. Stand 22, Buchanan Street Bus Station. I am now on the bus for Bellshill. It is a grey, overcast morning. I hoofed it up the road to get a bus.

I wish to express my appreciation to this firm for the pro bono assistance that TNT Ltd gave to SESF on 26 April in delivering boxes to Unit 12 (see www.haitirelief.org.uk). I wish to determine whether this international transport firm might be willing to sponsor and work with me and SESF in pursuit of the charitable foundation's objectives, and to seek information about introductions to other sources of corporate social responsibility assistance.

11:15 a.m. I am in the reception room of TNT Ltd headquarters in Scotland, main office. I have met a representative of the firm, who has taken my file and information from a pen drive and said she will post it back to me. I told her that I was looking for continuing goodwill assistance from other firms in the haulage, logistics and transport industry.

I wanted to find out if this firm would be willing to support my initiative on a limited, one-off basis in the removal, collection, storage, delivery and shipment of fit-for-purpose, surplus to Scottish education system requirements resources to deserving beneficiaries in the impoverished natural-disaster prone and rapidly developing world?

Earlier I got off the bus on what I thought was the London Road and had a good long walk through the vast maze of warehouses and small industries all dependent on the road haulage industry, and I ignored the tempting purvey being offered at that time of day by the many snack vans on my way to find the TNT HQ.

My interlocutor returned after what seemed a long while and returned my main SESF file, which she said had been photocopied, and told me that they were very busy. I have achieved goal one, and whether goals two and three pan out remains to be seen. I then walked up to the main road at the boundary of the Righead Industrial Estate and eventually got a slow bus back to Glasgow.

I got off on St Vincent Street, I walked down Renfield Street and into Central to await the Wemyss Bay train.

2:26 p.m. The engines of the MV *Argyle* are throbbing below me. I have had a cup of soup. I stopped in at the Wemyss Bay Station Café and gave the pleasant proprietress some of the SESF flyers and sheets of SESF publicity. *'You have some influential friends,'* she said.

Have I now? And who might they be? I asked myself.

Thursday 19/08/2010

8:20 a.m. I am on the ScotRail service for Edinburgh Waverley. £11.50. I can get the No. 16 bus to Granton Square and should be able to walk along West Harbour Road to the West Shore Business Centre by 10 a.m. I am beginning another day of self-employment.

'Are you doing this full time?' asked George's mum, of the Plan Farm, Isle of Bute, as we were waiting to disembark from the MV *Bute*. Tony turned to me and said, *'You are hanging on by the skin of your teeth.'* I did not say anything, but thought *'true enough, but what else can I do but to persevere with this initiative until I have seen it through to completion?'*

I continue to climb the hill with difficulty. I am heading back across the Clyde as I look across to the Nautical College where David will be studying today; there is a cloudy grey sky interspersed with a few blue patches. I am going over to meet a delivery of educational resources from the Erskine Stewart's Melville

Thursday 19/08/2010

Schools Consortium, and I hope to meet with Bahram, who said to me at our last meeting, *'I have some questions to ask you.'* 'Go ahead,' I said. We pass by Cambuslang, Newton, Uddingston, Bellshill, Holy Town, Carfin, Cleland, Shotts, Fauldhouse, Breich, Addiewell, West Calder, Livingston, South Kirknewton, Curriehill, WesterHailes, Kingsknowe, Slateford, and Haymarket.

10:15 a.m. I got a taxi from Haymarket Station: £12.50 to be able to meet Malcom and Grant Removals at Unit 12, where we unloaded 200 metal-legged plastic-seated conference chairs. They are away to collect more resources and return with 12 heavy computer desks in excellent condition, possibly out of fashion, and 7 filing cabinets with keys, also in good nick.

11 a.m. Bahram's office. He's gone next door to make me a coffee. Kind hospitality. The sun is shining brightly on Edinburgh this morning. I was sweating from the shifting of furniture from Pettigrew's large removal van and have changed out of my boiler suit. I am now *un homme d'affaire.* He said he would call me when he has prepared the numbers; he thinks SESF needs funding.

I returned to Unit 12 to tidy up and appreciate the loan of this space. It is far to travel, but this beggar can't be too choosy. I closed the unit and walked up West Harbour Road to the bus stop past Granton Square to get a No. 16 bus. I am on the bus for Glasgow with some treats to enjoy.

I achieved what I set out to do this morning. I am now on the train for Wemyss Bay. I met a fellow traveller who knew about my work and seemed interested, perhaps just curious as so many of my fellow travellers have been, so I gave him a flyer; and one to Rory who is studying architecture at Glasgow School of Art and who is working as a steward on the MV *Bute* for the summer. I am tired and can only keep on, keeping on course.

I am Confronted with Problems of My Own Making

Friday 20/08/2010

9 a.m. Home. It is wet and grey this morning and I am trying to get started. *'I'll put you in my diary and I will probably call you up in a couple of months' time,'* said Bob, Head of Business Studies at the College.

11:45 a.m. *'All to a good cause, but I wouldn't hold my breath, the lease for the unit does not extend to repairs,'* said Alasdair. I called to ask him whether the leaking roof of Unit 12 could be repaired and I suggested that the roofing company in the unit across the way might do it gratis.

2:37 p.m. The sun continues to shine so I am going to walk over the top of Canada Hill into the town, collect my prescription and purchase some messages for supper.

Monday 23/08/2010

3:44 p.m. Home. It has been drizzling wet all day. I set off this morning to walk around and over Canada Hill. I am glad that I made the effort. I went along to One2One Accountancy Services Ltd to collect two VAT returns, which I sent to Ross & Co from the post office. I got the goldfish their food and headed home. Last night I wrote to the principal of St George's School in Grenada in reply to a letter from them requesting a shipment of educational resources.

Wednesday 25/08/2010

5:10 p.m. MV *Argyle*. I am waiting for Robert and Frank to appear. They are teachers from Malawi visiting Scotland and Inverkip Primary School, who I had been taking with me to Edinburgh. I am becoming anxious. *Where are they? Are they on the boat?*

Wednesday 01/09/2010

I went over with them at 6:30 a.m. Train up to Glasgow Central Station. I walked over to the taxi rank with them, took a taxi up to Buchanan Street Bus Station and got the 8:30 a.m. Edinburgh bus. We walked out of Saint Andrew Square Bus Station and across to another taxi rank and took a taxi to the Scottish Parliament at Holyrood. A beautiful morning, and we waited for the Rothesay Academy Jazz Band. We were given a conducted tour of this amazing building, then the three of us walked up the Royal Mile to the castle. We declined the exorbitant entrance fee of £14 and walked down the hill into Princes Street Gardens, across to Princes Street, and up to George Street. I treated them to lunch at the Undercroft Café, having also paid their travelling fares. After lunch it was back across Saint Andrew Square and the bus back to Glasgow. Where are they now? As it turned out they were left behind at Wemyss Bay.

Wednesday 01/09/2010

---

9 p.m. Home. I am sitting here in the living room where Johanna is working at her laptop. Marion is doing teacher preparation; David is staying with Gran in Kilbarchan and travelling in to the Nautical College; Amy is also with them as she had her Speech and Language group work at the Chest and Heart Centre in Barlanark.

I set off before 6 a.m. A mild morning to deliver the pen which Robert, teacher from Malawi, had dropped in our car on Saturday, and so up the road I cycled to the Sunnyside Boarding House where he and Frank were staying. I awoke the landlady, who was not well pleased, to deliver it, then it was on to the MV *Argyle* ferry. On the way over I chatted with Alan of A&M Transport Ltd removals.

I am now on the train and feeling smart: shoes shined, suited, white shirt and tie – feeling and looking the part. Those who ken my face after all these years perhaps are curious, as many have asked me where I am going. I walked up to Queen Street Station and got the 8:30 a.m. train to Edinburgh. I sat across from Annabel Goldie, current leader of the Scottish Conservatives, and I took the liberty before leaving the train at Waverley Station of quickly introducing myself. I gave her an SESF flyer and my business card. I heard a voice in my head saying, *'Who do you think you are, buttonholing one of the great and good like that?'* I have got to try and step out and above myself since no one is going to invite me to do so; some influence from the right quarter at Holyrood would not go amiss. I am wasting my time there.

It is a morning of bright sunshine on Princes Street as I wait for the green man at the corner of the same spot as in 1974–1975, on my return from lectures at Moray House College of Education then situated at the bottom of the Royal Mile. I walk back across the city to 65 Northumberland Street, a converted New Town residence, which was then, behind the Georgian façade, a mental health hostel run by the Lothian Regional Council's Department of Social Work, who had employed me temporarily as an assistant to the warden, Pipe Major Calum McPhee. I crossed the busy road and went into Waterstone's bookstore where prime minister's Blair's autobiography was being promoted, and got a book with a book token that had been given to me by David.

I had a long wait for a No. 16 bus outside Jenner's. I was on the top deck as always and got off at the Granton Square bus stop near the roundabout, and in to the Len Lothian Ltd self-storage premises where I met Stephen, who gave me the figures. His associate standing beside him said my library shelves were worthless. I trudged further along West Harbour Road and stopped off at Pickford's, who gave me a friendly reception. I gave my details and explained what I was after and they told me that I would be contacted. I stopped in at the plant-hire firm, who advised me to write to their property services.

I arrived finally at the West Shore Business Centre. In to see Bahram, who did not have the numbers for an SESF budget as

Wednesday 01/09/2010

promised but would do so next week. Over to Unit 12. I am dismayed, and pleased at the same time, as I see how much good quality useful stuff, good kit, and essential classroom furniture I have collected over last five years, and presently there are also at least five, or is it six, ocean freight containers with educational resources at five different road haulage depots the length and breadth of Scotland. I have inundated myself with a vast quantity of fit-for-purpose, good quality, educational resources. Where and to whom is the Surplus Educational Supplies Foundation (Scottish Registered Charity SCO39331) going to distribute it all to?

I don my boiler suit and I am glad that I have made another monumental effort to get over here and begin to tidy up, to make room for the shelving which is stored in container MSKU6311690 over in Coatbridge. At which depot? I have now lost track of the resources that have been collected and stored in ocean freight containers that were purchased at my expense; albeit grateful that handling and temporary parking charges where containers are located have been waived.

Shortly after noon, Scott, the team leader from the Muirhouse Social Work Centre Community Services Criminal Justice Department, appeared. I showed him around and explained to him what I was trying to do. I said that apart from delivering much-needed educational resources to devastated and inadequately equipped schools in the developing world, I also hoped to make a small contribution to the rehabilitation of young offenders by providing them with opportunities for meaningful work in the collection, storage, refurbishment and the shipment of educational resources, and possibly involvement in their delivery. I gave Scott my SESF memory stick, with digitals of the various activities that young offenders had contributed to (see *Diary of a Shipping Clerk, Volume Two, published 27 October 2023, www.haitirelief.org.uk),* my CV and social enterprise business plan, current SESF accounts etc. I had given him and his social work colleagues more than enough information to vet my suitability, or otherwise, to collaborate with their clients. He said he would return with my dossier at 2 p.m. I carried on working. Alan at Forth Engineering Ltd let me have a bucket of water to wash the windows of the Unit 12 office that I was unable to reach. 2 p.m. came and no Scott.

I had to phone him. *'Could I let you have your information next week?'* he asked, *'I would appreciate if you returned it to me today.' 'I will be down at 3 p.m.,'* he said.

I have made an appointment with Scott, acting on behalf of Community Services who will provide the Surplus Educational Supplies Foundation with one of their teams who will come to Unit 12 at 10:15 a.m. on Monday, 11 September. Check date; when together we will inventory the entire stock and arrange in apple pie order.

I asked him to drop me off at Granton Square and got a No. 16 bus back to Saint Andrew Square. I stopped in Kodak on Rose Street corner to have digitals of the Jubilee Gardens Library shelves copied by a helpful sales lady. I walked on down the road to Haymarket Station with sunshine on my face.

I met Neville, the seagoing chef, in Central Station and we chatted all the way back across the watta to Rothesay harbour. I am tired out.

Monday 13/09/2010

10:09 a.m. Unit 12, West Shore Business Centre, below the Granton Gas Works. It is a grey, wet and windy day. I walked from the Granton Square bus stop. So far no one has showed up from Community Services: *'Some of our clients lead chaotic lives, I don't know whether they will show up or not,'* said Nicola at the Muirhouse Crescent Community Centre. I change into my boiler suit. Marion drove me in from Kilbarchan to Johnstone Railway Station and I got the train to Glasgow Central and walked up to

Monday 20/09/2010

Buchanan Street Bus Station. I got a 7:45 a.m. bus for Edinburgh, got off on Princes Street and walked up to Jenners and got a No. 16. I shall get to work.

11:15 a.m. The team from Community Services showed up and got stuck in; they are all great workers who stacked the metal-legged conference chairs and rearranged the school furniture. I went and saw Bahram, and he tells me he has prepared a budget based on my accounts and will call me later in the week.

1:50 p.m. The team from Muirhouse Crescent returned from their lunch break and with little ado got back to work.

2:40 p.m. The team have just left; they have done a grand job, which has allowed me to see my way through all this stuff, which is great. One had her eye on an antique china doll, and I gave it to her. *'I am going to call her Kimberley,'* she said. Bless her and all the team, and may each be able to turn their fragile and precious lives around for good.

I called Alasdair, Head of Security and Estates Supervisor, Waterfront Edinburgh Ltd, to let him know that I had spoken to someone at Roofing and Cladding Ltd at the unit across from Unit 12, who said that they would repair the roof for £250. I asked this firm to confirm with Alasdair that it was alright for them to go ahead and do the necessary repair on the roof of the unit. It is time to climb out of my boiler suit, which could do with a good wash, and head for home.

Monday 20/09/2010

8:53 a.m. Home. Here I go again, pushing, struggling through the barrier of my own inertia and feelings of inadequacy.

I am calling Andrew of React Transport Ltd, who have a depot on West Harbour Road in Granton. Will they allow SESF to temporarily park its containers on their property? The receptionist said, *'I will ask him to call you.'*

I left a message for Bahram in Unit 5; he had said he would be in touch. So far, he has not done so. I had great expectations of him and still do. I am waiting expectantly for him to call; would that I did not need to be so dependent on the help of others. How can I become less so? It would be great if I was able to work in an area, a field, an environment, an occupation, where I could just get on with it, like I have been able to do for more than three decades in the garden at the back of Blacksmith's Bothy at the foot of Creag Mhor cliff.

I called Carnegie College in Dunfermline. What are you after now, skip raker? I am trying to enlist the collaboration, cooperation and inspiration of some students who have not lost their enthusiasm, and who have not become cynical and apathetic. I speak to Marian in their office, who said she will pass on my enquiry to John.

12:25 p.m. Someone in the Faculty of Business and Society will call me back. I am still waiting for a reply. The corporate and public sectors are moribund and seem to have lost their vision and drive. I have returned with some clean laundry, which I had taken to the launderette in the town and did some shopping for messages. I stopped in at Ghillies Bar in the Victoria Hotel for an Americano. Amy is home and is preparing lunch. Bless her.

3:05 p.m. Andrew of React Transport Ltd called me. He is approachable regarding my request for the temporary use of their depot's yard, which is not far up the West Harbour road from Unit 12, to park SESF containers to load and unload. He tells me to call after 3 p.m. next week.

4:09 p.m. I have made an appointment to see Neil, manager at Biffa, tomorrow morning about the possibility of parking SESF containers at their depot, which is across the road from the West Shore Business Centre. Andrew had suggested I contact Clockwork Transport Ltd further up the road. I made an appointment to see the Apfelsnapz team, Unit 5, before noon tomorrow, who will help me put together a budget for SESF. I spoke with John at Carnegie College Faculty of Business and Society, who said he would get back to me with arrangements for me to speak to the students.

Tuesday 21/09/2010

11:45 a.m. I am in the office of Apfelsnapz Crisps Ltd, sitting at their boardroom table in an upstairs room of this large warehouse unit with big windows and with views across the Firth of Forth. I was welcomed by James, with a Barbados connection, and Iain the accountant.

Earlier I had gone across to the Biffa depot and met Neil the manager, who was affable and has a positive attitude to what I am trying to accomplish. He is willing to let me store the SESF containers in the Biffa yard but cannot let me have regular access to them.

Bahram has disappeared with a mobile telephone stuck to his ear; if nothing else I have made another supreme effort of will to get over to Unit 12.

I cycled into Rothesay town in the dark and on the way over to Wemyss Bay I was in conversation with Neville, local chef and merchant navy cook who comes from the Emerald Isle. I travelled up to Central Station on the train, for how else would I have gotten there, and walked up to Buchanan Street Station. I go the 8:45 a.m. bus to Saint Andrew Bus Station and walked across the square to get a No. 16 to Granton Square. I walked along Weston Harbour Road to the West Shore Business Centre. I opened up Unit 12 and walked across the road to the Biffa reception Portakabin and then retraced my steps to collect my fluorescent waistcoat, which I had left in the office. I am now in Bahram's office, Iain the accountant is on the phone and I am looking across the car park to Unit 12 and the Granton Gas Works behind Unit 12. I'm wondering what have I come all this way across the Central Belt of Scotland for?

Wednesday 22/09/2010

Home. I am down in the dumps. It has been raining all day, so I got on the phone and began making contact with the firms and organisations that I intend to talk to tomorrow at the Scottish Learning Festival at the Scottish Exhibition Centre, Glasgow. I don't feel like it; the prospect does not beckon. Why bother? Well because if you don't, no one else will bother.

Thursday 23/09/2010

6:40 a.m. MV *Argyle*. I forced myself off the bed, shaved, and under a warm shower began to look forward to a new day. On awakening I had to quickly get rid of all the baggage that I dump on myself at first consciousness.

'*Where are you going today?*' asked Dougie, the pier master ex-policeman. We had a brief chat and I told him where I was going. '*I would not be standing in front of you this morning if I did not bother,*' I said. '*You are right,*' he said, as much to say, '*On ye go then.*'

3 p.m. Home. I had a call from Holly, TNT Transport Ltd Special Services, which I returned but she was in another meeting.

As I was leaving the SEC concourse at around 11:45 a.m. a voice shouts out, '*Do ye no remember me?*' A character in denim jacket, jeans and cowboy boots seated at a café table. '*I'm Eddy Edwards, ah know you from somewhere years ago,*' he said. I turned around and went over to him and shook his hand, racking my brain to recall the time and place.

Thursday 23/09/2010

I arrived at the SEC shortly after 9 a.m. and handed my haversack in at the coatroom. *'I'm sorry you can't come in until it actually opens, unless you are an exhibitor,'* she said. *'I am exhibiting,'* I think to myself. I am a walking real-life exhibit. I went and had a coffee. Later that morning I met the marketing development manager of the consortium based in Trowbridge, who had worked for Findel the educational resources supplier in Wiltshire; she had travelled all over Africa and was on my wavelength, and just as the conversation, which I initiated, had begun to get interesting I spilt my coffee.

Later I had another cup of coffee with a representative of Dunbartonshire Community Services, who told me that she was related by marriage to the Duncan Adams Transport Ltd family; it is a small world in Scotland. I pitched my patter to many stall holders: some were indifferent and others showed a bemused interest. On the whole it was worth my effort to get out and about. A trainer and expedition leader from the Lochgoilhead Outdoor Centre, who was bound for Malawi with a party of trekkers, quizzed me about shipping containers. There was Sian's mum, from the Ben More Centre, who came over to speak to me and I recalled the time when we had last met in 2005, when they had dropped off a carload of toys at the Caribbean Hurricane Relief Depot at the Boat Yard in Port Bannatyne. I also met Peter from the Outdoor Centre over on the Cowal Peninsula, at which point it was time to quit while I was ahead as it was becoming too crowded with teachers and their pupils all milling about, unsure of how to get a hold on the purpose of their day, out of place, just as I was in this commercial milieu.

On the return journey aboard the MV *Argyle* I met Neville, who is now a ship's catering manager with Maersk, who bought me a coffee and we chatted away perched on Cabin Café bar stools.

I AM CONFRONTED WITH PROBLEMS OF MY OWN MAKING

Friday 24/09/2010

4:26 p.m. Home. Alasdair, the head of security and estates supervisor, has called to tell me that the roofers have surveyed the Unit 12 roof and it will cost me £250. I said that this would be fine and there were sufficient funds in the SESF charity account to cover it (I knew that I would personally have to make up the difference), so would he tell them for me to go ahead and make the necessary repairs. It is a beautiful autumn of full-on sunshine. I went up the road on my bicycle to the High Kirk Church of Scotland to attend Janet, our former next-door neighbour's funeral service, which was taken by the Reverend Iain Laing. I met John, Johanna's friend Samantha's dad and we stopped to chat. He is a great man for a number of reasons: he told me that his family are going to foster two children; he is heavily involved in raising funds for Spirit Aid, and has been out to Malawi. He became seriously ill while jogging to raise funds for that charity, and if all of those good deeds were not enough, he later donated one of his kidneys.

Monday 27/09/10

4:27 p.m. Home. I have returned from dropping Marion, who is on her way to Malawi, off at Glasgow Airport. I received a return call from Spencer of Texas Instruments based in Northampton, who I met at the Learning Festival last week. He is keen to assist SESF. He is going to follow up my query regarding the possibility of his firm donating their surplus to requirements IT equipment.

Tuesday 28/09/201

09:16 a.m. Home. It is overcast and windy. We are heading into winter. I am about to call Habib, who is a fundraiser for a Pakistan charity. *'It has not been possible to connect you,'* he said.

Friday 01/10/2010

10:01 a.m. *'That's Mum arrived in Johannesburg,'* said Amy.

Wednesday 29/09/2010

6:25 p.m. Home. I received a call from Marion earlier to say that they had arrived safely in Malawi. Great! May the journeying mercies continue for her. I spent the day preparing two SESF flyers by cutting and pasting the old way. I have no IT expertise and I'm awaiting the arrival of Zeb, the washing machine engineer; there is a clear sky overhead and I must stay put.

The common good, the UBUNTU, ALOHA spirit, benefits for all; the Surplus Educational Supplies Foundation is a self-funded social venture. I call Rosetta, head teacher St George's Anglican School, Grenada W. I. No result. I don't know when to give up and leave well enough alone. *'G-D does not expect you to do everything,'* Roland said to me in his office on 18 December 2009, Miami, Florida. I must get wise – less is often more.

Friday 01/10/2010

1 p.m. Home. I am eating a banana and it is raining heavily. I cycled to Port Bannatyne and stopped off at what was the Tea Pot, now rebranded as The Tea Room, to say hello to Janet and Sharyn. I was not quite wringing wet. They gave me a warm welcome and in return I gave them some SESF flyers, which the former placed one on each table. Thanks for the publicity. I want action on deliverables.

3:52 p.m. It is still raining. I have been reading Clement Freud's autobiography. I called Bahram, who said he would call me last night, and he said his accountant had done some work on preparing a budget for SESF.

I am Confronted with Problems of My Own Making

Tuesday 05/10/2010

7:45 p.m. Home. It has been a long day. I travelled over to Edinburgh to attend the OSCR AGM, which held in the Murrayfield Conference Centre, where there was no gain for my effort and the expense of attending. I was a fish out of water in that milieu; I had no opportunity to chat, to network. It was a beautiful day that I spent indoors. For what? I am just going through the motions. I am barely hanging on.

Thursday 07/10/2010

9:53 a.m. Home. I arrived back on the MV *Argyle* and walked up the road in the drizzle. I have been over to The Grove, Kilbarchan, where I was weeding the driveway. Yesterday morning I got stuck into some energetic manual labour of which, thankfully, I am still capable when the need arises. This morning, as I walked out to the bus stop on Wheatlands Drive, I looked back at my piecework with at least a clear conscience, if not satisfaction, as there was so much more weeding still to do in the garden that Marion's dad had put so much effort into.

9:56 a.m. I called Bahram about the SESF budget and business plan and the application for a grant – funding.

10:43 a.m. I spoke to Iain the accountant, who said he would call me back next week.

Wednesday 13/10/2010

10:54 a.m. Home. David is back safely from doing his sea time and is studying. Marion and Amy left earlier for her studies on the mainland. I spoke to Iain, who I am to call next week to arrange a time when he will help me to put a budget together.

Thursday 21/10/2010

3:45 p.m. I called the head teacher of Blackhall Primary School, Edinburgh, to discuss with her the school's offer of tables and educational resources that were surplus to their requirements (*see their email, 6 October*). I received a positive response from her. I suggested that the Community Services Criminal Justice Department teams, based at Muirhouse Social Work, might be able to help me with the uplift and told her that I would call the centre to see if they could make this collection. A few moments later, I spoke to Scott at the Muirhouse Social Work Centre to determine if they could make this collection, and he said that they could make this collection. He told me that their Community Services Criminal Justice Department is now based in one of the units in the West Shore Business Centre. *'We are neighbours,'* Scott said. I then called the head teacher to let her know that a collection of resources from her school had been arranged and gave her Scott's mobile number; hopefully this uplift will take place after the holidays.

Yet again, I have had to respond and act in an entrepreneurial fashion. I have had to make the initial move. I take the risk, seize the opportunity, and suffer the consequences. If there is anything worthwhile that I have achieved in this project, now going into its sixth year of operation, it has only been achieved because I took the initiative and made it happen at no little cost to my family and myself.

Thursday 21/10/2010

Home. I have been outside helping our neighbours reassemble their garden shed. It is grey and damp today. I am going to call Iain the accountant: he told me to call him on Monday 25th. He said he might see me on Tuesday.

I call the High Commission for Jamaica in London and try to speak to their education attaché. I call Forest Furnishing Ltd: the receptionist answers and says, *'You had better speak with one of our directors. You are through to the IT department.'* I push myself out the door and go into the town for some messages from the Co-op. It had been raining earlier. I stopped at The Bike Shed. *'You can only try,'* said Liam, who has taped my fraying bicycle seat.

9:03 a.m. Home. A beautiful day. There is not a cloud in the sky. I am showered and ready to do battle. I called Iain the accountant. *'This person's phone is switched off.'*

Tuesday 26/10/2010

6:30 a.m. I was over on the MV *Bute*. As I was walking into Rothesay, Zeb the washing machine engineer kindly paused to offer me a lift to the pier. It was the first blessing of the day.

11:15 a.m. Unit 5 office, West Shore Business Centre, Granton. I am attending a meeting with Iain the accountant, who is sitting in front of me with his laptop with the appropriate spreadsheet software, helping me prepare a budget of projected costs for 2010–2013 that will be part of a business plan to apply for funding and investment in the social enterprise of what will be a revenue generating and self-sustainable social enterprise.

I am grateful for his help this morning and that of Bahram, who has just brought me a mug of coffee. Just as I felt we were getting into the nitty-gritty of the budget of costs, a hale and hearty Jim of Scottish Enterprise Ltd appears at the door, unannounced, who Bahram and Iain tells me is a 'high up' in that organisation: my tutorial, a masterclass in basic bookkeeping, comes to an end. The visitor says he would like to have a look at my financial statements, CV and the story of SESF, and he leaves with copies of those documents. I have yet to hear from him.

1:40 p.m. I am now back in Unit 12. Both Iain and Bahram couldn't have been more helpful to me. I take another faltering step along the road. I am going to head for home; hopefully the ferries are sailing to schedule.

Wednesday 27/10/2010

10:04 a.m. Home. I call Zak the SCVO IT person applications developer to find out how his trip to his homeland of Ghana, West Africa, went. He tells me that he spent a fortune in order to release his container of educational resources from Scotland; he has spent all of the funds he took with him in order for Port of Tema customs, Ghana, to release the container. He tells me *'Ah got some pitchas foh yah.'*

10:34 a.m. I called Ross & Co to discuss the SESF company's accounts. They tell me to call Companies House in Edinburgh – a direct line who will send me form AAO2 for a 'dormant account'.

11:03 a.m. I call the Ghana High Commission, London, and speak to Edward their welfare officer, who says he will come up to Scotland to see what SESF has to offer in Unit 12; but first I must contact their Ministry of Education in Ghana.

Thursday 28/10/2010

1:32 p.m. Home. It is wet and grey. Sian, a contemporary of Amy, has not long appeared to have a look at the rabbit hutch, which Dan had made for Amy and Johanna's rabbits. She has come in response to an advertisement that I had asked the pet shop in Rothesay to display; she would like to have it and will call and collect it some time. It has been up the back under the Craigmore escarpment, the big cliff, for not a few years now.

I am in limbo. In the doldrums. I am holding on, just. Martin, the person responsible for Viridor operations in Scotland, the waste collectors, builders of incinerator plants and waste recyclers, has returned my call to tell me he is on annual leave. His firm have a large skip outside Unit 12. This skip is always overflowing with rubbish and blocks the front door of the Surplus Educational Supplies Foundation office. I have been trying to get this firm to park it somewhere else.

Friday 29/10/2010

5:30 p.m. Home. Alasdair, head of security, estates supervisor at Waterfront Edinburgh Ltd, has just called to let me know that it may be possible to park a couple of ocean freight containers on a vacant site adjacent to their security office. He asked me if the repairs to the Unit 12 roof had been carried out. I told him that while I was in the unit on the morning of Tuesday 26 October I could not tell. I said that after the heavy showers of today I will be able to tell the next time I am over, and if there are no leaks I will settle my account with Roofing and Cladding Ltd.

I have done little today apart from calling Carnegie College, Dunfermline and I left a message with Emma, administrative.

Wednesday 03/11/2010

12:45 p.m. At this moment I am on the top deck of a No. 16 shoogling vibrating bus, with panoramic vistas of the Firth of Forth's distant shoreline. I have come from a meeting with Alasdair, the security and estates supervisor, Waterfront, Edinburgh at 11:30 a.m. I paid the roofer bill; it would appear that their handiwork on the roof of Unit 12 has been satisfactory. The Rotary chapter here in Rothesay made a donation to Scottish Registered Charity SCO 39331, The Surplus Educational Supplies Foundation, which defrayed the cost of this necessary repair. Thank you, Rothesay Rotarians.

I had a brief impromptu meeting with Alasdair and they have offered me a large fenced-off vacant site, where they will allow me to park the SESF containers, adjacent to Waterfront Avenue, directly across from the huge modern multistorey flats across from the Waterfront Edinburgh Ltd Security Portakabin, where the security guards train their dogs. He tells me, *'I have five Gurkhas working for me.'* I asked after Gumon from Nepal.

I had a meeting with Jan, Telford College, Faculty of Community Studies, who was receptive to my pitch; I was wondering if any of the students might like to become involved in the work of the Surplus Educational Supplies Foundation. I struggle, and the struggle goes on for every single one of us in Blue Planet Global Village. I am heading back to Saint Andrew Bus Station.

(And today, this unseasonably wet day of spring, as I copyedit Diary of a Shipping Clerk, Volume Three, 4 p.m. Wednesday, 27 March 2024, the people, the men, women and children of Ukraine, Gaza and Sudan are being rocketed and bombed to destruction.)

Thursday 04/11/2010

9:36 a.m. I am over the watta once again. There is a thick blanket of wispy mist sitting on top of Skelmorelie. I cycled into Rothesay town and would have been almost soaked to the skin had I not worn showerproof overtrousers.

I stopped off at Print Point to collect a copy of the SESF annual report, with budget. I chatted briefly with Dougie, a supporter, ex-policeman and now assistant harbour master. I told about him my trip over to Granton, Edinburgh, yesterday and the former ex-Gurkha security team and their dogs. *'Well you won't have to worry about security.'*

I am heading off this morning to a social media promotional event being held in Springfield Court, Princes Square, Glasgow: somewhere I have never been before. I am keen to get up to speed with this digital means of instant communication with a goal of somehow raising the profile of the work of the Surplus Educational Supplies Foundation.

10:55 a.m. Inverclyde Royal Infirmary, Greenock. Admissions waiting room.

Roll it back from the river of time. *'You don't step into the same river twice',* said the clever Greek Heraclitus. Change is constant. I try to keep some kind of a record of the changes that occur in its flow.

I was slow in getting off the boat and I nearly made the round trip; as I was walking up the pier on my own, a gentleman came up to me and asked me, *'Are you David Hanschell?'*

'Yes,' I replied, hesitantly, thinking to myself where is this leading?

'My name is Sam, and I am the Inverkip School janitor and I have come to collect you. Your wife has had an accident at the school,' he said.

I was stunned. How serious is this accident, I wondered?

He drove me up the road. On arrival I find Marion lying on the floor of the school gym, with two Scottish Ambulance crew in attendance and a number of colleagues standing around. *'What's wrong?'* I ask. On up the road to the hospital.

Friday 05/11/2010

10:25 a.m. Home. Marion has a broken arm, in plaster to her shoulder. I am going to make her cup of tea. I call Hannah, International Development Team. *'I am going to a meeting at 11 a.m. When would it be convenient to call you?'* she said. *'Any time that would suit you,'* I reply.

5 p.m. I receive a call back from George, ex bus driver and HGV artic driver with Duncan Adams Transport Ltd, who came on Saturday, 9 December 2006 to collect educational resources from what was the former Inverkeithing Primary School; that was the first collection of many more to follow.

I wrote a letter to James, my friend, lad o'pairts, former physician with the Scottish Office who has moved to a new address in London. I called the International Development Team, Scottish Government, Edinburgh. Pass the parcel: I was told to call Gillian and then I call John, Social Enterprise/Third Sector, at the North Edinburgh Business Incubator. I received an encouraging email wishing me the best of luck with the project.

This afternoon I met Tony on my way from the Co-op car park over to collect Marion's prescription and I told him that I did not think much of quangos. I met him on my return again and he was not well pleased with my dumb, totally unnecessary remark; I make unintended enemies easily – keep your mouth shut. Why, do I wind people up and annoy them so?

7:10 p.m. I have left a message on his mobile apologising for my unjustified off-the-cuff criticism of his employer.

(Some years later, I had to make that apology to him again, in person, when we had unintentionally sat beside each other one morning while travelling on the ferry across to Wemyss Bay.)

Chapter Fourteen
The Shipping Clerk Settles into New Quarters

Tuesday 15/11/2010

9 a.m. Unit 12, West Shore Business Centre, Granton, Edinburgh. I call the Muirhouse Community Social Work Centre supervisor to make arrangements for their collection of educational resources from Blackhall Primary School, Midlothian and delivery to Unit 12. I have already made arrangements with the chairperson of the School Council.

Deliver my Social Enterprise Academy Report for the Surplus Educational Supplies Foundation to the High Growth Adviser, Edinburgh Chamber of Commerce, who I had met some time ago at a social enterprise conference that was held at the Caledonia Hotel.

I am on the train for Glasgow Central Station; the sun is shining down on beautiful countryside. I bought a copy of *The Big Issue* from a seller outside Haymarket Station and an espresso for him; he tells me that he is from Romania. On my arrival at Unit 12 I found an envelope with my rough draft of a business plan from the Edinburgh councillor with no comment. I did what I set out to do this morning. I am now going to take a swig of water and polish my shoes.

Saturday 04/12/2010

The meeting for 12:30–1:30 p.m. was cancelled. Because of the weather. The British Tanzania Society, 6 West Haddington. Bring lunch. I met Kingsley of The African Scottish Development Organisation (ASDO) c/o The Africa Centre Scotland, Edinburgh.

Saturday 04/12/2010

Unit 12, West Shore Business Centre, SESF Depot and HQ, Edinburgh. Tuesday 05/11/2010. A place of my own? Ha, ha. The roller door was never repaired.

Meeting of ASDO rescheduled for 6 December at 11 a.m. British Home Stores Café, Rose Street.

Monday 06/12/2010

11 a.m. British Home Stores Café, Rose Street, Edinburgh. Meeting with Kingsley of The African Scottish Development Organisation, who tells me that he is a qualified physician, an Ibo from Sokoto State, North Nigeria. I admire his entrepreneurial spirit and enthusiasm. He was keen to take me up on my offer to show him the educational resources that I had in Unit 12, so after coffee we walked out to the taxi rank, but there were no taxis. I was anxious of returning to Wemyss Bay in time to board the last sailing of the day, and he cheerfully accepted my decision to make his inspection of the educational resources in Unit 12 for another day. I left Kingsley with a Surplus Educational Supplies Foundation flyer, business plan and budget for 2011–2013.

5:38 p.m. Home. I left home early to catch the 6:30 a.m. ferry; cycled into Rothesay in the dark, and got myself a hot chocolate and a roll with two links. I am trying to recall now if I met anyone on the crossing; yes, I chatted to Iain, one of the stewards who was interested in my destination. *'Where are you going today?'* I proceeded to tell him and gave him an Surplus Educational Supplies Foundation brochure, which ought to satisfy his curiosity for the time being.

On the train to Glasgow Central then walked it up to Buchanan Street Bus Station. I stopped to chat briefly with a young open-faced African at the corner of Renfield and West Nile Streets who was selling *The Sun* newspaper, and who told me he was from Nigeria. *'It just so happens that I have an appointment to meet a man from your country.'*

I left the bus station in driving, sleety rain and before long we were crawling bumper to bumper along the M8. Marion called me, bless her. *'You will have to turn around and come back.'* By midday we had only got as far as the roundabout at Gogarburn. I then called Kingsley and arranged to meet him at the Haymarket Starbucks Café. Young chap, alert, entrepreneurial; he likes his hot chocolate and appears to be a fellow believer, un croyant, a Christian who is full of the joys of our common faith, quoting Holy Scripture, is studying at Queen Margaret University on a scholarship to do a PhD and tells me that he is an Ibo. He is from northern Nigeria, near the border with the Republic of Niger. He is keen to take me up on my offer to show him the educational resources in storage across the city in Unit 12, so, soon after quaffing a brew that cheers but does not inebriate, we leave the café for the taxi rank and stand in the queue: no taxis. He is a little too insistent to continue waiting but being mindful of being stuck on the mainland because of the weather he took my decision to make this visit another day. I left the prime mover of ASDO with the SESF dossier, business plan and budget for 2011–2013.

I managed to get a train back to Glasgow Queen Street, and a train later for Wemyss Bay and the last sailing of the day for the Isle of Bute.

Tuesday 07/12/2010.

12:17 p.m. Home. Marion and Amy are going into Rothesay town. I am working the telephone and I have not even got into the shower yet. Laura at the Scottish Office has returned my call. *'I am going out to Nicaragua on 19 January 2011 and I will do some detective work when I get to Bluefields. I will try and find out what has happened to your donation of library books,'* she said.

Thursday 09/12/2010

12:15 p.m. Home. I am returning a call from Stevie at Recycle Scotland, an RBS-based charity. He has asked me to contact Pah from the Gambia. I call him and he said he would like to look at the SESF educational resources in Unit 12, West Shore Business Centre, Granton and he will call me back: an interesting development from out of the blue, like so many of the contingent occurrences on my journey.

2:31 p.m. Call back from Bob of Forth Valley College, who will put me in touch with Bob, who has an idea of what educational resources will be surplus to the college's requirements when they move to their new campus in Stirling.

I called Simon who said that he had to speak to their bursar about their intended donation of educational resources from the Stewart's Melville Schools Consortium.

3:31 p.m. Call from Bert at the Edinburgh Social Enterprise Academy to prepare my application for a Scotland Unlimited Grant and ILM? Accreditation.

5:30 p.m. Back from a trip to Rothesay town. I stopped off at Bute Naturally and there met Michelle, digital artist, who is going to create the SESF calendar for 2011. Phil the proprietor made me a cup of tea, *'Is Earl Grey all right?' 'That is kind of you,'* I replied.

I thanked him for pitching for me at his Rotary meeting last Thursday at their usual venue at Kingarth Hotel. I then cycled around up Bishop Street and across to the Rothesay library to return what I thought were overdue books; they were not overdue. Patricia the librarian asked me if the Surplus Educational Supplies Foundation was interested in acquiring a donation of children's books, mainly paperbacks. Yes please! Then she mentioned that there were boxes of adult fiction and non-fiction books, part of their reserve library stock collection, upstairs in a Moat Centre store room. *'Do you want those as well?'* she asked. *'Yes Patricia, that would be wonderful. Many thanks,'* I replied. (At that point I did not know how I was going to uplift them, where I would store them, to whom I would send them, and how I would get them off the island. Social Entrepreneurs take risks at their own expense.) I asked her if she would make this donation of surplus library stock to SESF official, and she replied that she would contact the Argyll and Bute Library Services and *The Buteman* newspaper in due course.

Friday 10/12/2010

6:17 p.m. Home. Received a call from Pa; he is keen to see the educational resources in Unit 12. I have arranged to meet him there next week.

Wednesday 15/12/2010

11:45 a.m. I called Bute Community Links about someone on their team who might be able to help me vet the accounts for the Surplus Educational Supplies Foundation (Registered Scottish Charity SCO39331) and help with the necessary OSCR (Office of Charity Regulator) paperwork before I return it back to them in Dundee. The person I spoke to was very helpful.

Friday 17/12/2010

9 a.m. I am on the train for Edinburgh Waverley Station. The sun is beginning to break through. It is a cold and fresh winter's morning. I am going to meet Pah from the Gambia. I have just called him, and it sounds as if he has just woken up. He said he would meet me at Waverley Station; we will see what this meeting holds for us both.

2:45 p.m. I am now on the train for Wemyss Bay; while I was on the way over I told Pah I would meet him in front of the WH Smith newsagent in Waverley Station; a smartly dressed gentleman strode confidently towards me and we seemed to hit it off immediately. We walked to his car, which was parked just opposite the taxi rank, and we drove down to Leith and back towards Granton. He had never been in the West Shore Business Centre before. I showed him the educational resources on offer. We seemed to establish mutual trust and respect right from the start. He has come on a long journey from the Gambia. He spoke fondly of his 'Daddy' and how he had let him down when he left home for Europe. I have heard that before and his description of his relationship to his father struck close to home, and the wasted years that I, too, had spent in Canada 1961–1973. He has lived all over Europe; he has a Global Village attitude and describes himself as a businessman and freight forwarder to trade.

He said he was aware of his corporate social responsibility to aid those he had left behind in the Gambia, who had not had his opportunities for self-advancement at home or abroad. He went on to tell me that he was mindful of his good fortune from early on, and that his Daddy had studied in the United Kingdom when the Gambia was a colony of the British Empire. This fact had presumably contributed to Pah's success. His grandfather, he told me, was also a member of the privileged class.

I pitched what I thought SESF could offer his fellow countrymen and in particular the schools. I told him that the ball, so to speak, was now in his court, and went on to stress that what he could see in front of him in Unit 12 was not for trade, but material that would be donated to equip classrooms with basic classroom furniture, the bare minimum necessary, to equip them and that he especially, with all that he had already told me about his background, surely would be well suited to facilitate their safe delivery and handover to the beneficiaries, free of charge. I suggested that he might be able to put SESF in touch with a deserving school in the Gambia that would be able to take advantage of what I could offer. I suspect that he will want to do some sort of a deal. He said he would get back to me and spoke highly of Stevie at Recycle Scotland, based in Livingston, because it was him who Pah said had given him a leg up.

We had a good chat and then I asked him if he wouldn't mind dropping me off at Pickford's warehouse on West Harbour Road as I thought I would drop by and see their officer manager, who had kindly offered, on a call to that firm some weeks back, to let me have some cardboard boxes which they had said they would drop off at Unit 12. Pah from the Gambia drove me up the road and kindly said he would wait for me. *'Yes, certainly we will give you some boxes,'* said Eddie from the Pickfords team who let me have 20 new boxes.

Pah then drove me back to Unit 12 to drop them off and gave me another lift to Waverley Station, and soon I was back to Glasgow Queen Street Station. I will have to wait and see what transpires from this meeting. *'We are approaching Paisley Gilmour Street Station. Please mind the gap when alighting from this train,'* she said.

Thursday 30/12/2010

7:14 p.m. Home. I have been speaking to Kingsley who comes from Nigeria, who tells me, *'You must come to our home in Edinburgh and we will eat some fish and pounded yam, call me in the New Year.'* I left a message for John of the Edinburgh Chamber of Commerce and Pah from the Gambia.

I went into the town to get messages for Marion; there is a smoky mist stifling low over the Crosbie Hills. I left excerpts of my diary with Anne Marie, a supporter at RBS, to photocopy and collect tomorrow: these I will send to Ken, vice principal of Forth Valley College of Education and Higher Education, to add another dimension to the discussion – as a contributor to their discussion – about a strategy for the college's sustainable policy for the disposal of their surplus resources, of which there will be a large amount when the college moves to its new campus. In his letter to me of 16 February 2009 he had written, *'We will have a*

substantial surplus equipment and although its early days and we do not have a strategy as yet for disposal, the College will be in touch to see whether there will be a potential for the good cause we discussed.'
This letter had raised my hopes and made all the difficulties I had so far experienced worthwhile.

(The possibilities promised in this letter that I envisaged, like so many on this journey, did not come to fruition and it was not for lack of commitment on my part.)

12:52 p.m. Pah from the Gambia has returned my call and we will meet in the New Year.

Wednesday 12/01/2011

11:19 a.m. BHS Cafeteria, Rose Street, Edinburgh. I have called Hannah at Scottish Office International Development, who put me onto NIDOS. Pass the parcel. I called Kingsley, who will meet me at 1 p.m.

I did not get into Waverley Station until 9:30 a.m. I walked up the steep steps, the slopes of Sisyphus, a symbol of my interminable efforts to make something worthwhile out of my life. I cross Princes Street, along Saint Andrew Square, and back to Rose Street to meet with the executive coach in the offices of the Scottish Enterprise Academy. I got nowhere with him. Why do I always expect more from people, or more than they are able or scheduled to give me? He kept on asking me questions, interrogating me on the progress of SESF and would not let me finish one story or account of the stage it was at, constantly interrupting the flow of my part in the conversation. He would not let me finish one 'story' till he was onto quizzing and challenging me about something else. Then he started to tell me about a business associate who is with an oil company that is drilling for oil somewhere off the coast of West Africa. It was a short meeting, which I brought to a close when I came to my senses that I was going to

Monday 17/01/2011

get nowhere with him. He said he could offer me more 'coaching sessions'. No more, thank you, and he was not well pleased.

I then had another meeting with Bert which went a little better. I apologised for being late – 10 minutes after 10 a.m. I gave him my dossier and he said he would let me know if I qualified for the ILM certificate, but did not tell me what that was! *(I learned later it was my licence to run a social enterprise business.)* He brought this meeting to a close to tell me that he had another appointment, video conferencing. I have finally got around to drinking my coffee, now cold, and digesting a stodgy roll and two sausages.

3:40 p.m. I am now on the train returning to Glasgow Queen Street. Kingsley arrived at 1 p.m. and we walked up through BHS to Princes Street and got a taxi, which cost me £20, across the city to Unit 12.

I showed him what was on offer. The taxi waited for us and then we were driven to his home, where I met his wife and baby son. They gave me a bowl of pounded yam and roast turkey. I was not hungry, but not to offend I ate what was put in front of me. We discussed a possible way forward but he had to report to the Fire on the Mountain Pentecostal Church. He and his wife are Ibos from Cross River State in Nigeria. Time will tell whether anything will come from this meeting.

I enjoyed the kind hospitality from this young family who are well on their way to making a success of their new life in El Dorado Britain. I called the elusive John of the Edinburgh Chamber of Commerce, who has not replied to my calls; he had seemed interested in what I was doing when we had met at the social enterprise conference at the Caledonian Hotel way back when.

Monday 17/01/2011

12:01 p.m. Unit 12, West Shore Business Centre, Granton. I got the No. 16 bus from outside Jenners department store. Earlier I had gone into the BHS cafeteria. On my arrival in Edinburgh on the 8:45 a.m. bus from Buchanan Street Bus Station I got off at a Princes Street. I had then got myself a restorative mug of coffee and a roll 'n' fried egg, bottom side up, sunny side down. The sun is shining in a cloudless blue sky, which always helps to make my day.

Unit 12: I went across to Unit 5 to say hello to Bahram, who comes from Iran, and Iain the accountant who is a Paisley Buddie. There is now a chill breeze blowing in from off the Firth of Forth. I am awaiting the arrival of Pah from the Gambia, wheeler-dealer par excellence and freight forwarder.

1:36 p.m. Pah has just left with his van and 200 metal-legged plastic-seated conference chairs at £1 each – a bargain; he paid me £200 cash, which I need for current expenses. I was reluctant to go against my decision not to sell him anything, but there you are. I am strapped for cash.

I met Shaz from Turkey, who works for Mitie who had brought building materials to dump in the overflowing Viridor skip a couple of yards away. I gave him an SESF flyer and I am going to make my way homeward.

Wednesday 19/01/2011

12:21 p.m. I am on the train from Falkirk High Station. Gordon the taxi driver drove me up from Duncan Adams Transport Ltd at Grange Dock. I had hailed him from outside the Wetherspoon's pub on main street in Grangemouth. After my meeting at the college with Bob and Tom, I got a bus which took the long indirect route into Grangemouth. I will now have to wait and see what they come up with: both of them said they would have to refer to their senior management! No decision taken and they said, *'You are pushing at an open door.'* They were receptive to my pitch but non-committal. A waste of our time.

Monday 24/01/2011

10 a.m. Unit 12. I am awaiting the arrival of the Scottish Water inspector. Why does he want to inspect these premises? There is no water being piped into the premises apart from a once leaking roof.

10:37 a.m. The Scottish Water inspector has come and just left.

I left Rothesay harbour at 6:30 a.m. and half an hour later I was on the train from Wemyss Bay Station for Glasgow Central and then I walked briskly up to Queen Street Station. Single fare £12.20 to Edinburgh Waverley. I got the No. 44 Ocean Terminal bus to leafy Trinity, walked down to Starbank Road and continued walking, and soon realised I was further from Longcraig Rigg Road than I thought, so I hailed a taxi and here I am facing a chill breeze off the Firth of Forth and the time has come for me to head back up the road and home.

Tuesday 25/01/2011

10:16 a.m. Home. Up, shaved and showered, and now I am going to fix a bowl of cereal. No milk. I have plugged in my hearing aid but I don't want to start using the telephone just yet.

10:30 p.m. I touch base with Pah from the Gambia. I make arrangements to collect the boxes of library books from the Rothesay library. I start that process with a call to A&M Transport. I speak to Alan to get a price for uplift; free lift? Nae chance. Charity tariff? Not likely. He said he would call me back on Wednesday with his price and I told him that in the interim I would not be calling anyone else. I will need, however, to make arrangements with MacKirdy Haulage, if they will shift them off the island. Where to? I will cross that bridge when I come to it.

10:04 a.m. I finally get through to Pah. *'Can I call you in the next 15 minutes?'* he asks.

11:05 a.m. I called UNICEF Scotland, based in London, and left a message. Called Oxfam Scotland, speak to Anne, responsible for curriculum. I call World Vision, Milton Keynes, regarding possibility of sponsoring a child in Sierra Leone. £18 per month.

Wednesday 26/01/2011

---

3 p.m. Home. I called Galt Transport Ltd, Dumbarton, to see if they can shift 40-foot ocean freight container INBU4923875 in their yard across to the WH Malcolm Transport Ltd container base at Linwood. Billy, the multi-skilled janitor at Saint Andrew's Primary School, called to offer me roll-top chalkboards, which are being replaced by digital whiteboard technology. I thanked him for getting in touch with me but I no longer had any storage space on the island.

2:37 p.m. I called WH Malcolm Transport Ltd, Linwood depot, to speak to John who is a friend of Tom Walker, container surveyor and my friend. John told me that his firm would let me store the SESF containers at their Linwood container base which has a railway link to the Port of Grangemouth. I am grateful beyond words.

I arranged to meet Pah from the Gambia outside Falkirk High railway station at 10 a.m. on Friday 28 January. My goals are synonymous with the Surplus Educational Supplies Foundation. I must try to identify deserving beneficiaries soon. Who? Where? How? When? Why? (See my efforts to contact Scottish Office, DFID, British Council and the charities. Their response? Not interested.)

3:30 p.m. I called Carson Transport Ltd, Cumbernauld, to see if they will shift MSKU6311690 from their yard to WH Malcolm Transport Ltd, Linwood depot.

To do: contact Alan about his price to shift books from Rothesay Library to Linwood; confirm appointment on Friday 28 January with Pah for him to see what educational resources are currently held in the SESF containers at Duncan Adams Transport Ltd at Grange Dock depot; call Eric to confirm that I will be able to show contents of containers GATU4033193, SEAU4272551 and TRIU5079422 to Pah; make an appointment at health centre to see GP to arrange appointment with an audiologist.

Thursday 27/01/2011

9:32 a.m. Home. Billy the janitor has called to tell me know that there is the possibility of shifting the chalkboards down to Father Michael's garage, where they be stored temporarily.

I called Alan, who tells me that he does not think he can manage to shift the large number of boxes of Rothesay Library donations and shelving up to an SESF container at the Linwood container base, so I will have to see if John MacKirdy Haulage Ltd can move them. Alan says he will help Billy the janitor to move the chalkboards from Saint Andrew's Primary School to the RC Chapel rectory garage.

I call Galt Transport Ltd and Simon answered the phone. *'I'll stop you right there. It is Allan you are to speak to.'* Allan comes on the phone said, *'We'll see what we can do for you.'*

Thanks to them the SESF 40-foot ocean freight container INBU4923875 is going to be moved to the WH Malcolm Ltd Linwood/Elderslie container base. This 40-foot ocean freight container, which has the educational resources, mainly classroom furniture, uplifted from Golden Hill Primary School, Clydebank, some months ago and from which Zak from West Africa and now from Edinburgh picked the conference chairs and left SESF with the rest.

The Shipping Clerk Settles into New Quarters

9:43 a.m. Call Carson Transport Ltd. No joy.

10:21 a.m. I called my friends at Duncan Adams Transport Ltd, Grange Dock, and spoke to Shirley to see if it would be okay for me and Pah, the businessman and freight forwarder from the Gambia, to view the SESF educational resources stored in the two containers. *'That won't be a problem,'* she said, and tells me that we will need our ID at the Port of Grangemouth security gate.

I called Carson Transport Ltd and spoke to John, who was not well pleased, and understandably so, on learning from me that I wanted one of the containers at their depot in Cumbernauld moved yet again to Linwood. I called John Russell Transport Ltd Hillington depot to call me back at 1 p.m. Hopefully, the two 40-foot containers riddled with pinholes, past their sell by date, which I had covered with my tarpaulins are still in the yard.

2:43 p.m. I have had a call from Johanna, who is going into Lloyds Pharmacy in the town to help out. I had a call earlier from Michelle the pharmacist asking if she would come in. I have been inside the house for a bacon and egg toasted sandwich and a pot of tea. I had been outside round the back raking leaves and tidying up. The sun is shining this afternoon.

I called Bute Community Links. I have high hopes that their team will help SESF/me get my OSCR and Company's House documentation up to speed.

4:31 p.m. I call John Russell Transport Ltd Coatbridge depot and speak to David. *'I'll see if I can dig one out for you.'* *'That will be great.'*

I will visit Saint Andrew's Primary School after 9 a.m. tomorrow and the janitor, Billy, will show me what's in the dunny. *'Ah didnae think you knew what that wurd meant,'* said he to the dunny raker, skip raker, and waste-stream miner.

Friday 28/01/2011

11:40 a.m. I am in a carriage of the train for Wemyss Bay having walked down from Queen Street Station. I had got the train from Falkirk High Station where I had met Pah at 9:30 a.m. He drove us in his car up to Grangemouth and down to Grange Dock and into the Duncan Adams Transport Ltd depot and reception, where I introduced him to Elizabeth, who looked at him quizzically over the top of her spectacles. She was civil to him. While they were chatting, I went across the foyer to the reception counter and asked to speak to Eric, who could see me from his desk, which faced the door. I introduced him to Pah and then we went out into the yard where the sun shone to see TRIU5079422, which had been brought out from among hundreds of 'boxes' and was looking worse for wear. At least it had been brought out from under many 40-foot ocean freight containers so we could look at the contents – all of it had been uplifted many months ago (see diary entry) from Dunshalt Village Primary School and had been stored in a Glenrothes warehouse until loaded.

This container will also have to be emptied, and the educational resources sorted and inventoried, which Pah said he would help me do when he returns from the Gambia; he tells me that he is regarded almost like a king in that West African country. I am hoping that he will assist me in directing these resources into the right hands. *(However, as I was to discover later, he had other plans for their disposal. My vision and Christian faith energise my motivation, stickability and perseverance when disappointments and difficulties are encountered on this journey that would otherwise have caused me to jack it in long ago.)* Pah and I were shown the other two *boxes*, which were also in a bit of a state showing many rust bumps, and I doubted that either would ever get an ISO certificate. What I could with is a grinder and some paint for these ocean freight containers which I loaded and unloaded last summer.

Unit 12, West Shore Business Centre, Granton. Friday, 28/01/2011. Pah, a freight forwarder businessman from the Gambia, inspected SESF resources. Pah told me that his Daddy had studied in the United Kingdom when the Gambia was a colony.

Resources salvaged from the Dunshalt Village Primary School, Fife. Eventually these were delivered to Ecole Dame Marie, Republic of Haiti, in April 2017.

I cannot expect too much given that these three 40-foot freight containers have been parked in this Duncan Adams Transport Ltd Grange Dock depot all that time. The dilemma is, if I had not gone to the trouble of collecting these educational resources, I would not have them to deliver. Pah and I agreed to leave things as they were until he returns from West Africa.

We walked back to the office to say goodbye to Eric, Elizabeth and Duncan, who said, *'You are welcome here any time.'* These words from Duncan made me feel really good. Pah then drove me back up to Falkirk High. Pah has seen for himself what SESF has to offer at Unit 12 and out here in the three containers at Grange Dock. The sun is shining brightly, which always keeps my spirits up. I can see no further ahead than the next step in front of me; there are other possible links which I can investigate.

Monday 31/01/2011
___

4 p.m. Home. Earlier, when I came ashore, I cycled up to the John MacKirdy Haulage Ltd depot at the top of the High Street, Rothesay, to see if they will deliver the boxes of Rothesay Library reserve stock library books (which need to be palleted) across to the WH Malcolm Transport Ltd Linwood container base, where I will store them temporarily in an SESF container. They can do it, they tell me, but not pro bono.

I stopped off at Bute Naturally to order some more flyers. Phil and Anne were helpful and welcoming as ever. I called David at Russell Transport Ltd, Coatbridge, to see if they can dig me out a box. *'They are very scarce at the moment,'* he tells me. I then called Alan to arrange the uplift of the boxes of reserve library stock from the Rothesay library to John MacKirdy Haulage Ltd. where they will be palleted and shrink-wrapped and taken up to WH Malcolm Transport Ltd, Linwood, to be temporarily stored in an SESF container.

1:33 p.m. Call Carson Transport Ltd to speak to John. *'He's in a meeting,'* he said.

Tuesday 01/02/2011

10:05 a.m. Home. I called Duncan Adams Transport Ltd, Grange Dock, Port of Grangemouth, to see if it was possible for them to move GATU4033193 to the Linwood container base. I spoke to Bryan. *'I'll see about that for you, no worries.'* I then called Carson Transport Ltd about moving MSKU6311690 to Linwood – no one is answering the phone. I called the editor of *The Buteman* newspaper, who said he will give the donation of Rothesay Library some publicity.

I called the Ministry of Education in Grenada, West Indies, trying to contact Dessima who was supportive in 2005 when I was trying to make the first shipment of educational resources to Grand Roy Government School in Grand Roy. I learned that she is now working at the United Nations in New York. I called the editor of *History Scotland* about information on Scotland's links to the slave trade in the Caribbean. I called the first secretary chargé d'affaires, Nicaragua, about the possibility of further shipments of resources to schools in Bluefields and Costa Caribena.

11:58 a.m. I am sitting here with my fluorescent jacket on waiting for Alan of A&M Transport Ltd to call to let me know if he will need me to lend a hand uplifting the boxes of library books from the Rothesay library up to John MacKirdy Haulage Ltd.

He has just called and he will need my help. Here I go on my bicycle up the road. Alan, young David, his helper, and I took 250 boxes up to John MacKirdy Haulage Ltd warehouse and put them on pallets. The Rothesay librarians will let me know when they have got more boxes of their reserve library stock of books ready to be collected. Pah called to arrange for him to collect the rest of the conference chairs from Unit 12. Meet Pah on 4 February at 10 a.m.

Wednesday 02/02/2011

10:22 a.m. Home. Nicky from John MacKirdy Haulage Ltd called to let me know that the 10 pallets of library books would be delivered to the WH Malcolm Transport Ltd container base, Linwood, within the next 10 minutes. I did not expect them to be delivered so soon. I called John Murray at WH Malcolm's office in Linwood to let him know; the empty SESF container from Duncan Adams, Grange Dock, would not have been brought over to the container base so soon. I make apologies to John for the confusion I have caused; he is gracious as ever and helpful. I am dependent on good will and I don't want to run out of favours until I have seen this initiative through to a tidy conclusion.

It is a wet, dreich morning. There seems to be always potholes along this road. I call Bryan at Duncan Adams Transport Ltd and he tells me, *'We have it under control. The container has not been delivered yet.'*

11 a.m. John has called to let me know that the 10 pallets of library books have been delivered and he will call me tomorrow to let me know when the container across at Grange Dock has been delivered.

3:50 p.m. I have received a call from John to tell me that the container at Grange Dock has been delivered a short while ago to the WH Malcolm Transport Ltd container base. Great! I had only called Duncan Adams and his team this morning. I told John that I would be over to the Linwood container base first thing tomorrow morning.

The Shipping Clerk Settles into New Quarters

Thursday 03/02/2011

11:01 a.m. WH Malcolm Transport Ltd container base, Linwood/Eldersie depot with a rail link to Grangemouth. I arrived to find that Duncan Adams Transport Ltd had not sent the container I had asked for. It was SEAU4272551 that I needed: go with the flow. Keep calm and fight on.

I am with Hugh, driver of the big box lifter, and Brian – the team who are helping me to load the eight pallets of reserve library stock into container INBU4923875 until it is box tight. Brian and Hugh have invited me to the gatehouse office, security gate and weighbridge for coffee, where they introduce me to Frank, the checker. Later John appeared with a firm handshake: he tells me, *'You can keep your boxes here'*. Those word of his and the unconditional welcome I had just received lifted me off my skinny pins.

12:01 p.m. I have boarded the train at Paisley Gilmour Street Station for Wemyss Bay. Brian, the manager of the container base, has given me lift to the station. Time for reflection.

When I saw that the wrong loaded container had been brought across from Grange Dock I despaired, but Hugh and Brian stepped into the breach and helped me to move the large chalkboards to make room for boxes of books. GATU4033193 was loaded with classroom furniture; there is a waste of space in the container and the contents will need to be inventoried and reloaded in due course.

On my arrival at Paisley Gilmour Street Station at 8:45 a.m. I had a coffee in the café, former post office, opposite. I got a No. 36 bus out to Eldersie, where I got off and walked along the SUSTRANS cycle path until I could no longer walk along the former railway line. I then had to retrace my steps to be able to find the main WH Malcolm Transport Ltd security gate at Linwood, where they told me to go into the reception room and wait. A short while later Brian, manager of the Elderslie container base, came to collect me in the Malcolm van.

(My contacts with the Scottish road haulage industry have so far been way beyond my expectations or my deserts, and a cause for acknowledgement and gratitude, which has been the primary motivation to keep this diary over many days and see Diary of a Shipping Clerk, Volume Three *through to publication.)*

It is grey damp day but it shone bright with goodwill, hospitality, pro bono assistance and a favour from the team at the Elderslie container base. There is indeed nothing else for it but to press on in faith.

'We know who you are doing it for,' said Brian the manager.

Friday 04/02/2011

7:49 a.m. I am on the bus from Buchanan Street Bus Station, Glasgow, for Edinburgh. I left Marion earlier at The Grove, Kilbarchan, and waited at the foot of the drive for a bus to Johnstone, where I spent the night for a kip in the police station back in August 1975: I had walked up from Ayr where I had spent a fortnight working as a kitchen porter in the Darlington Hotel en route to take up my first teaching post at Sunnyside Primary School in Craigend, Easterhouse, August 1975.

I walked up to the bus station. I am on my way to meet Pah the Gambian dealer in things reusable. Pah has told me that he wishes to purchase the remaining conference chairs and I am uneasy about selling the stuff which I intend to be used for charitable purposes, but the truth of the matter is, I am not far from poverty street, where Eric warned me a while back is where I would end up if I did not get myself *'a charity and get some lottery money'*. He had told me this several times. My scruples and idealism have made me reluctant, in fact, averse to pursuing that route for funds; gambling is a curse and the charities are anything but, charities in name only, and are business oriented, using tainted lucre from taxes on gambling. I see only what is front of me and it is in retrospect and looking over my diary notes that I see how far I have travelled with this venture, the successful resolution of which is not assured.

12:46 p.m. Unit 12. I have been chatting to three young lads who are working for the Port of Leith Housing Association driving a Mitie transit van: Matt, one of the lads, tells me that he and his wife, who is a nurse, went on holiday recently to the Gambia; Craig, who remembers me from somewhere is switched on like me to saving the Blue Planet; and Scott, who has a firm grip. Meeting all three of these young men has lifted my spirit. There is a gale coming up the Firth of Forth and rain is falling heavily on the roof. There are no leaks that I can see.

I paid to have the roof repaired with some of the money that I got from Rothesay Rotary. I am waiting for Pah to appear. Pah showed up at 11 a.m. with a Condor Rent-a-Van. He tells me that he goes out to the Gambia next week. Earlier, I had brought 80 of the remaining conference chairs to the main entrance to the unit and he, with my help, stacked them in with other stuff he had collected from elsewhere. He will be taking them down to Leeds from where they will be freight forwarded to Africa, where of course he will have no problems with Gambian government bureaucracy.

Pah tells me that he is driving down to England this evening. He paid me and I put the cash in my boiler suit pocket. He gave me a lift to what was supposed to be walking distance up to Leith Walk, and instead I was left on Bonnington Road. I walked across a bridge over the River of Leith and trudged up to Leith Walk and along up to the Saint Andrew Square Bus station, where I had just enough time to purchase a treat of purvey for my journey back to home city – a small Americano, savoury cheese sandwich, a packet of salt and vinegar crisps and a bottle of juice. I achieved something today for my effort: the SESF

Friday 04/02/2011

banner had come almost off the metal grill in front of Unit 12 and I fixed it back on.

I continue to build a working relationship and mutual trust between myself and Pah, in the hope that he might source genuine beneficiaries for the Surplus Educational Supplies Foundation stockpile of educational resources which has become my problem. What else was good today? It was my pleasure in meeting three straight, on the level, young millennial lads, about David's age, who are making every effort and straining sinew to earn an honest crust and who, to a man, voiced support for my work for the Surplus Educational Supplies Foundation. Boy that is some wind blowing in hard from the West.

3:35 p.m. I am on the bus, which is shuddering and rumbling along Princes Street heading for the M8. The wind is driving the rain into our path. I'm wondering whether there will be a ferry to take us across the Clyde – we will have to wait and see.

I got as far as Wemyss Bay to learn that the ferry to Rothesay Port had been cancelled on account of the gale-force winds blowing up the Firth of Clyde. I met Joyce, the home help, and her son, who used to make me a cup of tea when I visited Bob McEwen; like me a friend of Cuba. Bob told me once about rescuing a drowning man from the Clyde. *'My only claim to fame,'* he said.

Joyce and her son agreed to share a taxi to Gourock pier, and on arrival we learned that the ferry to Dunoon had been cancelled. I then got us another taxi to get the Western Ferries from Hunter's Quay, where the three Isle of Bute residents waited in the windswept kiosk to be told that that ferry had also been cancelled.

I bid my fellow travellers adieu and I walked around the queue of parked cars to find another taxi to take me up to Gourock railway station and a train to Paisley Gilmour Street, where Marion met me at the Marks and Spencer checkout. We got the bus back to Kilbarchan to have supper with Mum; such are the twists and turns of this eccentric road, whose goal is to meet the educational resource needs of teachers and their students somewhere in the developing world, impoverished and ravaged by natural and man-made disasters.

Saturday 05/02/2011

8:15 a.m. I am on the train for Edinburgh Waverley. *'The next stop is Falkirk High,'* she said.

I walked up from Glasgow Central Station after a comfort stop. I woke Amy at 6:15 a.m., who made me a cup of tea and three pieces of toast. Bless her. I walked in from The Grove, Kilbarchan to Johnstone Station and got the 7:29 a.m. train. I am off to a British Tanzanian Society meeting at the Old Drill Hall on Dalmeny Street at the bottom end of Leith Walk; for what purpose you may ask? I am not quite sure really, but I hope to meet like-minded folk who are smarter than I am, Africa Hands, and perhaps we can work together to direct surplus educational resources currently being trucked into landfill into the right hands, of teachers and their students in Tanzania. I travel as always, in hope.

11:20 a.m. The Old Drill Hall, Dalmeny Street, Edinburgh. I am attending a meeting of BTS. In attendance are mainly expatriates. People who retired from working in Africa when much of it was part of the British Empire; Tanzanian expatriates who have made Scotland their new home. Discussion is all about when they should hold their next meeting and an evening of entertainment and fundraiser on 19 March. Do I attend? It would be an opportunity for me to network but I cannae dance or sing, and I don't bevvy.

Wednesday 09/02/2011

4:30 p.m. Home. I received a call from Rachel, the business manager of Tidemill Primary School, Franklin Street, London. They are offering the furniture from 10 classrooms; against my better judgement I said, '*Yes please*'. There is a problem, of course. Where to store it? A London warehouse in the vicinity. Don't be daft. Not feasible, but worth a try.

Thursday 10/02/2011

9:49 a.m. Home. I receive an email confirming the offer of educational resources from the Lewisham Council, London Borough of Lewisham. I don't want to see this offer go down to the dump, so I call Mitch, a London contact of Howard's, who gives me an earful. *'Are you tyking the effin' piss, after all I did for yew last toime?'* This unrepeatable and great offer I know will be impossible to accept, and I experience great dissatisfaction at witnessing so much unsustainable fit-for-purpose surplus educational resources going to waste. My reach continues to exceed my grasp.

(My enthusiasm and commitment to this seat-of-the-pants, social entrepreneurial, recycling initiative was causing problems within the family circle and would continue to do so for the next six years. I did not know when to say. 'Enough is enough.')

3:54 p.m. Home. I called the Office of the Scottish Charities Regulator in Dundee, which has become a nuisance, and I spoke to helpful Ann who informs me that the accounts of the Surplus Educational Supplies Foundation (SCO39331) for 2010 must be in, and will have to be signed by an independent examiner; I do not know what that means and I need to send the trustees report as soon possible, and this puts me under more pressure. This report basically tells them what happened to the Surplus Educational Supplies Foundation during that year. I am glad that because I keep an almost daily account of its activities that should not be a problem. Who are the trustees you speak of? Me! The Prime Mover.

I then called John Russell Transport Ltd, Coatbridge office. Here I go again with my begging bowl. Do they have any 'boxes' to spare?

Tuesday 15/02/2011

10:50 a.m. Home. I sent emails to Bruce and Olivia preparing for tomorrow's meeting at Telford College, and with the team of students from Edinburgh University who will help me to sort and inventory the large collection of educational resources in Unit 12 gathered by Elspeth of Bishopbriggs from primary schools in the Borders, much of it unused. I have not been feeling well all day, and as a consequence I missed the opportunity of helping Alan and David, his assistant, to dismantle the Rothesay Library shelving and deliver the seven pallets of books from the Rothesay Library reserve library stock. I was going to set off at 11 a.m. when Ronnie, of Cowal Builders Ltd, appeared as promised with the Honda power-wash kit.

I ignored my discomfort and got stuck into power-washing the slabs and did not stop until the petrol ran out. I then set off to cycle into Rothesay town library. I had to pay Alan £80 for dismantling the library shelving and delivery of it up the High Street to John MacKirdy Haulage Ltd. On my arrival I did not feel physically able to help him and was much relieved that they could manage the uplift.

On return home I got a message from Zak, the Ghanaian chief. *'Mr David, would you call me please.' 'Yes Zak, how can I help?'* I ask. I am to meet with the students from Edinburgh University tomorrow outside Telford College (since rebranded as Edinburgh College) at 10 a.m. They will give me a hand to sort through a collection of curricular and classroom stationery materials which came from schools in the Borders. Thanks, Elspeth: a worker with the Church of Scotland.

Wednesday 16/02/2011

1:35 p.m. I have boarded the Citylink bus for Glasgow. It is a wet morning. Earlier I got a No. 8 bus along the road from Telford College. I had walked up from Unit 12 at West Shore Business Centre, West Harbour Road, past what was the Granton Gas Works tower. I walked up to the bus stop with Olivia and Lucy. When we got on the bus Finn and Garett were sitting at the back and we joined them; Finn was quizzing me about my involvement with SESF, how it started from small beginnings and was still small. He asked if there was any other young folk involvement, and I told him about teams from the Criminal Justice Community Services and Pay Back Schemes from Rothesay, Glenrothes, Barrhead and Muirhouse, who had been a great help over the past five years, and that they were the first university students (Edinburgh) and their initial contribution was an opportunity for further collaboration.

Roll it back as I scribble this note aboard the bus. I got the 8:50 a.m. bus from Buchanan Street Bus Station and when I boarded discovered that I had either lost or misplaced my bus pass. Oh no! Hard lines, Cyril. Take it on the chin. Get off the floor. Come off the ropes. Do not quit now! Now you will appreciate how useful your Pension Travel Free Bus card has been in all journeying to and fro, and hopefully you have not lost it, but have left it at home.

I got off at the west end of Princes Street and got a taxi across the city to Telford College. I waited and waited, among the young puffers of tobacco smoke at the main entrance. I introduced myself at reception to ensure that the presence of this old geezer did not have malevolent intent and he had legitimate reason to be at the college; I became impatient and went outside the building and from a distance became aware of the better-off youth,

The Shipping Clerk Settles into New Quarters

Unit 12 West Shore Business Centre Granton, Edinburgh. Wednesday 16/02/2011. Edinburgh University Students HELO team.
Top: Finn and Garret taking inventory and boxing curricular materials. These were salvaged by Elspeth many months ago from primary schools in the Borders (due for closure as part of the Private Finance Initiative fiasco).
Bottom: Fay, Lucy, Elizabeth and Olivia. They are doing this volunteer charitable work for a school in Tanzania. SESF made the arrangements with Reed International to have them delivered.

Wednesday 16/02/2011

the favoured private-school educated, whose life chances had been determined at birth and who would never need to put a fag in their mouth to bolster their confidence.

Along came Olivia and Elizabeth striding confidently out in the vanguard, followed by Fay, Lucy, Finn and Garrett, all studying at my Dad's alma mater – who was in the College of Agriculture, botany (see class photograph 1934–1935). I stood them all their choice of breakfast purvey in the crowded Telford College cafeteria, and explained to them what the Surplus Educational Supplies Foundation was and what I was attempting to achieve. We then walked down past the futuristic British Gas headquarters, past the Granton Gas tower and along to Unit 12 in the West Shore Business Centre, opened up the office and went next door into the large industrial unit, to hear one of the students behind me comment, *'This is awesome.'*

I was right chuffed to hear someone say those words. I set up the computer tables donated from the Stewart's Melville Schools Consortium and brought in from next door the boxes of curricular materials that Elspeth had salvaged off her own bat from the skips of Borders primary schools. They all got down to the task in hand of sorting these almost new resources and inventorying them. They boxed three Pickford's boxes for a charity in Tanzania, which some of them have had contact with and had made arrangements with while on holiday visits to that country. Where will this meeting of these six young ones and an auld yin lead? Their enthusiasm, energy and optimism today has refreshed and encouraged me; time will tell.

1:50 p.m. I am now going to have my en route picnic scoff and welcome treat. It has been a productive morning's work.

Friday 18/02/2011

3:55 p.m. Home. Message from Scottish International Relief. I have returned the call and left a message.

11:30 a.m. Bute Community Links office, Bishop Street, Rothesay. The manager has gone to photocopy SESF accounts for 2010. The meeting began at 10 a.m. and I set out my stall, and she said with encouragement, *'If your initiative does not succeed it will not be for want of trying.'* The manager was welcoming from the start and offered to look over the Surplus Educational Supplies Foundation dossier and business plan, and said she would like to become involved and offered to assist. Her response has encouraged me; I said I needed a structure, a strategy, governance and due diligence. The manager wanted to have a look at the business plan that I had prepared for the Edinburgh Social Enterprise Academy. I said that I was looking to take a step back and others, possibly a patron, a board, or a social investor might wish to come on the bus. There was no harm in attempting to make a wish list, an ideal scenario of what could be; after six years I have a track record, and usually those applying for funding have nothing but plans on paper.

We arranged to meet again Monday 21 February at 2:30 p.m. Bute Community Links, with the chief executive. At long last it seems that there is someone who can advise me in this social entrepreneurial initiative of the Surplus Educational Supplies Foundation. She mentioned that her dad came from Baillieston in Easterhouse, part of the Glasgow conurbation, and took notes throughout the whole meeting. She was positive about my venture and keen to be of help. I have to wait and see and not raise my hopes too high for a good outcome.

For the meeting on Monday 21 February:
1. Get the OSCR Charity Regulator forms ready to send to Ross & Co Accountants to be signed.

Friday 18/02/2011

2. Companies House, Annual Return now sorted with help from Bute Community Links.
3. The chief executive's response. What has been achieved to date, and what do we hope to achieve in the future? Formulate a strategy for achieving it. How do I turn a lame duck into a cash cow? Is this feasible? Potential for development.
4. Ideas. Possible recipients of educational resources to be identified in the resource and underdeveloped poverty stricken Third World Global Villages.
5. Marketing. SESF advertisement through social media. Publicity necessary to set out the SESF stall. Raise the profile of SESF with what has been achieved since 1 July 2005 and still hopes to accomplish.
6. What have I learned from the failures?
7. Sources of funding: who are they and what is the best way to approach them? Possible ethical funders who might wish a vehicle for their corporate social responsibility image and their requirements.
8. The time has come to build a team, a board and a support network, because I can no longer afford to continue to be a solo, one-man band – so create a forum for SESF governance that is credible and transparent.

2:27 p.m. I paid the delivery tariff that I owed to Duncan Adams Transport Ltd from Grange dock to WH Malcom Transport Ltd Container Base, Elderslie, for 40-foot containers SEAU4272551 and TRIU5079422, and I spoke with Richard the accountant at Duncan Adams Transport Ltd. Shortly after, I received a call from Nicky at John MacKirdy Haulage Ltd, Rothesay, Isle of Bute, to say that the rest of the palleted boxes of library books, together with shelving, will be going up from here on the island on Monday 21 February to WH Malcom Transport Ltd Container Base, Linwood/Elderslie. I told her that I would be there to offload the resources and would it be possible for the driver to give me a lift?

I asked her to call John, the container manager, to let him know of the delivery and I would do so as well.

I am now calling Duncan Adams Transport Ltd, Grange Dock to confirm whether or not the two 40-foot SESF containers from their depot had been delivered. I called Carson Transport Ltd, Cumbernauld, to find out if MSKU6311690 had been delivered. All SESF 40-foot ocean freight containers will now be in the one place.

3:45 p.m. Call John at Malcolm's head office in Linwood, who said to me, *'I'll see you on Monday, nae bother.'*

Monday 21/02/2011

6:49 a.m. MV *Bute. T*he engines are throbbing away under foot. I met Duncan the artic driver from John MacKirdy Haulage Ltd, who will allow me to accompany him with the Surplus Educational Supplies Foundation donation load of Rothesay Library books and library shelving. At this moment I am supping a hot chocolate having scoffed a bacon roll; the purvey treats of the journey.

2:30 p.m. Bute Community Links office, above the post office, Bishop Street. I have arrived here for a meeting with their chief executive. I have cycled in from Delhi Cottage. It has been snowing with sleety rain; a grey day. I have been informed that the CEO of Bute Community Links cannot make the meeting. Hard lines, Cyril. I go with the flow up to a point. I told the office manager that I was disappointed: not showing up does not augur well for the future. I must not complain.

Earlier today I got a lift across the watta and up the road to the Malcolm Group Container Base Depot at Elderslie with artic HGV driver Duncan of John MacKirdy Haulage Ltd. On arrival this morning, Hughie, the big box lifter and avid falconer, Frank the brain and Brian the manager, and clay pigeon shooter, gave me a lot of slack. We had container MSKU6311690, which already has library furniture along with the remaining seven pallet loads of library books, loaded with what had been brought up from the island. I could not have managed without the help of Hughie and Brian. The latter was expertly stacking the boxes off the pallets as I passed them up to him and the former was driving the hold all.

They invited me back to Frank's gate office for a coffee, where the artics are checked in and out of the container base by Frank. Then Brian, in a Malcolm van, drove me back in to Paisley Gilmour Street Station. I got the 11:01 a.m. train for Wemyss.

Back home, I took Toffee, the neighbour's dog, for a walk along the Craigmore Road grass verge all the way up and then down the road and let him off the leash. I came in, fed and watered him. I changed into formal attire for my meeting at Community Links. I dropped off the book *The Forgotten Soldier* by Alasdair Urquhart for Pan at his local, beside the wee Co-op and there I met Gordon. Then, a short way up the road for the meeting that did not transpire. I then came along to the Victoria Hotel where I have been since 3 p.m.

Wednesday 23/02/2011

9:30 a.m. I am in a meeting with the CEO and manager of Bute Community Links. Together we are going over the OSCR forms that I must return to Ross & Co the accountants in Dunoon with my Trustees Report and SESF Accounts.

9:40 a.m. She disappeared to check the existing OSCR entry on the office computer and is now discussing the SESF business plan with me.

10:10 a.m. Meeting ended. I am grateful for this help. To do:
1. List all contacts and sort into potential board members and offers of help.

2. List all the pro bono assistance: who have helped the Surplus Educational Supplies Foundation.
3. Prepare an SESF Exit Strategy.

2:19 p.m. I called Food for The Poor in Miami, USA, and left a message for Art with the intention of establishing a link with the Republic of Haiti. *'He is not at his desk. We use their shipping line,'* she said, referring to SeaFreight Agencies Lines Inc. Miami, Florida.

I have already approached Mary's Meals here in Scotland but they were not interested. This charity, which feeds school pupils, might have been a possible recipient of educational resources. To do:
1. Do SESF Companies Annual Return for OSCR to send off.
2. Give some serious thought to consider where do I go from here?
3. Discuss fresh information about SESF that I bring to meeting on 25 February.

3:10 p.m. I called John the freight forwarder. John, who is based at the Port of Liverpool, is always glad to give me the time of day; he told me that he had been out to India. *'I have got my own office now.'* Good on you, John. Our telephone-linked friendship has remained strong since he talked me through our first container shipment of educational resources. *(See Diary of a Shipping Clerk, Volume One, the entry for Friday 1 July 2005.)*

Friday 25/02/2011

3 p.m. I am meeting with the manager of Bute Community Links, who tells me that I need trustees for the Surplus Educational Supplies Foundation to be considered a charity. I tell her that OSCR simply requests my accounts, which thankfully are prepared by Ross & Co free of charge; the manager was throwing up more obstacles when I told her that all I had to do was send back to OSCR a copy of the SESF audited accounts.

3:10 p.m. I have put the documents for OSCR in an envelope to be posted. Stay cool dude, because at this stage some help is better than no help at all. Next meeting is for Wednesday 2 March.

3:35 p.m. The manager wanted to look over Iain's financial budget forecast for 2011–2103, which we did together.
'You are going to look at the viability of the whole operation of the Surplus Educational Supplies Foundation and come up with a proposition that will demonstrate that you have a rationale, okay?' she tells me. I nod in assent. The meeting ended at 3:40 p.m.

Wednesday 02/03/2011

2:30 p.m. Bute Community Links office. I have a meeting with another member of the team who is, at this moment, filing SESF accounts and the report for Companies House. I am immensely grateful for this professional assistance. It is a beautiful afternoon outside on Bishop Street.

2:50 p.m. The helpful member of the Bute Community Links team is being sent around in circles by the Companies Online registration procedures; control and regulations have become counter-productive.

Tuesday 15/03/2011

3:15 p.m. Meeting with the manager at Bute Community Links. We discussed the way forward for the Surplus Educational Supplies Foundation. She said she would contact the organisations and individuals who had provided pro bono support to SESF since 2005 with a view to determining whether or not they would be willing to continue their support. I mentioned that the Office of the Scottish Charities Regulator (OSCR) had not received my annual return and the Bute Community Links manager said she would send another. She told me that her assistant was on sick leave and would assist me with this on her return to work. I told her that I had spoken to Phil, proprietor of Picture Bute, Rothesay, who said he would be glad to come on the board of SESF.

3:45 p.m. The meeting ended.

Wednesday 16/03/2011

7:35 a.m. I am on a new train, Siemens, made in Germany, bound for Glasgow Central Station. I was up at 5 a.m. and cycled through cold mist. I hope to meet Olivia and her team of fellow Edinburgh University students at Unit 12, West Shore Business Centre, Granton, who will lend a hand to sort through the wonderful collection of educational resources, inventory, and box some more of these primary school curricular materials for the charity's orphanage school in Tanzania, East Africa, that they support. I am becoming weary of the struggle to salvage fit-for-purpose educational resources from destruction; for the time being, I can do no other than persevere and just get on with what I have been doing non-stop for the past six years. (*Read* Diary of a Shipping Clerk, Volume One, *published 25 September 2022;* Diary of a Shipping Clerk, Volume Two, *published 27 October 2023.*)

I have not long boarded this shoogling bumpy bus for Glasgow, which has just stopped at the Frederick Street traffic lights. What's new? I arrived at Waverley Station shortly after 9 a.m. and got a taxi to the Turkish tailors in Great Junction Street, off Leith Walk, where they are replacing the zip in one of my boiler suits. The helpful and friendly taxi driver waited for me and took me from there to Telford College, where I met Olivia, Elizabeth, Lucy and Hanna. I stood them coffee and then we walked down to

Unit 12. They were thrilled and enthusiastic to be able to box more resources for their orphanage's school in Tanzania. Hanna and Lucy left at 1:30 p.m. I and the rest packed up at 2:15 p.m. I got a No. 16 Colinton bus up to Saint Andrew Bus Station and I did not have time to get my travelling treat. I am hungry, as are many millions of my fellow suffering inhabitants of Blue Planet. It has been a successful day with the HELO team, all worthy representatives of the University.

To do: make arrangements next week to visit Inveralmond Community High School, Livingston, to collect container and later meet Sanjay at Braehead M&S Café at midday.

Monday 21/03/2011

12:59 p.m. Home. I call Leslie, editor of the *Grenada Voice*, who, when I mention the name of a Grenada government official, tells me, *'We were in prison together. I'll speak with the Prime Minister.'*

Tuesday 22/03/2011

11:54 a.m. I received a call from Sandy, of Pass IT, with an offer of about a dozen about-to-be refurbished computers with UBUNTU free software. He will contact me when they are ready. I received another call from Joanne, the Head of the English Department at Gourock High School, offering English textbooks, who tells me, *'I have just been handed one of your Surplus Educational Supplies Foundation flyers.'*

Soon after, I was speaking to Hugh, operations manager at Peel Ports Ltd, Clydeport Ocean Terminal, Greenock, who has told me that, providing I get the educational resources inventoried, boxed, palleted and shrink-wrapped, they will store them in one of their containers at their container base. I am immensely encouraged at these wonderful offers of assistance. I then called Galt Transport Ltd, who tell me that they will not accept payment for taking the

SESF 40-foot ocean freight container over to WH Malcolm's container base at Elderslie. I am so grateful; I asked if they had any 40-foot boxes for sale. They said they would speak to Alan.

Tuesday 29/03/2011

3:02 p.m. I have just this minute boarded the Wemyss Bay train at Paisley Gilmour Street station, where I had a square slice wi' brown sauce in a roll, an Americano, and a packet of crisps. About an hour ago, Pah from the Gambia dropped me off in Paisley having come from the WH Malcolm Transport Ltd container base at Linwood/Elderslie. It was thanks to Brian, Hugh and Frank, that Pah and I were able to inspect the contents of the following containers:
- GATU4033193: classroom chairs
- SEAU4272551: tables – Formica-topped metal legs
- TRIU5079422: varied classroom resources and gym equipment from Dunshalt Village Primary School
- INBU4923875: Rothesay Library books and school furniture from Golden Hill P. S Clydebank
- SEAU4272551: chairs

Pah has told me that he has a recipient school in the Gambia for all of these fit-for-purpose, surplus to requirements, educational resources, all of which are in good condition, but he wants to do a deal. What does that mean?

This morning I left home at 5:50 a.m., cycled into Rothesay, was aboard the ferry MV *Bute* at 6:15 a.m. bound for Wemyss Bay and left on the train for Glasgow Central at 7:15 a.m. I then walked up to Queen Street Station, got the 8:30 a.m. to Edinburgh Haymarket Station and took a taxi from there to Unit 12, West Shore Business Centre, Granton. Pah was there to meet me. I introduced him to the people at Charlie Stamper Fruit and Vegetable Wholesalers and Apfelsnapz Crisps. He then

Tuesday 29/03/2011

wanted me to start touting for educational resources scrap. I told him that my primary focus, passion, commitment and goal, was to ensure that all of the educational resources that I had gone to the trouble and personal expense to acquire previously had gone to schools in Grenada, West Indies, that had been devastated by Hurricane Ivan in 2004, and that any further resources collected would be at some point delivered gratis to deserving schools in the underdeveloped world, and for the time being I did not wish to be sidetracked. He kept on mentioning the people at Recycling Scotland; he told me he could move into Unit 12 and do his business from there. Well for the time being that is not possible or desirable. He tells me that he would like to turn the stacked tables and chairs that he saw before him and remove the metal legs for scrap. He persists in his attempts to persuade me to change course.

He has a scheme, whereby he wants me to approach solicitors and real estate agents supervising house sales to obtain any metal scrapped from building refurbishment. I can only play along with him for the time being, hoping against hope that I can establish a link with a deserving school in West Africa. This is a great disappointment to me – welcome to the world of business.

After he had chatted to James at Apfelsnapz I asked him if he wouldn't mind driving back to Leith to stop off at JUST SEW to collect my boiler suits with new zips. As he drove out of Edinburgh on our way to view the contents of the containers at Malcolm's container base he caught me off guard, and asked me if I would put £30 worth of petrol in his car. I should have, at that point, terminated any further contact with him – I did not, because I was desperate to get all of those good school resources delivered into classrooms, and the Gambian school that might be a beneficiary of a shipment, and I had now become a victim of my own desire to do good. I only discovered later that I must have dropped my credit card on the filling station forecourt.

The Shipping Clerk Settles into New Quarters

Wednesday 30/03/2011

10:35 a.m. Home. I called Conrad, of Box Trade, who said he would purchase all of the SESF containers; he also tells me that he supports a charity called Work Aid.

I will need to transfer all of the educational resources they contain to Unit 12. I am now cash-strapped and in another pickle of my own making.

Thursday 31/03/2011

11:57 a.m. Home. I called Saint Andrew's Primary School, who have told me that they have their donation of boxes of curricular materials ready, but have not sealed them or taken an inventory of contents. Their school secretary said they will inventory and label the boxes and will contact *The Buteman* newspaper about their donation to the Surplus Educational Supplies Foundation. I had had a call from their janitor, Billy, yesterday to come and get my boxes.

1:49 p.m. I had a call from Steve, representing the Order of St John. Never heard of them before about ocean freight containers. A possible offer of assistance. I contacted CMI Trading (UK) Ltd, Avondale Business Centre, Hampshire .

Saturday 02/04/2011

9:07 a.m. I have just inadvertently boarded the slow train from Glasgow Central Station for Edinburgh Waverley; my hearing aid is plugged in and I have seated myself where I can scribble these lines. We have just recrossed the River Clyde. I purchased a ticket for £11.30. The conductress is pleasant and curious. She tells me that she has been to Tanzania, after I tell her I am going to attend a meeting of BTZ. *'Fantastic. I travelled around the country and I*

Saturday 02/04/2011

handed out pens, and when I left the country I gave the Tanzanians that I met everything I had,' she said. She approves of my mission. Then I asked for a receipt, which I should have been doing right from the beginning of my 'mission' – another one of the failures that lead to my downfall. Rolling ahead into sunbeams.

I cycled out in the darkness, having to stand on the pedals, into the wind blowing hard out of the west; the train has just arrived at Bellshill Station. *'The next stop is Shotts,'* he said.

11:01 a.m. I am attending a meeting of the British Tanzania Society, Old Dalmeny Street Hall, Edinburgh; sederunt. DMH, Neil, Jim, Maggie, Anne, and Lesley welcoming the new High Commissioner to Britain.

Other events: buffet night bringing together the Tanzanian diaspora groups in Scotland and an opportunity for expatriate Tanganyika hands to meet. NIDOS and DFID networking – Anne suggests that better links could be made with other organisations working in East Africa. Neil begins to tell us about his experience of working with women in Tanzania who were becoming economically independent: some of the issues where there is potential for change and difficulties that women in the country face if they wish to start a business, for example printing cloth, women being change makers when given access to microfinance and experience of gender inequality that women face in Tanzania.

I listen in with my hearing aid plugged in and jot down what is being discussed. The chat continues. *'Our assistance from the British Tanzania Society should be directed by empowering women and men to do something for themselves. Such as microbusiness income generating activities,'* she said, and mentions the Kateza organisation at the Moffat Centre. Jim suggests that requests for help should come from the beneficiaries. I pose a question to the group: *'How do you get educational materials to Tanzania?'* And I tell them briefly about the HELO Team of Edinburgh University students who have recently prepared 12 boxes of educational materials at

Unit 12, West Shore Business Centre, Granton, for the orphanage school in Tanzania, which this team of students supports; but the response I get from this group of seasoned African hands is indifference. I had hoped that by attending these meetings I might have been able to move the work of my initiative forward, since I have no links with East Africa. And then I recall all the friends I made with students from Kenya, Zambia, Botswana and Malawi, while I resided at Lindsay House Hostel, Kittoch Street, East Kilbride from 1984 to 1986.

For week 4 April:
- Rothesay Library donation of library books and shelving to the Girls School in the Gambia capital. This will only happen if Pah, the Gambian freight forwarder, wishes to cooperate and make this shipment happen.
- Arrange for the sale of the six ocean freight containers at WH Malcolm Transport Ltd container base.
- Disposal of the educational resources stored at The Fife Warehousing Company Ltd in Dunfermline.
- Obtain a storage warehouse facility in the West of Scotland.
- Contact Gourock High School about their offer of textbooks; I have not recently heard from them.
- Review the generous offer from the operations manager, Hugh, on behalf of Peel Ports at Clydeport Ocean Terminal in Greenock to allow the SESF to store, temporarily, educational resources gathered from Inverclyde schools prior to shipment, provided they are inventoried, boxed and shrink-wrapped first.

It is imperative that I need to cultivate beneficiaries and a funder before much longer. It is a donor culture at the recipient end. I heard this comment, in a strong West African accent, *'Weh is de donah?'* I know in my gut that I shall continue to be a mug before I can wrap all this up.

(I did not know it then, that it would be another six years before I could walk away: at least with my head high, but with empty pockets.)

Wednesday 06/04/2011

1:03 p.m. I spoke with Rose of Reed International, who will take the HELO team's Unit 12 boxes to Tanzania in one of Reed International's containers leaving Newcastle, and must away by 25 April. I will need to cover the costs to deliver boxes to their depot in that city; another of my contributions to International Development. Fool me.

1:21 p.m. I received a call from Tom Walker, the container inspector, who said he will look over the five boxes at the Malcolm container base, Elderslie, and would contact Conrad at Container Brokerage Ltd and let me know which ones are seaworthy. They have got one of their representatives in Scotland to look at the boxes. It is wet and grey today, but these positive exchanges between cooperative human beings have brightened up the day and I am grateful for this assistance, from Tom especially.

Thursday 07/04/2011

1:22 p.m. I received a call earlier from Yvonne at Eldapoint Ltd, Grangemouth, who told me that they were keen to purchase my containers but they have to be emptied first.

Monday 11/04/2011

I call Cameron Bookbinders Ltd in Glasgow, in The Arches across from the Bridge Street underground. They told me that I can come and collect my *Diary of a Shipping Clerk* on Friday 15 April. *The current edition once published is going to run to a lot more pages.*

The Shipping Clerk Settles into New Quarters

(Diary of a Shipping Clerk, Volume One was published 25 September 2022; Volume Two was published 27 October 2023.)

Friday 15/04/2011

6:45 a.m. MV *Argyle*. I am en route for Wemyss Bay, Glasgow Central and Strathclyde University Campus to attend the 'Back to the Future' lecture. The Firth of Clyde is flat calm. I have not long swallowed a roll and sausage, a link sausage slice that is, and I am supping a hot chocolate and about to swallow my two prostate tablets.

Were it not for the fact I have in this journal-cum-diary of sorts, a record of not a few trips across the watta and up the main road, I would not be mindful of the extent to which I have put such a great deal of time, expense and unstinting effort into the Surplus Educational Supplies Foundation. *'We will shortly be arriving at our destination,'* he said over the vessel's intercom.

2:40 p.m. I am sitting in a new railway carriage, which I see was made in Germany, bound for Wemyss Bay.

I walked along the City of Glasgow streets for Strathclyde University Campus up on Rottenrow and attended a lecture by Jack Black, former Easterhouse social worker, who is a life coach, motivational speaker and proud to be a Glaswegian. Initially I found him interesting and knowledgeable but, as I write these words, I cannot recall anything he said, except that somewhere in his talk he said he lived in Kilmacolm. The sun was shining brightly this afternoon when I quickly finished my lunch, after 1:35 p.m. The lecture show had recommenced at 1:30 p.m.: I was going to be late. My left brain and right brain had had a chat, and weighing it all up I decided that listening, inactive, to this feisty Weegie go on about how smart he was was enough for one morning.

After the first session I went across to the student refectory-cum-restaurant where I hurriedly ate my poached salmon, veg and mashed potato. Between mouthfuls I was chatting to two third-year marketing students, Derek and Cameron – I had slipped away from the Jack Black 'Back to The Future' Alumni Events Lecture to have a bite. Then I walked down the steep hill to Cathedral Street. I walked up to Glasgow Cathedral, where I hoped to get a taxi that would take me over to Cameron Bookbinders Ltd under the railway Arches.

Be positive, stay happy, above all keep calm, breathe deep breaths and develop resilience to be able to bounce back no matter what hits you. The sun is shining brightly onto this page. I am heading home.

Thursday 21/04/2011

8:55 a.m. I am on the slow train from Glasgow Central to Edinburgh Waverley. I walked up from Glasgow Central to Glasgow Queen Street; the upper level line is closed – there has been a fire. I am down to the lower-level Platform 9 to get this train. I have just called Olivia, one of the HELO Edinburgh University team of students who had prepared 12 boxes of curricular materials for an orphanage's school in Tanzania, to let her know the van man she had organised to collect the boxes from Unit 12, West Shore Business Centre, Granton, who was to take them down the road to Reed International's container in Newcastle, should arrive at Unit 12 no later than 11 a.m. Olivia tells me that all hymn books are to be removed from the boxes. Why is that I wonder?

'Now approaching Coatbridge Sunnyside,' he said. The train has just whizzed past Freightliner Ltd Coatbridge Container Base, Gartsherrie Road. I wonder how helpful Raymond from Garthamlock in the John G Russell Transport Ltd yard is getting on, he who made me a Scottish breakfast in their canteen one morning. May I never forget the many undeserved kindnesses I have received from the team at John G Russell Transport Ltd, which have enabled me to continue with this project for so long.

The Shipping Clerk Settles into New Quarters

10:10 a.m. I have just arrived at Unit 12, West Shore Business Centre, Granton, by taxi from Edinburgh Haymarket station. I had left Glasgow Queen Street at 8:44 a.m. Press on and label the boxes with the labels that Marion had prepared for me. (See inventory in appendix of these almost new curricular materials that were rescued from skips outside primary schools in the Borders and, at long last, are being delivered to a school in Tanzania.) The sun is shining brightly out there in the car park.

A curious passer-by looks in and asks me where do I come from, and when I tell him he wants to know how long I have lived in Scotland and why did I come to the United Kingdom. I don't mind being rudely questioned in this manner, as it takes my mind off the anxiety of worrying whether the van is coming to collect the boxes or not.

1 p.m. David the van man arrived and I helped him to load the boxes and paid him. *'May the LORD bless this export without hymn books.'*

Glasgow Central. I can still move my legs to catch the train in the nick of time. I am on the train for Wemyss Bay. I got a taxi from Unit 12 to the McDonald Library in Leith, where I meet Sandra, the chief librarian. I received a pleasant welcome from her, and some of her first words to me, when we were introduced by her mum at the Port Gala Day at the Port Park in 2005, told me, *'Edinburgh is awash with books.'* I gave her update news about the long-awaited delivery of their donation of 100 boxes of library books to anglophone schools in the city of Bluefields, Costa Caribena, Nicaragua, Central America. I tell her that it had taken over 14 months from the time that John G Russell Transport Ltd uplifted them from the Muirhouse Community Centre's Elizafield Industrial storage unit, which had been in storage for over a year. When they were collected from the Morningside Library, the social work department had probably thought I had forgotten about them, instead I had been trying to find a beneficiary; this

Wednesday 27/04/2011

transport firm had collected the boxes, palleted them and shrink-wrapped the pallets at their Gartsherrie Road, Coatbridge, depot. The pallets were then collected by Vanguard Freight Logistics Ltd and delivered to the Warrant Freight depot in Liverpool, and subsequently loaded on a ship for a Nicaraguan port – that stage of the journey took about a month. The pallets were to remain in a Ministerio de Educacion warehouse in the capital Managua for over a year and eventually most of the boxes arrived in Bluefields. This shipment was confirmed by Bruce Callow of the Foreign and Commonwealth Office at the British Embassy in San Jose, Costa Rica. Sandra said she would pass this information on to her colleagues at the Morningside Library who had boxed these books many, months ago.

It has been another beautiful day. I have made another supreme effort of will to overcome personal feelings of inadequacy to just get out of bed, get out there and *'Do it!'* I have accomplished what I set out to do. I will now have to wait and see what happens to yet another first-class shipment of fit-for-purpose educational resources, five boxes of primary school curricular materials salvaged by Elspeth from skips outside schools in the Borders.

(The resources were inventoried and carefully boxed by a team of enthusiastic, well-organised students, the HELO team who came from Edinburgh University, who were: Olivia, the prime mover, Lucy, Fay, Hannah, Lisa, Garrett and Finn. Many thanks again and many blessings on each of you, in these reset post-Covid days of the Global Pandemic.)

Wednesday 27/04/2011

2:20 p.m. Home. It is a glorious afternoon of full sunshine. I have cycled back from the town of Rothesay where I had an appointment with the Bute Community Links manager. She, poor soul, is recovering from bronchitis. I left my OSCR forms to be filled in and they were returned to be filled in again. Mea culpa. I should have gone over them first.

The Shipping Clerk Settles into New Quarters

Thursday 28/04/2011

9:20 a.m. I called Simon at Education for All, which is the charitable arm of the firm Thorpe Kilworth, which is based in Corby. *'I am on holiday at the moment. I'll be back on the third,'* he said, giving me short shrift. The last time I spoke to him he was keen to accept SESF's offer of resources. So what? Move on.

I left a message for the Head of the English Department of the Gourock High School. I have had no word from them since I accepted their kind offer of surplus-to-requirements English textbooks.

11:01 a.m. I have returned from a brief meeting with the Bute Community Links team, who said that they would contact OSCR to sort out the confusion over the incorrectly filled SESF forms. I looked them over and they seemed all in order. Two SESF questionnaires have been returned. Some good news from both. Forth Ports Plc will provide storage of containers at the port of Grangemouth; Brian, the port manager, remembers when I nearly crashed Martin Stirling's van, which I cannot for the life of me ever remember doing: some incidents perhaps are best forgotten. There was also a reply from Waterfront Edinburgh Ltd, their manager, Nina, has indicated that they will continue to provide storage of educational resources and there was no word from them that my lease of Unit 12, West Shore Business Centre, had expired. This morning I visited the Shanks cowp – both Robert and Richard are supporters of the work of the Surplus Educational Supplies Foundation.

11:40 a.m. Joanne, Head of the English Department, Gourock High School, called to tell me that if I still wanted to accept their offer of textbooks I would have to provide boxes. No problem. I will supply them and sticky labels with the SESF logo. I asked if they could give me a list of titles and the amount of textbooks on offer. No reply. I guess that will be too much trouble for them. Where am I going to get boxes from?

Tuesday 03/05/2011

8:03 a.m. I have not long taken the moving stairway, escalator you mean, up to the Tesco café, Greenock, where I have now before me a roll and fried egg, and a mug of strong coffee.

I got the early ferry: it is a beautiful summer's morning. I met Iain from along the road at Madras House, who invited me to join him and his wife, Sarah, for coffee. On arrival at Wemyss Bay I bought a ticket to Drumfrochar Station and walked down the steep hill. I thought it would be wise to anticipate the need for a comfort stop and here I am.

I intend to walk along to the box manufacturer (that's what I think it is) on Laurence Street that runs parallel to Clydeport Ocean Terminal. I hope to purchase some cardboard boxes if possible, with Surplus Educational Supplies Foundation funds, and take them up to Gourock High School; that's the immediate task in front of me.

9:45 a.m. Station Café, Wemyss Bay: that's the café in the world heritage site railway station. I have been dropped off by Jim the taxi driver from Greenock, who I hired as he was first in the rank when I walked out of Tesco's and who drove me down to the DEVOL Engineering (Polymers) factory across the road from the Clydeport Container Base Ocean Terminal. A gentleman was getting out of his car, which was parked beside the factory premises. Did he know where the box manufacturers were? He kindly said he would find out for me. I was mistaken; it was this factory that I had walked past several years ago and thought that they manufactured boxes. Shortly after, another gentleman appeared, Jerry, who was very helpful when I told him what I was about and why I wanted to purchase boxes. He said he would go and speak to the higher-ups to get permission to donate 25 boxes. I waited and waited; Jim the taxi driver had switched off the meter. Jerry reappeared with 25 new large flat-packed cardboard boxes. I thanked him. I was speechless with gratitude. He helped me to load them into Jim's new white taxi, then we drove up to Gourock High School: a magnificent site with panoramic views across to the Argyllshire hills and up and down the Costa Clyde.

At reception I asked to the see the Head of the English Department, Joanne, who eventually appeared and told me that they will not be able to seal the boxes. I then asked her, if it would be possible, if her department could inventory or give me a rough idea of the titles of the textbooks – any help and any donation will be welcome and received from my quarter with gratitude. This beggar, raker of school skips, cupboards, stockrooms and basements, can't be too particular and fussy. All donations gratefully received.

I gave her the SESF company report, dossier folder and some SESF flyers to distribute. I wanted to give her and her school an idea of what was going to be done with their surplus-to-requirements textbooks, which were going to be binned anyway. She said she would contact me when the boxes were ready to be collected.

That small mission of the morning has gone according to plan, meanwhile, my pot of tea and bacon roll are now stone cold and I can see the ferry approaching with sunshine glinting off part of its white-sided hull. Enough of this scribbling.

10:20 a.m. MV *Argyle* heading back tae Rossay wi' a hot chocolate from the Coffee Cabin. I meet Karen from Print Point, who is always friendly, who asked, *'Have you been away? You are awfy brun.' 'No Karen, I have just been across and up to Greenock. I am still on the Costa Clyde where for not a few years now I try to catch as many sunbeams on my skin as I can,'* I reply.

George, the purser and steward, tells me they will change

shifts on Thursday. I say hello to Tom who drives for MacKirdy Haulage. I met young Scott, a Rothesay Academy contemporary of our bairns, who tells me that he is now a fully qualified tractor mechanic and is now employed by the aforementioned firm as a driver mechanic. I get into conversation with a gentleman at the Coffee Cabin, where I am usually perched on a bar stool. He tells me that he comes from a small fishing village on the Northumberland coast and has moved to Sunderland. He discusses the variations in the dialect in the British Isles. He is unable to understand his uncle who lives in Stirling. He gives me some advice about the retirement experience. *'It is whole new way of life, you must rediscover your youth,'* he tells me: advice which I take to heart. You bet. I have to reinvent myself every day, and this initiative has enabled me to do just that; I must keep my chin up. Brand new. I am trying and making the effort to look at the life before me with fresh eyes and not be mired in the past. *'Davide, ces't toujours le present,'* Madame La Rochelle, my landlady, said to me, winter, Quebec 1972!

11:57 a.m. Home. On my return I called James at DEVOL Engineering Ltd, human relations to say thank you. I left a message and sent an email acknowledging their donation of boxes. They replied with the offer of a possibility of more boxes if required. The sun continues to shine brightly – another beautiful day.

Wednesday 04/05/2011

Home. I contact the Greenock Chamber of Commerce and speak to Michelle. I then speak to Hugh. I call Riverside Inverclyde Ltd and speak to David, time-served roofer and slater from Bridgeton now their surveyor, to ask him, *'Do they have any industrial units I might be able to use?'* The meeting with Ailsa of Fyne Futures Ltd and Tony, to be held at Lochgilphead High School, is back on track.

The Shipping Clerk Settles into New Quarters

Thursday 05/05/2011

9:44 a.m. I call Elaine at Greenock Chamber of Commerce about premises for the Surplus Educational Supplies Foundation charity shop. I speak to Jennifer, who is responsible for corporate social responsibility at National Semi-Conductor, which has recently been bought by Texas Instruments Ltd, who says she will call me back. I called the *Greenock Telegraph* and spoke to David Goodwin their senior reporter, who says, *'Ping me some stuff.'*

3:01 p.m. Home. I called Pah, the businessman from the Gambia, who gives me short shrift. *'Ah loadin' two containahs,'* he said. I leave him to his business and put the phone down. *'I'm a sole trader,'* says Pah, who is stonewalling me because I will not let him use Unit 12, West Shore Business Centre, Granton.

Funds paid out to: Duncan Adams Transport Ltd £247.25 for delivery of container; Bute Naturally £60 for flyers; Print Point £21.36 for ink; post office £4.95 postage. *(Just a fraction to what I spent 2005–2017.)*

Friday 06/05/2011

11:21 a.m. Home. I have just returned from the little town of Rothesay. I posted a recorded-delivery letter to the Gambia High Commission in London offering, on behalf of the Surplus Educational Supplies Foundation, any assistance where appropriate and donations of educational resources. I contact the chief executive at Bute Community Links about OSCR forms and SESF accounts, regarding their resubmission and to discuss responses to questionnaire resources.

Earlier today, before getting under the shower, I received an email from Hannah, the principal of St Joseph's Secondary School for Girls in Banjul, the capital of the Gambia. In her email she

Monday 09/05/2011

clearly outlined the needs of her school and welcomed any help from the Surplus Educational Supplies Foundation.

I stopped off at the Musicker Café and there I met Jim and Margaret, and their grandchildren and daughter Fiona, who works for Thomas Cook in East Kilbride. On my return home I called Pah, the Gambian sole trader and freight forwarder, and made my peace with him. He is my link and the one who, at this stage I think, might be able to facilitate the delivery of much needed educational resources to St Joseph's School for Girls and other schools in the Gambia. Will he cooperate? That's the question. I asked him if he would liaise with the Surplus Educational Supplies Foundation on this shipment to his country: he says he will be available after 18 May. He knows I am begging for assistance, and I count for naught basically. He could quite easily help me if he wanted to; I am a bottom feeder at the end of his food chain.

11:28 a.m. I call ZIM to speak to Stephen. *'I will transfer you to sales,'* she said. *'Have you heard of Bennet and McMahon? They ship a lot of charity stuff to schools in the Gambia,'* he said.

12:15 p.m. It's time I stopped for some lunch.

2:45 p.m. I call Philip of the Grenada Boys Secondary School in Grenada, West Indies. *'He is not back in de office as yet,'* she said.

Monday 09/05/2011

---

11 a.m. Home. I am printing off the digitals from 28 April of the Bluefields, El Bluff, Costa Caribena teacher purchase of resources with the money that the Surplus Educational Supplies Foundation sent to Bruce, Foreign and Commonwealth Office, British Embassy, San Jose, Costa Rica. I have just had a voicemail from Jennifer, Texas Instruments, Greenock, to inform me that they will be able to store the donation of textbooks, and pallet and shrink-wrap them. I will now call them to thank and confirm my acceptance of their kind offer.

I spoke to Jennifer, who will get back to me next week. This offer of assistance is a great encouragement to me.

3 p.m. Print Point, Bishop Street, Rothesay. I am having a lukewarm hot chocolate and have come from the official reopening of the Rothesay town library, where I listened to Sheriff Irvine Smith give an eloquent and interesting address extolling the value of libraries. I chatted with him briefly and gave him an SESF flyer and an annual report. I used to give him a wave whenever the family went down to St Blane's to climb the big hill that overlooked his property. I viewed him with respect as he strolled up and down the road with his dogs. Later, while in the library, I took the opportunity to pitch my off-the-cuff spiel, to the annoyance of gathered guests.

3:15 p.m. I have just pinned Andrew, a Rothesay resident's, ears back. He was curious so I gave him my elevator pitch. I was desperate to spring a leak and had to leave the unfinished hot chocolate, now stone cold, and walk up Bishop Street to see if the Bute Community Links door was open. There is a toilet outside their office; that door was shut. I walked back down the street, said cheerio to Matt, collected my bicycle and went across to the Co-op. Helpful folk, and I used their loo with great relief and gratitude.

The sun is shining bright this afternoon. David had wanted me to get some potatoes for supper, and I had forgotten to purchase them, also there's Marion's card and cheque for Rothesay Motors to post, so it was back into the town. *'You are too old to ride a bicycle,'* he shouts at me from the pub across the street. I ignore his advice.

Tuesday 10/05/2011

9:33 a.m. Home. I have just spoken to the Greenock Academy's English Department. *'Will you take novellas?'* she asks. *'Yes please,'* I reply. I told her that I would be over there tomorrow with cardboard boxes. I am now going to call DEVOL Engineering Ltd, to see whether or not they will let me have some more boxes. First call Pickford's. I will try them first.

9:40 a.m. I call Bute Community Links to see if they will help me to get this OSCR accounts form filled in correctly.

9:51 a.m. It is a grey and wet morning. I am trying to keep my spirits up here on my own.

11:41 a.m. DEVOL Engineering Ltd has called to tell me that their operations director has authorised the donation to the Surplus Educational Supplies Foundation of another 25 new cardboard boxes. Wonderful! My spirits are lifted.

12:23 p.m. I am heading off to Bute Community Links for a meeting to see if I we can get the SESF accounts for OSCR sorted once and for all.

1 p.m. Meeting with BCL. I have handed in the recently returned from OSCR SESF accounts. There are three desks piled high with folders and loose papers of one description or another. There is a member of staff at one desk in the corner of the office who is the real person in control, at another desk sits their chief executive and at another her assistant, to whom I have been passed on to. I make myself cheerful and treat them with jocular respect; the fact that I have sought their help over many hours is beginning to wear, but to who else can I turn? There is some good news, however, for a number of replies have come back to the questionnaire they had prepared and which I had posted a month ago, and I am grateful for this assistance. I loaned Fiona my copy of Boswell and Johnson's *Tour of the Hebrides* and she told me that she was reading of their stay on the island of Coll, where she has relatives. I will have to wait on them and see if this Bute Community Links team can help me with creating some proper governance for SESF. I'm implementing the advice long overdue given to me by executive coach Barry.

Wednesday 11/05/2011

7:20 a.m. *'The next stop is IBM.'* Today, I get off at Drumfrochar and walk down the hill into Greenock town centre and into the Tesco café to chill for a bit, and then get a taxi from the rank along to DEVOL Engineering Ltd, collect the donation of new cardboard boxes and deliver them to Greenock Academy. I will then return to the Oak Mall in the Greenock town centre to deposit a cheque at the Santander branch and head for home. Don't forget to purchase supper at Marks & Spencer.

11:25 a.m. Wemyss Bay Station Café. I have not long walked in here. Let me roll it back in time, before I partake of the purvey treat in front of me.

I got off the bus from Greenock. I left the Oak Mall, where I had gone to Santander to bank the cheque and then to Marks & Spencer to purchase supper for the family. Prior to that I walked down from the Greenock Academy having left their Head of the English Department and her helper, Stewart, who told me that his mother does a lot of work for Malawi. I had dropped off another pile of flat-packed cardboard boxes, thanks to the operations director of DEVOL Engineering Ltd. I had arrived at the school by taxi shortly before 9 a.m. and was kept waiting for a spell at reception. This is an area of Greenock, the west end, that I had never ventured into before. I paid Jim of Inverclyde Taxi

Thursday 12/05/2011

and left the Head of the English Department to it with the SESF Nicaraguan file and two dossiers about the prime mover, which I asked especially that they be returned. After getting the train to Drumfrochar Station I walked down the hill.

I had to stop at the bus depot toilet for a comfort break, then went further along to Tesco where I purchased some stationery and up to their café for a roll and links and a pot of tea. '*That will make you fat,*' said a soul sitting at a table nearby, who was sitting at the same place the last time I dropped by. Then I went to shop for brews that cheer but don't inebriate, and some Tunnock's wafer logs and biscuits, a minder for my supporters at DEVOL Ltd, and got Jim the taxi, who was the only taxi in the rank.

I had better stop scribbling or I shall miss the boat.

Thursday 12/05/2011

11:54 a.m. Home. I have had a call from the Head of the Greenock Academy English Department saying that they wanted the boxes of books collected by tomorrow! A bit off the wall, an out-of-left-field surprise. Why the hurry all of a sudden? I told her that I would do my best to collect the boxes. Here we go again another session of the Generation Game.

Immediately after receiving that unexpected phone call, I call Ronnie at Pickford's in Glasgow, who is helpful and suggested I speak to John at Inverclyde Removals who, when I do, passes me on to David. I am now waiting to call him back.

I then call Greenock Academy and I spoke to a member of staff. '*The bell goes in 10 minutes and she will probably phone you then. I will try the English base for you okay?*' she said. The pressure is on me to get the one o'clock boat. Why is Greenock Academy making it difficult for me to collect these precious English textbooks? Here they are, throwing up an obstacle course by giving me this impromptu ultimatum to collect or they bin them. Tough. If you don't like it, we will just chuck the lot into one of the many skips in the school car park, which are currently being filled with fit-for-purpose educational resources.

12:50 p.m. I am still waiting for the Head of the English Department to call me back.

1:06 p.m. The phone rings. *'Did you not receive my message? I was teaching,'* she said, in spite of the fact that someone in the school's reception had gone along to tell her that I had managed to organise the collection of these boxes of books at such short notice. It's your problem Goody Two Shoes; you can take it or leave it chum.

She hummed and hawed, while carrying on a conversation as we spoke. I feel they are not playing fair, but I have no other choice but to play along if I wish to collect these books; they are cutting me no slack whatsoever. I told her that I would be over to their school before 3 p.m. tomorrow. I then called David, the van man, who said, *'We will have a van for you at Greenock Academy at 1 p.m. tomorrow.'*

The trouble I have gone to over the past six years, to make collections of fit-for-purpose quality educational resources from schools all over Scotland, is a cause for celebration, if only I had been able to do it with more support and not at my own expense. I must not whinge; I chose to do something about this profligate and totally unnecessary waste of valuable resources six years ago, and these uncooperative hiccups go with the territory, so I must carry on regardless.

4 p.m. I have returned from the town through drizzle and some rays of sunshine to receive a pleasant call from the Head of the English Department at Greenock Academy to say that the boxes will be ready to collect tomorrow from the tradesmen's entrance and the school's janitors will assist, and she said that their school will also be donating three bags of football strips.

Friday 13/05/2011

6:05 p.m. I received a call from Pah, the sole trader from the Gambia, who asks me, *'Have you any funding?' 'No, is the short answer,'* was my reply.

Friday 13/05/2011

8:05 a.m. I am in the Wemyss Bay Station aboard the train bound for Drumfrochar. I have called Inverclyde Removals to confirm that it will be okay for me to keep the 30 boxes of English textbooks from Greenock Academy in their premises until next week, when National Semi-Conductor, now Texas Instruments, at Larkfield will store the boxes for somewhat longer.

I then left a message for David, the van man carrier, that I will meet his van at Greenock Academy at 1 p.m. It is a beautiful day of clear blue sky, after that rain. I am not feeling too good but I am quite determined to see another collection successfully accomplished.

10:24 a.m. Tesco café. Greenock town centre. I have walked along the road from the barber shop over the road from the James Watt College, where I had my usual trim. I had stopped off at the Inverclyde Volunteer Centre, where I spoke about the Surplus Educational Supplies Foundation. They told me that they have a group of volunteers. She said, *'We will do the uplift, delivery and storage for you.'* I am to let her know, possibly a week in advance, when I want a collection to be made. I thanked her for her kind offer, but thought to myself, *'Sorry, it does not work like that, it's more a case of just-in-time collection, just-in-time delivery and just-in-time storage. As recent events have shown.'*

What do I do now in Greenock City till 1 p.m.?

I received a voicemail on my mobile phone, it was Joanne at Gourock High School to tell me that they will need more boxes. One would have thought that in a secondary school of that size, collecting empty cardboard boxes was not a problem.

The Shipping Clerk Settles into New Quarters

12:30 p.m. Sunshine on the page as I sit here on the steps of the entrance to Greenock Academy. I have met Sheila, who has given me instructions as to where I am to take the van, which I hope will arrive at 1 p.m. as arranged. Reception has returned my file from my visit to Bluefields, Nicaragua, Central America. I have walked up here from the Oak Mall Shopping Centre complex where I had gone for a pit stop after Jim the taxi had dropped me off at Tesco's. Earlier, he had been very helpful and had driven me all the way up Baker Street to the Booker Cash and Carry to get some 'help'. There I received a donation of six rolls of parcel tape and boxes; the manager said he would call me when they had some more boxes. Jim the taxi driver then drove me back down the road to Morrisons supermarket, where the fruit and vegetable manager said they would let me have some more boxes if I came back later.

I am sitting here now under the welcome rays of the sun waiting to take the next step of this collection process.

3:55 p.m. MV *Argyle*. Homeward bound. Roll it back.

David the van man and his co-worker, Gary, dropped me off at the Larkfield roundabout at the west end of Greenock. We have unloaded the boxes of textbooks into a large plywood container at the Inverclyde Removals depot, where I met John, who was civil, even friendly. I told him that all being well I would be collecting the boxes within a couple of weeks and would be taking them further along the road to the Larkfield Industrial Estate to National Semi-Conductor Ltd, who were going to store them.

I had arrived at Greenock Academy at 12:30 p.m. and waited and waited. I could wait no longer so I called the van man and spoke to someone with a strong Irish accent who assured me that he was on his way. At 1:30 p.m. I called again and she told me that his van had broken down. Meanwhile, two Greenock Academy janitors and a party of S1 boy pupils brought their English Department's donation of textbooks to the rear of the main building. I called the *Greenock Telegraph* and left a message saying where I was and that it would be newsworthy to get a photograph of the handover of textbooks from Greenock Academy to the Surplus Educational Supplies Foundation. Not long after making this phone call their photographer appeared. *'David told me to come,'* he said.

(See article, Greenock Telegraph*, Tuesday, 17 May 2011, 'Pupils book in to help African kids: Greenock and Gourock youngsters save novels from bin' by David Goodwin.)*

I kept my eyes open for a van to appear, which it finally did at around 1:50 p.m. I thanked him for their support and he said, *'All of this will be razed to the ground and they will build a lot of houses on this site.'*

I am heading back across the Firth of Clyde. I cannot say *'Mission accomplished'* until I see this collection of textbooks being put to further good use in a classroom somewhere in the Third World. At least I have saved this collection of English set books and texts from being thrown away.

Monday 16/05/2011

8:50 a.m. Here I am in the Tesco café in Greenock city. I ordered my roll and twa links and a small pot of tea. I was dropped off here by ABC taxi, who collected me and my 10 banana boxes from Morrisons supermarket, up the road to Port Glasgow and took me up to Gourock High School. I was given a friendly reception. Taxi driver in cab 493, ABC, brought me back to Tesco, opposite the Oak Mall Shopping Centre, and here I am.

I set out this morning in the smirry rain, took the train to Drumfrochar and walked from there down the hill to Morrisons supermarket, which has now become a familiar route. So far so good; nothing worthwhile achieved without sustained effort on my part.

11:25 a.m. I called David to let him know that I would bring something home for lunch. It is a grey, wet and windy day, so carry on moving ever forward. On the way out of the Oak Mall Shopping Centre, where I had gone to Vodaphone to have my mobile phone account topped up, I stopped off at Millets and bought a pair of hillwalking boots, a pair of socks and a headlamp.

4:53 p.m. I called The High Commission for the Gambia in London to follow up on why my letter to the High Commissioner has not been replied to. I was told that my email of 5 May would be brought to her attention. Why not before now? They have not received my snail mail letter; the individual at the other end of the phone went looking for my email and found it.

For tomorrow: Office for Scottish Charities Regulator to remind Bute Community Links – have they sent off the fresh accounts? Call the *Greenock Telegraph* to get my SESF dossier returned and possibly a copy of their newspaper with the article of the handover of textbooks and football strips from Greenock Academy: 'Pupils book in to help African kids, Greenock and Gourock youngsters save novels from the bin' by David Goodwin. *Greenock Telegraph*, Tuesday 17 May 2011.

Tuesday 17/05/2011

Home. I have a meeting with Ross & Co, the accountants, Dunoon, at 11 a.m. 18 May.

Discuss: can the money I have spent, invested, in the Surplus Educational Supplies Foundation be counted as a loan? Is there some way round, and through, recovering the funds I spent? Are there ways of recovering this money?

10:04 a.m. Home. I received a call from Gourock High School asking if they could have some more boxes and with an offer of shelving. I called Morrisons supermarket in Greenock, who will have some boxes for me to collect tomorrow morning. I called Bute Community Links and left a message regarding the SESF accounts form for OSCR.

Wednesday 18/05/2011

8:45 a.m. Tesco café. The helpful ABC 559 taxi driver has just dropped me off.

I left home early, cycling against the breezy wind. Damp and grey. MV *Bute* across the watta. I received words of encouragement from steward Callum. Train up to Drumfrochar and hoofed it along Cornhaddock Street looking out for signs of what was the Tate & Lyle Sugar Refinery. I wondered what Dad would think about my movements and negotiations in this part of the world? He had been an employee of a Tate & Lyle subsidiary Caroni Ltd, Brechin Castle Estate, from 1955 to 1970, producing sugar from sugar cane on the island of Trinidad, WI. *'My son is serving another apprenticeship.'*

I walked down Baker Street, passed the Bri-Mac incinerating plant and arrived at Morrisons, a few minutes before 8 a.m. to find they had a stack of banana boxes for me. I then called a taxi, which arrived within a few minutes, and it was back up the road to Gourock High School, who told me that they had more boxes of books for me to collect, and now here I am.

10:25 a.m. MV *Bute*. I scoffed a roll and twa links and a hot chocolate. Look after the inner man and away doon the hatch. Roll it back.

I conceived the plan in the sleepless hours before dawn, and now I reflect on the flow, and it came to pass. As I was out of the Gift Box, *Greenock Telegraph* newsagents, where I get the bus for Skelmorelie, Largs, Ardrossan to Wemyss Bay, who should I meet but a recent settler from South Africa, who immediately reaches into her handbag and gives me the address of a trust in that I should write to. She told me that she had sent the address to Unit 12 in Edinburgh, but had another typewritten address to hand, to give to me whenever we might chance to meet. *'Lay it on thick, tell them about the resources you are collecting and wish to donate,'* she said. I said I would write to them. *'No. Send them an email,'* she said.

11:17 a.m. Home. Office work. I call the *Inverclyde Volunteer*, the Community Task Force.

'I will give your number to Ross, who coordinates the different volunteer groups,' she said. *'That is good of you,'* I said.

11:28 a.m. I received a call from the English Department, Greenock Academy, offering books from their school library. *'Yes please,'* I said.

4:05 p.m. The Victoria Hotel. I am in the upstairs dining room, sitting at a table before a large picture window with a magnificent view looking out over the putting green, floral beds, Rothesay Bay and, beyond, the hills of the Cowal Peninsula.

I am here for a 2:20 p.m. appointment with Artur, the webmaster from Poland. I had stopped off earlier at Print Point to send a fax with my letter, email and CV introduction to the trustees of the DG Murray Trust in Claremont, Cape Town, South Africa, as was suggested I do by my chum from South Africa. Oddly enough, the waitress here in the hotel, who is welcoming, tells me that they have not long arrived in Scotland from South Africa, only two weeks ago. *'The economic situation is not good,'* she said. I wished her and her family good luck and a good innings in Scotland. I had my meeting from 2:20 p.m. to 3:30 p.m. with Artur, who appears to be keen and competent. I gave him my file and memory sticks, which he said he would return tomorrow. He was recommended to me by Kevin, who some years ago built www.grenadarelief.org.uk pro bono.

Thursday 19/05/2011

9:10 a.m. Home. It is a beautiful morning. The sunshine has removed the thick grey blanket of cloud cover and I can see a clear blue sky through the skylight window, and my spirit soars once more. I make an appointment to meet the surveyor for Inverclyde Properties Ltd up at the Lynedoch Industrial Estate.

1:15 p.m. MV *Bute*, returning to Rothesay; Rothesay Collegiate School 1961–1963, Rothesay New Brunswick, Canada, not ever likely I should return there, but you never know. I have met the chief executive of Bute Community Links, who has assured me that the SESF accounts have been sent to the OSCR office in Dundee.

I was able to give her the letter, which I received last week, reminding me that my SESF accounts must be completed correctly and returned forthwith; how long will this toing and froing go on for?

What of the last few hours? I met Joanne's sister as I was disembarking at Wemyss Bay. I told her that I would be hiring a taxi to take me to the Lynedoch Industrial Estate and would she like a lift on my fare; she was grateful and there was a people carrier in the car park and she asked if she could be dropped off at the Cardwell Bay Garden Centre. Certainly, jump in! No sooner were we out of the station and along up the road past Pearson's Garage than we found ourselves in a traffic jam. Gridlock: the taxi driver had the presence of mind to turn around and said he could drive up through the Wemyss Bay Caravan Park and along a back road that would take us onto the main road, and there were magnificent views of the Firth of Clyde from up there. As we drove past the Inverkip Power Station, John the driver–owner of the taxi, a former mechanical engineer at the power station now due for demolition, said, *'I would like to put a revolving restaurant at the top of the chimney.'*

He dropped me off at the Lynedoch Industrial Estate and there I waited in the rain for the surveyor to show up. I had my mobile with me and I could remember Inverclyde Properties Ltd's number without much fuss; he showed up eventually and opened up Unit 18 for me, which is about a quarter of the size of Unit 12, but it will suit the purposes of SESF for the time being. Martin will let me know when I can sign the lease. The premises are rent and rates free for six months. Brilliant! No electricity, but it will be somewhere to prepare, store, and inventory the donations of textbooks for export from Inverclyde schools. And so, it goes.

2:30 p.m. Home. David has made me a coffee. Bless him! I collected my bicycle, which needed some repairs, from The Bike Shed and met Betty (my friend from Port Bannatyne who set up and maintained the memorial there, His Majesty's Ship Verbel and Submarines, and which was opened on Sunday, 26 June 2005) and her daughter Sandra on their way back to Edinburgh, and we stood and chatted.

2:35 p.m. I was speaking to Inverclyde Volunteers, who tells me that Ross will call me regarding the logistics of collecting boxes of books from schools. I am waiting for Ross to call. Tomorrow at 1 p.m. Port Bannatyne Post Office, I have an appointment with the Scottish Education Secretary, Michael Russell; this meeting has been arranged by the Argyll and Bute SNP councillor Isabel Strong.

Friday 20/05/2011

1 p.m. Meeting with Michael Russell, the Minister for Education and Life Long Learning.

The meeting was brief as he was in a hurry to meet with his constituents on the Isle of Bute, but he said he would write a letter on my behalf to the recently appointed individual who would look into the work of the Surplus Educational Supplies Foundation. Michael Russell said their policy was to support relief work in Scotland and not to export educational resources to the underdeveloped poor countries. I explained to him why I thought that, sometimes, it was a better use of aid as educational resources could be put to use immediately. I argued that from recent reports in the press, UK Government aid funds to a number of countries in the developing world were being misappropriated. He reiterated that he would write to the new person concerned, but was not at liberty to identify the individual. I gave him, for the second time, a copy of my dossier and prior to this meeting I had obtained a letter from Bute Community Links, which endorsed the work of the SESF and the positive response from the questionnaire from benefactors to determine the level of their continuing support.

Monday 23/05/2011

8:03 a.m. Home. It is another very wet morning and I am going to have some breakfast.

Follow up with the surveyor at Inverclyde Riverside Properties Ltd and Jennifer, Texas Instruments Ltd, about possible temporary storage sites. The SESF board members: one possible so far, the proprietor of Bute Naturally.

10:56 a.m. I am chasing up the Gambia High Commission about my email of 5 May and letter; mention Principal Hannah's request for educational resources and library books.

3:04 p.m. I can collect some boxes from Morrisons supermarket tomorrow morning.

The Shipping Clerk Settles into New Quarters

Tuesday 24/05/2011

8:44 a.m. Tesco café. I have ordered a pot of tea and roll and sausage. I walked down the hill from the Notre Dame High School, Dempster Street campus, where I had delivered a dozen banana boxes that I had collected earlier from Morrisons supermarket, thanks to helpful Harry, ABC Taxis N0234. He shut the meter off at £2.30. When I had got in the cab he said, '*It is just up the road.*'

I was out early this morning; the wind had died down but the trains were off. Bus to Greenock. I walked through the Oak Mall Shopping Centre and along to Cathcart Square and further along to Morrisons supermarket to collect the banana boxes and deliver them.

1:45 p.m. The sun is shining. There is a strong wind blowing up the Clyde. I got a taxi from Tesco to the Riverside Business Park. I am here awaiting an appointment with the surveyor of Riverside Inverclyde Properties (Holdings) Ltd to sign a one-month lease to Unit 18 in the Lynedoch Industrial Estate, which is better than nothing. I take it one step at a time. '*You have taken the trouble to collect these valuable educational resources, you could be bothered,*' he said.

I had a stringy toasted cheese sandwich and a mug of tea in Leo's Café in the Oak Mall. I had walked round from the Greenock Central Library, where I had gone to find out some useful information about the links between West Africa and this port city of Greenock.

The time has come this day, as I try make sense of all my efforts, and that of many others, to salvage fit-for-purpose educational resources from this fast-flowing waste stream of reusable and fit-for-purpose educational resources.

Wednesday 25/05/2011

*

Monday 14/02/2022

Home. Here I am today, 11 years later, in semi-isolation, nationally imposed quarantine due to the Covid pandemic. I have been reluctant to risk travel off the island for almost two years. I have had the time to record the numbers, since I started this initiative way back in September 2005 How many containers? Collected from how many schools? How many collections/uplifts? How many trips across the Clyde? How many phone calls? How many road haulage firms? How many collection teams? How many shipments? What was the total tonnage of educational resources shipped from 2005 to 2017 to how many countries? Does all that costly personal effort matter now? It does matter to me, for it has given me something to do, writing up, and editing *The Diary of a Shipping Clerk* in these post-Covid pandemic days of self-imposed isolation since March 2020.

Roll it forward; *The Diary of a Shipping Clerk, Volume One* was published 25 September 2022; *Diary of a Shipping Clerk, Volume Two* was published 27 October 2023.

*

Wednesday 25/05/2011

8:34 a.m. Home. I have made a mug of coffee and have a piece of toast and marmalade ready and I must make these calls. Gourock High School, Head of the English Department: left a message. Greenock Academy Head of English Department: left a message. I call Notre Dame High School.

9 a.m. Home. I called the operations director of National Semi-Conductor, now Texas Instruments, who I had called yesterday.

This firm have offered to store boxes and will help SESF with the packing, which is absolutely brilliant; the pro bono goodwill and encouragement from such individuals always cheers me up. I asked him if their company could keep the offer on hold as the Inverclyde Council's property, assets and facilities management were about to offer some storage and collection assistance. He said that would not be a problem.

1:29 p.m. I called Mike, who gave me the number of Bennet and McMahon Freight Forwarders Ltd. £2,454 for a 40-foot standard high cube to Banjul, the Gambia. *'Make sure you give me all the elements,'* he said. Did he quote me everything? Haulage to port and the handling charges at the port?

Thursday 26/05/2011

9:21 a.m. Home. The senior reporter at the *Greenock Telegraph* has returned my call. He is a supporter of the SESF initiative. I have an appointment at that newspaper tomorrow at 9:30 a.m.

10:08 a.m. Call from Davina in Rothesay offering a video tape recording set. Yes, please. Another supporter. I called Sandbank Primary School where I taught from 1991 to 1992. They have some chalkboards for me to collect and I have no means to collect them.

12:35 p.m. I have been here revising my list of benefactors for Artur, who is going to add the firms' links to his website version of www.grenadarelief.org.uk *(which, for the record, some years later, he demolished and it was rebuilt by Sam Tweedlie junior www.hati-relief.org.uk)*. It is time to take a break.

1:40 p.m. I have spoken to Graeme, who has agreed to meet me at Unit 18 Lynedoch Industrial Estate tomorrow – a volunteer recommended by Bute Community Links.

Friday 27/05/2011

1:47 p.m. I have left a message for the Community Services Manager, Dunoon, about the possibility of one of her teams to assist in the sorting, inventorying and reloading of the educational resources stored in the five 40-foot ocean freight containers at the WH Malcolm Transport Ltd container base in Elderslie. I call A&M Transport Ltd.

2:32 p.m. Ross, the coordinator at Inverclyde Volunteer Centre, called to tell me that he would send an email to other community groups about my request for volunteers to assist.

Friday 27/05/2011

8:49 a.m. Here I am once again in the Tesco café with a cup of black coffee and a roll and egg. *'May I have the sunny side turned over please.'*

I have walked down from Drumfrochar Station. I stopped off at Homebase to purchase a couple of pairs of work gloves. In for a comfort stop at the bus rank toilet, and along and across the main road and here I am. I have an appointment with the senior reporter of the *Greenock Telegraph* in half an hour and then to find my way back up the hill to Unit 18 in the Lynedoch Industrial Estate to await the arrival of container TRLU2519369, purchased for £900 plus VAT from Freight Container Services (Scotland) Ltd, which I will unload of primary school furniture. The container is coming from WH Malcolm (Transport) Ltd at their Fouldubs depot in Grangemouth.

10:36 a.m. Unit 18, Lynedoch Industrial Estate, Greenock. I have not long walked up the hill past the Greenock Central Railway Station. I met some youngsters from Learn Direct, who are based in a unit here on the estate. I introduced myself to their manager and invited him to see the unit and told him what SESF was about. The unit is spotless; I am well pleased, for at long last I have premises, albeit temporary, that are closer to home. Get cracking.

Monday 30/05/2011

8 a.m. Unit 18, Lynedoch Industrial Estate. I am not long in here. I have walked in from the Dellingburn Road entrance to find a Duncan Adams Transport Ltd artic with a 20-foot ocean freight container with the 'bovine waste' of holy cows from India. Said hello to the driver.

I opened up and began to shift the furniture to make room for the arrival of bookshelves.

9:15 a.m. I have completed a wee task of rearranging a 40-foot container-load of primary school classroom furniture. I call Graeme, who said he would be here sometime!

10:15 a.m. That's me sitting on a vintage wooden classroom chair – they don't make them like that anymore. I scoffed a bacon roll with brown sauce from the café on Dellingburn Road and sipped my coffee. I am pleased with myself. I left an SESF flyer with Bri-Mac reception across the road. That's the second container of toxic waste delivered by Duncan Adams Transport Ltd this morning. Squawking gulls and whistling blackbirds and nothing more for me to do here at the moment. I left a message with Graeme to let him know I would be here until 11:30 a.m.

Tuesday 31/05/2011

9:56 a.m. Home. I called RBS Rothesay to see if the Murrays' donation and FCS Ltd funds for the purchase of their container are in the charity's account. RBS don't take calls anymore and I am put through to Edinburgh.

10:11 a.m. I left another message with Community Services Criminal Justice Department, Dunoon. I spoke once more with the Gambia High Commission and they have not replied to my correspondence. I have walked up not a few blind alleys and been led up some garden paths on this journey and there were difficulties to be faced head-on and overcome; sometimes the sun has been able to shine through, but at this moment there are thick, damp, grey clouds overhead.

Wednesday 01/06/2011

9:50 a.m. Home. I am having a piece of toast and marmalade and a mug of coffee. Ready to roll.

I have called Freight Container Services (Scotland) Ltd, Grange Dock, Port of Grangemouth, who assures me that the sale of the SESF container has gone into the account via BACS, Bank of Scotland, Grangemouth.

10:16 a.m. I called Graeme to arrange to meet me at Unit 18 on Friday, 3 June. Artur is coming here tomorrow from 4:30 p.m. to 6:30 p.m. to discuss the website.

Thursday 02/06/2011

8:50 a.m. Home. I called Greenock Academy to let them know that Inverclyde Council, Head of Property, Assets and Facilities Management, Cathcart House, Greenock, has delegated one of his officers to collect and store textbooks from them in one of the facilities that they use to store surplus educational resources from the council's educational system. This assistance from Inverclyde Council was most helpful.

12:35 p.m. It is still damp and overcast. I am calling Bute Community Links to see if they can recruit another volunteer to assist the Surplus Educational Supplies Foundation (see Facebook page for photographs).

Friday 03/06/2011

8:15 a.m. Tesco café, Greenock. I left home at 6 a.m. Rothesay Bay and the Firth of Clyde was flat calm, not a cloud in the sky. It is a beautiful warm morning, the birds were singing their throats out as I cycled up the road. I parked the bicycle, took off my fluorescent road safety vest and bought a return ticket from Wemyss Bay. On the way over, I met Argyll & Bute councillor Jean Moffat, full of the joys, who was taking her mum up to the Western Infirmary, and who kindly offered me a lift. I told her that I was only going as far as Drumfrochar.

I also chatted with John 'Speedy' McMillan, who was telling me that he cannot get parts for his construction and farm machinery because the production factories in Japan have been affected by the recent earthquake and tsunami.

I walked down the hill from Drumfrochar Station and had to have an immediate comfort stop at the McGill Bus Terminal public toilet, and here I am in the Tesco café, where I am going to sit, drink my cup of tea, enjoy my roll and fried egg, have a look at *The Herald* and prepare myself for today: visit Tool Hire up the road, rent skids, a barrow or a trolley, whichever is best to shift the bookshelves; head up to Unit 18 in the Lynedoch Industrial Estate and take an inventory of all the school furniture that came out of TRLU2519369 last week; prepare for the arrival of Rothesay Library books and the Jubilee Gardens bookshelves.

9:45 a.m. I have just rented two barras from Tool Hire on Dalrymple Street and Inverclyde Taxi No. 204 has delivered me and this 'kit' to Unit 18.

10:30 a.m. I have completed an inventory of all the items of

Friday 03/06/2011

classroom furniture that were unloaded from the container that was brought over from WH Malcolm Ltd, Fouldubs depot, Grangemouth. What do I do now? It is a good thing that I have brought some of my own reading matter, the history of the Atlantic slave trade by Hugh Thomas.

10:40 a.m. The surveyor from Riverside Inverclyde Property Holdings Ltd has arrived and remarked how tidy everything looked in Unit 18. I appreciated the compliment. I keep going forward and watch my step, giving full attention and maximum effort to what I am doing for the present, my best shot as they say. I am heading down Baker Street for elevenses. The sun is shining and not a cloud in the sky.

11 a.m. That's me back to Unit 18 wi' a crispy roll 'n' bacon and a white coffee, nae sugar please.

11:15 a.m. I call the trader in boxes. *'Ello Divid, I fink it's gone into yer account give me a call and let me know how you got on. I fink Eric's on 'oliday,'* he said. I am now going to call Brian at Duncan Adams Transport Ltd.

1:51 p.m. I am waiting for the big one, the big box that is. I have been sorting the three boxes of classroom library books and school textbooks that came from the Greyfriars Primary School in St Andrews.

3 p.m. Graeme, Bute Community Links volunteer, has showed up and I tried to keep him busy.

5:20 p.m. He is sitting on the tarmac outside the unit having a smoke. The container should have been here at 3 p.m.

7:25 p.m. Mark, the artic driver, has just left the container with no paperwork. I called FCS Ltd, who tells me that the SESF funds from Freight Container Services (Scotland) Ltd for the purchase of the container had been deposited in the bank.

8:58 p.m. MV *Bute* is sliding across the watta. I was chatting to Artur, digital artisan, earlier. Graeme and I hailed a taxi from Hope Street, off Lynedoch Street, to Wemyss Bay. It has been a long day. *'However, we will soon be arriving at our destination.'*

I have left a 40-foot ocean freight container with doors left open backed into Unit 18. I called DCL Security Consultants Ltd when I got home and they said they would check it out.

Saturday 04/06/2011

11:35 a.m. Unit 18. I bought a pie from the butchers on Lynedoch Street, and a coffee and an Irn Bru from Aulds, the bakery further up the road. On my arrival in Greenock City I stopped in at the British Heart Foundation, Barnardo's and Sense Scotland charity shops on West Blackhall Street to see if I could enlist some volunteers to help me unload the Jubilee Gardens Southall library furniture from the container: there is no way I can do it on my own. The manager in the Sense Scotland charity shop was very helpful, she is going to supply a team to assist me.

I then went into the Oak Mall Shopping Centre and had a new SIM card put in my mobile at Vodaphone, then I hoofed up the hill, along the road, and stopped for lunch purvey and here I am.

3:20 p.m. Today, a team of the following individuals assisted the prime mover to unload the heavy-duty bespoke shelving donated by the Jubilee Gardens Library. The lot! John, Ricky, John, from Port Glasgow, and the two Colins.

4:19 p.m. MV *Argyle*. The sun is shining on the page and I am facing the Isle of Bute once more.

Saturday 04/06/2011

This morning, I got the eight o'clock ferry boat with Marion, who was off to join her chums in Edinburgh. I got the bus from Wemyss Bay to Greenock and went across to Tool Hire and the young lad who served me said it was okay to return the barras on Monday. He suggested I try BHF for volunteers with the lifting. I went in and they couldn't help me. I then stopped off at Sense Scotland, who were sympathetic, and the manager said she would make some phone calls and try to enlist some help. I then went along to Vodaphone in Oak Mall, the helpful Gillian replaced my SIM card and I chatted with Phil from Paisley about the rapid changes taking place in mobile phone technology every two months as a result of the increasing power of silicon chips. Moore's Law. *'Hate to think what they do with the technology that becomes out of date,'* said Phil.

I then walked back to Sense Scotland and donated £20 to the charity, and from there it was back through the Oak Mall and up the hill and into the memorial park and to the butchers on Lynedoch Street for a pie, which they heated for me in Aulds Bakery Shop while I bought a takeaway coffee and a bottle of Irn Bru. I walked down Hope Street into Lynedoch Industrial Estate to Unit 18, changed into my boiler suit and had my elevenses.

I was daunted by the task that lay ahead of me; I couldn't shift the library shelving but I could begin by unloading the boxes. I knew that I would have to get some help or I was sunk, however, as I was about to despair, along came a team of five gentlemen, who were soon tired out. I said I would get some refreshment for them. I asked them what brand of soft drinks they would like, and one of them said, *'Tennent's lager please, ah dinnae drink Irn Bru.'* I set out, leaving the Sense Scotland team behind having their smoke, up through the industrial estate, out on to Lynedoch Street and into the Lynedoch Pub to see if I could persuade the afternoon clientele to lend us a hand; there was an understandably cynical and indifferent response to my off-the-street apologetic pitch, from a complete stranger.

I said I would keep trying to get some help, and a gentleman standing at the bar turned to me and said, *'You'll be effing lucky!'* I was beginning to despair, but I thought I might be able to strengthen the weak hands back at Unit 18 once they had quaffed their bevvy, so on down the street and into the off-licence. *'May I have six cans of Tennent's Lager, please.'* Who else can I ask? I am desperate.

It was back into the friendly butcher shop, perhaps they could direct me to some folk who would lend a hand – and there I met Big Colin, Desperate Dan for real, buying his butcher meat, and who had overheard what I had said. *'No problem, ah'll help yuz, wish you luck you huvnae been told to f— off,'* he said.

Monday 06/06/2011

8:30 a.m. Tesco café. Greenock. I am sipping a mug of hot tea having scoffed a fry up, which was not quite the full Scottish, but it will fill a hole. The trains were not running, so I got the bus for Greenock and walked over to the Tesco café, which was not open, so I got an Inverclyde Taxi to take me up to Unit 18. Agreeable driver, who put the trolley barras in the boot of the taxi and drove back down to HSS Hire on Dalrymple Street. I chat with the young lad with classic features and back over here.

To do: call Duncan Adams Transport Ltd to find out when are they coming to pick up the empty container and RBS to see if the £1,000 from the purchase of the Surplus Educational Supplies Foundation container has been deposited into the account; hoof it up the hill to the 'office' and begin to shift and sort through what needs to be done; post letters at WH Smith, Oak Mall post office.

11 a.m. I am back up at Unit 18. On the way up steep Bank Street and into the Memorial Gardens and Park of Remembrance and across the busy road and into the Euronics Service Centre electrical shop, where I pitched again to the helpful manager and left him

Tuesday 07/06/2011

with an SESF flyer and also left flyers at the off-licence, butcher shop, Clydeside Electrical Components and Aulds Bakery Shop, where I bought a ham roll and coffee to go, and here I am. *'Now is no time to think of what you don't have, think of what you can do with what there is.' – Ernest Hemingway.*

12:50 p.m. I called Duncan Adams Transport Ltd, Grange Dock, and spoke to Mick, who assured me that the container would be picked up some time today, but he couldn't say when. I called Howard in Newark who said to give them a look, which I will do. I then called RBS Wimbledon and spoke to Daniella, who comes from Jamaica, who assures me that the £1,000 had gone into the SESF account. She is sympathetic to my mission, and had checked the website.

I had gone into the InverStore Home and Business Storage Unit to meet Brian and pitched to another gentleman. I also pitched to Keenan, the joiner next door, who said, *'Ah take that stuff out of banks and shops every day and ye cannae give it away.'* Okay big man, I know that the waste of good stuff is endless. Why should it bother me? But it does. The time has come for me to pack it in and head for home.

4:34 p.m. Home. On the way over I met Irene, librarian from the Rothesay library, a supporter, who tells me about her grandfather, who was a boy soldier at 14 in WWI. *'He was an eccentric,'* she said. I was interested to learn more as to why she thought him to be out of the ordinary.

Tuesday 07/06/2011

7:10 a.m. Home. I call John at Inverclyde Council Property and Assets about the possibility of leasing, for free, Unit 29, which is the largest unit in the industrial estate. Where do I go from here? Proximity of units across the car park. Can SESF use them?

Send an email to the solicitor to arrange a review of my initiative and get some advice as to what might be the way forward. *(I did not realise it at the time, but I had been walking up the garden path on that front. The registration paperwork undertaken by solicitors was not necessary; he could have told me – he saw a bear of little brain coming, a mile up the road.)*

Later today I will go over to Ettrick Bay to prepare for Marion's visit with her Primary 1 class, and contact the Gambia and Sierra High Commissions in London. I have not long dropped Marion off at the ferry. I am trying to get my head round what to do next.

8:53 a.m. I received a call from Pah, the Gambian, to tell me, *'I on de motah way to London. I got containah of sea food comin', de name of countin' is money. I wit my cousin.'*

1:31 p.m. I call DC Removals, who tell me that there are over 100 boxes of books to be collected from Port Glasgow High School. The shuttering at the council property across from Unit 18 is not working. I called Colin at Texas Instruments Ltd, who tells me that they will store boxes and deliver them after 1 p.m. on Friday. I am grateful and encouraged by their support.

Wednesday 08/06/2011

8:59 a.m. I make arrangements for the transport of boxes from Port Glasgow High School. I call Arnold Clark.

9:38 a.m. I speak to Lee Ann at the marketing department who says, *'I'll see what I can do for you and I will call you back.'*

9:45 a.m. I left a message with marketing at Strathclyde University and speak about the possible exposure of SESF, an initiative of David Miles-Hanschell, up-and-coming social entrepreneur and a former alumnus, class of 1995. Ross tells me that the magazine is inundated by alumni seeking publicity for their own projects.

Thursday 09/06/2011

10:30 a.m. I am going to make Johanna a mug of tea and some toast. The sun is shining and its time I got outside into the garden.

4:15 p.m. I received a call from Sense Scotland, Greenock, to tell me that they can supply transport and helpers to uplift the boxes from Port Glasgow High School on Friday and transport them to National Semi-Conductor, now Texas Instruments Ltd, Larkfield Industrial Estate.

2:03 p.m. I call Inverclyde Council and speak to John about entry to the Port Glasgow High School building. He tells me that the shuttering of their Lynedoch Industrial storage unit does not work – so much for the council's offer of storage. He said that I can collect the boxes from Port Glasgow High School.

2:11 p.m. I call the *Greenock Telegraph* to tell them about the uplift of boxes of textbooks made possible by the Sense Scotland team of volunteers. I am to call Arnold Clark and Rent-a-Van tomorrow.

For Friday: be at Port Glasgow High School before twelve o'clock on Friday, and remember to collect the letter from Fiona, the depute head teacher, authorising the handover of the boxes of books. Meet team at Sense Scotland, West Blackhall Street at 9:30 a.m. Friday, 10 June.

Thursday 09/06/2011

11:17 a.m. Home. I called Gourock High School and Notre Dame High School to see if I can get official letters from them stating that the boxes of resources from their schools are donations. Someone said to me recently, I can't remember who, '*You must spend a lot of time just moving stuff around.*' And I agreed, because I have no other choice at the moment if I want to salvage these textbooks from being pulped, or simply dumped in landfill sites. I am at the mercy of unplanned and unexpected contingencies.

For tomorrow: call David the surveyor on arrival at Port Glasgow High School; remember to collect letter from depute teacher and David the journalist at the *Greenock Telegraph*.

Friday 10/06/2011

8:12 a.m. Tesco café. I have met a supporter from the *Greenock Telegraph* who was in here to have his full Scottish breakfast. I was out at 6 a.m. with a pain behind my left eyeball. It was overcast and damp on the road again. I met Claire, P3/4 2000 class, North Bute Primary School, on her way to her printing and design course at Kilwinning College in Ayrshire. She is a former pupil who told me that she finishes her course in three weeks' time.

I walked down the hill from Drumfrochar Station, past the ducks and seagulls on Murdieston Loch, and here I am with a pot of tea, a roll and two sausages. The slog of the journey is behind me and now there is nothing else for it but to persist. To do: meet with the Sense Scotland team at 9:30 a.m.; collect boxes from Port Glasgow High School and deliver them to Texas Instruments Ltd.

12:19 p.m. Wemyss Bay Café. I will capture some of the past moments before they slip away into oblivion.

I have not long got off the McGill bus from Greenock. I went up the road this morning and into the Oak Mall Shopping Centre, withdrew some cash and back out paid the manager of Sense Scotland on West Blackhall Street a £50 donation. She introduced me to the team of helpers and I pitched to them as a van with half a dozen young gentleman arrived and we all piled in. The only place for me was to lie on the floor of the van: I squeezed in by the legs of the passengers and saw the Greenock Town Hall from a fresh perspective as I chatted on the road up to Port Glasgow High School to one of the hard-faced helpers, who was dressed in a shell suit. I caught glimpses of beautiful panoramic views of the hills on the other side of the Clyde.

Monday 13/06/2011

Out of the van we tumbled and went into reception and were met by a friendly janny – initially I mistook him for a teacher – and he gave me the depute head teacher's letter. Soon a teacher appeared, who from his casual dress could have been the janitor, accompanied by a class of pupils who proceeded to load the boxes into the van. He tells me that I can only have some of them; I am disappointed as I was told that there were a hundred boxes to collect. I don't make a fuss: this beggar takes what he is given with a grateful smile. I ask the driver of the van to take me up to National Semi-Conductor, now Texas Instruments, Larkfield Industrial Estate, and en route I change the plan – easy peasy: we will drop off the much-reduced collection of boxes at Unit 18, Lynedoch Industrial Estate,

On arrival at Unit 18, I put £20 each in the hands of the helpers, which puts a big smile on their solemn faces. They are all in their twenties, and I feel for them and the opportunities they have so far missed or that presented and were not taken advantage of in life's roulette casino; there you go again, bountiful, shallow-pocket philanthropist – perhaps they, too, will be imbued with a spirit of unconditional generosity to their fellow human beings.

I sort the boxes and walk back to the Sense Scotland charity shop and touch base with the manager, and meet another charity worker who was part of the team last week, who were shifting the heavy-duty library furniture out of the container. He is working as a volunteer in the shop. I had withdrawn some more cash on my way through the Oak Mall to pay him for his labour last week and to pay the driver. I know, my lack of judgement hurts me more.

Monday 13/06/2011

9:45 a.m. Home. I called Marketing Placements, Strathclyde University Careers Service.

9:55 a.m. I received a call from Stirling Furniture, to whom I had sent an email.

10:45 a.m. I called the Gambia High Commission and speak to Her Excellency, who is stonewalling; her fine words will butter no parsnips.

11:30 a.m. I speak to someone in the office of Talent Scotland and was told to send them an email. I am trying to enlist some smarts with skill sets that, given my time left on Blue Planet, I will never have the time to acquire.

Wednesday 15/06/2011

10 a.m. Wesley Owen's Bookstore café, once Pickering and Inglis in them days 1975–1982, a former haunt, Bothwell Street, Glasgow, and I order a small black coffee. *'Would you like anything else?'* she asks me in a welcoming voice. *'Yes, please.'* I am tempted. *'I'll have a fruit slice, if I may please.'* A fly cemetery.

I am looking out the door onto Bothwell Street. I have an appointment with the solicitors up the street to discuss:
1. What happens to the Surplus Educational Supplies Foundation (registered Scottish Charity SCO39331, company registered in Scotland No. 37345) should the chief executive and sole trustee not be around or compos mentis to run the show? What are the procedures necessary to wrap it up, liquidate, dissolve the attempt at social enterprise?
2. Could the solicitor give me some advice as to how I might build on what has been accomplished and become a more effective organisation?
3. Can he give me advice as to how I might approach potential sponsors? How best to dispose of all the educational resources in Units 12, and 18 and the ocean freight containers should I dissolve the charity and limited company?

Friday 28/01/2022

10:45 a.m. I was shown to the lift by a gentleman at reception and on the way up I met the solicitor and was whisked up to the 9th Floor.

11:30 a.m. I felt that the meeting went well. He is keen that I should persevere with the work of SESF and should not 'burst the bubble' at this stage. He said he would look over my dossier and record of shipments. He talked of possible linkages with other charities, *'synergies'*, was the word he used. The meeting with him was pro bono, and he said he would get back to me.

*

Friday 28/01/2022

9:16 p.m. Home. I always find it worthwhile to talk with anyone, more so now in these days of locked down self-isolation for two years, and more than anything I miss that spontaneous interaction. It's the price we pay to obey the protocols that enforce this national quarantine, so that we social creatures might reduce the risk of catching the virus variants of this 21st century plague, possibly unintentionally created in a Wuhan laboratory; who wants to end up in an ICU ward and be intubated?

I typed those words just now. Back to the past, to past days.

*

11:50 a.m. I am on the train for Wemyss Bay and meet Rosetta, from South Africa, one of the encouragers.

4:45 p.m. Meeting the digital artisan to go over grenadarelief.org.uk, who was here till 5:45 p.m. I asked him to make a correction on the section 'about me' in the gallery: I was not born in Grenada, but in Barbados, West Indies.

THE SHIPPING CLERK SETTLES INTO NEW QUARTERS

Saturday 25/06/2011. Frederick Longino, PhD student at Edinburgh University, from Dar es Salaam, is here at Unit 12 to collect several pallets of books for the Ngulla Community School in Tanzania.

Tuesday 21/06/2011

11:45 a.m. Home. I received a call from Business Gateway in Dunoon, who thinks my SESF project is great and is going to try and pitch for me. I need a team to get cracking and market all this stuff, of quality school furniture, for a start. She knows what I am trying to achieve and will contact with me within the next fortnight.

I call the Sierra Leone High Commission, London, England.

Thursday 23/06/2011

11 a.m. Home. I have called the Sierra Leone High Commission and left a message.

I spoke to Michael, of the Peace and Hope Trust, who tells me that his personal assistant has returned from West Africa and that he is travelling to 'Nica' (Nicaragua, Central America, to you and me) in July and will call me on his return with any information about the SESF shipment of library books to schools in Bluefields City, Dinamarca, and El Bluff in the Costa Caribena, Central America.

Saturday 25/06/2011

7:04 a.m. MV *Argyle*. It is grey and damp. A thick grey blanket hangs heavily low over the hills on both sides of the Kyles of Bute and on the Cowal Peninsula.

I am leaving Rothesay for the day and I hope to meet Marion, who is also travelling to Edinburgh, outside WH Smith's Newsagents in Queen Street Station, Glasgow. I am over to attend another Scottish Tanzania British Society meeting. The town is slowly receding and I am leaving three of the most important people in my life behind, and I hope to meet another en route. I have munched my way through a roll and two links and am sipping my hot chocolate, without sprinkles. '*Is that you over to Edinburgh?*' asks Robert, who is the foreman of the town's recycling centre and who I have known for some time. '*Yes, Robert, I am not finished with the work of my initiative just yet; I hope to meet some representatives of a country in Africa, who might be able to direct me to a school that is interested in receiving a shipment of salvaged educational resources.*'

Rothesay folk love to know where you are going. I have brought *Capitalism and Slavery* by Eric Williams to read to try and keep my mind engaged.

8:30 a.m. The train from Wemyss Bay had been cancelled, so I shared a taxi up to Greenock West with a settler. '*We are now approaching Greenock Central. The next stop is Cartsdyke,*' she said.

9:45 a.m. '*This train is for Edinburgh Waverley,*' she said. £11.40. As instructed by Marion, I stopped off at a sports shop in Gordon Street and got a rain jacket.

11:20 a.m. I am attending the STBS meeting. Discussion about Jubilee Scotland and applying debt relief. I had met Apollo some time ago. Cross-generational partnerships and the Twende Pamona 'Let us walk together' scheme. '*There are a lot of people going to East Africa on relational visits,*' said another.

A report was presented from a community in Portobello connected to a community in Tanzania. Folk from Scotland going to live in a Tanzanian community. Exchange visits.

(*The effort that I made to attend these Saturday morning meetings in Edinburgh was to have a positive result, though, that afternoon. I did not think they would lead to any constructive action. Fast forward.* 'Education charity spreads its wings with Africa donations. Tanzanian School to get Scots books' by Craig Borland, Friday, 14, September 2012. The Buteman. '*Rothesay resident David Hanschell, the founder of The Surplus Educational Supplies Foundation, presented a donation of textbooks books recently to Frederick Longino, a student from Dar es Salaam who is completing his PhD at Edinburgh University. The books are destined for the Ngulla Community Secondary School in the East African country, of which Frederick is a patron. 'It was very humbling to see just how excited Frederick was to receive all the materials,' David told* The Buteman.*')*

Thursday 07/07/2011

4 p.m. Home. I was speaking to the container dealer, Freight Container Services (Scotland) Ltd, who had called and left a message for me to call him. He told me his business partner had been to see him. He is keen to buy my remaining four boxes.

Bob of Forth Valley College can now meet me next week. My meeting with them, at long last, is on 11 July at 10 a.m. I have a meeting at Bute Youth Project, 12 Tower Street, on 13 July. I spoke to Business Gateway, who will call me next week: she would like a list of all the educational resources that Forth Valley College, Falkirk, wish to dispose of, and suggests that I 'enhance' their value and generate a revenue from their waste stream. How? Does Forth Valley College have enough educational resources on offer to make such a scheme worthwhile? And will the college assist SESF in any way?

Monday 11/07/2011

9:15 a.m. Forth Valley College, Falkirk Campus. It is a beautiful summer morning: puffy clouds in a blue sky. I arrived here by taxi from Falkirk High Station – better to be early for the appointment than late. I have a meeting with the Director of Building Services and the Depute Principal of Business Studies.

Issues and topics to discuss:
1. Is there storage in the Falkirk, Stirlingshire, area close to the port of Grangemouth?

2. Who will bear the costs of collection, because SESF can't.
3. Beneficiaries of these resources?
4. Does the college have any links with similar institutions in the Third World?
5. Can the college's students and staff collaborate?

Bob and Iris are committed, they tell me, to aiding the developing world. Tom's strategy is to wait and see what's left. I have been waiting months for them to tell me what SESF can have. *'I have got a campus full of furniture,'* he said. I am to call Elaine in Tom's office to arrange to view the furniture. Iris said she would try and arrange a meeting with Michael Matheson MSP. They tell me that FVC is a Fairtrade college. What does that mean?

'I can see a situation arising where you will have to empty, decant, dump and get rid of all the educational supplies you have collected so far,' said Iris.

'Yes, what you foresee is more than likely, however I am determined, before that happens, to make every effort to source deserving beneficiaries for the fit-for-purpose educational resources that I currently have in storage, and it is a great shame that our Scottish Government, COSLA and the colleges were not supportive of SESF,' I said.

The meeting began at 10 a.m. and ended at 11:15 a.m. The college representatives were non-committal and left me no further ahead. At the end of that meeting Iris said, *'I know where you are coming from.'* I had been in contact with them over two months ago. They were apologetic about not contacting me sooner, which was an afterthought. They told me that they were at the fourth stage of their resources disposal policy. Will Forth Valley College leave me with what is worth uplifting? Will they be willing to establish an ongoing reciprocal link with SESF, FVC, the local education authorities and deserving recipients? I must get cracking to shift what I have already collected. Sell it, if I can, as this would have to be the last resort.

Thursday 14/07/2011

12:36 p.m. I am on the train to Wemyss Bay. While walking up the road to Falkirk High Station, on the way back, I stopped off at the Salvation Army Citadel in Falkirk. I met Captain Philip, their commanding officer, introduced myself and gave him my card and an SESF flyer. He was helpful and he suggests I contact Major Heather of the Salvation Army International Development Department in London.

I have slight nippy pains across my chest. What does that indicate? The warning given to me months ago: '*You are going to die doing this work,*' he said.

Thursday 14/07/2011

---

2 p.m. Meeting at Bute Youth Project: Bob, Rhuiraidh and Chris. As soon as I hear from Alan I will be in touch with the team leader.

3:25 p.m. I had a meeting with the Business Gateway representative at 13 Argyle Street. She appeared to be impressed with my initiative but came up with no suggestions for its development. She did, however, say she would look further into the possibility as to whether I could formulate a viable business model that would generate revenue, and did mention the possibility of my pitching to MBA students for help preparing a plan for marketing surplus educational resources for the circular economy; a suggestion I had already followed up, having approached the Strathclyde University Business School, whose students come from all over the world.

9:15 p.m. I called the Bute Youth Project team leader. He has been unable to contact the two youngsters who said at the meeting today that they would like to volunteer to work with the Surplus Educational Supplies Foundation. I will have to put that project on hold, which is just as well for I feel terrible at the moment: severe pain in my stomach on the left side below my ribs.

The Shipping Clerk Settles into New Quarters

Tuesday 26/07/2011

9:25 a.m. Phoenix Park Hotel, Linwood, Renfrewshire, which is directly under the flight paths flying out from Glasgow Airport. The patio.

I am in the midst of the 21st century commercial world: KFC, Burger King, Pizza Hut. The hotel did not appear to be open for business. I left home shortly after 6 a.m. and while buying a ticket I met the master mariner and island supporter from the Boat Yard, who is on his way to Dubai. He invited me to come and sit with him. He showed me a picture on his mobile phone of his 'ship': a jack-up rig, a massive seagoing barge used for assembling offshore wind turbines and other installations. He asked me how David was getting on, and I told him that he had just qualified from the Glasgow Nautical College as a watch officer. *'Tell him to call me,'* he said. *'Donald, I have given him your telephone number, ages ago, and I know he will not call you.' 'What is your telephone number?'* he asked and I gave Donald our telephone number.

(It was good to chat with him, little did I know then where this brief encounter with a Rothesay resident would lead. Donald, who comes from the Isle of Barra, has always had time to speak with me, for over a number of years now, from the day we met at the Port Bannatyne boatyard.)

I got the train to Paisley Gilmour Street. As I approached the Rothesay ferry terminal, I decided to take the bicycle and cycle through Paisley, and I have hazarded the main high way out to Linwood. I stopped off at ASDA in Linwood to get some beverages that cheer but do not inebriate for Frank, Brian and Hugh at the WH Malcolm Transport Ltd container base, Elderslie, where I am heading to in a short while. While making these purchases I succeeded in dropping a large jar of Nescafé Gold Blend – get another jar. I put on my boiler suit in the car park and cycled across to the Malcolm Group container base. Frank greeted me warmly, and told me that they are shifting containers onto rail

Tuesday 26/07/2011

cars, and will be until 11 a.m. What do I do now? Do I cancel arrangements or not?

I called Tom, container dealer from Bathgate, who I had spoken to yesterday afternoon and who had agreed to meet me here between 10 a.m. and 11 a.m. He told me that he preferred to come at 11 a.m. and he was bringing two men from Bathgate to assist me in unloading the container that he wished to purchase. I called home and spoke to David, who was working for Sam at a construction site. I decided to push off over here to the Phoenix Hotel and chill out in some style. Here I am, on the patio of the hotel, and I have a bacon roll and coffee before me, which have grown cold while I scribbled.

11:45 a.m. I was met at the container base by Tom, Stephen and Chris at the gate and they were signed in. I had no time to finish the coffee that Hughie had made me. The sun is cracking the sky and we three are all set to unload and reload two 40-foot high cube ocean freight containers, with the words of Eric ringing in my ears: *'David you only want to move it once.'*

2 p.m. Stephen, Chris and myself had some lunch from Stewart's Snack Bar down the road. The sun is still cracking the sky. We are beginning to empty GATU4033193 into aluminium container SEAU4272551.

That removal and storage was exhausting.

7:02 p.m. MV *Argyle* is chugging its way across the Clyde. I was chased by the crew, who were sweeping up and are now hosing down the deck, while I was scoffing a poke of chips and washing them down the hatch with a bottle of Irn Bru.

Roll it back. Stephen and Christopher, who are from Coatbridge, and the Nutter from the West Coast – we finished unloading and reloading school furniture into container SEAU4272551, a rather battered and patched 40-foot aluminium container. I paid

Stephen and Christopher with a sum of which they both deserved every penny; they were chuffed and it was obvious by their reaction of surprise and delight that it was unexpected. Hughie, ever his friendly and concerned self for my welfare, tells me that steel containers now fetch £3,000 for scrap. I bid goodbye to Brian, Hughie and Frank and set off for Paisley Gilmour Street Station.

I stopped at Coffee Kiosk on Platform 2 and bought a Fanta juice, a bottle of water, an egg sandwich, and lost the plot. In my haste to board the train for Wemyss Bay, I left my haversack behind on a platform bench: blunders. I only discovered what I had done halfway down the track to Bishopton. What do I do now? I missed the chance to alight there and got off at Port Glasgow, crossed over and spoke to the helpful station master, who phoned through to Paisley Gilmour Street, while I sat on a bench and waited anxiously. She called me half an hour later to tell me that the engine driver for the train to Gourock would have my haversack for me. Such are the trials and tribulations and joys; I kept calm through detachment. The steps, stops and mishaps of this righteous idiot are sometimes my own fault.

Wednesday 27/07/2011

1:41 p.m. Home. I called McIntyre Brothers Ltd, St George's, Grenada, West Indies, and he said, '*Ah have you in front of me now. I will speak wid de Ministah of Education, ah know de ministah.*' I am trying to locate a deserving school for another shipment of fit-for-purpose educational resources. I am a persistent soul. I had spoken earlier to his secretary, who had recommended that I gift the educational resources in the container we had recently loaded to her school, the Samaritan Presbyterian School in Union, St Mark, Grenada, West Indies.

Wednesday 03/08/2011

5:25 p.m. Home. For the past couple of hours I have been on the phone to Anne in Grenada, the businesswoman who described me as 'someone working on a shoestring'. I am grateful to her for putting me in touch with Roland Malins-Smith of SeaFreight Agencies Inc, Miami, Florida, some years ago now and Salim, businessman, of Spice Isle Retreaders Ltd, who said, *'David, you can trust me.'* Salim had purchased the last four 40-foot ocean freight containers that I shipped to schools in Grenada. I am trying to arrange, set up, the delivery of another container of educational resources, SEAU4272551, to the aforementioned school. Expensive transatlantic telephone calls.

I also called Knight Watson Ltd, Freight Forwarders, Grangemouth, who will give me a quote for shipping the container to Kingston, Jamaica, West Indies, and from there SeaFreight Agencies Lines will ship the container pro bono to St George's, Grenada.

Thursday 04/08/2011

8:33 p.m. Home. This morning Marion and Amy dropped me off at Unit 18, Lynedoch Industrial Estate, Greenock. I donned my boiler suit and slowly began to put some shelving into the unit and I unpacked the boxes of books that we had collected from Port Glasgow High School several months ago, which were mainly English and geography textbooks, all in mint condition. I had rented a porter's barrow, a trolley, from the tool rental business in the unit across from Unit 18. I stopped work at 1 p.m. and walked down into the town and through the Oak Mall Shopping Centre to get the bus to Wemyss Bay, boarded the ferry MV *Bute* for Rothesay, and walked home.

For tomorrow: contact: Inverclyde Council Estates; contact Knight Watson Ltd and their freight forwarder about the usual tariff to Kingston, Jamaica, from the Port of Grangemouth.

Chapter Fifteen
Will There Be Some Light at the End of This Tunnel?

Monday 08/08/2011

8 a.m. I am now in Unit 18, Lynedoch Industrial Estate, Greenock. I walked from Drumfrochar Station along Cornhaddock Street and down the hill to here. It is a cool grey morning, but the sky is clearing up over the big warehouse, Unit 29, across the road. I was chatting to Tony Edwards on the train up from Wemyss Bay, and Michael the Geordie, who now drives a bus for McGill's and was in education supplies for the Newcastle Education Authority.

Tuesday 09/08/2011

2:46 p.m. Home. I am sitting in full sunshine at the back door of Delhi Cottage. Marion has just gone indoors to cool down.

I set off on the bicycle to get the 6:15 a.m. ferry. Train to Drumfrochar Station, I walked along Cornhaddock Street to Lynedoch Street and I arrived at Unit 18 just in time to reach the loo. I donned my boiler suit and began tidying up, moving the superb collection of Dexion system metal shelving, salvaged from the refurbishment of Argyll and Bute Council's Rothesay Town Library.

8:45 a.m. Jim arrived to open up Inverclyde Council's large warehouse unit across the road. Before long, the photographer accompanied by the journalist, Paul from the *Greenock Telegraph* newspaper, appeared along with the education convener on the education committee of Inverclyde Council: Terry Loughran is switched on to the value and importance of what I am trying to do. I assisted the Inverclyde Council official and his team of Craig and Paul from the removals Harrow Green Ltd, in unloading their van of the boxes of textbooks from Gourock High School.

I reminded him about the collection of boxes to be uplifted from Greenock Academy that were still up at the Inverclyde Transport Ltd depot in the Larkfield Estate. He said he would let me know when he would be able to have them uplifted. I thanked him and his team for their help, without which these books would have been on their way to be pulped.

Terry is aware of how difficult my initiative is. He gave a long quote for the newspaper. He is an ally and a wonderful encouragement to me to see this whole project through to completion. *'What you are trying to do is insurmountable. All problems have a solution,'* he said. I have to persevere; how often have I used that word since that Friday afternoon, way back in August 1974, when I came upon a pub, The Perseverance, in Leith, called by the name of that supreme virtue and took the courage and determination to make success of every day of my new life in Scotland.

It was 10 a.m. and I decided to call it a day and made my way back to Stewart Street and got the Largs bus, but missed the eleven o'clock ferry.

Wednesday 10/08/2011

2:04 p.m. Home. Forth Valley College, Alloa campus, is going to arrange for me to visit the remaining educational resources in their former Alloa campus buildings. They have moved into a new build and have left a message with Elaine in Falkirk to contact me.

2:14 p.m. I called Knight Watson Freight Forwarders Ltd in Grangemouth and spoke to their director, who told me that they are working on a quote for shipping a 40-foot ocean freight container from Grange Dock, Port of Grangemouth, to Kingston, Jamaica, West Indies.

1:30 p.m. I am at Saint Andrew's Primary School to collect a donation of educational resources. How? I have to work that one out. I have received, this afternoon, a copy of the Thursday, 11 August 2011 *Greenock Telegraph* article written by Paul John Coulter 'School books saved for kids in Africa'

Monday 22/08/2011

10 a.m. Home. I have spoken to Ryan, the fitness trainer, who tells me that he has decided to put my fitness programme on hold until I get further medical tests. He thinks my blood pressure is not what it should be.

I call the Grenada High Commission in London enquiring whether the government will grant SESF (registered charity SCO39331) a concession from the Ministry of Education, on the import duty on a 40-foot ocean freight container shipment donation to one of their government's schools. I await their response. I will seek to acquire practical skills in building construction while continuing to further the objectives of the Surplus Educational Supplies Foundation

Thursday 25/08/2011

10:20 a.m. Home. I left a message for Business Gateway about applying for a 'Start Up Grant'. I spoke with Irene about the remaining educational resources at Alloa College, and with A&M Transport Ltd about assisting me to reassemble some of the Rothesay Library shelving the next time he is on the mainland. I have been unable to figure out how it's done.

Monday 29/08/2011

2:55 p.m. Argyll College, Isle of Bute campus. Access to Construction Skills, Scottish Qualifications Authority course, Level 5. I am up the road at the joint campus and have been offered a coffee by the welcoming Learning Manager. The Technical IT manager has also made me welcome.

1:05 p.m. What am I waiting for? The sun is shining bright on the new joint campus buildings. New beginnings. I am never too old to learn new skills.

1:10 p.m. Induction process has begun. Administration details and filling in registration forms. I am the perennial student who refuses to be old and meets young fellow students. We are told what we need to know and are to meet at 11 a.m.

Tuesday 30/08/2011

11:10 a.m. Construction Centre, Industrial Estate. My student days have begun again. The multi-skilled instructor has introduced himself and has worked on large construction projects in countries all over the world. *'My experience is 40 years in building and you all want to learn how to do things,'* he said.

'That is just why I am here today, to learn how to do lots of stuff,' I think to myself. He has set out the regulations regarding safety practice in the workshop and the course time table which is as follows:

Monday   1:30–4:30
Wednesday   8:30–1:00
Thursday   10:30–4:30
Friday   8:30–4:30

He tells us to *'Look out for one another!'*

It is a wet morning and I cycled from home and arrived on

time, raring to go. As I was cycling up the road I passed by Jack, local tradesman and former mainland clerk of works, out for a walk with his dog, and I paused to speak with him. He asked me where I was going. When I told him he said, *'You are staring at the bottom.'* Jack had done the tiling by the kitchen sink and in the bathroom of Delhi Cottage when we had not long arrived on the island, and to him I owe a debt of gratitude, which I may be able to acknowledge elsewhere.

The instructor goes on to tell us about what we are to expect from the course; there will be a self-study requirement and we will need to have this documented in some form. The skills to be acquired are as follows: half-brick walling; decorative painting; intermediate plumbing; plastering; roof tiling; one-brick walling; bench joinery; sanitary plumbing; cavity walling circulation; painting undercoats; door frames; wallpapering; how to calculate copper piping; pressure plumbing; and gravity plumbing.

'All of this stuff links in with each other. Over a period of time you will get to know where everything is,' he said.

Wednesday 31/08/2011

8:05 a.m. It is dry and cool here at Unit 5 and I am ready to go. *'Is everything all right?'* asks the instructor. *'No complaints,'* I reply. At the tea break I jot down a little of what he said: *'Near enough is not good enough. If you are not happy with yourself, don't give it to someone else or a customer. If you make a mistake fix it. Measure twice and cut once, look twice and double check. Put yourself out to everyone. 95% of any job is preparation.'*

10:41 a.m. Paperwork. The team are collating SQA files. The instructor talks about safety instructions, the rules and regulations of the workshop, and the safety officer's responsibilities.

1 p.m. Time to go. This has been a paperwork session, and here I am wanting to get down to doing, to making stuff, and this is not quite what I had bargained for. We will have to wait and see what this self-imposed series of hoops and hurdles is going to be like.

Thursday 01/09/2011

10:20 a.m. On the way I met Paul, so I got off my bike and we walked up the hill together. He was telling me about his experiences living in Barcelona, Spain, in 1982, and he's been a paramedic in London.

'The idea is we all work together. In the real world, you work together as a group. You have to be truthful within yourself. Near enough, is not good enough. I will show you how to fix it,' said the multi-skilled instructor. He then launches into an account about his journey to become a member of the Guild of Master Craftsmen. *'When I did my apprenticeship, I did the whole thing,'* he said, describing the various places he had worked on his journey to become a skilled tradesman.

11:10 a.m. He tells us what he expects from us and introduces what we will be making on the hinged wall.

Friday 02/09/2011

3:10 p.m. Home. It has been slow day, which began at 8:30 a.m. and finished early at 2:30 p.m. We spent most of the time watching the instructor assemble a large four-sided seven-shelf display unit, which had been commissioned by the local jam factory to display their products. Occasionally he would call on members of the class to assist him by applying glue, drilling holes for screws and tidying up.

I cycled back down the hill and stopped in for coffee and a toasted cheese sandwich at the Musicker Café on Castle Street. It has been a dry but overcast day. I slept poorly last night. I was up often to go to the toilet. Press on. I foresee a long haul with this course; my attempt to acquire some skill with 'The Tools' and techniques of the building trade. *'What are you doing up here?'* asks my chum, Jim the bus driver. *'I hope to go and build a school somewhere,'* I replied. *'You are getting on a bit, but now that would be something,'* he said.

Monday 05/09/2011

1:15 p.m. I am always showing up earlier than I need to and some of the team are on deck. The sun is shining pleasantly outside. I would much prefer to be working out of doors. This course portends to be too much like being in a classroom for my liking. I am ready to learn how to dovetail the joints, but instead we spend the entire afternoon getting his project, his homer, the jam jar cabinet ready for the big house. I did some sanding and sweeping up. I am going into the 'please everybody in the ever-cheerful smiley face and helpful' mode, by making myself agreeable and helpful. I am old enough to be their father and grandfather. This lot spend a lot of their time fooling around.

Wednesday 07/09/2011

8 a.m. As I stood on the pedals to climb the steep Barone Hill there was a rainbow encircling the top of the hill.

'You wet your bed or something?' asks the instructor, who remarks on my early arrival. I let the veiled criticism, or joke, pass without comment. I will work round you.

'What was the Scotland score last night?' asks the instructor. I haven't got a clue nor am I interested: to confess that opinion would have me burnt at the stake, I think to myself.

8:40 a.m. He is handing out the boiler suits. I have my own. The boots with steel toecaps are too big for my feet, but I will wear them without complaint; we are going to go through the drawers under the benches and learn how to use the tools. *'Planning and preparation,'* repeats the instructor.

Thursday 08/09/2011

Not long after 8 a.m. I'm earlier than I need to be. *'Coffee and a biscuit?'* he asks. *'Thanks Derek,'* I reply. The instructor gives a talk on timekeeping and the importance of looking busy. When, later this morning, there is a lull in the work and the rest of the team are on their iPhones, I take this to heart and start cleaning the washroom/toilet, which is filthy.

10:55 a.m. The team is just hanging about waiting to be told what we are going to do and this inaction is more than I had bargained for.

The jet-setting digital savant, who kindly built the website pro bono for me, is over grenadarelief.org.uk: he has dropped by to see the instructor, who is making him another homer. Last week, the instructor had repaired a split stand with what he called 'biscuits' – slivers of wood glued in between the split rail. The multi-skilled instructor takes a photograph of the team and the jam cabinet, which will be taken to the big house for the island food festival at the weekend.

1:15 p.m. I am back from what was the newsagents on the High Street and is now the 'Polish Shop' with a cheese roll and salad, and a packet of crisps.

2 p.m. The sun is shining outside. I am ready and waiting for instructions.

Will There Be Some Light at the End of This Tunnel?

Friday 09/09/2011

8 a.m. I am here before everyone. The instructor tells me that the patron was pleased with the jam cabinet. *'This what we are making today. You can't kid a kidder,'* he said. Lap joints to measure twice and cut once. That's me for another week.

I let the instructor know that I will not be able to make it on Wednesday 14 September, but I will try to get back in time for the afternoon session; I have a hospital appointment at Golden Jubilee, Clydebank, for tests.

Tuesday 13/09/2011

12:05 p.m. Home. Inverclyde Council has called to let me know he has some boxes from Greenock Academy. He has made an appointment to meet me on Tuesday, 20 September. He said that the surveyor of Riverside Inverclyde Properties (Holdings) Ltd was trying to contact me, so I called him. He tells me that he has prospective tenants for Unit 18, so I said that I would be happy to move. I cannot be otherwise, as he has alternative units that I might wish to view. I just have to go with the flow and that's all there is to it.

Wednesday 14/09/2011

11:05 a.m. Wemyss Bay Café. I got a taxi from the Inverclyde Hospital, having attended Sister Liz's Level C prostate assessment clinic. Blood taken and urine flow measurement etc.

I have had this test done before. I thought I would make the eleven o'clock boat. Hard lines David Miles-Hanschell; as I write this, the sun is shining on the big round table at the far end of the café. I have made the effort to try and get back before the end of my class, and before me I have a bacon roll with HP sauce and a mug of tea to shift. Go with the flow, and I must keep it flowing.

Thursday 15/09/2011

10 a.m. I had a long wait standing about outside the unit. I am just so eager, for what? The sun shone today; the team were present and we were making a frame. Focused on the task in hand there was an ambience of collaborative camaraderie; the group I was in worked well together today.

Friday 16/09/2011

I am early again. I can't help it, being so keen I am always over the top; keen as mustard ever since I was a little lad. The instructor arrives and opens up. I go into the unit after he has turned the lights on. I put on my boiler suit and oversize boots and feel comfortable. I am looking forward to today. I spent the day correcting the mistakes that I had made on my frame. *'It is precision work,'* said the instructor. We were dismissed early as we all agreed to shorten our lunch hour. I have enjoyed the day.

Monday 19/09/2011

5:20 p.m. Home. I goofed again. I was standing outside the unit at 8 a.m. and after a while it dawned on me that I only needed to be there by 1:30 p.m. Oh, hell! When will I ever get it right?

The team were finishing up the bench joinery Module One and were later introduced to the plumbing module. It has been a grey and damp day and I am plodding forward, soldiering on.

Tuesday 20/09/2011

6:31 a.m. MV *Argyle*. I cycled through the drizzle with drookit troosers. I had to purchase a ballpoint pen from the Coffee Cabin, 'For all Your Journey's Needs'.

I am looking across to the street lights of Largs, under a cloudy sky with some patches of blue. Well, will you tell us why you are journeying this morning? I had called the surveyor and factor of Riverside Inverclyde Properties Ltd several weeks ago at the suggestion of the Inverclyde Properties estates and assets manager, who had told me that the factor was trying to get in touch with me and I had done so immediately. He had told me that there were empty units in the Lynedoch Industrial Estate that were beginning to be reoccupied, and I knew that I would have to vacate Unit 18. He suggested that they might be able to offer me alternative premises on a temporary basis. I have an appointment to see him first thing this morning and an appointment to meet the latter official at the Lynedoch Industrial Estate. There are still problems and challenges ahead, in spite of the opposition I will overcome them somehow or other. For the past three weeks I have been on a Scottish Qualifications Level 5 course, an activity which has kept me focused. Today is our day off and it has given me the chance to see the aforementioned individuals. Later on today I have a dentist appointment.

7:45 a.m. Unit 18. I have been over to Aulds Bakery on Lynedoch Street for a takeaway coffee with hot milk, and further up the street to the newsagents for a cheese and salad roll then back down cobbled Hope Street. The sun is shining out of a misty sky. I have put on my boiler suit. I feel comfortable in it, and think to myself that I look the part of … what? I have been wearing it thin for a few years now.

The stinking fumes are coming downwind from the organic waste incinerating plant across the road – all that's left of what was once a thriving area of industrial activity. There was once a sugar refinery not far away that had links to my past, when my dad, David Manning-Hanschell, worked at the Brechin Castle, Caroni Ltd sugar estate, which was a subsidiary company of Tate & Lyle from 1955 to 1970. He died suddenly of a heart attack, while on holiday in Barbados. On this huge sugar estate, he worked for some years as the agricultural superintendent, helping to produce raw sugar from sugar cane in Trinidad, West Indies, which was shipped in bulk to refineries in Liverpool and here in Greenock.

Stop reflecting, and get started. Someone has been let into the unit and left a pile of boxes with secondary school textbooks. I will clear them to the rear of the unit.

10:30 a.m. There is a cool breeze blowing in from the west. There is sunshine on the cloudy rooftop of the big shed across the way. I have been sorting, boxing and labelling the magnificent donation of secondary school texts from what was the Gourock High School. Thank you Head of the English Department and your colleagues.

2:35 p.m. Home in the sunshine.

2:53 p.m. I called Vanessa at the Cranfield Trust and Amanda tells me that she is on holiday.

Wednesday 21/09/2011

I was on time. Hooray! Pressing forward.

Thursday 22/09/2011

10:15 a.m. More downtime. A visitor is chatting away to the gaffer while we sit here waiting.

11:20 a.m. The class recommences. The plumbing module practical. We are fitting pipe sizes, 2 x 40 mm, 1 x 110 mm, 2 elbows, 2 reducers, single trap, double trap. Water tank, septic tank. *'We are going to do a soil pipe ... that drawing does not do anything ... real problems, real solutions,'* he said.

Friday 23/09/2011

8:20 a.m. *'Davey, you wanna a coffee?'* asks Derek. *'Yes, please. Black,'* I reply.

We are signing off yesterday's assignment, which was a crash course in plastering. Lathe and plaster. Thin strips of timber. Sheet of plasterboard 2.4 m x 120 mm (1.2 x 2.4) standard imperial sheet 8 ft x 4 ft. L x B = A. We will learn how to calculate how much plaster is required. The standard height of a ceiling is 2.4 metres. Sticks and dwangs. Lath and plaster in the old days. Lime plus sand plus horse hair. Plasterboard and how to calculate things.

9:45 a.m. How much of X does it take to cover Y? A x B = M to the power of 2. L x B = A Surface AREA 2.4 m x 1.2 m = 2. 88 m to the power of 2.

Anything we do here we must look, read, learn and inwardly digest (LRLID). Always look at the bottom right-hand corner of a plan. 5.6 m x 4.6 m = 26.22 m to the power of 2. The cutting list for this workshop room is 65 sheets of plasterboard. Everything we do is approximate. This workshop room is 14.72 m x 3.2 m = ? 16 bags of bonding, coat anything you do, start off with the *datum point*.

Monday 26/09/2011

1:25 p.m. I am ready to go. Plaster work. *'Ah gonnae show yeh a bit of plastering. You get what you pay for. Get the best if you can afford it,'* said the instructor.

He holds up a plasterer's hawk. There are different trowels. Use the edges, the rest is to hold the plaster. Run your fingers down both sides and edges looking and feeling for the imperfections. The instructor is holding up a finishing-tool-type trowel: *'You pay me by the wall,'* said the instructor, pretending to be a skilled plasterer.

Tuesday 27/09/2011

First step is preparation. Bare coat. You are basically trying to make everything level and as smooth as possible. Making sure that the tools are clean at all times. Try not to put too much plaster on the handle. When mixing the plaster make sure use to little amounts, it's easier to add some water than take it out. A rule of thumb off or in at a time. *'Commonsense prevails,'* he said. *'Read the instructions. Go slow. Take your time.'*

The instructor is showing us bags of bare coat. Make sure the walls are prepared properly.

Tuesday 27/09/2011

---

8 a.m. Unit 18, Lynedoch Industrial Estate, Greenock. Here I am once again. Roll it back.

I cycled through the drizzle from home. I am aboard the MV *Bute* ferry, where I meet Robert and Adam, the former from one of my classes at North Bute Primary School, Port Bannatyne, 1992–2008. They are on their way to Anniesland College in Glasgow and are studying to become marine engineers. *'You have spread yourself out from the Boat Yard,'* said Adam, who always greets me with a smile. His grandfather owns the Boat Yard. I have put on the same boiler suit, it is grey, that I wore then, when I moved with a 20-foot Grey Adams ex-refrigerated container, which became the Caribbean Hurricane Relief Depot 2005–2010. For the record it never was sponsored by Cowal Building Supplies, they reneged on an agreement to do that.

I will sort through this jumble of boxes of precious books from Gourock High School.

9:45 a.m. The Harrow Green van from Kinning Park has just arrived, along with Tony and Scott and another jumbled load of boxes from Gourock High School. The council man has just told me that he has more 'stuff' up at Gourock HS.

10:30 a.m. I have received a call from Apollo from Tanzania, who I met one Saturday at a Scottish British Tanzania Society meeting. I told him that he could meet me here if he wished and I would be here until midday. The mobile went while I was across to the wee shop for a crispy roll and corned beef. And into Aulds Bakery Shop for a coffee with hot milk and a packet of the Real McCoy ridge-cut cheese and onion crisps, accept no imitation, which I have scoffed. There is a strong breeze blowing in from the west, tugging the browning leaves off the few trees.

11:15 a.m. The surveyor-cum-factor arrived and took me up in his car to view a vacant unit in Drumfrochar, which had no toilet and the shutter doors, which are electrically powered, were not working. I decided without hesitation that it was not suitable. He suggested that half of Unit 29, which is a largest unit across from Unit 18, might become temporarily available, though I would be sharing it with the Greenock Arts Guild, who have stored props in half of it. He said he would be in touch.

Midday. It is time to call it a morning: press on trapper.

Wednesday 28/09/2011

1:51 p.m. Home. The sun is shining brightly on Delhi Cottage, once the blacksmith's bothy, on the road to Mount Stuart. I have returned from another Access to Construction Skills class. I am now going to try and set in motion the shipment of 40-foot ocean freight container SEAU4272551, to be loaded with educational resources which will be gifted to the Samaritan Presbyterian Primary School, Union, St Mark, Grenada, West Indies.

Call Tom Walker, the container inspector, to see if he will determine whether the container is seaworthy.

2:08 p.m. Tom Walker will inspect the container tomorrow. I am

Thursday 29/09/2011

now going to call John at WH Malcolm Transport Ltd, having just spoken to Brian the manager at this firm's container base. *'Is it not time you were slowing down, David?'* said Brian. 'No way, man. I am going to go out with a bang. It is far better to burn out, than to rust out,' I said. What else is there for me to do anyway? Sit meekly in a rocking chair and while away the rest of my days? No way! I discuss with him the possibility of delivering the container from the container base to the Port of Grangemouth via rail freight. I then spoke with John, who said, *'No problem, we can move the container to the port for you.'*

I have called Derek, Port Manager, Forth Ports Plc, Grangemouth and left a message. I then called Forth Valley College and left a message. I am following up their 'offer' of educational resources from their former campus in Alloa.

5:58 p.m. I have been here a while working the phone and it is time to stop. I sent an email to Roland, president, chief executive of SeaFreight Lines Inc, Miami, Florida, USA, bringing him up to date and pitching (surely you mean begging) him, to see whether his shipping line will take the SESF container pro bono from Kingston, Jamaica to St George's, Grenada. I can only ask, and I hope to receive some more assistance from that corporation before I can bring the Surplus Educational Supplies Foundation initiative to a satisfactory conclusion.

Thursday 29/09/2011

9:45 a.m. Home. Tom the container inspector has called to let me know that SEAU4272551 is not CSC plated and cannot be shipped, but it could go deck cargo. Problems! I have lost track from whom I bought it: check my invoices. Tom said he would look at the other SESF containers that I have in storage at the WH Malcom Ltd Elderslie container base. I am now going to set off for my construction skills class.

10:25 a.m. Painting and Decorating Module. '*It is all common sense to my way of thinking. If you do exactly what it says on the tin you have no recourse,*' said the multi-skilled instructor, who is talking his way through the support sheets. He is now pointing out where the fire extinguishers are. No water on an oil-based flame; use CO_2. Check symbols on the tin of paint to see if the paint is inflammable. '*If the safety officer walks in the door, we then pass the responsibility on to you. Obey the rules and regulations,*' said the instructor.

There are several types of paint, water-based and oil-based. You put one coat on the surface and let it dry. Emulsion surface first and then gloss after.

The instructor is now talking about brushes and how to take care of them. How to clean paint off a brush. '*Push the paint out with a palette scraper squeezed off the brush, then use the white spirit or, using a wire brush, remove excess paint and then clean. Brushes that are used with an emulsion paint are washed in cold water. Use clingfilm to keep air off the roller or brush. Brushes are designed for different purposes. Don't try and thicken your first coat. The next thing is the paint kettle. Don't paint from the tin. Decant. Less is more. Paint roller. The base coat must …*' The instructor is recounting an anecdote from his wide and varied experience to illustrate what he has been talking about.

12:30 p.m. I have been talking to Paul, who tells me, '*I am an unrepentant Stalinist.*' He is a time-served printer who began his apprenticeship in the local newspaper and a qualified paramedic. He has lived in Barcelona and has been through the mill. We have a lot to talk about. We both agree that this course has not turned out to be what we had expected.

Afternoon session. Decorative Paint Effects. Ground coat. Discussing paint. Additives that extend the life of paint. Special brush. '*I will show you a picture of what the class did last year,*' he said. '*Apply the paint lightly. All these brushes before you are used to produce a different texture. Everything you need to know is in this booklet,*' he said. Rag-rolling: '*I prefer to use newspaper lightly crushed with an even pressure. It is only as good as you are able to make it: and if you are not happy with a finish, do it again.*' Sponge stipling: you can apply paint and remove it? Dragging. Use a dragging brush. Stencilling. '*Remember how a stencil works,*' he said.

5:02 p.m. Home. I called Tom, who said container TRIU5079422 was okay; it is back to the drawing board. I will have to unload it and decant contents somewhere else; not again! I then called a container dealer in Bathgate. He has agreed to purchase SEAU4272551 for £1,000 and will meet me on Tuesday 4 October with help to unload it and reload TRIU5079422; he is cutting me some slack, for which I am grateful. '*You don't want to run out of favours, David,*' said executive coach Barry some time ago.

I called Brian at the WH Malcolm Transport Ltd container base at Elderslie to see if the proposed aforementioned arrangements would suit them. '*Where are you going to put the stuff?*' he asked. I then asked him if I could store the educational resources in one of their empty ocean freight containers. '*We will see if we can find something,*' he said.

I have gone from solving a few problems and have now become part of the problem, and a nuisance.

Friday 30/09/2011

8:25 a.m. It is a beautiful morning. There are three collared doves on the ground beside the car park.

12:30 p.m. We have all been tidying up outside. '*Everything in its place, and a place for everything in it place and a place for everything,*' said the instructor. Holidays 1–17 October.

Will There Be Some Light at the End of This Tunnel?

Monday 03/10/2011

1:32 a.m. Unit 12, West Shore Business Centre, Granton, Edinburgh. Here I am with a roll and sausage and a coffee from the wee van parked outside the Forth Valley Engineering Distribution Centre unit on West Harbour Road. I arrived here by taxi, to save my legs, which I hailed up the road in Newhaven.

I got the early ferry this morning. As I stepped out the back door of Delhi Cottage I paused to look up and see the sky dusted with stars, and took courage to face the day ahead of me. It is cloudy and windy here. While on the ferry it was announced that the train was off and Albert the roofer, the Good Samaritan, returned to where I was sitting to offer me a lift up to Glasgow. We had been chatting shortly after leaving the pier. Bless him and all his, for his kindness to me. He dropped me off along from Mandela Place, across from the Tron Church and George's Square just past the entrance to Queen Street Railway Station. I decided to get the 8:15 a.m. ScotRail to Edinburgh Waverley Station. The train was delayed en route.

I walked down Leith Walk, turned left into West Junction Street and stopped off at Just Sew Tailoring, Alterations and Repair Service; they had repaired my boiler suits with new zips some time ago. I left a jacket, which Marion gave me, with a broken zip and a pair of trousers to let out, and then got a bus which took me as far as Newhaven. I went over to the Apfelsnapz Crisps unit to touch base with Bahram, who continues to express support for my initiative, and got a welcome from James.

I am going to box some educational resources which had been missed some time ago by Olivia and her HELO team of fellow students from Edinburgh University. I am at peace with the world and continue to tidy things up a bit. It is quiet and a breeze is picking up.

2 p.m. Time to quit. I walked up through the waste ground at the

Tuesday 04/10/2011

back of West Shore Business Centre to get a No. 16 bus to North St David Street and got the train to Queen Street Station.

5:30 p.m. I am back on board the MV *Bute*. I cannot work any harder, that's for sure. How can I work smarter? Please tell me if you, dear reader, have come this far in my diary. I did what I wanted to accomplish today, which on reflection does not seem like much. I put in an appearance at Unit 12 and delivered a jacket to be repaired. Leave it now.

Tuesday 04/10/2011

6:25 a.m. MV? I am not sure which ferry it is this morning and here I am once again.

I cycled against the windy drizzle. I am tired and, to be honest, I am not looking forward to the prospect of unloading one 40-foot ocean freight container with educational resources, unloading another and reloading the former. I am exhausted by the thought. I am wondering, feeling, that I have indeed done more for the island of Grenada, West Indies, than I needed to, but I have to see this current shipment through to delivery before I can begin to think about how to bring the Surplus Educational Supplies Foundation to a close.

If Tom shows up at the Elderslie container base I will have one less container on my hands, and perhaps another container loaded with good quality fit-for-purpose educational resources and boxes of Rothesay library books will be on its way to Samaritan Presbyterian Primary School, Union, St Mark, Grenada, West Indies. My goal is to try and divest the Surplus Educational Supplies Foundation, registered Scottish Charity SCO39331, of all the educational resources that it has in storage in containers at Unit 18, Lynedoch Industrial Estate, Greenock, and in Unit 12, West Shore Business Centre, Granton, and do so in as efficient a way as possible. Some of the school furniture is steel-legged and may have to be sold for scrap: to do so will have defeated my purpose to salvage it, and I am reluctant to do this.

10:50 a.m. Steven, who works for Tom, has driven me here from Linwood. I am in a Portakabin office. Tom has left me here while he attends to some business in the yard outside. Roll it back.

I arrived in Paisley and walked across town to get a No. 7 Linwood bus. The bus driver was very helpful and dropped me off at the Linwood roundabout, and I walked from there up the road to WH Malcolm Transport Ltd, and on up the road to their container base. I received a welcome from Hughie and Brian, who asked their apprentice to make me a coffee. Brian told me that the empty containers belonging to the company that were available for temporary storage of the decanted educational resources had pinholes and leaked and I felt they would be unsuitable, at which point Steven, a member of the team from Bathgate, arrived ready to assist me in unloading TRIU5079422 and INBU4923875. Problems! The time has come to put GRIT and SALT on the road.

I then called the dealer to tell him of the pickle I was in: he said he would also purchase one of the steel containers as he had a buyer for it.

11:20 a.m. Tom has just dropped me off at the railway station and before he left I called Galt Transport Ltd. I left a message for him to call me back.

I will make arrangements for the three remaining containers to be brought from the WH Malcolm Transport Ltd container base to the Bathgate depot. Tom handed me £1,500, which I said I would deposit into the SESF RBS charity account, Rothesay branch.

11:45 a.m. Drumgelloch the next stop is Airdrie.

Thursday 06/10/2011

3:15 p.m. Home. I am off the MV *Argyle* and cycled back with the wind behind me and rain spray in my face.

Wednesday 05/10/2011

1:23 p.m. Home. I arrived here a little while ago. I left for the early ferry. I got the train from Wemyss Bay to Glasgow Central and down the steps to the lower level to get the train to Dumbarton. I walked from there over to Galt Transport Ltd in the Broadmeadow Industrial Estate. I met Simon and gave him £300 and five boxes of biscuits for shifting three 40-foot ocean freight containers from Malcolm's Elderslie container base to the depot in Bathgate. I did not hang around.

It was back to Glasgow and back to Wemyss Bay in time for the noon ferry. I met Sheriff Irvine Smith, who told me that he and his Mrs Smith had been away on a three-week Mediterranean cruise so he would not have his book *'Life, Love and the Law'*, which I had posted to him to autograph. His book was later returned to me, unsigned. Frank the steward gave me a second cup of soup. It is a grey, windy and wet day and I am glad to back sitting here.

1:38 p.m. I called Tom, who told me that container SEAU427551 had been collected and dropped off at his depot.

1:40 p.m. I called the surveyor and factor, Inverclyde Properties Ltd, Greenock, and left a message. I need to make arrangements to shift educational resources from Unit 18 into Unit 29 next door.

Thursday 06/10/2011

9:37 a.m. Home. I have had a call from Tom. I am to meet him and Steven at their depot in Bathgate tomorrow to unload

SEAU4272551 of its primary school furniture. Change of plans, so I must go with the flow.

9:52 a.m. I called the factor to confirm if they could offer me somewhere else, possibly a larger unit. Unit 29 next door would be great. He said he would get back to me.

3:20 p.m. I called Sense Scotland. *'I'll get in touch with the manager,'* she said.

3:27 p.m. I am now off up to the Rothesay Health Centre for an appointment with the GP to take my blood pressure.

Friday 07/10/2011

3:45 p.m. I am on the train for Wemyss Bay.

I left on the early boat and then got the train. I walked up to Queen Street Station and got the train for Bathgate. Tom met me and drove me to his yard to meet Steven and the towering Chick. We got stuck into emptying container TRIU5079422 and then container SEAU4272551. I could have wept because I and my helpers had to move these educational resources more than once and then again. The shifting of the school furniture seemed never-ending, but Chick and Stevie were great to work with in what was unstinting, tedious, heavy manual labour. Eventually we had loaded container TRIU5079422, bound for Samaritan Presbyterian School. This time the shipment had most of the adult and children's non-fiction from the Rothesay library reserve library stock. Boxes were all labelled and standard size, included were more chalkboards – all of which I hope will be appreciated by the school. Fortunately, the sun shone brightly on us all morning.

What do I do now with all the educational resources, chairs, and tables now stored at Tom's depot? I will cross that bridge when I come to it. Now I need to get this container out to Grenada.

Tuesday 11/10/2011

(For the record, this container never reached the intended beneficiary – it was impounded by the Grenada Port Authority, St George's, Grenada, West Indies and the cargo/contents were auctioned. I discovered this fiasco months later.)

Monday 10/10/2011

10:59 p.m. Home. I called Knight Watson Ltd freight forwarders in Grangemouth and Galt Transport Ltd in Dumbarton, who are to call me back.

12:06 p.m. I have a meeting tomorrow with Bob, client support at First Port, Cornerstone House, Melville Street, Edinburgh.

1:57 p.m. I have spoken to Jim at Knight Watson to let them know that a cheque for £1,410 will be in the post to cover the cost of shipment of the container to Kingston, Jamaica, where it will be trans-shipped by SeaFreight Agencies Lines to St George's Grenada, WI. I have spoken with Mr Allan Galt of Galt Transport Ltd, who will do a 'free lift' of the container from Bathgate to the Port of Grangemouth. I have called Tom in Bathgate to let him know that Allan will contact him. I sent an email to Derek, Port Manager, Forth Ports, Port of Grangemouth, to confirm whether or not they will waive quayside handling charges for container TRIU5079422. There were no handling charges!

Tuesday 11/10/2011

2:03 p.m. Central Station, Glasgow. I have boarded the train for Wemyss Bay. It was another early start this morning.

One train journey and then another. I got off at Haymarket and walked to Melville Street for my meeting with the adviser at First Port, who was amiable and laid back and who suggested I get some volunteers to do the 'running about' for the Surplus

Educational Supplies Foundation. Initially he gave me the impression that he might have a constructive suggestion to make, but he could come up with no imaginative suggestions and I knew then that I had wasted my time. He told me that First Port bank funding is directed towards activities based in Scotland. He could do nothing for me. I don't seem to meet the right people in these organisations.

I walked up the road to Princes Street and stopped for a cup of coffee in a pub at the corner of Princes Street and Lothian Road. I hailed a taxi to the Turkish tailors on Great Junction Street in Leith, collected Marion's jacket and continued on to Unit 12 where I met, by chance, Alasdair the security manager for Waterfront Edinburgh Ltd. It was good to let him know that I was still here for I have not come across for some time now; there was no mention from him of my having to vacate the premises.

I stopped in at Unit 5 to say hello to Bahram, and was given a smiling but short shrift from James, who told me, '*He's on the phone.*' Ah well, I should know by now to stop looking for, or expecting, a welcome from those who would prefer not to give me the time of day. So it was back home.

Wednesday 12/10/2011

1:52 p.m. Home. This morning I called Tom, who told me that Galt Transport Ltd had picked up TRIU5074922 from his yard in Bathgate to be delivered to the Port of Grangemouth. I called Alan, who told me that the container had got past the gate at Grange Dock without a seal. I then contacted Forth Ports and spoke to Jim, who helpfully said they would seal the container. I then called W. Knight Watson Ltd, the freight forwarding firm in Grangemouth, and spoke to Jim, who asked me for the seal number. I then got back to the Forth Ports office and he said he would let them know what it was.

Monday 17/10/2011

1:59 p.m. I am now going to go back up the road to the Rothesay Health Centre for an electrocardiogram.

Monday 17/10/2011

I return to the Access to Construction Skills SQA Level 5 Class.

9:01 a.m. Home. It is wet and very windy this morning. Call Jennifer and Colin at Texas Instruments Ltd in Greenock.

I need help – volunteers to assist me with the inventory, packing and shipping of the textbooks that SESF has managed to salvage from four of Inverclyde Council's secondary schools: Gourock High School, Greenock Academy, Notre Dame High School and Port Glasgow High School, and at least that number of their feeder primary schools.

12:15 p.m. I finally got through to the Head of Chancery of the Sierra Leone High Commission in London, who said I might be able to meet with her and the High Commissioner in December to discuss the SESF and Greenock Schools donation of educational resources for their government schools in Sierra Leone.

12:34 p.m. It is still grey and windswept. I called Containerlift Ltd and spoke to Chris to get a quote for a 40-foot second-hand ocean freight container to ship from Greenock to Freetown, Sierra Leone, West Africa.

This morning at the bank I met Mary, who was kind and supportive when my teaching career at the Port School began to unravel. She said she would let her listeners know about the work of the Surplus Educational Supplies Foundation the next time she is on the island's FM radio station. I met Gordon and the local allotments manager over coffee and I shopped later for messages. This morning I saw Dr K. Mather at Rothesay Health Centre for my ECG results, who tells me I need more tests and may need a pacemaker. I hope not.

I called Knight Watson Ltd freight forwarders in Grangemouth; they want a bill of lading; they have cashed my SESF cheque.

5:11 p.m. Home. I have cycled back home, as I did earlier, in the rain. The choice to begin this course once more, or rather to continue with it, presents me with a choice and the decision is mine.

I arrived at 1 p.m. and the instructor grumpily complained about my early arrival. I shall not worry for the time being about his attitude to my wholehearted commitment. We were applying different textures of paint on boards, not the most demanding, or interesting, of tasks but I gave it my full attention and effort. I will just have to dig deep and tough it out for the time being. The Surplus Educational Supplies Foundation is going nowhere at the moment and there is nothing else for me to work at here on the island.

Wednesday 19/10/2011

8:50 a.m. I am ready to go. It is a day of a bright blue sky and is cold. Paul and I, the subversives, are chewing the fat while we wait to be told what we are going to do next. He speaks Spanish and refers to us as the '*Confederacion Nacional de Trabajadores CNT or Federacion Anarchista y Birrica y professor Señor gassato.*'

Thursday 20/10/2011

10:30 a.m. I am ready to roll: coffee, tea and a biscuit. We are continuing to work through the practical assignments of the painting and stencilling module.

Friday 21/10/2011

8:30 a.m. *'Coffee please,'* I said. Paul teaches me some more Spanish phrases. '*Yo se me acabo la gasolina.* I have run out of gas. *La camino sin salida.* A dead end. *La leyenda negra.* The shitty past. *Muy trieste pero mucho tiempo.* Very sad but it was a long time ago. *Vaya mas lento por favor, David.'*

9 a.m. We are hanging about while the instructor is laminating our stencils.

Monday 24/10/2011

Not long after 8 a.m. *'What is a break? Gie us a break. Gie me a break!'* For me, there is tension in the air.

I start the brickwork module. Flemish bond. Footing. Flemish bond. The different kinds of brickwork foundations; dimensions of a brick 65 mm x 102.5 mm. The Leaning Tower of Pisa had a poor foundation. *'The preparation must be right and then everything follows; the idea is to always check your level,'* he said. Half-brick wall; the standard brick wall. 10 mm space brick, width of a plastic ruler.

2:10 p.m. More downtime! We, all nine of us, are standing around while the instructor is chatting away to our regular visitor. *'That's how ah got that scar on ma heid, it was on London Bridge.'* Paul is regaling us about his football gang fights in London in the 1980s.

'Set your levels first, make sure the footing is level before laying the bricks,' said the instructor.

3:10 p.m. We are hanging about again. I think the instructor enjoys the total control that he has over the class; take it or leave it old guy.

Will There Be Some Light at the End of This Tunnel?

Wednesday 26/10/2011

8:30 a.m. I am outside with chums at the cement mixer mixing sand and lime mortar, while the rest of the team are getting the floor of the workshop ready: setting out where we are to carry out our bricklaying assignment. I am getting stuck in or, more aptly, bricked in.

Thursday 27/10/2011

10:15 a.m. Into the boiler suit and on with the oversize boots and I am ready to begin again. I am not looking forward to making another brick wall; not that I don't want to learn how to do it properly, it's just at the start the prospect before me causes me to crumble.

I have got the will, motivation, commitment and enthusiasm, it is the fact that I lack the physical agility and strength: I have yet to come to terms with the fact that I am an old man; I have had my three score and ten years. I will make up for it with endurance and experience. Soon PK and chum arrive, the former lends me a book, *Defenders of The Faith. The Spanish Civil War in Colour*: a DVD by Russell Palmer. We make a coffee and the instructor sets out the task he requires us to perform. We all set to work on, and work through until 4 p.m. with a few 15-minute breaks.

Friday 28/11/2011

3:55 p.m. Home. It has been non-stop brick work all day; at times I was exhausted but I kept going by focusing on the task before me, which was to complete a corner brick wall. The instructor was pleased with our handiwork.

Monday 31/10/2011

5:13 p.m. Home. I arrived at Unit 5 shortly after 1 p.m. The instructor was not well pleased with my timekeeping, and this time I reacted and did not turn the other cheek. He told me to go and not come back; perhaps I should have left at that point, instead in a split second I backtracked and ate the humble pie, and said I was too eager, over the top, gung-ho enthusiastic, which is one of my besetting sins. Blessed, are the meek for they shall inherit the earth, for their faces are already in it. This afternoon, I deliberately hung back. When will I learn? For me, the name of this game is to complete the course. Seven months to go.

Wednesday 02/11/2011

4:03 p.m. Home. I have been here since 2 p.m. to let my construction course chum have a couple of bags of kindling.

'Another day in paradise,' exclaimed the multi-skilled instructor. I made sure that I was not early; apart from putting a lid on my energy and enthusiasm, I now have to be conscious, self-aware, of working around this master craftsman, who has been everywhere and can perform a myriad of tasks associated with a number of trades. I will have to play along. Today I was building a double-brick Flemish bond wall and remained focused throughout the task.

Thursday 03/11/2011

Today it is a double half-brick Flemish bond wall.

I walked up the hill with PK and chum. We were in at 10:15 a.m. For me it was a long day. I found it exhausting – the banter, the swearing, the time wasted hanging about awaiting instructions, and not least the instructor's hypercriticism of my puny efforts, are wearing me down. I was determined to complete the task in hand for this day successfully.

Friday 04/11/2011

2:35 p.m. Home. Hooray! I cracked another day with the bricks and mortar.

Monday 07/11/2011

5:32 p.m. Home! More bricks and yet more bricks. I dismantled my painstaking handiwork and cleaned the mortar off the bricks that I had used and restacked them. I made sure that I arrived when other members of the team did. I just got stuck in and did my share of exactly what was required of me, no more and no less. There was a clear blue sky this afternoon with sunshine, which is always welcome and lifts my spirit; the survival of my self-esteem is the whole point of my commitment to completing this course.

Tuesday 08/11/2011

6:08 a.m. MV *Coruisk*. I am on the high seas once more. I have just looked over an *'Espana Banos'* lesson. I am going over to Unit 18 to meet John to receive a van-load of boxes from the Gourock High School. I have to keep going.

Yesterday I returned home to the bills for TRIU5079422, which is now on its way to the Samaritan Presbyterian School, St George's, Grenada via Kingston, Jamaica. I received an email from Roland, chief executive, president and company founder at SeaFreight Lines in Miami, acknowledging that he had received the scanned paperwork and bills of lading, which had been done thanks to the SESF company secretary, Amy's information technology expertise.

The time has come, sailor, to disembark at Wemyss Bay.

8 a.m. Unit 18. I walked up from Drumfrochar Station while the traffic was building up in both directions on Cornhaddock Street.

Thursday 10/11/2011

It is damp and grey and there is fog over the high and low flats. A strong, acrid, nauseous, sweet stink is floating in the air from the incinerator plant that sits between Dellingburn Street and Baker Street; I will have to suck it up, put up with it or leave it, since I am here to make the most of this opportunity given to me for storage. I have a pile of good stuff to be sorted.

Wednesday 09/11/2011

3:08 p.m. Home. I got to my class on my willpower. I kept fully on task and meekly hung about until given instructions. There is no scope for using one's initiative here. I was barrowing bricks to the end of the yard-cum-car park and restacking them in preparation for the next module – Roofing.

3:16 p.m. Alan said he would meet me at Unit 29 next Tuesday.

Thursday 10/11/2011

5:58 p.m. Home. The instructor let me away at noon. When I left the team were working on a mock roof frame. I was barrowing slates and roof tiles and was attempting to power-screw battens to the roof surface.

12:30 p.m. Waiting room, Rothesay Pier Ferry Terminal. The sun is shining bright. I am catching my breath while I wait for the one o'clock boat. I had asked the course instructor, who is a member of the Guild of Master Craftsmen, if I could get away a little earlier.

I stopped off at Print Point to fax the Bills of Lading to SeaFreight Agencies Lines, Miami, and to Salim of Spice Isle Retreaders Ltd, St George's, Grenada, who in the past had kept his eye on the arrival of SESF container shipments in the port in St George's. *'You are on a mission,'* said Karen, the manager at Print

Point, who has been a source of great help and encouragement to me for some time now.

However, earlier today, PK the paramedic was telling me in class that it was time I stopped. *'Don't you think you should just retire now and stay put?'* he said. I tried to explain to him that I needed to bring the affairs of the SESF initiative together with no loose ends, because I still had container loads of fit-for-purpose educational resources in storage all over Scotland, which required delivery to deserving beneficiaries in the developing world.

2 p.m. I am on the Greenock bus. I meet Brian the brickie, who asks what I am doing these days and he says, *'As long as your two corners are plumb.'*

2:30 p.m. I am at HSS Hire on Dalrymple Street to meet the Mark who wants to see the Jubilee Gardens Library furniture.

3:22 p.m. Customs House, Riverside, Inverclyde Properties Holdings Ltd. I am here to sign a short-term lease of Unit 29 in the Lynedoch Industrial Estate.

6:02 p.m. Home. The surveyor drove me up to the Lynedoch Industrial Estate and showed me around Unit 29. A lot of space for a short lease for one month, with a week's notice to pack my bags, but it is more than adequate to bring all of the salvaged donations from Inverclyde Council's schools together, inventory, box, pallet and shrink-wrap them and by then I will have located a deserving beneficiary somewhere in the ill-equipped Third World.

It is better than nothing, and if I am going to be able to inventory and box this massive collection of textbooks and school library texts I will require space large enough to set up the metal library shelving and the Jubilee Gardens Library shelving units. This space is ideal for the time being. I intend to take full advantage of this fresh opportunity to power Surplus Educational Supplies Foundation to a successful finish. *(Little did I know then that it would take me another six years to ship my final consignment of fit-for-purpose educational resources.)*

The factor presented me with the keys and kindly drove me down to the Greenock Bus Terminal where I took the bus to Wemyss Bay. I met Marion on the boat and joined her with a pie and a hot chocolate.

Friday 11/11/2011

I am back on the island. I stopped off at the Co-op for a paper, some washing-up liquid and some chocolate biscuits. I told the instructor, the teacher, the boss, about Unit 29 and what I hoped to achieve during my absence from the class. I changed into my boiler suit and my safety boots and I began to concentrate on what was in front of me. A slated, or rather a tiled section, of a roof, the frame of which we had assembled earlier in the week. The rest of the team had been busy yesterday, and soon I got into the swing. I was glad later to be back on my bicycle and moving at a rate of knots down Barone Hill.

Saturday 12/11/2011

4:40 p.m. Home. Returned to home base on the MV *Argyle*. Got the bus from Greenock to Wemyss Bay. Roll it back.

The taxi met me at Unit 29 at noon. I kept him waiting. While I quickly closed Unit 29's electric-powered shutter doors, the taxi driver put a barra in the boot of his cab, I ran across to Unit 18, changed out of my boiler suit, hung it up and closed the hand-operated roller-shutter door. I asked the taxi driver to stop briefly at Inverclyde Aquatics to see Jim, who told me that he used to be a taxi driver on the island and had said he knows my face. I guess after three decades a lot of people do. I recall Jimmy, Glen Sannox tie-up crew, saying to me in the Seaman's Mission Café, during that summer in Oban 1974, *'Davie, they're aye watchin' yer.'*

I had gone into Jim's Lynedoch Street shop to let him have the two aquarium fish books that I had said I would let him have when I dropped by his shop this morning to say hello, when I was on my way up the street in my usual routine to get my take-away coffee from Aulds Bakery Shop. She asked kindly, *'Wi' hot milk?' 'Yes. Please.'* And then further up the street to Cowden's for a crusty roll and corned beef, and a packet of cheese and onion crisps. The sun was shining brightly out of a cloudless blue sky.

The kind taxi driver dropped me off at HSS Hire on Dalrymple Street to return the barra wheels, which I had collected this morning on my arrival in Greenock City at 8:45 a.m. Mark, the manager, would not charge me for them.

Rolling it back up time's stream: after I had my treat, I went across to Unit 29 and opened up. I found the trolley that I had dropped off several days ago and began to bring the boxes of books from Unit 18 across to Unit 29, and was happy to get on with it. I stopped at noon. I had made a start, enough was enough, and I now had an idea of how best to utilise this vastly increased area of storage space.

4:57 p.m. I am tired, whacked, knackered and I am going to have a lie down.

Monday 14/11/2011

9:04 a.m. Home. I am munching porridge and a mixture of breakfast cereals, and when I finish I am going to call the Tomorrow's People charity.

9:34 a.m. I called A&M Transport Ltd, who said, *'I am on my way tae Ayr tomorra.'* I asked him if he would drop in on me at Unit 29 to help me reassemble some of what was the island's library shelving rescued from the skip.

10:50 a.m. I called Sense Scotland, who are supportive. Heather said she would rally the troops to assist me in removing the educational resources from Unit 18 across to Unit 29.

11:30 a.m. Call from Louise of the Duncan of Jordanstone College of Art, Dundee, enquiring about the SESF donation of resources and the resources that the HELO Team of Edinburgh University students had boxed from Unit 12 and SESF had shipped to that East African country of Tanzania. I told her her charity could take the pick of resources in the Fife Warehouse Company Ltd warehouse in Dunfermline. I had forgotten that I had spoken to her before.

12:35 p.m. I called Inverclyde Council Properties and Assets who said, *'I may have some stuff from Sacred Heart Primary tomorra.'*

1 p.m. Unit 5. I made a coffee and had my composite sardine sandwich; the rest of the team arrived within the next 15 minutes. I hope they are raring to continue the present assignment, which is putting smaller slates on the roof but leaving a space for a skylight window. The instructor has a contract, a 'homer', to complete and has given us the next three days off, providing we all pull out the stops to complete this 'mojul'.

5:18 p.m. Home. Message from the Head of Estates and Facilities, Forth Valley College about an offer of containers. He is to call me tomorrow.

Will There Be Some Light at the End of This Tunnel?

Tuesday 15/11/2011

8:25 a.m. Unit 18, Lynedoch Industrial Estate, Greenock. Pat the joiner with Maxwell Joinery has invited me round to view their shopfitting of Unit 17. They have made considerable progress since they invited me round last Tuesday for coffee, which was kind of them. I had got a taxi from the Tesco cab rank, stopping by HSS Hire Shop. Mark the manager arrived as we pulled up to collect three dollies and a barra. Get started!

12:30 p.m. John has arrived with boxes of educational resources from Sacred Heart Primary School. The team from Sense Scotland; John senior and John junior have worked with me before, the latter likes books on archaeology and cooking; ex-army Kevin has worked with me before, and David and Alan from James Watt College are on the painting and decorating course.

12:35 p.m. It is just me and John senior; all of us together have made a good start. Scott has just left. Bless them all!

1:30 p.m. John senior has just left. Hopefully they will all be here tomorrow, including me. Meanwhile I steer the vessel on my own.

1:40 p.m. Alan, one of the supporters from early days, the removal man, has just left. He has shown me how to put the salvaged Rothesay Public Library shelving together; bless him for his trouble. It was simple once you knew how. I can do the rest of it on my own.

Alan was astonished at the amount of fit-for-purpose educational resources that are going to waste, just thrown away, dumped, while teachers in many local authority schools in Scotland must go shopping for their classroom basics. *'It's no rocket science that yeh cannae keep on chuckin' good stuff away. It's just common sense,'* he said. I am going to close the roller door and get myself a coffee and a roll and something.

Tuesday 15/11/2011

5:15 p.m. It is now dark; Pat and the Maxwell Joinery team are still shopfitting in Unit 17. I have shut Unit 18 and I am in Unit 29 surveying a day of shifting top-quality fit-for-purpose educational resources. We have made a hole in the stuff in Unit 18. Bring on tomorrow, that we might complete the flit. I am waiting for Mark, the HSS Hire shop manager, who wants to take some digitals of the Jubilee Gardens Library furniture. I am about to change out of my boiler suit. That smell is wafting on a gentle breeze from the incinerator plant's chimney across on Dellingburn Street.

5:17 p.m. I called Riverside Inverclyde Properties Ltd. Their factor and surveyor told me once that he had served his time as a roofer in Bridgeton, where I served part of my time as a security guard with Waterloo Guards Ltd, on the site that was once Possill Shot Blasters Ltd, during the winter of 1985. Later the following year I had the good fortune of a temporary supply teacher post at Dalmarnock Primary School.

I had found their email offering SESF temporary occupation of Unit 29. I agreed to meet with him and sign the lease at their Greenock Customs House office before 5 p.m. Get your skates on dude!

7:16 p.m. MV *Argyle*. Mark arrived at 6 p.m. as he said he would, but his digital camera had no battery power. I opened up Unit 18 and showed him the bespoke beech bookcases. I let him have Wilmot Dixon Construction pix and he will scan them for his woodworker friend. Mark kindly gave me a lift down to the Oak Mall bus rank and I got the 6:30 p.m. Ardrossan bus.

The team and I managed to make a successful start at clearing Unit 18. I had told the factor, as I said I would, and I managed to continue working on my own until after dark. Pat the joiner brought his son Patrick round to meet me. He is studying at the Nautical College in Glasgow. He is on the same course that David was on before graduating this year. I can only continue to take one day at a time, as it comes, and continue trying to give it my best shot with everything. I will continue to build on all the work and effort, at personal cost, that I have put into the Surplus Educational Supplies Foundation (Registered Scottish charity SCO39331) since 2005.

Wednesday 16/11/2011

6:35 p.m. Home. That was David, recent merchant navy graduate of the Glasgow Nautical College, calling me from Great Yarmouth, England, to let me know that his course on an MV *Kraken* survival vessel lifeboat is going well. He faces more practical tests out in the North Sea tomorrow morning; good to hear his voice.

I was up and out into the crisp morning and into the little town on the bicycle, and just made it in the nick of time to board the MV *Coruisk*. I got the bus to Greenock and walked up from the bus depot around the back of the Oak Mall Shopping Centre, past the Greenock City Chambers, up the steep cobbled street, up the steps and through the memorial park, and on to cross the busy road to Lynedoch Street. I stopped in at Cowden's sandwich-cum-wee groceries-cum-newsagents shop for a crispy roll and a cheese roll, a cup of tea and milk and a drap o' sugar, and down another cobbled street and through into the Lynedoch Industrial Estate. Sunshine on the surrounding hills was beckoning me forward.

Over the past few months, this ever green, ever young, youthful stripling is beginning to appreciate the topography of the Green Oak Town. I went into Unit 29 and changed into my boiler suit and then went across the yard and opened Unit 18. I shifted the metal-legged classroom chairs over to Unit 29 before I had my piece, and by then the tea was cold but still satisfying. Before long young John arrived, he barrowed the plywood chairs over and I showed him where I wanted them set out. Then, sometime later, John senior (known as Mint) appeared and he and I, using HSS Hire dollies/wheelies, got stuck in. We were shifting the rest of the

Thursday 17/11/2011

former Ealing Borough Council Jubilee Gardens Library shelving and so it went. *'It's getting close to Christmas,'* he said.

I got John senior and myself a roll and slice and tea at noon and he quit at 12:30 p.m. Archie the spark came in to read the meter: he tells me he goes out to the Dominican Republic and loves the island Columbus, called Hispaniola. Archie was appalled by the poverty, especially the schoolchildren. I wonder how he would feel about the children on the other half of the island, which is the Republic of Haiti? He went on to tell me that he was enjoying his retirement. *'I am doing a bit of this and that,'* he said. I got back to work after he had left.

Later that afternoon I met Peter, the managing director of Rainbow International Cleaners, who have a big unit at the top end of the industrial estate. He reminded me that I had dropped in to visit him on my arrival last year in the Lynedoch Industrial Estate. He has kindly offered to lend me one of his teams to clean up Unit 18 when I vacate the premises, which, all being well, will be by tomorrow lunchtime. I packed up and was away and back down the hill by 2:50 p.m. I stopped in at Vodaphone in the Oak Mall and went across to the HSS Hire shop, and got the bus and ferry home.

Thursday 17/11/2011

1:15 p.m. Unit 29. That was Robert and Bernie from Rainbow International Contract Cleaners and Restoration. They had come by to tell me that they had finished mopping the floor of Unit 18. They came by around 11 a.m. and pitched in to lend us a hand removing all of the metal shelving and tables and bring them round to Unit 29. Without their cheerful assistance John senior and I would still be working away. I am going back over to collect my high-viz jacket and shut up. My corned beef crispy crusty roll and cold tea awaits.

I walked across to Unit 2 to Inverclyde Tool Hire to touch base

Will There Be Some Light at the End of This Tunnel?

Unit 29, Lynedoch Industrial Estate, Greenock. Thursday 17/11/2011. Large warehouse with resources recently collected. Chief executive pauses for a coffee break. A growing accumulation of fit for purpose surplus to requirements resources was being salvaged and uplifted from Inverclyde Council Education Department school system.

The Shipping Clerk is in his element having stepped up to the plate, and accepted total responsibility, for the success and failure of the Surplus Educational Supplies Foundation.

Friday 18/11/2011

with Paul and Big Iain, and then I got a taxi to take me down to Customs House Quay to hand in the Unit 18 key to Heather. There I met Neil, the Bob Dylan fan. It is a case of moving ever forward. I have done all I can to ensure that I was out of Unit 18 within a week. Had it not been for the instructor and his homer's need to postpone the Wednesday and Thursday class I would still be in that unit; many have helped me to make this a prompt and efficient removal of educational resources.

After paying HSS for the hire of three dollies and a porter's barrow I walked up to the bus rank to catch a Largs bus, just in time.

3:15 p.m. MV *Bute*. It has been another long day of modest collaborative achievement.

Friday 18/11/2011

9:50 a.m. Home. I am about to return a call from Bob. His colleague Maria tells me that he and Kim have gone to an event. I was speaking to Ann at Clydeport Ocean Terminal, who told me that Andrew had suggested I contact Fraser Haulage in Coatbridge, who might have a container for sale.

4:16 p.m. I called them and someone told me, *'They are very expensive right now.'*

4:23 p.m. I spoke to Forth Valley, who told me that the Surplus Educational Supplies Foundation can have gratis the two containers that remain on the building site of their new college in Alloa, but so far it has been all talk.

4:43 p.m. Spoke to Simon of the Container Brokerage Company (Europe) Ltd, who said he would try and get me a container from Rotterdam, which could be brought over to Grangemouth as this would be much cheaper than bringing it up from London.

4:47 p.m. I then called Simon at the Education For All charity in Corby. '*Hello Simon, David here, from the Surplus Educational Supplies Foundation. Did you by any chance follow up those leads I gave you some time ago*'. '*I am just in from a meeting, I will check, and call you on Monday,*' he said.

I achieved little today.

Monday 21/11/2011

5:57 p.m. Home. I was back in Unit 5 for more self-inflicted punishment this afternoon. The multi-skilled instructor was showing us how to put the flashings around the skylight window frame correctly, and so it went. I tried the eager beaver, willing old horse to make myself useful, drilling the tiles on the battens etc.

Tuesday 22/11/2011

8:30 a.m. Unit 29, Lynedoch Industrial Estate, Dellingburn Road. I got a taxi up the road from the lower end of the bus rank on Stewart Street and was dropped off on Lynedoch Street. I did not wish to be late for the helpers.

10:50 a.m. James Watt College student David away to his class. '*We are playing the lecturers at football this afternoon,*' he said. He had been helping me to set up the metal library shelving. I had had gone earlier to Cowden's for our pieces: two teas and a roll and slice for him and a crusty roll and corned beef for me. I am now going to slot some more shelves into place.

2:15 p.m. I have tidied the floor: a place for everything, and everything in its place. All of the metal shelving has been assembled and now begins the next task of sorting the educational resources stationery and box files and shelving the textbooks. I will take an inventory, box, pallet, shrink-wrap and finally arrange the shipment to deserving recipients. It is time to call it a day's work.

Wednesday 23/11/2011

3:35 p.m. Home. Almost half of the team were absent and were greatly missed by me; many hands make light work. I was taking the tiles off the 'roof' and preparing to disassemble the roof and move on to the next module. It was wet and overcast with thick grey clouds, but I was just getting on with it regardless, pleased with myself and able to do all that was expected of me.

3:07 p.m. Home. I called Jim the accountant, who told me that they were doing the accounts pro bono for the Surplus Educational Supplies Foundation, and he told me that if the Office of the Scottish Charities Regulator gave me any more hassle to tell them to get in touch with him.

I am so grateful to him, Alyson and his team for enabling me to keep this shoestring initiative on a reputable and transparent basis, if not a financially viable one. My coat continues to hang on a shoogly peg.

3:20 p.m. I finally get to speak to Florence, Head of Chancery at the Sierra Leone High Commission in London, who tells me that she is going to come up to Greenock to see for herself what the Surplus Educational Supplies Foundation has to offer the schools that have been destroyed by the civil war in her beleaguered West African state. I am encouraged by this development. I am to call her on Wednesday, 30 November.

13:54 p.m. I called Andy at Pentalver Ltd in Leeds about the purchase of a container for the next shipment of all the resources in Unit 29. *'You are looking at a couple of grand,'* he said.

I have a dentist appointment at 11:30 a.m. and a meeting with the Tomorrow's People charity at Unit 29, sometime before or after?

Thursday 24/11/2011

5:33 p.m. Home. We stood about while the instructor did all the necessary paperwork that is supposed to record our progress, or lack of it, through the Access to Construction Skills SQA Level 5 curriculum. We then answered questions that related to the roofing and tiling module and carried out the employability skills assessments.

I was chatting with different members of the team while drinking the brews that cheer but do not inebriate. I am quite happy so far, to be there, each day of the course, and don't regret the time and effort that I have invested in it so far.

Friday 25/11/2011

2:25 p.m. Home. I spent the whole time of this class just hanging about restraining my eagerness and enthusiasm to learn new skills. I spent my time answering multiple-choice questions. I finished off the afternoon barrowing tiles to the storage area at the far end of the car park. I missed the help of those who were absent. The instructor asked me if I wanted to go to the college graduation ceremony to be held in Oban next year? No thanks.

Monday 28/11/2011

6:04 p.m. Home. I cycled out with the wind against me and back in the drizzle. The instructor was showing the team how to assemble a toilet unit and discussing how the fittings are connected up and the principle of the crappers.

Tuesday 29/11/2011

9:08 a.m. The office, Unit 29. Thanks to Muriel, who gave me a lift in her car a short while ago as far as the roundabout across from the Greenock City Chambers, Oak Mall Shopping Centre and Tesco – otherwise, I would still be back there at the Wemyss Bay bus stop, with rain bucketing on my baldy heid.

I went into supermarket to purchase Marion's Christmas cake mixed peel and then tried to hire a taxi from the rank. '*Ye cannae get up there, you'll huv tae tap it,*' he said. I walked from there back out onto Dalrymple Street in the pouring rain and I thought I had better retrace my steps and got myself a golf umbrella, on sale for £7.50. I walked from there through the park, up Lynedoch Street and into Aulds for a takeaway coffee, and further along to Cowden's for corned beef in a crusty roll. Rainwater is gushing down the street and my trousers and feet are wringing wet. I am now into my boiler suit and I am going to enjoy ma 'tea break' before it gets cold.

10:45 a.m. The team of helpers from James Watt College have not showed up. I am going to assemble some more metal shelving and then I'm going to walk back down the hill and across to for my dentist's appointment.

Midday. MV *Coruisk*. I just made it – I am puffed oot. I am about to enjoy a packet of crisps and hot chocolate as I watch raindrops bounce off the windaes of this toy-town ferry.

Wednesday 30/11/2011

3:17 p.m. Back home. I was out into the wind under a sky of thick grey cloud. I was waiting around, trying to look interested, until it came to my turn to assemble a toilet unit. The instructor was watching me attempting to do it the correct way; it takes me a while to figure out from the paperwork where all the elbows, olives and O rings go. I need to actually do it, that is how my concrete, operational brain is hard-wired: tell me, and I forget; let me have a go, and then show me how, again and again, until I can do what is required.

I call the Sierra Leone High Commission in London, as I said I would at this time, as requested to do so by their Head of Chancery. She has left a message with reception to tell me that she is in a meeting and will call me back, which she never does. I am wasting my time with these people, but I persist and continue to clutch at straws.

Thursday 01/12/2011

The sink unit. I was fiddling with bits of plumbing and connecting bits made of plastic, the new material and some of copper.

Friday 02/12/2012

3:21 p.m. I am catching my breath while sitting in the ferry terminal waiting room. Roll it back.

I went up the road this morning powered by my will. I was assembling the connecting 'copa' pipework for the sink unit, answering multiple-choice questions, standing about, and taking my cues from the instructor. I mopped the toilet floor and cleaned the pan: no one else keeps it clean. All members of the team were on deck today.

Saturday 03/12/2011

8:35 a.m. I am on the train for Edinburgh. Marion and I have not long said goodbye to each other. *'You have five minutes to get the train,'* she said.

Why am I making this journey? I hope to attend a meeting

Saturday 03/12/2011

with Ken Campbell. I am exploring the possibility of working with Pilot Light Scotland together with the Small Charities Coalition, which exists to help give small charities access to skills, experience and the resources that they need to fulfil their aims. They are like a free voluntary-sector match-making service, enabling small charities to help each other achieve their aims and objectives by exchanging the skills and experience they have with the ones they don't. Here's hoping. I also hope to return with my porter's barra and the roll of Visqueen that I took over to Unit 12 some time ago.

The sun shed its golden beams over the top of the clouds. *'It is better to journey than to arrive,'* said RLS, a native of that fair city. Drink up yer coffee and stop trying to be literary, just enjoy the ride, your ride to the finish, and tell it like it was for you.

9:45 a.m. Unit 12, West Shore Business Centre, Granton. I got a taxi across the city from Haymarket Street Station, drove past Stuart Melville and Fettes private schools and I recall the long walks from 65 Northumberland Street, New Town, over to Silverknowes Primary School in Pilton, North Edinburgh in September 1974, where I did my first teaching practice as part of the Postgraduate Certificate in Education at Moray House College of Education. Later, in the spring of 1975, I did another teaching practice session at Victoria Primary School in Newhaven.

I asked the taxi driver to let me get out at the modern British Gas Headquarters, back of the Granton Gas Works tower. I walked past secluded Granton House into the waste ground beside it, strewn with litter, paused for a pee in the bushes, and on down to West Harbour Road, past the Edinburgh Council Skills Academy building site and here I am for my appointment. Here's hoping for a breakthrough, a collaborative stepping-up-a-notch stone. There is a cold blustery wind in the car park coming from the nearby Firth of Forth.

10:55 a.m. The Pilot Light official has come and gone. He arrived about three-quarters of an hour ago; he was non-committal, laid back. I offered to donate the sports equipment in Unit 29, all of which is new, unused and was salvaged from Gourock High School. '*Tell Bob at First Port that you met me,*' I said. Now to pack up and head back tae hame city.

1 p.m. Uphall North Livingston via Bathgate. I am on the train from Haymarket to Queen Street Station via Milngavie. I had walked up from Unit 12 to Telford College, now rebranded as Edinburgh College, to the main road and got a No. 16 bus. I was travelling with my porter's barra and roll of Visqueen to Constitution Street in Leith, where I got off and hailed a taxi. Another tenner. I thought it was worth it. Friendly driver, so I gave him my spiel when he asked me what Visqueen was and what I had been doing with it. '*Do you know anyone who plays the bagpipes?*' I asked. '*My nephew does,*' he said. '*You can ask him to play Amazing GRACE and Highland Cathedral over my coffin, which will be draped with the Barbados flag,*' I said, and he laughed.

2:19 p.m. Glasgow Central Station. I am now on the train for Port Glasgow. I called Marion and Amy, who are in the Buchanan Street Centre, and they told me to meet them in Kilbarchan. I thought that I would get this gear of trolley and roll of plastic sheeting offloaded at Unit 29 in Greenock first. While I was thinking this, I got off at the High Street Station – the wrong stop – so I walked down Cathedral Street in the rain and hailed another taxi to Central Station. Go with the flow, but don't go down the drain.

I have a Cornish pasty and cup of tea. The purvey beckons, so get my chops into it before yuh have to get aff.

3:36 p.m. Job done! I am now on the train from Port Glasgow, back up the line to Paisley Gilmour Street to get a train from there to Johnstone.

Tuesday 06/11/2011

I got a taxi up to Unit 29, dropped off the barra and roll of blue plastic sheeting and showed John the taxi driver Unit 29. He was interested in what I was trying to achieve. It has been a long day.

Monday 05/12/2011

Home. I was in class on time. I made it back from my hospital appointment at Inverclyde Royal Infirmary with time to spare, and had an Americano at the Musicker Café. I was answering multiple-choice questions and filling in forms. The instructor recorded in his observations of my work practice, *'He works well with others.'* There, you see.

We are being held up as the roof assembly framework needs to be dismantled. I am required to put together a toilet and sink unit once more. Practice makes perfect.

Tuesday 06/11/2011

2:05 p.m. Unit 29. I have arrived to find that there is no power for the roller door. I got a taxi up the road: I had been to the dentist and had had major work done. I had double jags from a dentist, who ought to have become a veterinarian. She told me that I had to pay the bill next time, so I wrote a cheque there and then on the SESF account, for she would never again touch my remaining gnashers. I thought it was time I used some of the SESF funds to keep the fabric of the Prime Remover together.

I am going to assemble some more shelving and take some more wonderful books out of the boxes and on to the shelves.

2:10 p.m. I have done enough in here on my own – an area the size of several basketball courts and a hockey rink. It is sleeting and raining outside: the very time I need my new umbrella and did not bring it. Nothing has been easy for me today; it can only get worse or better.

Will There Be Some Light at the End of This Tunnel?

Wednesday 07/12/2011

2:38 p.m. Home. Review of the class activity. I went into class prepared to disassemble the roof mock-up. Stephen and I barrowed the roof tiles back to the storage area at the far end of the car park. I was wise to use a bit of forethought, but at the same time, wisely, was not being over eager as I knew that the rest of the team would be reluctant to do the mundane and heavy shifting task; by doing so willingly, I could get out of the instructor's road. The rest of the team helped the instructor to move parts of the roof assembly, the rafters etc., up to a storage area in the attic space above Unit 5's washroom and toilets. I washed the coffee cups and other wee chores to keep myself busy.

We then moved the work benches back into place and the team took a break. Ally made the coffee and teas. After the break we got the pipework in place for the toilet and hand washbasin, ready to be plumbed in tomorrow. Holidays beckon: Term 2 back on Monday, 9 January 2012. *Deo volente*.

I stopped at 1:15 p.m. and whizzed back down the road. I bought a *Herald* newspaper at Toffoletti's, the Montagu Street newsagents, and stopped off at Bute Naturally to assist Phil in designing the Surplus Educational Supplies Foundation banner. While in the shop I went out and across the road to get a coffee each, and also for Anne and her friend.

Tuesday 13/12/2011

11 a.m. Unit 29. I have walked up from the Oak Mall Shopping Centre. The helpful opticians at Vision Express had repaired my spectacles. I met the efficiently friendly Gillian at Vodaphone, who recharged my mobile phone account.

I stopped off at Aulds the Bakers on Lynedoch Street to get a coffee and a savoury cream cheese roll. Prior to that pause for the purchase of the purvey, I stopped in at the Fish Tank Aquarium shop and received a welcome. They got my note from last week, that I could not make it on 10 December.

I have called Texas Instruments Ltd to speak to Colin, the operations manager, who told me that he is going to come round sometime and see what SESF is all about.

11:50 a.m. Jim the Fish Tank came by with his partner Julie and her daughter Nicola to lend a hand, which is very kind of them.

2:10 p.m. We were unpacking boxes and stacking textbooks on the shelving. I am going up to Lynedoch Street with an order for our purvey – it is the least I can do to show my appreciation for their voluntary assistance.

4:29 p.m. It is blowing a gale. Marion, bless her, is coming back up the road from Inverkip to collect me. Colin is unable to make it; he will contact me next time I am over. He said he will see if he can recruit some volunteers from his team at Texas Instruments Ltd, which used to be National Semi-Conductor Ltd, to assist in the inventory and packaging of this marvellous collection of top-quality secondary and primary school textbooks. He is a great encouragement to me. He is on my wavelength. *Get oot yer biler sute.*

Thursday 15/12/2011

3:22 p.m. Home. I was out before 10 a.m. The sun was shining down for a change. I was working with PK and we just got on with it, making the box for the ventilation pipe for the toilet with assistance from the instructor whenever we needed it.

Will There Be Some Light at the End of This Tunnel?

Friday 16/12/2011

3:59 p.m. Home. It has been a good day with an atmosphere of camaraderie and solidarity. PK and I finished our ventilation pipe box and we got oor fotie taken; there was welcome sunshine and snow on the hills.

Sunday 18/12/2011

2:24 p.m. Home. I have had a call from Mary, who started the knitting club with Davina, offering SESF an Epson Printer. *'Yes, please, thank you very much.'*

Monday 19/12/2011

11 a.m. Home. On the telephone. Call Bahram at Unit 5, West Shore Business Centre, and left a message, asking him if he would call me back. I left a message with the Lord Lieutenant of Hampshire about her correspondence with the British Council on behalf of SESF. I called Greenock Chamber of Commerce, who is helpful, about marketing the Surplus Educational Supplies Foundation. *'My job is to spend Inverclyde Council money to find and create employment,'* she said, and she is going to send someone round to Unit 29 at 11 a.m. tomorrow.

I left a message with John about the collection of educational resources from Saint Michael's Primary School, and to confirm SESF's acceptance and appreciation of their offer of resources. I spoke with Lorraine of Inverclyde Removals Ltd about the resources that were collected from Greenock Academy and stored in their Larkfield Industrial Estate container way back in May; she tells me they are busy. I will contact them again.

5:42 p.m. Home. *'You are only half way there, see you next year,'* said the multi-skilled instructor. I was in before 1:30 p.m. and there was time for me to have a coffee and scoff a cheese and salad roll from the wee Polish dairy-cum-paper shop on the High Street.

I was tidying up the workshop, sweeping the floor and cleaning the toilet. I will be back on 9 January 2012.

Tuesday 20/12/2011

7:02 a.m. I am on the train for Unit 29 via Drumfrochar Station.

I was out from early and cycled into the chilly wind on the road into the little town; it was not too bad and I was mindful of a skid. Over the watta on the MV *Bute*. I met bonnie Jean, all cheery in red, one of my supporters from way back, who insisted on buying me a hot chocolate, and I purchased a roll and slice. Later I hope to meet with a representative of the marketing department of the Greenock Chamber of Commerce and the operations manager of National Semi-Conductor; I can but only continue to try and garner support for my initiative from all sectors, private, public and corporate.

7:50 a.m. On my arrival I found that I had unintentionally locked the office door, so I called the locksmith and I am waiting.

12:35 p.m. I have had a meeting here with the business development officer and a representative of the Economic Development Team, leader of the Inverclyde Council Regeneration and Environment Department. They were positive and interested. On their arrival they found me unpacking, sorting and shelving textbooks.

3:10 p.m. Do you want to know the truth? I am knackered. I have shelved a lot of textbooks and I have plenty more shelf space. I think that I have done enough for one day. I shall now call Colin to see if he is going to make it.

3:40 p.m. The security man has just shouldered the office door open for me, with no little force, I shan't mess with him. I saw what I presumed were his children sitting in his car parked outside the big roller door, and I asked him if they would like to come inside and choose some children's books that I had shelved. *'No thanks, we are wealthy,'* he said. It is raining again.

4:15 p.m. Colin showed up; he has taken away my blue folder with the latest SESF company accounts and information about the charity's shipments to six Grenada government schools. He went over a possible business model for SESF with me, which demonstrated his capacity for systems analysis.

He is a gentleman who knows the score, an aristo of quality, a real toff in my books and a great supporter. Before he left, he said, *'Let me be the first person to solve your next problem.'*

Thursday 22/12/2011

8:15 a.m. Tesco café, Greenock City. I am keeping track. I set out from home shortly after 5:15 a.m. so I had enough time to remove the SESF banner, which I had tied to the railings opposite the new Cab Man's Rest on the pier. I got the 7:15 a.m. bus from Wemyss Bay and I am sitting down to a roll 'n' black pudding and a coffee, and catching my breath, so to speak.

From here I hope to make my way over to Customs House Quay, Inverclyde Properties Ltd office with a gift of shortbread, brews that cheer but don't inebriate and my SESF 2012 calendar for the factor and his team in the office: a token of my appreciation for allowing me to use Units 18 and 29 rent and rates free. I will then go up the road to Swordfish Signs Ltd, across from the fire station, and then up the hill to Unit 29 to do some work.

9:52 a.m. Switched the lights on. Before leaving the Tesco café I met George, the *Greenock Telegraph* snapper, who had taken foties of the Greenock Academy collection with councillor Terry. He asked me how I was getting on, and when I told him what my plans were, having collected educational resources from more Inverclyde Council schools, he said, 'If there is anybody who can do it, you will.'

10:20 a.m. I have come from the MOT and Tyre Garage on the corner of Hope and Dellingburn Streets, where a helpful young mechanic put some air in the tyres of my porter's barrow – like so many who have put air into my tyres. It is time to quit for today. I have emptied and shelved plenty of boxes of secondary school English curriculum material; there were masses of set books (uncut), plays, poetry, and anthologies of prose and poetry. Here is a treasure trove for any teacher worthy of the name.

My purpose from day one 2005 has been vindicated. I have managed to salvage a trickle, from what has swept into the waste stream. I have lit my candle rather than curse the darkness all around me on nano Blue Planet.

I stopped at noon to get some lunch; soup and tea from Aulds Bakery Shop, cheese and onion crisps, crusty roll and corned beef from Cowden's. Yum! Enjoy! Get out of my boiler suit, polish my shoes and head down Dellingburn Street.

Monday 02/01/2012

9:37 a.m. Unit 29. I have been dropped off here by Paul of Clyde Cabs. I gave some folk from the island, who were waiting at the Wemyss Bay bus stop, a lift up the road: a gentleman from Skelmorelie, who is going to visit his son, a doctor in Cairns Western Eastern Australia; a young lad, who is a digger operator; and a lady and her two sons, who works alongside Johanna in the chemists. What goes round comes round. I am going to get stuck into shelving books.

11:45 a.m. I think it is time to call it a morning; I have not stopped unpacking boxes of textbooks, paperback books, almost new, and boxes of new stationery (binders and box files). I am going to walk down to the Oak Mall, post correspondence, get the bus that stops at Wemyss Bay and hopefully get a ferry across the watta.

Thursday 05/01/2012

1:15 p.m. Unit 29. The sun is shining at long last and I am looking out of the office window, where I can just make out the hills on the other side of the Clyde.

I cycled into town and barely made the 11 a.m. ferry. I got the bus up to Greenock and walked up to the Lynedoch memorial park, which gives me cause to reflect on the lives of those who gave the ultimate sacrifice.

I stopped in to see Jim the Fish Tank aquarist who was busy decorating his Inverclyde Aquaria Aquatic shop, and met his son who lives on the island. Into Aulds for a cup of takeaway soup and further along the road and into Cowden's for a corned beef in a crusty roll, a packet of crisps and a bottle of water, and here I am. What's next? I will have my break for the purvey and get stuck into the usual unpacking boxes of textbooks, shelving them ready to be inventoried.

4:15 p.m. There is no sign of Inverclyde Removals Ltd, who had told me that they would be here between 1 p.m. and 2 p.m.. That's me, I have emptied a few more boxes. There was a lot of stationery that had not been used and here's hoping I will be able to get it into appreciative hands; the time has come for me to push off.

Monday 09/01/2012

Term 2.
1:25 p.m. On deck. The Bench Joinery module. Half lap, haunch and mortice.

Tuesday 10/01/2012

8 a.m. Unit 29. I am here and into my boiler suit. Michael, the bus driver who comes from Geordieland, had kindly offered me a lift up the road in *'My wee banger.'* He dropped me off in Branchton, where after a while I got a bus into Greenock, walked along to Morrisons supermarket and up Dellingburn Street, and then up cobbled Hope Street. Both Cowden's and Aulds Bakery Shop were shut, so before I start work I am going to walk back up there and get me a roll and coffee.

11:30 a.m. I have been working non-stop, emptying boxes and shelving books and prior to that I assembled another row of shelving. I think I have done enough for one day and it is time for me to knock off.

Noon. I have to drag myself away from this purposeful innerdirected activity, and out of the limelight. Who cares? I do.

I am enjoying – well perhaps that is too strong a word, because I miss the company of my fellow human beings – I certainly believe in what I am doing and achieving the goal, which is way in the distance, and I am prepared to put everything I have within me into the achievement of it. Enough is enough of my unstinting effort for one day; the appearance of the textbooks, fiction and non-fiction sections of this collection, has improved as more books are shelved.

Wednesday 11/01/2012

'You are going ahead of yourself,' said the instructor to me.

Will There Be Some Light at the End of This Tunnel?

Thursday 12/01/2012

4:50 p.m. Home. This was another good class. More joinery; there was only one member of the team absent, we were all working together to keep each other right. The sun shone out of a clear blue sky. *Camaraderie, spirit of familiarity and trust existing between friends – from the French comrade.*

Friday 13/01/2012

Home. I was struggling this morning to align the brace and bit (electrical) to the place where the tenon fits the mortice. My hands are shaking. The team were being helpful to each other. The instructor let me off at noon so I could get the one o'clock ferry.

3:15 p.m. Unit 29. I came in here 15 minutes ago accompanied by Raymond, a neighbour from a couple of houses along the Craigmore Road, who said, *'I would like to have a look at your operation.'* I met him on the boat and we got the bus from Wemyss Bay up to Greenock; we stopped to speak to Jim and Julie and their friend at the aquarium shop, and then into Aulds for a coffee and macaroni pie each. Raymond is going to snap some digitals of the Treasure Trove.

5 p.m. The Inverclyde Removals Ltd van arrived; they had parked opposite the Inverclyde Council unit and I beckoned to them to come over. They backed the two and half tonne lorry into Unit 29 and unloaded the boxes of books, which I had paid to be uplifted from Greenock Academy way back on Tuesday, 11 May 2011.

I gave each of the unloaders £20 for their trouble, with which they seemed pleased, but I received a shock when they told me that I owed the firm £450 for storing the boxes. They had not brought an invoice and stupidly I wrote out an SESF cheque for that amount. I had slipped up.

5:30 p.m. I have unpacked and shelved some more books. Lots of geography texts – one of my favourite subjects. I have switched off the main lights and I am heading home. *'All of that knowledge came out of books,'* said Professor Sir Brian Cox, who is another book lover.

Monday 16/01/2012

10:07 a.m. Home. I am on the phone. I called Colin, general manager at Texas Instruments Ltd, who said he would get back to me next week.

11:54 a.m. I called the executive coach, Barry. *'I am about to catch a plane. I am speaking at a conference in Turkey, call me next week,'* he said.

Earlier I had called Simon of Container Brokerage Ltd, who told me that he has not been well and he was not pleased to hear that I had sold the SESF containers at the WH Malcolm Transport Ltd container base, and he had paid a container surveyor to inspect them. I was sorry about that, but my foundation was short of cash.

I call Inverclyde Council Facilities and Assets Management about my having to pay for the storage of boxes that had come from Greenock Academy in May 2011. *'We no longer have a standing account for this job. I don't want to get into the politics of it all,'* said John. He tells me to get a receipt of payment from Inverclyde Removals Ltd and send it to them. I just might be able to recoup these funds, I will have to wait and see.

I call the Sierra Leone High Commission in London. I am making a concerted attempt to establish a working relationship with these people, to see if I can get them interested in receiving this huge collection of fit-for-purpose educational resources for a school or college in Sierra Leone, West Africa. The person I wish to speak with, I am told, is in a meeting. What else is new?

I have arranged to meet the team leaders John and Liz of the Tomorrow's People charity on Tuesday, 24 January at 2:30 p.m. in Unit 29.

Back to Unit 5. *'Are you alright, Davey?'* Ally keeps asking me as he plays with his iPhone. I was making the mortice holes, drilling and chiselling. All members of the team were on deck today, some more collaborative than others. The multi-skilled instructor and busy tradesman was showing me and the rest of the team how, by demonstrating the correct method. I have got the idea and my practice has improved.

Tuesday 17/01/2012

Late morning. I am on the train for Glasgow Queen Street. I left home a little after 6 a.m. with a cool fresh breeze coming past my ears and just made the boat. Train up Glasgow Central. I swithered on whether to walk up to Buchanan Street Bus Station and settled for the 9:15 a.m. train, for the usual fare, and sat on a stool in the Costa Café with an Americano and a cold croissant.

On my arrival at Edinburgh Waverley I got a taxi up to the former Royal High School on Regent Road. Alastair, the Edinburgh City Council surveyor, and his colleague Daimon were waiting for me. They gave me a tour of the building. They could not tell me what was, and what was not, furniture the Surplus Educational School Supplies Foundation could uplift. I made it clear to them that I had to know for sure what I could collect. I told them that I had to make sure I could arrange transport and I would let them know, and they could let me know what educational resources mainly furniture I could take away.

I walked back down Regent Road and passed the Christian Science Reading Room window, still there after 38 years of my new life in Scotland: I read that afternoon, in late spring

1974, a text from the Bible which advised me not to worry about anything. I had got off the train into Waverley Station from Eley, totally lost and without purpose – vague memories; I do remember the daffodils on the slope beside Edinburgh Castle overlooking Princes Street Gardens, and how I got the bus to Perth; enough recollection or you will get run over. I walked round Saint Andrew Square, along Rose Street then back onto Princes Street and walked all the way to Haymarket Street Station. I am a different person to the homeless, and rootless, soul I was then.

3:17 p.m. Home. Journeying mercies.

Wednesday 18/01/2012

9:05 a.m. *'It is worth asking for help,'* he said. The hardest part, for me, is admitting my ignorance, helplessness and inadequacy. We looked at the drawings. Recognition of prior learning, more form filling. *'Tell me what you have done,'* he said. The instructor is talking us through the drawing.

Bench joinery. *'Are you are happy with that? Sign it. Date it. Now I will take your photograph,'* said the instructor. I made up a cut list. Look at the drawing.

Thursday 19/01/2012

6:25 p.m. Home. Today I worked steadily through the assignment preparing a mortice and tenon joint and remained focused on the task, with occasional help from the instructor.

Friday 20/01/2012

2:42 p.m. Home. I spent some of the time in class completing frame and tenon joints. The rest of the time was spent hanging about trying to be useful, alert to how I could be of some help to another member of the team when I had completed what was required of me. *'Don't make things difficult for yourself, slow down, David,'* said the instructor.

Monday 23/01/2012

10:14 p.m. Home. I set out for the afternoon class and began tidying up the frame and getting my photograph taken. Onward and upward Davey my lad.

Tuesday 24/01/2012

8:07 a.m. Tesco café. I am one of the regulars in here at this time of day. I have scoffed a roll with two links and brown sauce. I am not sure I needed that nourishment; I should last the day.

I cycled in the rain to board the MV *Argyle* in a hurry. I had not been standing at the Wemyss Bay bus stop for long when Jim, friend of Michael the Geordie bus driver, came by and offered me a lift up to Unit 29, where I showed him the works; he was on his way to Edinburgh, to where he travels every day. He insisted on giving me a lift down to Tesco.

8:10 a.m. Marion has just arrived.

10:55 a.m. Unit 29. I walked up Dellingburn Street in the drizzle and I am drookit, prior to purchasing a potato peeler from Aitken's, the ironmonger and hardware, opposite the wee Co-op on Cathcart Street. I then stopped in at the Business Gateway office further along the road and gave my pitch. *'Is that your elevator pitch?'* asked the receptionist, and at that moment one of the business advisers who had said they would contact me walked past.

The gatekeeper was interested in what I had to say and told

Wednesday 25/01/2012

me that she had connections with Nicaragua. Another individual standing by said that the operations manager at Clydeport Ocean Terminal was her brother-in-law, and an active supporter of the SESF project. I gave each of them a flyer and continued my pitching at a charity headquarters further along the street. I thought I might as well continue on to the Oak Mall Shopping Centre where I met the security manager, whose attitude towards me changed when he learned that I was not complaining but only seeking commercial expertise from someone in the mall's management structure. The two men took my flyer and said they would pass on my request for assistance.

Now to change into my boiler suit and make myself useful. All of those boxes which I uplifted from Greenock Academy and Gourock High School last year and paid to be delivered and stored temporarily at Inverclyde Removals Ltd await my attention; if I hadn't collected those books they would have been pulped.

2:15 p.m. I have had a meeting with John and Liz from the Tomorrow's People charity. They seemed pleased with the prospect of involving one of their work experience teams in the task of inventorying, cataloguing and boxing the educational resources from the five Inverclyde Council schools. We arranged to meet for 10:30 a.m. Tuesday, 31 January, when they would bring one of their teams. I gave them a copy of my CV and a flyer.

2:30 p.m. It is time to head home.

Wednesday 25/01/2012

1:17 p.m. Home. I cycled back through the wind. The instructor went over the half-term Independent Assessment of our progress to date and, so far, all our work was to a standard above average. We discussed the Winter Gardens Floral Clock project and we later went down to the site at the Winter Gardens and took measurements, and returned back up the road to calculate the amount of concrete required for the base of the retaining garden bed wall and the number of granite setts that were required. We are at long last onto a real project. It is a pity it has taken so long.

Thursday 26/01/2012

2:30 p.m. Plastering module. Lathe lime, horse hair and gypsum sheets of plasterboard. Dimensions of plasterboard: 2.4 x 8.4 m, 8 ft x 4 ft sheet.

'We are getting away from plastering nowadays. Anything you buy has got a sell by date on it. You need to try and at look at things and be able to estimate correctly the length and width. The size of material sheets are there for a reason. You don't just slap the plaster on, but apply a little bit and then build it up. What we do in Australia is ... I need so many sheets of plasterboard. They supply one sheet 2.4 m x 1.2 m. We would plasterboard a whole house in one day. The craft of plastering has become obsolescent as a result of the changes, development in materials,' said the instructor.

The instructor talks about plastering aids. *'This thing here. What is this stuff here: a tape, this is a bead, a spirit level for the corner, what we use for corners. The use of different types of materials. Now the tools: a hawk, buck, trowel. It has no point. How to use them correctly is a different matter. If you have the right tools for the job and the best that you can afford. Make sure you keep the trowel clean; only put a small amount of plaster on the trowel ... keep your hawk and trowel level, just try to do small amounts at a time,'* said the instructor.

1:01 p.m. Home. I called Riverside Inverclyde Properties Ltd to ask if water for the toilets in Unit 29 could be turned on. I left a message for the factor. I arranged to meet with Inverclyde Council business advisers on Tuesday, 31 January at 11:30 a.m., Unit 9, 20 Pottery Street.

Friday 27/01/2012

Plastering. I am trying to get the sequence of the process in motion: making sure that the battens on the wall are lined up and plumb; mixing the plaster, only a little water at a time; the application of plaster using a hawk and a trowel. I have yet to acquire the knack, the skill and technique of doing it correctly. I am too much in a hurry and inclined to slap the plaster on, to the great irritation of the instructor. I might get there eventually. The team are all pulling their weight today.

Monday 30/01/2012

1:30 p.m. We are discussing the arrangements for next week. More plastering today.

Tuesday 31/01/2012

9:45 a.m. Unit 29. I got a taxi at the rank beside the Wemyss Bay bus stop. On arrival I found Liz and John, team leaders of the Tomorrow's People charity, and their team who were waiting for me. The leaders got them organised.

10:35 a.m. Liz is making coffee and tea for her team.

10:55 a.m. The lads are back on task.

11:30 a.m. I am in a meeting with representatives of CVS Ltd, 9 Pottery Street. One of them is looking over my OSCR form and accounts; he tells me that I must focus on getting a board and a group of volunteers to do things. *'Once you have a board, get a flip chart and list activities, plot different routes, identify costs. You are to float ideas, share the load and suggest potential sources of funds; look for commitment from them to meet with you on a regular basis;*

prioritise the actions you take. Once you get a board get back to me,' he said.

5:09 p.m. Home. On the way back to the island I was chatting to two young residents – a care-home worker and the other a blacksmith.

The Tomorrow's People and their team showed up, as had been arranged, and did not waste any time getting down to shelving textbooks. They all worked away diligently with their team leaders, who worked alongside; they have been booked to return on 14 February. *'The guys were happy with the challenge,'* said one of team leaders.

I left them at 11 a.m. to attend a meeting with CSV Ltd, where I pitched to their manager. I had counted on the business development manager being there, having already discussed with her what my objectives were. The office called me a taxi. On arrival back at Unit 29 I showed the driver around the unit and gave him some flyers, as I had done with Jim the taxi driver this morning. The Tomorrow's People team had shut up the unit.

Wednesday 01/02/2012

11:35 a.m. The instructor has left us to take a break. We have plastered the wall, cleaned the tools, hawk, trowel and derby and tidied up. Days off next week – 9th and 10th, Thursday and Friday. We will work all day Monday and Wednesday.

Thursday 02/02/2012

7:23 p.m. Home. We were completing the process of plastering the wall – applying the finishing coat. The team were working well together, taking it in turns on each step. *'David, David, stop! Listen. I've already shown you how! Use the leading edge of the trowel, you put too much plaster on the hawk,'* said the instructor.

Monday 06/02/2012

    I am slowly getting the hang of the technique, preparation and attention to detail and ensuring that all of the tools are cleaned properly after use. It has been a beautiful day, the is sun shining out of a clear blue winter's day sky. I will strive to get better.

Friday 03/02/2012

The instructor spent most of the class time talking about the different kinds of moulding, and what we were going to do to the wallpapering and skirting boards.
    There was yet more hanging around as the instructor worked his mobile phone; I find this inactivity a real bore and I have to be conscious of not showing my displeasure. I am trying to stay alert, focused and aware that I just have to accept things as they are. I am determined to see this course through to the finish. It has been a bright and freezing cold morning – stick with it my old son.

Monday 06/02/2012

9:42 a.m. Home. I spoke to Clive at Book Aid International Ltd about their work; new books from publishers to libraries worldwide. I called Sonia at Computer Aid International, and left a message. I spoke with admin at Cluff Gold. I spoke with supportive staff at the Glenburn School, Greenock, about educational resources that will become available when they have moved to their new build school; it is an ECO school and when I pass by on the bus I can see the flag fluttering in the wind. I make arrangements with them to visit the school to tell the children about the work of the Surplus Educational Supplies Foundation.

2 p.m. I am in class and we have been given a list of materials to price. Quantity. Price a job and give the instructor a quote for it. How many sheets of plasterboard? 12.5 mm thick. Area of wall?

5.7 m x 3 m = 17.1 m squared. Plaster, how many bags? Labour, £14 per hour.

'How long will it take to do the job?' asked the instructor.

- Area of one sheet of plasterboard: 2.4 m x 1.2 m = 4.88 m squared.
- 1 bag of plaster covers: 2.75 m squared.
- 3 bags of bonding plaster: 5.7 m x 3 m = 17 m squared.
- Wall area: 2.4 m x 1.2 m = 2.88 m squared.
- Plasterboard: 17.1 m squared divided by 2.88 m squared = 6 sheets of plasterboard. 5.94 is divided by 2.75? = 2.16 m squared.
- 3 bags of bonding plaster 5.94 divided by 10 = 0.594.
- Finishing plaster.

'All happy with the tasks in hand?' asks the instructor. My task tomorrow is to visit a builder and price these materials.

Tuesday 07/02/2012

8:30 a.m. Unit 29. Jim the roofer, who stays on the island and drives every day to a job in Grangemouth, had kindly offered once again to give me a lift up the road from Wemyss Bay. He dropped me of at M&J Builders and Timber Merchants Ltd, up on Drumfrochar Road where the Tate & Lyle Sugar Refinery used to be. I waited from 7:30 a.m. until it opened. I spoke with the manager/owner who gave me the prices of the materials required to do a plastering contract and fulfilled an assignment for the Access to Construction Skills course. SQA Level 5 course.

11:15 a.m. I had a discussion with the Inverclyde Council business adviser about retail properties that were available. I am thinking about opening a charity shop to create an 'income stream' which is a priority. A cash cow. I need to get a board and approach local industry for volunteers. I need a structure.

11:55 a.m. It is time to head down the road. The sun is shining. It is a cold winter's day; my next appointment is at 2 p.m. at Texas Instruments Ltd, Larkfield Industrial Estate.

Colin, the operations manager, kindly gave me some of his time to talk me through the process of creating an income stream. (See his flow chart, which is in my notes somewhere.)

Wednesday 08/02/2012

1:46 p.m. Home. I have just got in. It has been dry and cold. The wind is blowing in from the south. I have cracked another day. Hooray!

We were standing around, listening to the multi-skilled instructor talk about the preparation of a wall prior to papering it. I am persevering, keeping alert and aware and responding appropriately when I am required to do so. This close attention to the instructor and those in close proximity to me is a chore, but necessary under these circumstances if I am going to see this course through to the finish.

We don't come back until 8:30 a.m. on Monday, 13 February 2012.

Thursday 09/02/2012

9:57 a.m. Home. I called the council business adviser at Cathcart House, Cathcart Square, Greenock, regarding rental of a shop unit. She was positive and will get back to me. I must try and get my online marketing up and running. But how? Contact Careers, Strathclyde University and see a person who is up to speed about personal networking: the social marketing professor.

Will There Be Some Light at the End of This Tunnel?

Monday 13/02/2012

7:45 p.m. Home. I was out early from The Grove, Kilbarchan, Renfrewshire. Bus to Paisley to get the 8 a.m. ferry from Wemyss Bay to the Island of Bute. I arrived 15 minutes late to stand around listening to the instructor; later we were hanging wallpaper. I was waiting my turn and keeping alert; for me it was a long day in Unit 5. I have to grin and bear it, as there is nothing else for it.

Labour plus materials = Cost of the job. Plasterboard: 6 sheets x £14.75 = £85.50. Bonding plaster: 3 bags x £20.45 = £61.35. Finishing plaster: 1 bag x £16.75 = £16.75. Labour: 7 hours x £14.00 = £98. Cost of the job £261.60.

Tuesday 14/02/2012

4:23 p.m. Home. I was out by 8 a.m. I spent the entire class helping other members of the team with their wallpapering assignment, and I finally got to put my 2.3 m squared sheet up with a minimum of fuss. *'Slow down, David,'* said the instructor. Sorry, instructor, I think to myself. My respect for this individual is based, apart from anything else, on the mastery he has of the many skills in the building trade. I have to give everything to the work before me; I do, my all or nothing. I am not putting up with the pressure from you and company for recreation purposes.

Thursday 16/02/2012

5:55 p.m. Home. We were all standing about and there was more wallpapering.

Friday 17/02/2012

1:53 p.m. Home. It is great to be away. It has been a long morning. Some discord: as ever I am at fault – yes and no. I have won another round by eating another humble pie. I have not jacked it in. I kept my cool. I deferred meekly to the man in charge. *'Just go for a walk,'* he said. There was more papering and tidying up.

Monday 20/02/2012

7:10 p.m. Home. I have just got in. I got on with what I had to get on with today. There was more painting of the wall and standing about, and the instructor and I were chatting.

Tuesday 21/02/2012

8:30 a.m. Unit 29. I walked through the Oak Mall Shopping Centre into Cathcart Square, and past Well Park Church of Scotland kirk, which was shut. I walked up the steep cobbled street, up the park steps and past the war memorial; on this cold, drizzly morning I thought of the North Atlantic convoys and the many merchant seamen that did not survive. Across the busy main road and up Lynedoch Street, and stopped at Aulds the Bakers for a takeaway cup of tea and into Cowden's for a crusty roll and corned beef.

I have changed into my overalls. No sooner had I opened the big roller-shutter door than big Iain, ex-shipyard boilermaker from Inverclyde Tools Ltd, was walking over to say hello, offering to help me generate some revenue and showing me how to open PayPal and eBay accounts.

The big Iain reckons I could easily sell some of the educational resources online.

9:20 a.m. That's JP, David with the glasses, and John, the leader of Tomorrow's People, arrived. And now Craig and Jordan.

10:10 a.m. Liz, the manager and supervisor, arrives with Dean, Paul and Ryan. I gave them a volleyball and they had a kickabout among themselves at the far end of this massive unit. David has plugged into Radio 2; soon the Tomorrow's People team set to work sorting the books.

11:20 a.m. RP is a worker. He has been busy, non-stop, shelving library books and textbooks '*Ah got OCD like ma Ma,*' he tells me. Good on you, lad. Meanwhile the rest of the team, JP, Connor, Paul, Jordan and Dean are having their curry cups.

11:30 a.m. The entire team are now gainfully employed, having figured out how to assemble the shelves into the Jubilee Gardens Library units, that were salvaged from the Ealing Borough Council library prior to its demolition, thanks to Wilmot Dixon Ltd. *(See earlier diary entry in* Volume Two, The Diary of a Shipping Clerk, *published, Friday, 27 October 2023.)*

I am attempting, with the help of this great team of Young Folk of Today's World, to list, catalogue, the entire stock of English curricular textbooks that has come from Greenock Academy and Gourock High School.

Noon. The team have stopped and are having a kickabout.

7:25 p.m. Upstairs, The Grove, Kilbarchan. The Hanschell family home on the mainland. Roll it back.

I left Unit 29 at 12:30 p.m., first giving Iain a look, to let him know that supporter Mary, of Glenburn School, might drop by with my SESF folder and if that was okay with them to keep it for me. I then walked through the drizzle over to East Hamilton Street on the M8 to the Cappielow Industrial Estate, where once stood Kincaid's Shipyard, and there waited for the Inverclyde Council's business adviser, who was going to show me a property that I might be able use as a retail facility.

There was no sign of this individual, and I was getting soaked, when a gentleman who had driven past me earlier returned on foot to ask me if he could be of any help? I told him that I was waiting for someone from the council. He told me to follow him over to Jewson, the hardware and builders' merchant, and proceeded to use his iPhone to contact the business adviser, whose office in the council building he was able to get through to. I was able to speak to Gary, who said I could have an appointment at 3 p.m. John invited me back to his home on Brougham Street in the city centre, which he is renovating, for toast and coffee. Another totally unexpected, and not uncommon, welcome intervention of kindness that I have had the privilege to experience on my safari in the land of Caledonia from the day I arrived on the Air Canada flight at Prestwick, from Halifax, Nova Scotia, 18 May 1973.

I asked him if he would be interested in visiting the SESF storage unit at Unit 29. I left my business plan and CV with him. He told me that he attends the Tuesday Night Prayer Meeting at the small mission hall, Barnard Court, not far from where I was to have met with the Inverclyde Council official. I had forgotten that Marion had said she would meet me at Morrisons supermarket at the bottom of Dellingburn Street. I got an Upper Skelmorlie bus to Inverkip and met Marion at her school.

It has been a good day in spite of much effort. I am going to chill out for a bit.

Wednesday 22/02/2012

Home. I was in class shortly after 8:30 a.m. The instructor was demonstrating different electro-mechanical woodworking equipment; we were preparing for our next bricklaying assignment.

2:01 p.m. Home. I am checking my email correspondence. I have called Liz at Tomorrow's People, Unit 2, Ladyburn Business Centre, Greenock.

I spoke with Daimon, Services for Communities, Waverley Court, Market Street, Edinburgh. The Surplus Educational

Supplies Foundation is still interested in acquiring educational resources and furniture from the former Royal High School, depending on whether it can get pro bono assistance with removal and storage. I then called David of Bishops Removals Ltd. I sent an email to the operations manager of Texas Instruments Ltd with a pitch for volunteers for the SESF board, since he had said he and some of his colleagues might be able to lend a hand. I spoke to John, journalist with the *Greenock Telegraph* and the business development officer Inverclyde Council Regeneration and Environment to thank her for drafting my request for a retail space.

Thursday 23/02/2012

3:20 p.m. Home. I was out early in the smirry rain, under a thick grey blanket of mist hanging heavily over the bay and big watta, and returned with the wind at my back. It was a class day of heavy manual labour, except for a break answering multiple-choice questions related to brick work. The next module is cavity walls. Today it was barrowing the number of bricks required and stacking them on the floor of Unit 5, which we had cleared of the benches. I had teamed up with PK. I was conscious of trying to anticipate what the next move required of me without annoying the instructor

3:27 p.m. I am returning a call from Forth Valley College. They are offering me a 40-foot container. I call Galt Transport Ltd and speak to Simon to see if they can collect it for me. He tells me to call him back, which I do. *'Hold the line a little longer. We can do that for you, David,'* he said. I am humbled by his swift response to my request for assistance; they will pick up the ocean freight container on Monday. *(It was not to be a pro bono uplift.)*

Friday 24/02/2012

2:25 p.m. Home. I have called Inverclyde Tool Hire Ltd, my neighbours in the Lynedoch. *'No problem,'* he said. I explained that I had a college class that morning and would try to be there before 1 p.m., when the container was due to be delivered.

I was out against the wind at 8 a.m. It was a long day that dragged: the best of the team absent and I had to suffer the rest, who spend a lot of their time fooling around. *'It is just banter,'* said the instructor, who doesn't seem to care one way or the other. I can't bear wasting my time here, perhaps one day I will know why? I have my doubts. We spent some of the time lining out where the four walls were to go that we each had to build over the next two weeks.

Monday 27/02/2012

7:25 a.m. Unit 29. An early start. I met Jim the roofer on the boat, who has kindly dropped me off on his way across the Central Belt to a job in Falkirk. While on the boat I was chatting to Mike the bus driver, who is a man of many parts, and who in a previous life ran an IT training scheme in Newcastle.

9:05 a.m. I called Galt Transport Ltd in Dumbarton. *'Simon here, he's up there now to collect the container,'* he said. Hopefully the container will be here before midday. I have been up to Cowden's for the crusty roll and corned beef and takeaway coffee from Aulds Bakery Shop. My friend has torn the ligaments in her arm and has had to go home, but came in to open the shop. I stopped off at Unit 2, Inverclyde Tool Hire Ltd, to say *'Hi'* to Iain and Paul, and to confirm with them that it would be alright if I did not hang around and they could direct the artic driver to offload the container either behind Unit 29 or in the car park. *'No problem,'* he said.

11:30 a.m. I am preparing to leave. I call Galt Transport Ltd and someone in the office tells me that they were unable to extricate 'my' container from where it was situated at the Forth Valley College building site. I win some and lose some.

1 p.m. MV *Bute*. I got a voicemail from Simon at AGT Ltd to say that the container at the former Forth Valley College site in Alloa could not be got at, as a crane would be required to remove it. I had called Allan Galt at 11:30 a.m. to make an apology for the trouble I had caused. He was friendly. Why had the FVC staff I had dealt with over many months not indicated to me that there would be a problem in uplifting the container? I am gutted.

I got out of my overalls and went across to Unit 2 to let Paul and Iain know that there would be no container on its way. I walked down the hill and into the Oak Mall and posted Marion's letters to Amy and Johanna. I got the Largs bus just in time. I met Gillian and her friend Rhys, who was studying social care, and Rebecca, who is studying child care at James Watt College. They joined me for coffee on me in the Wemyss Bay Café. I am making every effort not to be late for the Access to Construction Skills course.

I received a message from John, Tomorrow's People team leader, to say that he and Liz had to attend an urgent meeting in Glasgow tomorrow and would be unable to bring their team to Unit 29 tomorrow. Oh well.

7:56 p.m. Home. I was half an hour late for this afternoon's class. I had to get the one o'clock boat and I called the instructor to let him know that I would not be in on time.

I was finding it hard to begin this next bricklaying module, but I kept at it. *'David, you are going too fast,'* he said. I was trying to slow down, take my time and follow the techniques. The process: levelling each brick and levelling the row of bricks as it progressed, with no spaces under the spirit level. I was glad to see four o'clock on the wall clock.

Tuesday 28/02/2012

10 a.m. Unit 29. I met Iain on his way out. It is a damp and grey morning.

9:30 a.m. Saved messages. Ian, Steel Removals Ltd, down in Enfield, is offering a full container's worth of office furniture, which the Surplus Educational Supplies Foundation is unable to accept. His firm had collected the Jubilee Gardens Library furniture and stored it prior to delivering it to my container at Tilbury and which is now set out in Unit 29. *(See account of that firm's kindness and crucial assistance in* Volume Two, The Diary of a Shipping Clerk.*)*

The volunteer has not shown up; I am leaving the premises having done enough on my own for one morning.

Wednesday 29/02/12

10:22 p.m. Home. *'Put the kettle on,'* said the instructor. I love to hear those words, because they mean that I can take a short break and catch my breath. I persevered and remained focused on the task of completing my end wall; the instructor was not satisfied with my handiwork. I am out of plumb, fair enough. I will try harder. I am becoming more confident handling the materials and approaching the task in a more methodical and workmanlike manner. I am mixing the mortar and tidying up, these are the easy bits. I continue to remain always aware, alert that there are tasks that require the assistance of a willing hand; knowing when to step in and when not to.

Thursday 01/03/2012

2:54 p.m. Home. I cycled back in the driving rain, sucking in the wind. I had barely made it through another day of classwork. The team was much reduced. I just had to get on with it and kept active.

Friday 02/03/2012

12:39 p.m. Home. I stumbled once more. The instructor calls me out from the group and asks what is wrong with me. He tells me that my attitude is upsetting the others; my persona, the real me when I lose control, I know full well I am not all peace and love. (*'You are either sugar or sh-1-t,'* said the cook to me one day back at the Northumberland Street Hostel, Edinburgh, autumn 1974–1975.)

I backtracked in a hurry and ate another humble pie. *'I am sorry for being unpleasant, please accept my apology.'* The instructor told me to leave for the rest of the class. It is the first time I have ever been told to leave a class, and it is the closest so far that I have come to quitting and telling him and the class where they all can go. Of course, there is no joy for me taking that precipitate action – I would have had the momentary pleasure of doing so, and would have excluded more possible and constructive options downstream, as so often happened in the past when I only did myself mischief by responding in many a fraught situation with more anger.

12:44 p.m. *'I have the keys to 38 East Hamilton Street,'* said the business adviser, Inverclyde Council, Cathcart House, Greenock, when I spoke to her just now.

12:48 p.m. I called the Sierra Leone High Commission and spoke to Florence, who is no longer Head of Chancery. I am to call again on 6 March.

I called the Muirhouse Social Work Community Services Centre: Graham is to call me back at 2 p.m. to arrange transport of furniture from the former Royal High School. Call Daimon at

3 p.m. to make arrangements to uplift. Call Bishop's Move on 12 March; Graham and his team from MCSSC will be available to uplift resources between 10 a.m. and midday on 25 February.

1:39 p.m. Call Donna at One2One Accountancy Services to obtain my VAT registration.

Monday 05/03/2012

8:30 a.m. Tesco café, Greenock. I am chatting to one of the regulars. Marion dropped me off at Morrisons supermarket. I am hanging around till 9 a.m. when I have an appointment with the business adviser to visit the shop unit, a former bank and post office at 38 East Hamilton Street opposite what was once Scott's shipyard. There is no harm in trying, for there is no other option for me at this stage of my journey except to keep on keeping on moving forward. It is a bright clear morning but it seems that we are back to winter again.

11 a.m. MV *Argyle* we are returning to the island in the sunshine. The business adviser drove me out to 38 East Hamilton Street. I have an appointment to meet her again on Thursday 8 March to collect the keys.

The shopfront is right on the main drag, part of the M8's non-stop traffic in and out of Greenock City. It is a derelict property, which apparently gets flooded from the main road; the business adviser tells me that this problem was sorted a while ago by AMEY the road people. I can't be too fussy. It is a great location in some ways: I can advertise on both sides of the ground floor premises. I will need to have the manually operated roller door repaired by a blacksmith.

The business adviser then took me up to Unit 29 to learn what the Surplus Educational Supplies Foundation is all about; while we were there the factor of Riverside Inverclyde Properties Ltd showed up with a party of prospective tenants, which gave me the opportunity to tell him that I was moving out. I got the bus back to Wemyss Bay. I must continue the collection, storage, inventorying and packaging of valuable fit-for-purpose educational resources, and at the same time identify deserving and suitable beneficiaries in the Third World.

2:56 p.m. Home. I made it through another session of the SQA Level 5 Access to Construction Skills course, building my corner wall. More bricklaying under the close scrutiny of the multi-skilled instructor. My exhausting efforts to attain perfection are never good enough. I think he expects me to quit. I was determined, however, from resources deep within my being to stay on top of what was required from the task in hand; needless to say I was glad to see four o'clock.

Tuesday 06/03/2012

7:50 a.m. Unit 29. A clear, cold morning. It is going to be a good day, I hope. That's the volunteer arrived and I've set him to task.

9:10 a.m. Tomorrow's People team leaders arrive.

10:15 a.m. I have returned from the Booker Cash and Carry up the road with rolls of boxing tape, which this firm has donated thanks to manager Richard, Sharon and James.

I returned to find Patrick, Ross, JP, Dean, Connor, Craig and David all working away. I am now going to take their orders for elevenses: Dean, roll and slice, tattie scone and can of Irn Bru; Ryan will have the same; JP, black pudding slice, tattie scone and Coke; Patrick, black pudding slice, tattie scone and Irn Bru; John, roll and slice and Irn Bru; Craig roll and slice and Coke; J ordered a roll and slice and Coke; Connor, chicken noodle and Irn Bru; David, roll and slice with tomato sauce and Irn Bru; Neil the volunteer, coffee.

I have introduced Joe and Neil, the volunteers, to Iain, the director of Inverclyde Tool Hire Ltd, with whom I will leave the key of Unit 29. The volunteers have agreed to come in on their own and continue the process of sorting, cataloguing and boxing of textbooks, library books and stationery.

12:45 p.m. That's Liz, John and their Tomorrow's People team finished another session of invaluable assistance. I hope to see them all again next Tuesday, 13 March.

Wednesday 07/03/2012

2:42 p.m. Home. A cold grey morning. I forced my ageing frame out of bed, and later got on my bicycle and was up along the main road into the little town and up the steep hill. I took a deep breath before entering Unit 5. I was focused and completed the task before me. I tidied and reckon I did more than my share, as per usual, which does not bother me as I don't need to hang about waiting on his instructions.

Chapter Sixteen
The Shipping Clerk Opens the Book Store

Thursday 08/03/2012

7:59 p.m. Home. An early start. More hanging about. We were filling in more forms to attest to our progress in the current module for the SQA bureaucracy. We were papering a ceiling, later we were cutting our plaster of Paris mouldings. I was pressing on with the tasks and was determined to complete this course of self-inflicted punishment.

Holidays beckon 29 March to 16 April. I managed to get away at 12:30 p.m. and went across to the mainland on the one o'clock boat and took a bus up the road to No. 38 East Hamilton Street.

3:41 p.m. I am sitting in the foyer of Cathcart House, Inverclyde Council headquarters. The business adviser has come down the stairs and handed me a bunch of keys to 38 East Hamilton Street. I told her that I would come by on Tuesday to sign the required documents. I asked her if she could recommend a locksmith – the front door needs a lock – and a builder to give me advice regarding refurbishment of the premises, which are in a parlous state. She has disappeared to obtain this information.

4 p.m. 38 East Hamilton Street. I met Paul, who comes from Dumbarton and knows some of the team at Galt Transport Ltd. He lives in the flat above the premises.

On arrival I thought I might introduce myself to occupants of the tenement. I went round on the McDougall Street side and went up the flight of stairs, and on the first landing I knocked

Thursday 08/03/2012

Lynedoch Industrial Estate Greenock. Friday 03/08/2012. Janitors from Glenburn School make another delivery of curricular resources. 'We don't want to see this stuff in a skip.'

on the door of the flat, from behind which a dog was barking loudly. It took some time before the door opened. I introduced myself, and Paul came back downstairs with me to see what I hoped would become The Book Store. He said he would like to come and work with me. I took some digitals of the shocking state of the disrepair.

Ian of Inverclyde Taxi had run me out. I got another taxi off the M8 back to Tesco and got some digitals of the Tomorrow's People at work and the shocking state of the No. 38 premises. I am thankful that the premises still has electricity.

Bus back to Wemyss Bay. I am knackered.

Friday 09/03/2012

2:22 p.m. Home. Today I was doing what had to be done, and there was more standing about doing absolutely nothing while the instructor ran his show from the Unit 5 office. I received a call from St Michael's Primary School to tell me that parents with a van would be bringing their donation of books from the school along to Unit 29 on Tuesday 13 March by 9 a.m.

At the moment I am feeling very fragile. I was up through the night, erupting at both ends, but I have showered and got some clothes on my skin and I am off to attend an exhibition of a collection of the work of George Wyllie at the Collins Gallery in Glasgow. I had the privilege of working with George on an art project with a class of P3/4 children at North Bute Primary School in September 2000 and we have kept in touch since.

Monday 12/03/2012

I was helping other members of the team to make their plaster mouldings.

Tuesday 13/03/2012

8:25 a.m. Unit 29. Marion has dropped me off up on the busy Drumfrochar Road, with non-stop traffic in both directions. On arrival at Unit 29 I met Iain and we paused to shoot the breeze for a few minutes.

Well, what is ahead of me today? I expect the Tomorrow's People team to be here for another session, which will be their last; that will be four two-hour sessions each Tuesday. I am grateful for their help and company. Alan the jack of all trades, another former shipyard worker, who describes himself as the problem solver, will be meeting me at 38 East Hamilton Street to see if he can assist me in refurbishing this derelict space. David the taxi driver had recommended him to me. I will sign the lease to these premises today. I had better drink my coffee before it gets any colder.

Wednesday 14/03/2012

1:45 p.m. I spent the morning helping Paul to make his piece of moulding and then had a go at making mine. Later I walked through the Meadows with two members of the team to an Argyll and Bute Council depot where we will be choosing granite setts for the floral clock's retaining garden wall – anything to get out in the fresh air.

2:20 p.m. Home. I called the Sierra Leone High Commission. The Head of Chancery is to call me back. How many times do I need to call them?

Thursday 15/03/2012

2:40 p.m. Home. I began the morning class with some members of the team, down at the council's builders' yard, sorting through a pile of granite setts to collect the number required to build the low wall around the garden bed with the mechanical clock. The instructor asked me to cycle back up to Unit 5 to put on my boots.

Friday 16/03/2012

3:39 p.m. Home. I called the Sierra Leone High Commission and managed to speak briefly with Demba, who said, *'We are busy with de presidential business.'* He tells me to call him at the same time and day next week. I have arranged to meet with Tomorrow's People in Edinburgh on Tuesday 27 March at Muirhouse Arts Centre, North Edinburgh. I am going to see if I can get a group to work with me at Unit 12, West Shore Business Centre, Granton, and that would be great.

Monday 19/03/2012

8:41 a.m. Home. I called Alan the problem solver, who said, *'I am doin' a bathroom suite. I will call you later.'* Later he calls me from 38 East Hamilton Street to tell me, *'I need scaffolding, it's four metres to the ceiling.'* This morning I was fitting parts of the door together and chiselling to make the joints fit more closely.

Tuesday 20/03/2012

6:35 a.m. I am on the ferry again. *'Don't forget to put on your foul weather gear,'* said Marion. I bid goodbye to David and tell him to hold the fort and remember to feed the fish. Have I got everything this time? A belt round my waist, spectacles, wallet, watch, hearing aid. I put on my showerproof trousers.

Rumble of the engines down below; I am into the unknown of another day, in which I hope to see the beginning of some refurbishment at 38 East Hamilton Street, opposite what was once Scott's shipyard. Alan the problem solver said he was going to show up. I will try and get the scaffolding from Brandon Tool

Thursday 22/03/2012

Hire just up the road in the Cappielow Industrial Estate, and I will need some help from them to set it up. I believe the officials from Inverclyde Council are coming with the lease for me to sign. What else can I do but continue to work away at this new development; a self-funded, independent, charity bookstore, in a location with constant road traffic but little footfall, with salvage and charity-donated books for export.

11:05 a.m. No. 38. 'The Book Store'. That's the business adviser been with the lease, and who tried to get the plumber to turn on the water. I signed the lease 8 March 2012 to 8 March 2013, for the storage of educational books, surplus educational resources and retail.

I arrived here by taxi from Tesco at around 8:33 a.m., changed into my boiler suit and walked up the busy main road to Brandon Tool Hire Ltd to return the vacuum cleaner and rent scaffolding. They said I could have the scaffolding when it had already been rented out in Coatbridge. I returned and started sweeping up the stoor. At around 10:15 a.m. Alan and his mate Paul arrived with tools and I had to tell them that the scaffolding was not available; they said they would be back tomorrow. I have made a start; the new broom sweeps clean. This is my side of the story for the Green Oak City dwellers.

(I gave The Book Store, my best shot.)

Thursday 22/03/2012

9:30 a.m. I called Property Services, Inverclyde Council, Cathcart House and they said they would call Quality Gas Plumbers to say it was okay for them to turn the water on at No. 38. I called Joe, who will meet me and Robert at Wemyss Bay on Saturday 24th to drive up to look at No. 38 and up to Unit 29. I called Iain who said he would put the keys to Unit 29 through the door of No. 38. *'No bother,'* he said.

3:59 p.m. Voicemail from Alan the problem solver to say that Paul had twisted his arm and they would not be able to start work.

Saturday 24/03/2012

3:41 p.m. Home. I called Alan to confirm that he will be able to put gypsum/gyprock panels on the ceiling.

On my arrival at 38 East Hamilton Street this morning I found the keys to Unit 29. The sun has been shining this spring day. While I was working in the premises of No. 38, John came by to say hello, and he came again, while I was putting red oxide paint on the roller door, to invite me round to the Barnard Court Mission Hall for a bacon roll and coffee. I thanked him and said I would come round as soon as I had finished the task before me. He came back later, while I was still painting, with the purvey.

Joe and Robert returned, they had been begging for materials in the Cappielow Industrial Estate, and with the two of them in tow I took them round, with my bacon roll and coffee, to the Mission Hall. They were looked after by John, who treated them to the same. Finlay, the kind neighbour from the top flat, filled my bucket so I could wash the entrance to the premises. Jim from the island came by to see what I was up to, and he tried to find the tap to turn on the water, but to no avail.

Monday 26/03/2012

11:15 a.m. On deck in full sunshine. There is a gaping hole in the top right of my remaining teeth, and I am facing another class in Unit 5 at 1:30 p.m.

I was over on the 7 a.m. boat with Marion. I got the bus up to Greenock, walked along to the dental practice and at 8:30 a.m. I was called in by a dentist and told that the tooth would abscess before too long and they administered three jags and brusquely extracted it. I was not happy, spitting blood, as I walked down

Dalrymple Street to the office of the *Greenock Telegraph* to see if I could get copies of photographs taken by their journalists. The receptionist told me that her family once lived in the tenement at 38 East Hamilton Street.

I then walked up to HSS Hire to say to 'Hi!' to Mark, and then on to the taxi rank at Tesco's and I got a taxi up the road to No. 38. Alan and his young assistant Stephen were on the job, trying to put the panels of gyprock on the ceiling with an unsteady scaffolding arrangement consisting of just a board to walk on. That did not look safe to me, so I walked up to Jewson's and bought a 9 ft x 2 in plank cut to two lengths. When I put them onto my shoulder I fell backwards onto my head. I thought that had finished me, but I was soon on my feet. I dropped the planks off so the professionals could have a more stable support on the scaffolding. I then bid them goodbye and hailed an ABC Taxi to Greenock and got the bus down the road.

Tuesday 27/03/2012

3:50 p.m. Platform 14, Glasgow Central Station. The train is underway for Wemyss Bay. A short while ago I was standing under the railway station clock when David came towards me. It was good to meet each other; he was on his way back to the North Sea aboard MV *Kraken*. Roll it back.

This morning I got the bus from Buchanan Street Bus Station for Edinburgh and got off the bus just before Roseberry Crescent, opposite Haymarket Street Station. I usually get off at a stop on Princes Street, but it had been closed off due to the construction of tram lines. I was nearly run over by the bus from which I had alighted, and was saved only by the instant response of the bus driver pressing the airbrakes, which caused the bus to stop within inches of me. A close shave which unsettled me for the rest of the day. I got a taxi from the rank outside Haymarket railway station; the taxi driver had witnessed my near-death experience and drove me over to Unit 12, West Shore Business Centre, Granton. The roads are being dug up all over this beautiful city.

I opened up Unit 12 and it was as I had left it months ago. I then called Kingsley to let him know that he could come and collect one of the filing cabinets that I had in stock, and which I said he could have. I met James, Bahram's assistant at Apfelsnapz Crisps, and we chatted briefly – he is semi-supportive of my initiative. He told me that their problem was getting paid for their unique product. Kingsley came by and I ordered a taxi, the driver happened to be agreeable to transporting ourselves and this piece of office furniture and they dropped me off at the Muirhouse Community Arts Centre for a 12 noon meeting with Kate and her Tomorrow's People colleagues. They were sceptical about what the Surplus Educational Supplies Foundation could contribute to the personal development of their clients, however they wanted to see what resources I had stored at Unit 12.

Would they determine whether or not there was sufficient challenge for their clients to organise and inventory the stock of resources in Unit 12? I gave them one of the keys to the unit and asked them to notify the estates manager of Waterfront Edinburgh that I had given them permission to access the unit and return the key to their office.

Friday 30/03/2012

4:08 p.m. Home. I am just in from the town. I was over the watta on the noon boat with Robert and we got the bus to Greenock and a taxi to 38 East Hamilton Street to find Joe, his brother Michael, and the plumber Alfie and his mate connecting the water, along with Alan the problem solver who I had paid £200 for plating parts of the ceiling that had fallen down. He still needs to use the remaining sheets of gyprock and plaster some of the walls.

I went up to Jewson's and barrowed back bags of plaster and 'Dot to Dot Adhesive', which Alan will use next week to finish the job. Robert and I got a taxi back to the bus depot and I got the Upper Skelmorelie bus to Wemyss Bay.

4:25 p.m. Home. I called Colin at Texas Instruments Ltd and they will let me have some pallets as and when required.

Saturday 31/03/2012

8:05 a.m. MV *Bute*. There is sunshine on the water, which is being rippled by a slight breeze. The boat is crowded with folk away for the day. What's ahead of me this morning? Get the bus to Greenock and another bus along to 38 East Hamilton Street, open up, put on my overalls and begin to shovel the rubble into the Jewson bags, which cost me nearly a tenner. Then, all being well, I shall put a coat of yellow metal paint on the roller door and I shall tidy up and begin the journey home.

12:30 p.m. Home. I accomplished what I had set out to do this morning. Alan the problem solver appeared and kindly gave me a lift in time to catch the one o'clock boat. He is a former shipyard worker and has spent some time in Cuba; I respect him.

Monday 02/04/2012

8:20 a.m. 38 East Hamilton Street. I set my mind to the task of refurbishment of these derelict premises last night as I sat in the rocking chair. I went outside, attached the saddlebags to my bicycle and loaded the two tins of paint into them, and tied a poly bag with a roller brush and paint trays behind the saddle. I feel, and look, like an idiot cycling with that lot. Who cares?

I got the 6:30 a.m. train to Drumfrochar and cycled down Cornhaddock Street, down Baker Street, and turned right at the lights. I then cycled up the hill, past the chapel and multistorey flats, due for demolition having only recently been renovated.

The Book Store, 48 East Hamilton Street, Oakmall Shopping Centre, Greenock. Many volunteers had made the Book Store an astounding success from start to finish.

The work of the Surplus Educational Supplies Foundation had become, after seven years of struggle and disappointment, a success. One customer told us that he had not expected to encounter such a quality bookstore in Greenock!

Monday 02/04/2012

Whose decision was that? Then along the ridge with views of the river and the hills beyond, and here I am.

There is a constant flow of traffic on my doorstep, and no parking spaces on this main road. How can I use this unsuitable location to my best advantage? I called Alan, who is taking Paul, his mate, to Wemyss Bay for a job. There is so much necessary refurbishment required. I have made a start.

I went to Jewson's to let them know that Alan will come by tomorrow to collect whatever materials he needs. The helpful guys there said that would be okay. I went into Howden's, who could not help me because I need an account with them, and then it was across to JW Carpets Ltd to see if I could get some offcuts to cover the floor. I left two of my SESF dossiers with the manager of J&W Maclean in the Cappielow Industrial Estate. I am trying to interest switched-on and successful business people who will attune to my wavelength.

I am waiting to hear from an island businessman who has my SESF folder and who is a close friend of two other island business people. I have already given another SESF folder to Peter, the managing director of Rainbow Cleaners Ltd based along from Unit 29 in the Lynedoch Industrial Estate. Bring it on! I am not sitting still. They were helpful and said they would give me a look tomorrow. I spoke to Phillip the signwriter, who said he would also come by tomorrow.

10:16 a.m. I am back at Drumfrochar Station, waiting for the 10:23 a.m. train to Wemyss Bay.

11:12 a.m. MV *Argyle*. I am back on a boat and I have put a cup of pea, beef and barley soup down my gullet. Spool it back.

As I was about to close the roller-shutter door, I met Martin, a neighbour from up the stairs in the tenement, who was friendly.

Tuesday 03/04/2012

7:13 a.m. MV *Bute* I made the ferry with seconds to spare; fortunately the wind was at my back once I got round Bogany Point. Wet and grey today. I was slow to move, and was wide awake from early. Joe is meeting me at 7:45 a.m. and we will work together to decide the next move. To discuss:
1. Seal the boxes, pallet and shrink-wrap and get them into one of the Clydeport Ocean Terminals empty containers.
2. Work on the two of us trying to source beneficiaries, for they don't know what they are missing resources.
3. Get No. 38, The Book Store, ready for opening.

1:30 p.m. Station Café, Wemyss Bay. This morning Joe showed up at 8:45 a.m. He drove us to Morrisons supermarket, where we had a Surplus Educational Supplies Foundation meeting in the café. At 9 a.m. Joe drove us to 38 East Hamilton Street and we put on our overalls and began removing the flaking plaster from the walls.

Alan the problem solver and Paul showed up, and then went away to look for cheap paint. The latter wanted £20, For what? But I gave it to him. I went up to the industrial estate to collect my SESF dossiers from J&W MacLean Hardware. The manager said, '*It is not something we wish to be involved in.*'

James the locksmith came and put new double locks in the double door; he did not wish to be paid, but I did pay him. Joe drove me to Morrisons where I got some biscuits, caramel wafers, snowballs, Scottish Blend Tea, and jar of Gold Blend Coffee as a token of my appreciation for the work the team at Rainbow International Ltd had carried out in Unit 18 and at 38 East Hamilton Street. I met the managing director, who said, '*You are doing interesting work.*' I replied, '*I am fortunate to get assistance from firms such as Rainbow International Ltd.*'

It was back to Jewson's to purchase more paint. I changed

out of my boiler suit and Joe drove me back to the Oak Mall Shopping Centre, where I bought a pair of shoes, had the frames of my specks adjusted, and headed home.

Thursday 05/04/2012

9:40 a.m. 38 East Hamilton Street. Alan the problem solver and his assistant Paul are busy painting. They have been here since 9:15 a.m. Iain from Inverweld, blacksmith in Port Glasgow, was here at 9 a.m. and took measurements for a metal protective strip (100 mm) on the door to prevent it from jimmied open. He will call me next week.

9:50 a.m. Swordfish Signs are away with my memory sticks. Time to leave the painters and head up to Unit 29 in the Lynedoch Industrial Estate.

11 a.m. I have been chatting to Iain over at Inverclyde Tool Hire Ltd, who suggests I access the cyberspace marketplace, such as Amazon and eBay, but it's an area of which I am ignorant. I am to meet with Paul of the *Greenock Telegraph at 10 a.m. 12 April.*

12:46 p.m. The Bon Appetit Restaurant, West Blackhall Street, with Rod Stewart belting out, 'We are sailing'. Fish is sizzling in the deep fat fryer. I could go a fish supper right now, but instead I had a scone and I am finishing my coffee. I was chatting to Al the friendly restaurateur and the waitress. *'You should get a sustainable business,'* she advises.

I stopped off at Carpet Rite to get a quote for some floor covering and I met John, who Iain recommended I speak to. I then crossed the busy main road part of the M8, with non-stop traffic flying past in both directions, to get a photograph of the Tomorrow's People team who assisted the Surplus Educational Supplies Foundation last month in the inventory and boxing of textbooks – a small token of my appreciation for the team leaders John, Liz and also their team. I met journalist Paul, who is supportive of the SESF objectives. I am going to have a meeting with him on Thursday next week.

3:35 p.m. Home. I am pricing floor covering. *'I'll phone you back in a wee second,'* he said. I then called the local businessman to whom I gave my SESF folder some weeks ago, and when I tell him about the latest development he says, *'I will give you my honest opinion about your project, she must be worried sick about you.'* He has nothing to offer and said he will leave my folder behind the bar at the pub where he is a regular.

Friday 06/04/2012

3:32 p.m. Home. I am eating a cheese and jalfrezi paste piece. Marion and Mum have gone for a drive and Johanna is studying upstairs.

I met Robert and Bobby the sheepdog at 10:50 a.m. to get the eleven o'clock boat. Bus to Greenock, and another bus to 38 East Hamilton Street to find Alan and Paul, who were about to leave. They have worked hard to cover most of the surfaces with paint, except for the office and toilets. I paid him £195. We then went along to JW Carpets to look at offcuts and then along up McDougall Street to A&J Removals to price shifting some of the library shelving from Unit 29. Robert hailed a taxi back to the bus rank and we got an Ardrossan bus to Wemyss Bay and the 2 p.m. ferry. I am now going to chill out for a bit.

Saturday 07/04/2012

8:19 a.m. MV *Argyle*. It was a bright and clear morning when I went to hang out my working jacket on the clothes line. There were high-flying aircraft streaking across the sky that left trails of

Wednesday 11/04/2012

exhaust fumes, which have now clouded the sky. I am on my way over to 38 East Hamilton Street where I intend to sweep up after the painters. The premises looks a lot smarter than it did a fortnight ago. I hope to open the bookstore by 19 April.

There are clouds over the hills above Skelmorelie and a string of pylons on the skyline. I have made many journeys on behalf of this venture, not all without some purpose.

9:35 a.m. No. 38. Jim, the roofer from Edinburgh, met me as passengers were about to disembark and kindly offered me a lift. I opened up and showed him the 'store', which is indeed looking a lot better. I have put on my overalls and begun tidying up.

11:20 a.m. I have removed the dust sheets and swept the floor and it is time to call it a morning. Should Alan and Paul return the decks will have been cleared. *'It's jist wan system afta another,'* said the problem solver.

12:10 a.m. I had gone up to Brandon Tool Hire Ltd, who were about to close. Alex said they would collect the scaffolding next week, but I managed to persuade them to collect it today if possible and Stephen came to collect it. While I was in the industrial estate I went into JW Carpets Ltd and a helpful individual suggested to leave the floor as it was or paint it, which is something I can do.

Wednesday 11/04/2012

8:30 a.m. Unit 29. I stopped in at Inverclyde Tool Hire Ltd to collect the keys from Paul, who is always welcoming and helpful. I had purchased a takeaway coffee from Cowden's to accompany the sandwiches Marion had made me before I left Kilbarchan, from where I had got the 7 a.m. bus to Paisley and the 7:40 a.m. Gourock train, and got off at Greenock Central. I walked up the hill and stopped in for the brew that cheers but does not inebriate. I am going to grab a few minutes to enjoy my piece before I begin to disassemble the metal shelving.

5:20 p.m. Home. I walked up the road from town. It has been a beautiful light-filled and busy day. Roll it back.

I got the bus from 38 East Hamilton Street to the bus rank in Greenock and another bus to Wemyss Bay. This morning A&J Transport collected two sets of metal shelving from Unit 29. Yesterday, while I was boxing some of the remaining boxes up at Unit 29, this young man appeared at the big door looking for work. He told me that he had come from Poland. I explained to him what SESF was trying to do and I could offer him some work, on a daily basis, if he was interested. He told me that his name was Gerald and that he had come originally from Port Harcourt in Nigeria, and he could meet me today at 38 East Hamilton Street.

Earlier, Nelson the taxi driver told me that the premises was originally a bank. Criminals had the flat in the tenement above the bank and had tried to tunnel their way into the safe below, but on their way in had burst a water main pipe, which had put an end to their tunnelling. A while later, a new occupant of the flat fell through the floor, which the criminals had covered over. The driver related this story to me on the way to No. 38. where Gerald from Port Harcourt, Nigeria via Poland, was waiting to assist me in the assembly of the shelving. We worked well together and Gerald said he would be happy to return tomorrow; he tells me he has come to Scotland to play for Celtic.

Thursday 12/04/2012

8:39 a.m. 38 East Hamilton Street. I have been here since 8 a.m. Joe, the Greenock volunteer, had met me off the 6:15 a.m. boat at Wemyss Bay in his car; he drove us up to Unit 29 Lynedoch Industrial Estate and collected five boxes of books, which I am

Thursday 12/04/2012

about to place on the shelves. He wanted to go up for more boxes but I told him that he had done enough; he is currently painting his house.

8:45 a.m. That's Gerald appeared on the look-out for work. I told him to do what he had to do and, if he wanted, I could give him a job of work too on the refurbishment of the premises.

9 a.m. The Quality Gas man arrived and has found the meter.

9:27 a.m. I have been up the road to Mclean Tool Box Ltd in the Cappielow Industrial Estate to purchase a ladder (£35.99) for Gerald, who is lightly scraping paint off the walls of one of the toilets.

10 a.m. The sun is shining down on East Hamilton Street and Robert the plumber has gone to the Quality Gas depot to see if he can get the parts to repair the boiler. Sheena, the journalist from the *Greenock Telegraph*, has arrived in lieu of Paul and she has snapped a photograph of Gerald from Port Harcourt, Nigeria via Warsaw to accompany her article in next week's edition.

11:30 a.m. Robert the plumber is giving us a demonstration of how to switch on the heating.

12:50 p.m. Robert and his inseparable companion Bobby, the English Sheepdog, arrived about an hour ago and is giving Gerald the third degree. '*Why have you come here?*'
  When Gerald told him that he had come to Scotland to play professional football, he took him away along with Bobby to show him the Morton football stadium at Cappielow.
  I then set off down the M8, with some reluctance, to a McDonald's at the roundabout, where a customer who was in the queue said, '*This is junk food, Burger King is better. What do you do?*'

He asked me what I was doing wearing a boiler suit. When I told him that I hoped to open a charity bookshop up the road, he said, *'You are a book merchant?'* *'I suppose so, among many other things, I have come here to collect some lunch for the team of what will be the bookstore charity shop,'* I said.

It is a beautiful afternoon and riven by the roar from the flow of traffic in and out of Greenock City. I am looking out of the west window, through the rusting wire-mesh grillwork, to the small park at the corner of MacDougall Street where there is a cherry tree in blossom, which cheers me up every time I look at it.

2:15 p.m. We are about to shut 'The Shop' when Karen from the top flat in the tenement, accompanied by her two bulldogs, has a gift of a large poly bag of books. Kindness from my new neighbours.

4:30 p.m. Wemyss Bay ferry terminal waiting room. We got the bus from Greenock having walked through a busy Oak Mall Shopping Centre. I had stopped in at Aitken the Ironmonger Ltd to let David know that James the locksmith had given the SESF bookstore good service. I had also stopped in at Swordfish Signs Ltd, where Stephen had drafted out signage for 'The Book Store'.

I am heading home, it has been a good day. I did what I set out to do with the help of Gerald the Polish Nigerian footballer, Joe the Greenock volunteer, Robert the interrogator, and a host of others, not forgetting the McGill bus drivers.

Saturday 14/04/2012

9:37 a.m. 38 East Hamilton Street. I have not long alighted from the No. 908 McGill's Glasgow Braehead bus. *'How is the wee shop going?'* asked the friendly bus driver when I boarded the bus at the Wemyss Bay bus stop. His recognition and his kindly interest will take me further along this road. It is a gorgeous day.

Saturday 14/04/2012

I am looking out through the window at the cherry blossom and the big shipyard crane towering over all that remains of Scott's shipyard. I am going to change into my boiler suit and see if I can rustle up some transport to ferry some more of the boxes of books up at Unit 29 down the road.

10:12 a.m. I have returned from Jewson's in the Cappielow Industrial Estate, where Mark and Gary behind the front desk were very helpful: they gave me a contact to call for transport. A short time before, as I was walking up East Hamilton Street, a horn beeped and it was Joe, who told me that he had been up at Unit 29 since 8 a.m. and thought he saw Gerald. So what does Joe do? He turns around and returns to look for him and soon he returns with a happy faced Gerald, who is now back on task completing the painting of the ladies toilet. Joe has returned to Unit 29 to continue to disassemble the remaining sections of metal shelving. I am holding the fort.

Joe has returned to tell me that he has taken apart the remaining shelving ready to be uplifted by me on Tuesday, 17 April.

2 p.m. Joe left with Robert, and Bobby the sheepdog, in his car.

2:19 p.m. Gerald has nearly scraped the flaking paint off the walls of the men's toilet and I paid him £30 for his work today. I am ready to call it a day.

Karen and Finlay from up the stairs brought some more books down while I was up the road in the Cartsdyke grocers getting rolls and gammon for a tea break with Robert, Bobby the sheepdog, Gerald and Joe. The former does not stop talking; I listen, but without my firm control he would take over.

The Shipping Clerk Opens the Book Store

Tuesday 17/04/2012

9:18 a.m. Unit 29, Lynedoch Industrial Estate. I arrived here in style by Inverclyde Taxi, moments before Gerald. It is a wet Scottish winter's day in spring and it will not stop me from pressing forward.

10:45 a.m. Stephen, Craig and Paddy showed up with two vans to uplift the boxes and shelving, which I had ready at the big door of Unit 29. I paid them £100 for transport to The Book Store and £10 to take the rubbish away. Out of the blue Stephen, who I have only just met, asks me, *'How do you know Joe?'*, which right away puts me on my guard. I tell him that he is a Surplus Educational Supplies Foundation volunteer, thanks to the *Greenock Telegraph*.

12:10 p.m. No. 38 East Hamilton Street, The Book Store. I walked up the road and into Pottery Row to the restaurant for a couple of sandwiches and two cans of Irn Bru for Gerald and myself; after a damp and grey morning, the sun is shining.

1:30 p.m. Joe arrived to give me a look and has gone back up the road to Unit 29 in the Lynedoch Industrial Estate to take apart the rest of the metal shelving.

1:41 p.m. Gerald has just set off. I paid him £25 and he has made a good start at painting the men's toilet, having scraped them down first. It is time for me to head home.

Friday 20/04/2012

2:31 p.m. Home. I called Inverweld blacksmiths in Port Glasgow and spoke to Iain, who dropped by to collect his payment for affixing a metal strip to the outer edge of one of the double doors. £80. *'Thank you.'*

Tuesday 24/04/201

I called Swordfish Signs Ltd and arranged to meet John at 11 a.m. tomorrow to discuss signage for The Book Store.

Saturday 21/04/2012

9:40 a.m. The Book Store. I got the 8 a.m. boat and was chatting to Rosetta, a recent settler on the island with Scottish roots, who has come from South Africa. She was on her way to the Cardwell Bay Garden Centre to buy a lawn mower. We had got on the No. 908 Braehead bus together. It is a beautiful sunlight-filled morning.

I arrived to find Gerald waiting patiently outside The Book Store, and he changed into the overalls that I had got for him. He tells me that his baby daughter, who had not been well, has had to go into hospital. I am going to change into my overalls.

10:22 a.m. Iain, the Inverweld blacksmith, came by for his £80 for putting a steel plate at the edge of one of the double doors.

12:05 p.m. Joe is showing Gerald how to turn the heat on. Earlier, John from Swordfish Signs Ltd came by. His firm are going to print a large banner which can be attached to the exterior wall of the book store.

Tuesday 24/04/201

10:45 a.m. Home. I made another call to the Sierra Leone High Commission in London and I spoke to Sahir, Minister, Counsellor and Head of Chancery.

11:04 a.m. I am to meet Stephen the scrap metal man and his team at Unit 29 on Saturday 28 April (time?). I called Gerald to ask him if he would meet me there.

Friday 27/04/2012

5 p.m. Home. I was over at noon: bus to Greenock, taxi to Swordfish Signs Ltd. I paid for the signage banner, £480, and I then walked up to the Lynedoch Industrial Estate and collected the keys from Paul at Inverclyde Tool Hire Ltd. I walked down the hill to the Oak Mall Shopping Centre, through it and over to the bus rank, and got the bus to Wemyss Bay.

Saturday 28/04/2012

Unit 29. I was over on the eight o'clock ferry. I walked up to Cowden's for a bacon roll and a cup of coffee. Gerald showed up, and Paddy and Paul with the van, and we loaded some more shelving and chairs and then it was back down the hill and along the M8 to 38 East Hamilton Street. The sun is shining brightly.

We loaded and unloaded the van by 11:30 a.m. I paid the removers £70 (I am overly generous) and Gerald £20, and arranged to meet him here on Tuesday morning. I shut The Book Store and walked up McDougall Street to get the train from Cartsdyke Station to Paisley Gilmour Street Station, where I have arranged to meet Marion at 1 p.m.

Monday 30/04/2012

11 a.m. Home. I received a call from Denis of the Edinburgh Direct Aid charity, to tell me that they have textbooks for schools in Gaza and are unable to send them, and he would like to pass them on to the Surplus Educational Supplies Foundation. I thanked him and gave him the head of Waterfront Edinburgh Ltd security's telephone number, who would allow EDA access to Unit 12.

Tuesday 01/05/2012

8:26 a.m. Tesco café, Greenock. On the way across on the ferry I met Wesley, the local barber, with his family and Nola the bulldog – they are on their way to the vet to have their pet neutered. It is a beautiful beauty filled morning. I am on my way to The Book Store, 38 East Hamilton on the road to Port Glasgow, to get on with it.

8:50 a.m. I have put on my boiler suit. I have great expectations. There is so much to play for.

9 a.m. Gerald has arrived and he tells me that he may have a job with Rainbow Cleaners Ltd; I told him to follow it up as they had told him to come back today and he has just left to go and see the firm's managing director. I will continue to assemble sections of shelving.

9:45 a.m. Gerald has returned to tell me that Rainbow Cleaners Ltd will call him – he knows that he has been fobbed off yet again. At least I can continue to give up some temporary employment. Willie, the car wash man, has come in to ask me if he can tie his sign to the wire-mesh grillwork on the McDougall Street side of the premises and I said, *'Go ahead.'*

I am going up to Brandon Tool Hire Ltd to get some scaffolding so Gerald and I can finish painting the office.

12:30 p.m. Joe has dropped by to discuss what still needs to be done before SESF vacates Unit 29. We agree to inventory and box the remaining stationery, and bring the rest of the shelving down to The Book Store. I gave him a key to 38 East Hamilton Street.

3:30 p.m. Gerald has left with £40, which he earned, and a fish supper got earlier from the Babylon Café up the road.

3:40 p.m. I am about to return the scaffolding to Brandon Tool Hire Ltd.

Saturday 05/05/2012

8:40 a.m. The Book Store. It is a beautiful day. I am going to put on my overalls and see what's next on the agenda.

9:30 a.m. Gerald has arrived and, after putting on his overalls, proceeded to complete the painting of the office.

10 a.m. A supporter has donated a magnificent collection of hockey gear and sports equipment.

11 a.m. Jim the locksmith, and supporter, has come by for a chat.

2:10 p.m. That's me and Gerald shutting the shop. The office is ready, except for the filthy carpet.

Tuesday 08/05/2012

6:34 a.m. MV *Bute*. I am sitting a couple of rows behind the MacKirdy Haulage drivers on the ledge beside the window with a cup of coffee. It is flat calm.

As I cycled down the driveway and out onto the Craigmore Road the sun was up, casting streams of light on the water. Words fail me here to describe the scene, but it made me feel good; I was in a hurry, pedalling as fast I could. The first ATM cashpoint was not working, so I went round the corner to the one on Montague Street, and reached into my pocket for my wallet. Oh no! I had dropped it. I cycled back round, hoping to pick it up and saw a gentleman, who was walking his dog, pick it up and was about to put it into his pocket. '*F— you are lucky!*' he said, and handed me the wallet.

Tuesday 08/05/2012

I got the cash from the machine and dropped four twenties on the pavement. *'Slow down, David!'* said the instructor, his words ringing in my ears. Here I am, into another new day, the prospect beckons and there is nothing else for it but to press forward; the mainland is shrouded in grey mist, with a hint of watery pale sunshine in the clouds above.

7:50 a.m. The Book Store. I have come off the Glasgow bus. The flow of traffic is non-stop, and I take my chances every time I have to cross that road. I put on my overalls and begin to wash down the dusty shelves.

9 a.m. Gerald has arrived and told me that the car wash people in Glasgow have let him down, so I suggested that he give Rainbow Cleaners Ltd another look. I have washed down the walls inside the doorway and I am going to make myself a piece and a mug of tea.

10:05 a.m. Gerald returns, no joy. I make him a mug of tea. I suggest he give the McGill's Bus Company a look tomorrow first thing. We start putting books on the shelves.

3 p.m. The factor from Inverclyde Council has come by with the lease for me to sign and is pleased with the refurbishment that has been wrought on the ground floor of their derelict property.

3:20 p.m. The friendly neighbour from up the stairs came by in a frantic state – a change from her pleasant happy self – told me that they have no gas or electricity, and taps me for £40. This development has unsettled me. I suspect there will be more donations in the future; I firmly believe that what goes round, in the scheme of life's give and take, comes round.

Thursday 10/05/2012

4:29 p.m. I was standing around (which is getting on my nerves) while the instructor was showing the others YouTube footage of Ferraris and tree-felling machinery. He finally got around to demonstrating the safe use of a variety of power tools for drilling and sanding, which was useful. As a class project we were engaged in sanding down the disassembled parts of what had been a hand-crafted garden chair; the instructor showed us how it could be repaired. He was telling us about his very interesting early career in the construction industry, which began in the seventies. He has had, without a doubt, a varied and fascinating career in the construction industry. Good on him!

Friday 11/05/2012

9:45 p.m. Home. This morning, once again, we stand around and wait on the instructor to tell us what we are going to do next. *'What's the matter, David?'* I have unintentionally expelled a big sigh; he has queried me about my huffing and puffing in classes past. I have told him I do this because of my heart condition – he knows full well about the previous classes that I have missed to attend Golden Jubilee Hospital for heart scans and medication etc. – however, this time I let him have my truth and admit to being fed up, hanging about during many classes, not doing anything. Immediately he gets on his high horse and becomes really fizzing furious, and tells me I can go home. Here I go again, doing myself another mischief. I tell him I want to do the paperwork and stick it out for the next four weeks. He is not well pleased when I tell him that his words to me, *'Tae F— off!'* were unacceptable. He then said, *'Don't speak to me like that!'* You should be talking, I think to myself. He tells me to go outside. I returned some minutes later and forced myself to eat yet another humble pie. You groveller! It was either that or kiss goodbye to a lot of effort, commitment and enthusiasm that I had for this course when I started out on my dream project of building a school, one day equipped with the massive amount of fit-for-purpose, surplus to requirements, educational resources that I had already salvaged from the educational system.

Eventually, we got around to filling in forms and review of progress sheets; the instructor sent us home at noon. I had come uncomfortably close, once again, to chucking myself off the course. I have won another round. Only four more weeks to go!

Saturday 12/05/2012

8:48 a.m. The Book Store. I am here off the No. 906 Greenock to Glasgow bus. I had a long wait at the Wemyss Bay bus stop. It is a morning of sunshine with a slight chill in the air. I am here to get on and bring it on, what I have to get on with.

9:15 a.m. Gerald has arrived and is still unable to find gainful employment. He tells me that his wife and children will have to return to Poland. They are living on the money that his father-in-law is able to send them. He has come to Scotland, like so many, with high hopes and dreams that are unfulfilled. There is little painting to be done, so I have given him the job of tidying up.

I met my chum, the McGhie's taxi driver, who was parked opposite Dingbro, the automotive spare-parts firm on McDougall Street. I walked up to Cartsdyke station, crossed the bridge over the railway line and asked the friendly proprietors of the small grocery if they could give Gerald, my Nigerian–Polish friend, some piecework. They said they would keep him in mind. I gave the son of proprietor the business my card.

10:10 a.m. At the moment there is little for me to do. I made myself and Gerald a coffee and I have scoffed two crusty rolls with corned beef. Gerald said he did not want a roll. I am sitting in what was, I presume, the bank manager's office. The room is a great improvement apart from the manky carpet, which I hope to get around to sorting next week.

10:35 a.m. It is too nice a day to remain indoors, the footfall past the door has been non-existent. Gerald has done the little that still required our attention. I suggested that he call on the trades that advertise in the *Greenock Telegraph* offering his service and current work as a painter and labourer for the Surplus Educational Supplies Foundation and take with him the article, *'Charity Book Project Opens New Chapter'* by Paul John Coulter, *Greenock Telegraph*, Tuesday, 17 April 2012. As this next attempt would be worth another try, his gloomy and non-committal nature makes it especially difficult for him to overcome the set-backs he has faced. *'Your attitude determines your altitude'*.

Monday 14/05/2012

22:23 p.m. Home. I am going to call the Sierra Leone High Commission in London.
   Someone comes on the line and says, *'For the Head of Chancery, press one … I am sorry there is no answer, unfortunately all our operators are busy at the moment, please hold,'* and I hold. Sahr comes on the line after a long wait on my part and says, *'We have finished our Independence Day celebrations and now I can look at it.'* He refers to the folder and with it my proposal to ship the next Surplus Educational Supplies Foundation donation of fit-for-purpose educational resources from Greenock City to Freetown, Sierra Leone, West Africa. He tells me that he may come up to Scotland to view for himself what SESF has to offer.
   I need to prepare notes for a proposal outlining the difficulties and possibilities that the SESF initiative presents to education systems in the Third World. Do I make another trip, this time to Sierra Leone, West Africa? *'Often this project has never had a hope of*

succeeding, right from the start. Little effort actually goes into identifying what is really needed and what can work.' The Economist's Tale, by Peter Griffiths, who is one of my supporters from early days.

Tuesday 15/05/2012

9:15 a.m. The Book Store. Gerald has arrived and is making the tea. Earlier, while walking up the main road opposite Morrisons supermarket, I tripped on a small step-like ledge on the pavement and came down with a clatter, landing with some force on the right side of my head. For a few seconds I could not move, meanwhile cars whizzed past in both directions; motorists indifferent to my accident. I managed to pick myself up and kept going until I got here. I wonder what the lasting effects of that knock on the right side of my head will be?

11:05 a.m. Gerald has left, returning to his family. We had another long conversation, in which I attempted to encourage him and suggested he take his family up to Glasgow for the day and said I would finance the trip; he is depressed that he has not found regular employment.

I took him up MacDougall Street to Willie the car wash, whose sign is now attached to the MacDougall Street side of The Book Store. I had noticed that Willie had a few cars in to wash, but he told me that business is slow. He did offer to take Gerald's phone number.

That was a representative from the *Greenock Telegraph*, who wants to sell SESF some advertising space on their website. *'Just a small ad on their website, only £40 per month,'* she said.

Thursday 17/05/2012

1:20 p.m. Home. I called Colin, the operations manager, Texas Instruments Ltd (formerly National Semi-Conductor Ltd), Larkfield Industrial Estate, who said they will let the Surplus

Educational Supplies Foundation have some pallets and boxes and will send me an email to let me know when they will deliver to Unit 29, Lynedoch Industrial Estate. This is another firm that has been absolutely brilliant in their support.

Friday 18/05/2012

10:50 a.m. The Book Store. A short while ago, John, who had sent me his CV, arrived and is shelving the donation of books which I had collected at 9:30 a.m. from the Wemyss Bay Railway Station bookshop. Thanks to you Sheila and to the very helpful Edward, from ABC Taxi, who ran me up the road in his van.

12:30 p.m. John has just left and I suggested he get in touch with Joe who, if they can work together, will be a boon to SESF. I called the Glenburn School to speak to their ECO coordinator, who asked me to follow up a letter of 24 February to contact the branch secretary of the Educational Institute for Scotland.

1 p.m. I called Opus Energy and they tell me to read the meter on the first day of each month.

Tuesday 22/05/2012

9:10 a.m. Unit 29. I arrived here by ABC Taxis 15 minutes ago. I then went over to Inverclyde Tool Hire Ltd to collect the keys from Paul, who is always helpful and supportive.

I got the 6:15 a.m. ferry and the bus at 7:15 a.m. to Greenock, walked across to Tesco and up the escalator to the café, and hung around until it opened at 8 a.m. A roll and link sausage and coffee, which will set me up for the rest of the morning. I later walked across to The Book Store, where I have scrubbed the carpet in the office and rented a Karcher carpet cleaner from Brandon Tool Hire Ltd. I have made some improvement.

Wednesday 30/05/2012

The sun is shining in the west, out of a bright blue sky. I am heading back down the road.

Thursday 24/05/2012

9:10 a.m. Home. The technical department of Park Mains High School in Erskine have called to confirm their offer of technical education textbooks.

Monday 28/05/2012

I was hanging around until midday; five of us were trying to keep busy, tidying up, while the instructor went off to a meeting at the college. In the afternoon we went down to the putting green to continue working on the construction of the small granite sett wall to the base of the floral clock. The sun shone brightly. I was hanging in there, determined to detach myself from the tedium of the whole experience, but at the same time alert and focused to ensure that I was pulling my weight. On the way down to the Winter Gardens I stopped in at the Electric Bakery and purchased a meat bridie, which I shared later with Bob.

Wednesday 30/05/2012

I stood about until I was told what to do. I walked down to the Argyll and Bute Council's builders' yard to collect more granite setts, which we loaded into the council's lorry. I then walked to the putting green, we unloaded the lorry and walked back up to Unit 5 and used the power drill to make our mark on the face of a small block of a granite sett, which would form part of the wall. Shortly after noon, I walked back down the road and we put another layer of setts on the garden wall. It stayed dry all day, but it was cool and overcast.

This morning, the instructor introduced me to the Hilti Power

Tool travelling salesman as someone who was going to build a school. I am glad that I am almost finished this course of daily obstacles, which I have overcome by sheer determination.

Thursday 31/05/2012

12:50 p.m. Home. Today I have completed the nine-month SQA, Level 5, Access to Construction Skills course. We returned to the floral clock garden bed wall to tidy up, and I walked back up the road with a load off my shoulders, mind and spirit. Where this course has led me, only time will tell. Has it been worth it? It certainly tested my capacity to persist and press on regardless to the end.

1:50 p.m. Home. I call Professor Williams in New York, who tells me about her Grenadian project 'Incubate, Education or Development' and is keen to set up something similar in Scotland. In early 2005 she sent some nutmegs from a tree that had survived Hurricane Ivan.

Friday 08/06/2012

3 p.m. Home. I received a telephone call from Jeeva who is the personal secretary to the Sierra Leone High Commissioner in London. *'Land that we love our Sierra Leone.'* She tells me that His Excellency can give me an appointment to see him on Tuesday 19 June at 3 p.m. I mentioned to her that in my email correspondence to the Head of Chancery I had had no acknowledgement of my written correspondence with a proposal to the High Commissioner. *'His Excellency was not interested in that and he did not even have time to read your email,'* said Jeeva.

3:45 p.m. Jeeva has called me to change the appointment. At least I am getting closer to presenting my case for contributing, in a modest way, to their nation's education system, on behalf of the Surplus Educational Supplies Foundation.

Monday 11/06/2012

2:35 p.m. Unit 29, Lynedoch Industrial Estate. I walked up the hill from Morrisons supermarket and dropped off two of my jars of bespoke marmalade to the team at Inverclyde Tool Hire Ltd, one for Iain and the other to Gary as Paul does not like it, and I left my angle grinder with them to see if they can get it to work.

Joe has been busy: he has got five pallets loaded with boxes, which need to be closed.

3:25 p.m. Brenda and Erica from the Wemyss Bay bookshop have arrived with a laptop and other IT equipment.

3:45 p.m. Paul at Inverclyde Tool Hire Ltd is going to show me how to use my angle grinder correctly.

4:15 p.m. Marion has arrived with a magnificent donation of non-fiction reference books from the Inverkip Primary School. Bless her LORD!

Home. She has helped me to make arrangements for my trip next week to London. Off-season peak return, Glasgow to Euston £127.60. Glasgow 5:40 a.m. ETA London 10:12 a.m. for Tuesday 19 June.

Thursday 14/06/2012

10:28 a.m. Home. Yesterday I received a voicemail message from the personal secretary to His Excellency, High Commissioner for Sierra Leone, to inform me that my pre-arranged meeting with him on Tuesday 19 June at 3 p.m. had been cancelled.

Where do go I from here? I have masses of fit-for-purpose educational resources such as games, sports equipment, school classroom library books, textbooks, the entire reserve library stock of the Rothesay Library, Isle of Bute, public library and school and college furniture. What am I going to do with it? Yesterday I called Tessa McKenzie, head teacher of the Samaritan Presbyterian School, Union, St Mark, Grenada, West Indies and spoke to her assistant, who told me that the SESF 40-foot ocean freight container TRIU5079422 had not been released by the Port Authority in St George's.

3:30 p.m. The personal secretary to the High Commissioner has called me to tell me that His Excellency has postponed his departure to Sierra Leone, West Africa, and will see me as arranged. I go with the flow, who am I to blow against the wind?

Monday 18/06/2012

9:40 p.m. Room 304, the Alexander Thomson Hotel, 320 Argyle Street, Glasgow. I have not long checked in and I have borrowed an iron from reception to press my good white shirt. After tea, Marion and Johanna drove me to the pier to get the boat, it was a calm crossing and a watery sun broke through the clouds to brighten the watta. Frank the steward, photographer and supporter from early days, wished me well when I told him where I was going; at this moment I feel inadequate to deal with what I have set in motion. I will take it one step at a time.

On my arrival at Central Station, I walked down the steps to the lower level and out to Argyle Street, under what is known as the Highland Man's Umbrella; here was where a kind soul, who I had met on the Air Canada flight from Halifax, Nova Scotia to Prestwick on 18 May 1973 (who had just graduated from Acadia University in the Annapolis Valley in Nova Scotia), had asked her family, who was at the airport to meet her, to give me a lift and had dropped me off. Culture shock! Where on earth had I landed up? This was definitely not the Scotland of my imagination, but some odiferous city many miles away to the east. Memories of that day in Glasgow city flooded back into my consciousness.

I have got plenty of reading matter with me, *The Times, The Spectator, The New Yorker* and a copy of *The Periodic Table* by Hugh Aldersey-Williams and, as ever, this amount of reading matter is beyond my capacity to read, absorb and inwardly digest, all at once. I am munching an apple. The room is clean and bright and overlooks Argyle Street. Marion has told me not to raise my hopes, all I want from the representatives of the Sierra Leone government is a fair hearing.

Tuesday 19/06/2012

4:55 a.m. Glasgow Central Station. There are not many souls about at this time of day. I will have a wait until 5:40 a.m. to get the London Euston train.

I did not sleep much. The noise of traffic throughout the night kept me wide awake, however, when I was called at 4 a.m. – I had asked the young lads at reception if they would call me in the morning, when I checked in last night – I was sound asleep, and still would be had they not knocked on my door; the luxuries of clean hot water and feeling fresh and ready to go once more out into the fray.

What is the purpose of this meeting with His Excellency the High Commissioner for Sierra Leone? I seek wholehearted commitment and support from the Government of Sierra Leone, West Africa, for a project by the Surplus Educational Supplies Foundation to refurbish a school in their country and supply it with fit-for-purpose educational resources.

'Get yourself a charity and some lottery money, we don't want to see you on poverty street,' said Eric, some five years ago now. I did go through the costly legal rigmarole of the Surplus Educational

Supplies Foundation becoming a Scottish registered charity, and have not applied for funds from the lottery as he had suggested. I am now on poverty street, as a result of purchasing all those containers and incurring the shipping costs and being inundated with educational resources that I am unable to dispose of. If there is some flicker of interest from this West African Government's Ministry of Education, after this meeting with their representatives, I will have explored that possibility; another dead end perhaps? I hope not.

11:20 a.m. I am now in Amigos basement restaurant, Eagle Street, Holborn, London. It is a beautiful day. I found my way here from Euston Station by way of seeking directions from passersby, all and sundry. I have taken up temporary residence in this welcoming establishment and am awaiting a black Americano and a salami sandwich with brown bread. The friendly waitress has given me an Americano on the house.

I found the Sierra Leone High Commission, which is just doors away. I rang the bell, introduced myself and made excuses for making myself known before the appointed time. I was hoping for a little unplanned-for welcome and was told by the hard-faced and tough looking gentleman at reception that His Excellency, who I learned from Wikipedia had once been a magistrate in Jamaica, West Indies, was fully booked until 3 p.m. I wandered around the leafy warren of law courts and exclusive chambers to settle here, where I will cool my heels for the time being.

1:20 p.m. Red Lion Square, ringed by London plane trees, is an oasis of civility and tranquillity, except for the roar and grinding gears of traffic from the main road, which is only a few blocks away and reminds me that I am in the Great Wen and not here for a picnic. I am sitting in the sunshine at the only unoccupied table near the open-air café. A pigeon has just strolled under my table.

The College of Anaesthetists is one of the many venerable institutes that front this square. A siren screams like a dentist's drill

Tuesday 19/06/2012

in my mouth; planes are coming in to land, and that pigeon has returned. The young insouciant, smartly dressed clientele appear to have got it made and do not need to be tied to their desks; do they know what it feels like, I wonder, to be an outsider all your life? It has got cooler now, like their indifference. A cloud has come between me and the sunshine. I have ordered a pot of tea and will be floating into the Thames if I don't watch out.

I bid the square folk adieu and walked around the block, not a few more times, and shortly after 2:30 p.m. I returned to the front door of the Sierra Leone High Commission, where the Sierra Leonean flag hung limply. I pressed the intercom button and I announced that I had an appointment to see His Excellency and was ushered into a small, crowded reception where there was an air of menace. Here, a group of casually dressed men sat on a large sofa, and moved over so I could sit down, but not for long. Gracious Jeeva, the personal secretary, came down the steep stairs and took me up to the office, where His Excellency sat behind a mahogany desk the size of a table tennis table, which had been raised several inches so when I sat down on a sofa in front of him I had to look up.

Immediately he informs me that he is keen to receive surplus educational resources on behalf of his nation's schools. '*You will know that many schools were destroyed in our country's civil war,*' he said. I told him that I was aware that the country had gone through turbulent times, and then he asked me, '*What do you expect from us?*' I told him that a commitment to collaboration and practical assistance with the shipment of educational resources from Scotland to Sierra Leone was what the Surplus Educational Supplies Foundation required. He then told me he could not commit one way or the other, since there were up-and-coming elections. He said he would give my proposal closer attention. I left my revised and up-to-date SESF folder, with my track record to date and the charity's accounts, and asked him to return the dossier to me. I can do no more here.

I called Marion to let her know that I was on my way back to Glasgow. The weather has been balmy. I walked back to Euston Station via more squares, Bloomsbury and Guildford and Camden Town in the flow of humanity, all preoccupied with their own agendas. I was so focused, with no time to dilly dally, to stop and stare where this nation's history emanated from every pore. I recalled my brief bedazzled sojourn in the city in 1965 when I had come from Canada to attend the wedding of my sister Diana. I was glad that I had least accomplished what I set out to do this morning.

Wednesday 20/06/2012

10:15 a.m. Home. Phil gave me a lift not long after I had left the ferry terminal. I received a call from Notre Dame High School asking me to come and collect the geography and English textbooks. I will try and do that tomorrow. I opened a letter from the Educational Institute of Scotland, Inverclyde Local Association executive committee, with a cheque for £500 for the Surplus Educational Supplies Foundation. I am speechless with gratitude.

Friday 22/06/2012

8:12 p.m. Home. I have written a thank you letter to Tom Tracey, the Secretary of the Inverclyde Association of the Educational Institute of Scotland.

Monday 25/06/2012

11:15 a.m. The Book Store, 38 East Hamilton Street. Jim the roofer gave me a lift up the road to meet Jim the Alba gas and boiler engineer; he took away a book about Rangers. I was glad that when plumber Jim called me I did not hesitate to make a point of meeting him – he told me that his sister lived in Easterhouse.

Monday 25/06/2012

Where would that be, I wondered, and when I asked him he told me Craigend. He was in too much of a hurry, but had spotted the book he wanted, he offered to give me something for my charity, but I gave it to him. I got the bus down the road from the bus stop in front of the new flats, built on the site of the Kincaid shipyard, and another bus across from the dentist.

12:01 p.m. I am heading home.

1:17 p.m. The MV *Argyle* is chuddering back to the island with wispy black smoke coming one of the funnels. I am on deck with a breeze at my back and the warmth of sunshine on my face. I have swallowed a cup of soup and a roll and two links.

I am now way out of my depth and have created burdens for myself by accepting more educational resources than I am able to deliver.

8:56 a.m. I spoke to Michele at the Inverclyde Council finance office about a form to pay the SESF The Book Store rates of £765, which I thought had been waived. She was helpful and had noticed The Book Store signage that had fallen onto the pavement.

Marion is in the living room with the vacuum cleaner; should I make that call now? I envisage her extreme displeasure on hearing that I am making arrangements to salvage another collection of textbooks. *'You promised me you would not accept any more,'* she said. I am in a quandary. I feel terrible. I am committed to this initiative, which has cost us both, and the children, so much. What am I going to do if I should bring my activities for the SESF project to a close? I know that I will have to bring it to a close sooner rather than later, but I cannot, not while I still have containers and large quantities of educational resources in storage to deliver to deserving recipients. I will postpone making this call until she is out of earshot. I can well understand the way she feels and her reasons for doing so. *'I don't want to be left with this,'* she said.

Yesterday afternoon I called the Sierra Leone High Commission and spoke to Jeeva. *'He is in Freetown,'* she said. I had been trying to contact him on the telephone numbers he gave me.

Thursday 28/06/2012

Home. I received a call from Park Mains High School, Erskine, to arrange collection of textbooks from the technical department: the building is due to be demolished. I am assailed by the fear of being inundated, swamped, buried under an avalanche of educational resources, which I am now no longer able to transfer into the hands that will further their use.

Tuesday 10/07/2012

12:55 p.m. Unit 29. Marion and Johanna brought me here at 11 a.m. with a load of books from Beverly and Len, which came, I think, from the Macmillan Cancer shop in Rothesay. There is a lot of good non-fiction.

11 a.m. The factor is showing a surveyor from Ryden's around the premises and there had been no indication from him that I should need to vacate Unit 29. He has remarked in the past how tidy the SESF operation looked, but my days are numbered here so I had better get my skates on.

I went over to see Iain and Paul at Inverclyde Tool Hire Ltd, where I always receive an open-handed and friendly welcome. Before setting out this morning I called Joe, who told me that he had driven all the way up to Park Mains High School in Erskine to collect the donation of what I thought were going to be books from their technical department, instead they gave him boxes of books from the home economics department; hopefully they will be put to good use somewhere.

1:05 p.m. I am going to have some lunch: a Scotch pie in a crispy roll and cheese, a cup of lentil soup and a coffee from Aulds the Bakers and Cowden's.

1:20 p.m. I have scoffed that. I am heading back down the road and back across the Clyde. I must now take full responsibility for this lot, which is a wonderful collection of educational resources that must be inventoried, boxed, palleted and shrink-wrapped, and keep a cheerful, positive and visionary disposition to the whole process until the shipment is delivered into deserving hands.

Thursday 12/07/2012

9:22 a.m. Unit 29. It is a beautiful summer's day. I got the early boat and bus from Wemyss Bay to Greenock town centre and walked up the hill and through the memorial park. The Clyde was sparkling before the blue-green hills on the shore beyond. I stopped at Cowden's for my tea-break takeaway. *'Milk and one sugar please,'* I said. And here I am, alone in this big space with good fit-for-purpose educational resources; the challenge is for me to get these educational resources into the right hands.

9:35 a.m. I am waiting for Stephen and Gavin take me up to Park Mains High School, Barnhill Road, Erskine, to see what textbooks remain from their technical department. I am now about to shut the side door, having already closed the roller door.

12:15 p.m. Steven in his Fisher rented van, along with Craig and John, who has been through the Greenock mill and come out the other side as a born-again believer, dropped me off with a load of books, which are not the best but they are bound to be useful. I gave Steven £70 and John and Craig £20 each.

It is a lovely day and I am going to get back down the road and to our home across the watta. I have accomplished what I set out to do this morning. The premises of what was the Park Mains

High School is in a disorganised state; there is no rhyme or reason to the way in which fit-for-purpose educational resources is being disposed of. I found it upsetting to know that what I have salvaged over the last seven years is only a nano, tiny amount from this tsunami wave of unsustainable and unnecessary waste. I must remain focused on the task that I have imposed on myself.

Friday 13/07/2012

8:40 a.m. Unit 29 at the top of Dellingburn Road, across from the incinerator rendering plant that has recently been rebranded from Bri-Mac to HAI Natural Ltd. I arrived here at 8:15 a.m. I walked up from Greenock centre and along Roxburgh Street looking for Rae the glazier, then back along Lynedoch Street and stopped in at Cowden's, where they sure ken ma smiley face. Crispy roll and corned beef, a packet of Walkers pickled onion crisps and a cup of tea, which is now cold.

I have been placing books on shelves; they are new and almost new, thanks to Marion and Inverkip Primary School. I cleaned the office windows. I was going to call Jamie, who I had met some time ago outside the Musicker Café in the island's town centre, to cancel the working appointment that I had made with him for today and I was unable to reach him. I had planned to head home early to relay the slab patio in the garden. I cannot do it all; this initiative is still top priority, no one else is going to do it, except me, so get on with it then.

1:50 p.m. Jamie has just left on his bicycle. He had been assisting me with unpacking and sorting through the donation of textbooks from the technical department of the Park Mains High School in Erskine, and except for our break for a bite, and a bevvy that cheers but does not inebriate, he has been working away and knows just what to do. He is appreciative of the immense value of these secondary school and post-secondary school textbooks.

He declined the offer of a roll and slice, '*I am vegetarian,*' he said. I am heading home.

Monday 16/07/2012

1:22 p.m. Unit 29. My tea is now ice cold, but it will quench my thirst and I look forward to having a packet of Golden Wonder full of flavour cheese and onion crisps with a crusty roll and corned beef. I have been here since 8:15 a.m.

Paul at Inverclyde Tool Hire Ltd sold me a hoe, with which I was later to remove the weeds from the side of this large warehouse. James the locksmith came to put Yale locks on the other two office doors. '*I will teach you how to weld,*' he said. I went back over to Inverclyde Tool Hire Ltd to return a small broom and dustpan – there was nothing else for it but to use what I could get to sweep and remove the weeds. Ian told me that The Book Store banner was down at 38 East Hamilton Street and he kindly lent me his van to go and collect it; bad news – I had locked myself out. Iain tried to contact Riverside Inverclyde Properties Ltd. No answer.

I stepped up to the plate and borrowed the van and borrowed a ladder from the scrapyard machine shop in the Cappielaw Industrial Estate and put the banner back up, which I think looks quite smart. I then drove down the road to the office of Riverside Inverclyde Properties Ltd at Customs House Quay. No answer: apparently, they have moved. I stayed calm. What do I do now?

I then got back into the van. I have just driven the wrong way round the roundabout before the Gourock line railway bridge before Baker Street. Journeying mercies prevailed; there was no traffic at that moment coming towards me. I was on the brink of disaster and was extremely lucky to return the van without incident. I called the security firm but they did not have a key for Unit 29. I saw a customer returning a strimmer to Inverclyde Tool Hire Ltd and went over and asked him if by any chance he was a locksmith? A safe cracker perhaps? Don't be cheeky. He was wearing a Scottish Prison Service jumper and he came to my aid, and fortunately it was just the Yale lock. I went over to Paul to ask him if he had a thin strip of metal: by the time I returned my Good Samaritan had opened the door. Brilliant! I breathed a big sigh of relief. I think it is time to just chill for a bit.

'*Slow down, David,*' he said. I will when I am ready and have a team of able-bodied, willing, honest, fun-loving and multi-skilled folk around me. I have been in enough self-inflicted trouble for one day.

2:15 p.m. John and his team from Harrow Green Transport Ltd arrived with seven boxes of textbooks.

2:49 p.m. Time to move. I have done enough for one day as a self-motivated, self-employed person. I have moved all of the Park Mains High School Technical Department textbook donation into an empty office room prior to having shifted one of the Jubilee Gardens, Ealing Borough Council, library bookshelves into it, where I hope to organise these texts for a display. It has been a busy day which at times was fraught with anxiety. I need to be more careful, and mindful of the task in hand.

Wednesday 18/07/2012

2:23 p.m. Home. I am on the phone again to His Excellency the High Commissioner for Sierra Leone in London. '*We will pursue the matter after elections in November,*' he said. What's the matter? I asked him for the return of my Surplus Educational Supplies Foundation dossier. I had expected some indication from him that his government would be interested in a shipment of educational resources for one of their schools that had been destroyed by the civil war. I am disappointed; where do go from here?

Friday 20/07/2012

12:32 p.m. I called Ross and Company Accountants and spoke to Alyson. I am grateful for their pro bono support.

Thursday 19/07/2012

8:15 a.m. Unit 29. I walked up the hill and along Lynedoch Street from the Greenock bus depot. I got a welcome from cheery Paul, who has arrived in his sports car and is about to open Inverclyde Tool Hire Ltd. My first task of the day is to turn the electricity on, open the roller door and set out the cones before the entrance. I am here to work and begin the task of inventorying the donation of textbooks from the technical department of what was once the Park Mains High School.

12:10 p.m. I am homeward bound. Joe came by at 11 a.m. and we had a good chat. He hopes to have permanent employment soon and his son David might be interested in carrying on where he has left off.

I boxed three large Shin Etsu Silicon Wafer Ltd boxes, a gift from Texas Instruments (UK) Ltd, of inventoried secondary school technical education textbooks, and that is enough work for one morning.

Friday 20/07/2012

8 a.m. Unit 29. The sun has got his hat on. Hip, hip, hooray; bike, the boat and bus, under a mixture of sunny skies and menacing clouds. I walked through the Oak Mall Shopping Centre, all swept and mopped clean, up the steps into Cathcart Square, turned right and up the cobbled streets to the steeper steps, and through the memorial park where the gardeners have shown off their skill and hard graft. I was picking up litter and went across the busy road to Lynedoch Street and into Aulds. *'Good morning, could I have an Americano with hot milk please,'* I said, and then went further along the street to Cowden's for a tuna and crispy roll, a packet of Walkers pickled onion crisps and the *Greenock Telegraph*, to see if there are any vessels sailing to countries where schools might like to receive a shipment of fit-for-purpose educational resources. I wave to Paul across the way as he gets out of his car and I open up. Am I able for this next challenge? I ask myself; in HIS STRENGTH, made perfect in my frailty, yes! I set out the traffic cones at the entrance to the big door. I am going to digest the purvey. I must confess that I have already had a bacon roll and coffee on the boat.

9:21 a.m. Scoffed the treat, now get to work. I am going to inventory the remaining donation of secondary school technical curriculum textbooks. I can hear the incinerators chugging away across on Dellingburn Street.

2:10 p.m. Joe and son David have just left. They have been here working away since 11:45 a.m.

3:10 p.m. I could easily work here all afternoon but the time has come to head homeward.

6:30 p.m. Jim the security guard has called to tell me that there was a baby seagull in Unit 29. Hopefully it will be alright until Monday.

Monday 23/07/2012

7:50 a.m. Unit 29. Jim the roofer fae Auld Reekie, who I met earlier on the ferry, kindly gave me a lift here and gently showed the young seagull the way out of the warehouse – and it was immediately attacked by other seagulls when I tried to feed it. Other seagulls snatched its provender away. It is a damp and grey morning.

2 p.m. It is still raining. I have been reorganising the pallets and emptying some of the boxes of tote trays. I shall have a stack of textbooks from the former Park Mains High School to inventory. I have a dentist appointment at 3 p.m., so it is time to punch the clock and hoof it doon the road.

Tuesday 24/07/2012

9:36 a.m. Unit 29. I arrived here at 8 a.m. I have stopped opening boxes that were not packed properly. I brought a couple more pallets in from outside. I have been putting off the inventory of another pile of technical textbooks, so here goes. I called the island health centre for more statins, aspirin and a waterworks prescription. Call the accountants.

11:20 a.m. I am taking a break. I went up to Cowden's for tea with milk, a packet of pickled onion crisps and a crispy roll and tuna.

2:10 p.m. It is time I stopped. I collected some more pallets from the rear of Lovell the house builders unit. I am going clear my desk and leave.

Wednesday 25/07/2012

8 a.m. I am on deck, for a change, in bright sunshine. I received an email yesterday from Martin, the Inverclyde Properties Ltd surveyor and factor, informing me that I will have to move from Unit 29 sooner rather than later. No sooner do I begin to feel settled enough to make some real progress, than something crops up. I now have to appeal to Inverclyde Council to waive the rates on 38 East Hamilton Street.

Some good news: I received an email from the Rotary in Grenada, West Indies, to say that they would like to receive a shipment of fit-for-purpose educational resources from the Surplus

Educational Supplies Foundation on behalf of a school for which, presumably, they will finance the delivery. For today: I must repack boxes if necessary, pallet and shrink-wrap them ready for removal, work harmoniously with Joe and his son David, and collect the laptop if it has been repaired.

8:10 a.m. The bay is flat calm and the sky is clear but for a few puffy clouds.

10:05 a.m. Unit 29. I walked up the steep cobbled street from the town centre, up the winding steps and through the park and across the road into the electrical appliances shop to purchase a transistor radio from my friend the manager, and went around the corner to Aulds for a treat: an egg and mayo roll, a packet of salted vinegar crisps and an Americano to go. I open up from across to say *'Hi'* to Ian and Paul, who are reassuringly solid positive chums. I am not alone here, so get on with what I have to do. Joe has left a message to say that he has gone to sign on and will be back.

2 p.m. The sun is shining brightly outside. Joe and David have just left. They came at midday and have been sorting through boxes of library books, children's fiction and non-fiction, hard and soft covers, which were all jumbled together, and we have been trying to organise this lot. John, the chip shop man, came over to have a look at what I was doing. He had asked me if I had had any donations of kitchen equipment; he knows Big Colin and the team of his mates who were instrumental last year in enabling me to empty the ocean freight container that held the heavy shelving that I had salvaged from the Jubilee Gardens, Ealing Borough Council Library.

    It's time to wrap up and shut up. Earlier today the factor came by with a prospective tenant to find me inventorying the donation of technical department texts, and he could see for himself that I had everything under control.

Thursday 26/07/2012

8 a.m. Unit 29. I arrived here 15 minutes ago; there is a strong unpleasant smell on the breeze coming from across the road. I wonder what this plant is incinerating today – don't ask. I can hear the roar of the furnaces as black smoke pours from the chimneys; the firm has rebranded itself after complaints from householders nearby. I am going to sort through the boxes of library books. It has to be done and there is no one apart from me to do it.

10:10 a.m. Time for a break. It is grey and cool outside and what a change in the weather from yesterday; you can never rely on the weather, which mirrors the constant change on many different levels that affects us all. I head over to Lynedoch Street and return with a tuna mayo and an Americano. I forgo the usual packet of crisps and have in addition Johanna's gift to me of an upmarket sandwich with brie and slow-roasted vegetables.

12:30 p.m. The time has come to say enough is enough for one day entirely on my own. Slowly, but surely, I am bringing order out of this mass of educational resources, which unfortunately had been boxed in a haphazard manner. The boxes will all have to be repackaged – their two-hour four-day stint, application to the task in hand, was not up to standard. I will be forever grateful for their company and input as they kick started this huge task that looms before me.

Friday 27/07/2012

7:45 a.m. Unit 29. Here I am again and the sun is shining brightly at the side-door entrance to Unit 29. I made the boat with a few minutes to spare. A bus up the road and walk through the town centre of Greenock, up cobbled Bank Street, up the steps and into the litter-free park with sunshine on my face, the across the busy road along Lynedoch Street to Hope Street. I am going to inventory and then pack books.

10:25 a.m. I have stopped work for a tea break. Americano coffee wi' a wee drap o' milk fae Aulds Bakery Shop and then into Cowden's for a tuna mayo in a crusty roll and a packet of Golden Wonder cheese and onion crisps.

10:45 a.m. I called the Sierra Leone High Commission. *'One moment please, unfortunately we are busy, please hold,'* she said, and when I did wait the receptionist returned to tell me to call back at 11 a.m. *'We do nothing until afta' de elections in Novemba.'*

My high hopes are dashed; why do I bother to keep on knocking at this door? I then return to the inventory of secondary school textbooks.

2:50 p.m. I have done enough for the day. I could easily work away until I had re-boxed and palleted the lot. I can only do so much. Home.

Saturday 28/07/2012

10:20 a.m. Greenock city centre church café. The sun is shining over the rooftops to the Clydeport container base cranes. I have just called John, who gave me hospitality and a lift into Greenock many months ago, and I am about to return his kindness to me that morning.

I had got the MV *Bute* 9 a.m. ferry and the McGill's Glasgow bus up the road. I posted letters in the Oak Mall post office and walked back to see if the computer repair shop was open, as Rizza said it would open at 10 a.m. I will return there in a wee while.

It is dreich outside. I walked up from the town centre a short while ago. John joined me for coffee at Struthers Café and then took me along to his upstairs flat to show me the massive amount of work he has taken on in rebuilding the premises and access stairs at the back of his property. I then returned to the computer shop and collected the laptop for David, the top Greenock volunteer, and hoofed it up Bank Street and through the memorial park to here. I called Joe, his dad: he can't make it up here to collect the laptop. I asked him if he could check out The Book Store at 38 East Hamilton Street and leave the keys behind the door. He is on a course for carers, so I feel that he is beginning to distance himself from SESF, and rightly so: he has done a lot of work that has kept this show on the road.

12:07 p.m. I am enjoying a coffee and a doughnut from Aulds the Bakers. That's the drizzle off. The roar of the incinerators in the waste disposal factory across the road is non-stop. A fly lands on my doughnut. *'Shew fly! Yoh mudda doan cook?'* Right, get down to the inventory of all these wonderful books.

3:10 p.m. I have just had three curious visitors. I let them choose a book each, gratis.

Monday 30/07/2012

7:20 a.m. Unit 29. Chilly, overcast grey skies but dry. Jim the roofer dropped me off at the corner of Hope Street. I walked up Dellingburn Street. The gates to the industrial estate were shut. Andy the Lovell Homes builder man said hello to me while waiting to drive in. I was about to walk round to the Hope Street entrance when Jim the security man appeared; he is friendly. I told him I was looking for containers and he told me that Bateman, up the back of the estate, rented them out. Here I am with another pile of secondary school technical subject textbooks to catalogue and place into Box 9. I told Marion that I would be back on the one o'clock boat. Gulls are screeching away.

10:15 a.m. That's all of the Park Mains High School Erskine collection of textbooks and miscellaneous texts that I salvaged weeks ago catalogued and boxed into nine Shin Etsu Handotai Ltd new boxes a gift from Texas Instruments, in all an incredible addition to any library. I am going to stop work and head for home.

Tuesday 31/07/2012

8 a.m. Unit 29. The smell of whatever they are burning next door is wafting on the gentle breeze past Unit 29.

I was on the early boat, MV *Bute*. Iain the steward asked me how it was going and I told him what my plans were for today and he gave me a white coffee. I sat up the stern end and read Amy's birthday present to me: The Boy who Harnessed the Wind by William Kamkwamba and Brian Mealer. I chatted briefly with Mike, the McGill's bus driver, who asked me if I knew the Peugeot dealer on the Drumfrochar Road. Then Ed, the Rothesay librarian, pitched in and said, 'I don't wish to be judgemental, but should you not be retired?' I tried to be civil in my reply, and mumbled something like *'I don't bowl, play golf or hang out in the local hostelry'*, instead of saying to him *'Why do you all have to be so curious, why can't you just mind your own business?'*

10:40 a.m. It is time to say enough is enough. I am on my own. I am heading home.

Wednesday 01/08/2012

8:20 a.m. I arrived at Unit 29 at 8 a.m. There is a smirry, non-stop drizzle from a blanket of thick grey cloud. I was chatting as usual to all and sundry on the way over: see that yon hail fellow well met geezer, he's aye bummin' his chat on the boat; it is all grist for my mill. I met Bruce the tree feller from Skye again, who I had met yesterday afternoon at the Mount Stuart Trust Bute Sawmill as I

Friday 03/08/2012

was about to leave with a pile of timber on the roof of Marion's motor. I also met the sister of Sandra, the Beachwatch Bute operative. *'You will know Tiger,'* she said.

I am not for being incinerated just yet; there are cries and screams, with cynical squawking chuckles, from the seagulls flying low above the roar and sooty, heavy smell from the chimneys. From across the street I engage the driver of Tracey Demolition Ltd of Linwood who is collecting one of the big skips round the back of Unit 29, and who expresses an interest and support for my salvage efforts. Stop your scribbling – there are 15 unopened boxes of books at the far end of the unit which must be opened and catalogued, so get on with it.

9:50 a.m. I walked over to Aulds the Bakers. A friendly soul who makes the sandwiches greets me. *'Can I have an egg mayo please,'* and I cashed in my card for an Americano.

2:05 p.m. Joe has arrived with the keys for The Book Store; David, top Greenock volunteer, has been here working away on the inventory of texts, re-boxing and then loading them onto pallets and shrink-wrapping them. His help, and that of his dad, has been invaluable. It is pouring with rain and I called a taxi for him. David has been here since 11:30 a.m. and I reckon that he has done enough voluntary labour for one day. I think it is time for me to drag myself away; together David and I have cleared another space out of this lot. Slowly but surely there is some order.

Friday 03/08/2012

8 a.m. Cool morning but dry, and there is sunshine on my face as I walk from the Greenock town centre.

10:15 a.m. Janet and Gordon from the science department of James Watt College have delivered a boxload of new textbooks that have been replaced by the new edition. *'All they have done is changed a couple of diagrams,'* she said.

11:30 a.m. David appeared and set to work with me sealing and shifting boxes of books onto pallets.

2:50 p.m. I am heading home and we have made another big step forward with this lot.

Saturday 04/08/2012

8:55 a.m. Unit 29. The Hope Street entrance gate was shut. I had to walk round and up Dellingburn Street with the stink of carbonised offal in my nostrils. I answered nature's call, cleaned the toilets and sinks, changed into my boiler suit and got to work.

10:45 a.m. David arrived for work.

11:30 a.m. Joe came and took us down to 38 East Hamilton Street, where I collected the mail, got a shovel and broom, and removed the weeds from around the outside edge of the building and swept up. Joe swept and washed down the entrance to the bookstore.

2:45 p.m. That's me and David getting ready to go. We have been working away steadily, cataloguing, labelling, repacking, packing, sealing boxes and placing the boxes on pallets to be shrink-wrapped later.

Monday 06/08/2012

8:15 a.m. Unit 29. I walked up from the corner of Hope and Dellingburn Streets, where Jim the roofer from Auld Reekie had dropped me off. It is grey and damp.

I came across the watta on the MV Bute early boat. I was

Tuesday 07/08/2012

chatting to Michael, from Aberdeen via Liverpool I think, who works for Subsea Leasing. *'Our office is next to Bibby,'* he tells me, and he went on to tell me about his time spent in Equatorial Guinea, which is controlled by a dictatorship, and that there are West African engineers in the firm that he works for. We first met seven years ago when I was based at the boat yard in Port Bannatyne. He kindly offered me a lift to Greenock. I thanked him as I knew that Jim the roofer, who I had seen earlier when I went to buy my ticket, would have a lift for me.

10:15 a.m. That's David on his way. He asked me if I was going to be here tomorrow, and I told him that I would be.

He came at 10:45 a.m. and together we have boxed and palleted all of the books except a donation of non-fiction library books from the primary school in Inverkip. The time has come for me to knock off; everything is slowly coming together.

Tuesday 07/08/2012

8:15 a.m. Unit 29. It is a beautiful day of sunshine and slightly cloudy skies. I arrived here 15 minutes ago and I have been footerin' aboot, so it is on with a clean boiler suit, thanks to Marion my love.

I travelled over with Johanna on her way to Aberdeen. She bought me a coffee and we sat looking back at the Isle of Bute as it disappeared into the distance. I am here, once again, to prepare this salvaged collection of educational resources, textbooks, reserve library stock books from the Rothesay library, school furniture and sports equipment for somewhere worth our joint effort, that myself and others have taken the trouble to bring together and prepare for shipment in one of the Surplus Educational Supplies Foundation's 40-foot ocean freight containers. There will be problems and difficulties in the way ahead but, for the time being, what needs to be done in the here and now is pretty straight forward.

To do today: shrink-wrap the pallets; reduce the large pile of empty cardboard boxes to be flattened; tidy the rest of the Unit 29 area allocated to the use of the SESF; and assemble the shelving on the Jubilee Gardens Library bookcases to make a display for visitors to the unit.

10:45 a.m. David arrived in good spirits and was keen to work; he brought with him bacon rolls and tea.

2:30 p.m. He left for home and so I am heading out; neither of us will be here tomorrow. A day off. I should record here that the voluntary help received from David and his dad, Joe, has been indispensable in making the prospect of another shipment of fit-for-purpose educational resources a success.

Wednesday 08/08/2012

10:35 a.m. I am calling the Sierra Leone High Commission in London. *'He said he has sent the document to you,'* said Jeeva.

Thursday 09/08/2012

8 a.m. Unit 29. Over on the MV *Argyle*, bus up to Greenock town centre, cross the busy main road. I walked past the craft butcher shop and I walked up the steep Sir Michael Street. It is cloudy and cool. Sunbeams are breaking through the clouds, as I walk along Lynedoch Street and down Hope Street, which is now a familiar route; for a change there is no putrid smell coming from the incinerator rendering plant across the road. I am going to box the home economics texts salvaged from Park Mains High School. I thought I had done the lot.

11:10 a.m. I go across the road to HAI Natural (Bri-Mac) to meet Chick, who Iain at Inverclyde Tool Hire Ltd had recommended I speak to. There I met Stephen, the aforementioned firm's operations manager, and his colleagues who have offered to assist SESF with the loan of a forklift.

11:15 a.m. Chick came by to see what was required and said he would return later with a forklift.

11:45 a.m. David has arrived with bacon rolls and two teas from John the Chip Shop at the corner of Lynedoch Street. I had already been up the road for my 'play piece' but I can still tuck in again. David has helped me to take a tally of the boxes: 186 boxes on 16 pallets.

12:05 p.m. I am going to complete the inventory and boxing of the home economics texts.

12:10 p.m. That's Chick with the Toyota Tonero 30 forklift to make spaces between the each of the pallets. I record here what is now before me.
- Pallet One: 12 boxes of children's paperback books
- Pallet Two: 12 boxes of children's library books
- Pallet Three: 18 boxes of mathematics textbooks and learning support texts
- Pallet Four: 14 boxes of adult fiction and non-fiction books
- Pallet Five: 10 boxes of new jotters/exercise books and stationery
- Pallet Six: 12 boxes of language curriculum textbooks
- Pallet Seven: 17 boxes of language textbooks
- Pallet Eight: 9 boxes of language textbooks
- Pallet Nine: 12 boxes of language textbooks
- Pallet Ten: 8 boxes of language textbooks
- Pallet Eleven: 8 boxes of binders
- Pallet Twelve: 12 boxes of binders and tote trays
- Pallet Thirteen: 12 boxes of binders and wallets

- Pallet Fourteen: 11 boxes of geography textbooks
- Pallet Fifteen: 9 boxes of science textbooks
- Pallet Sixteen: 10 boxes of science textbooks

12:50 p.m. Chick is brilliant and is a great encouragement to me! Nothing is too much trouble for this competent, helpful and friendly human being, who before this afternoon I had never had the privilege of meeting. *'He likes doin' that sort of stuff,'* the Bri-Mac operations manager said to me when he gave me his business card.

1:34 p.m. The sun is shining brightly between a few puffy clouds sitting over the Clyde flowing west before me. I am going to call it a day. Another significant step forward has been made today in preparation for shrink-wrapping each of the 16 pallets, thanks to Chick and Bri-Mac, who has shown me how and has brought the roll of polythene bags that go over the top of the pallets and a roll of Visqueen to wrap around them.

Friday 10/08/2012

8 a.m. Here I am again at Unit 29, with a whiff stink wafting on the breeze blowing in here. There are 16 pallets before me to be shrink-wrapped, so get started.

1 p.m. David has gone up to the chip shop. The surveyor has come by – he seemed pleased to know that some progress has been made with the packing and palleting of resources; they want me out of here pretty soon. I told him that I would need a smaller area for storage and wondered if they could offer me anything pro bono. Where to I wonder? I will cross that bridge when I come to it, is a beautiful day outside.

3:05 p.m. The time has come to head home.

Saturday 11/08/2012

9:21 a.m. Unit 29. Gary the forklift driver par excellence from across the road, 'The Plant', came over with the HAI Natural forklift and has just shifted 16 pallets and 3 with library books.

I went over shortly after I arrived, after changing into my boiler suit. *'He might do for you,'* he said as I was about to say goodbye to him at the main door of the unit. He had remembered the skid that I had asked him if he could repair in Bri-Mac's machine shop; I had taken it over earlier in the week, along with a box of 4 new castors purchased from Aitken the ironmongers. Gary took it up to the Bri-Mac office and Sandy the machinist came down with it, and he said he would do it right away.

1:30 p.m. Robert and Kenneth have moved into Unit 18. They were interrogating me until 2 p.m. David has had to leave, meeting with his family.

2:50 p.m. I could quite easily keep on keeping on, doing what has to be done. A lot has been achieved today thanks to the HAI Natural (Bri-Mac) team, and not least David, who has helped me to shift most of Jubilee Gardens heavy-duty library shelving units.

Monday 13/08/2012

8 a.m. An early boat. I chat at the bus stop with Ed the Rothesay librarian and power walk up Sir Michael Street, over to the newsagent on Roxburgh Street for *The Herald*, and put £10 on my phone. I walk down the road and meet Paul the mechanic at Unit 2, who tells me that it has been broken into. I take keys off my key ring, change into my boiler suit and am ready to roll.

10:25 a.m. I have stopped for a break. I called the factor and time-served roofer, who tells me that he is bringing the new tenants before lunchtime.

That's RIG Arts and Company here to make a film. I met Jason and David from the crew who are amiable millennials.

12:55 p.m. That's everything shifted into a more confined area. I have been working on my own non-stop; it is time to head home.

Tuesday 14/08/2012

9:10 a.m. The Star Café, High Street, Glasgow. Train up from Wemyss Bay. After a grey and wet morning, the sun is shining down on the High Street. I have an appointment at 1 p.m. with Dr Mozzamel M Huq, Chairman of Charity Education International, in Room 617, Department of Economics, Sir William Dunn Building, University of Strathclyde. I will call him and see if he will see me earlier.

Meeting with Dr Huq, who comes from Bangladesh. He wants IT kits and tells me that his charity set up the best library in North Bengal and works with the charity Books Abroad. *'Go to someone who knows how to make an application and apply to Awards for All,'* he said. He can't get over the personal funds that I expended on the Surplus Educational Supplies Foundation. He had expressed much interest in what I had accomplished during our telephone conversation weeks ago, but this meeting was a disappointment.

Wednesday 15/08/2012

8 a.m. Unit 29. It is a beautiful morning – there was a cool breeze at my back as I cycled into sleepy Rothesay town. I am carrying a recycling Bute Futures Ltd bag with a tarpaulin. Sunrise over Wemyss Bay. While at the bus stop I meet up with Ed the librarian, who is dressed for hillwalking, and asks me, *'How d'ya sleep at night?'* I ignore the query.

Friday 17/08/2012

On arrival in Greenock City I trudged up Sir Michael Street and here I am.

12:35 p.m. David has left: he came at 11:15 a.m. I make him welcome at whatever time he appears; he brought bacon rolls and tea. There is nothing more for me to do here for the time being.

I was aboard the MV *Argyle* early this morning with the breeze at my back and with the other tarpaulin balanced on the handle bars. George, the ace photographer and steward, did not have any string. *'I'll see what the boys can give you,'* he said. He returned with several metres of new nylon rope, which I can use to lace the two tarpaulins together.

Friday 17/08/2012

8 a.m. Unit 29. The kettle is boiling. Rain. I have changed into my clean boiler suit, which I had taken home on Monday.

It is a very wet and grey morning trudging up Sir Michael Street, off the busy roundabout across Roxburgh Street I cross the road to the newsagent beside the chemist and along from the Salvation Army Citadel, which is opposite the New Roxburgh Tavern. I bid good morning to the bearded proprietor, and two lads immediately get into a smart limousine and drive away. I purchase *The Herald* and as I get to Lyle Street the smell of burnt bovine flesh and bones, and whatever else, hits my nostrils.

I trudge and I trudge. I am wearing out this route to 'My Work' to Lynedoch Street. I turn up past Clyde Car Components Ltd and acknowledge the gaffer, the chief executive, the manager, in a crisp white shirt and tie, who is always standing behind the counter, and who invariably catches my eye as I walk past. Down Hope Street I take care to watch my step on these ancient cobbles. The gates this side of the Lynedoch Industrial Estate are shut, so I continue down the street and up Dellingburn Street and into the industrial estate, just in time. Relief.

I am going to make the most of Another day in Paradise. Yes, instructor, I will do that, exactly that. The Inverclyde Tool Hire proprietor roars in ahead of me. Here I am scribbling. What lies ahead of me today? Many thanks to Louise of the James Watt College's estates department, who is going to have some Formica-topped, solid metal-legged classroom tables delivered. There was a call from Janet of their science department offering more textbooks, and I am to let her know when I would like them delivered. David is going to come today to lend a hand.

I will soon have enough SESF educational resources palleted and ready for uplift. Where to? And who are the deserving beneficiaries who will get the maximum benefit from this marvellous and unique collection of educational resources? I am working on it.

8:25 a.m. I am sitting on the desk holding on, tenuously, to this space for a wee while longer.

9:19 a.m. Gerry and Taff, the janitors from James Watt College, have arrived with the tables.

9:52 a.m. I am having a mug of coffee and waiting for David to show up. I have returned from John's fish and chip shop with a can of Irn Bru and a single fish. '*I am going to give you some chips and two teas,*' said John. '*That's most kind of you, John,*' I said.

David, who came earlier with bacon rolls, is off to get his mum's messages. In the interim, Gerry and Taff, the janitors from James Watt College, have been backwards and forwards with more tables, which now number 64.

2:10 p.m. They have just delivered 41 chairs, brand new, and 4 big tables.

3 p.m. I am on the bus for Wemyss Bay. The sun is now cracking the sky and it is back to summer again. At 2:30 p.m. Taff, who comes from Anglesey and has been living in Scotland for 22 years, came by with another load of chairs and he kindly gave me an orange and a lift down to the bus stop opposite James Watt College. Well that's it for another day.

Saturday 18/08/2012

8:40 a.m. Unit 29. I was slow in getting off the island. I am so tired in every way. No support. I am pushing forward. There is a damp blanket of thick grey cloud sitting low on top of me. I am here to keep faith with all who have helped me this week: David, Iain, Paul, Gerry and Taff, Colin and team, David Martin and RIP Ltd, and Chick and Gary from across the road.

I am going to put on the boiler suit, don my cap and get back on to the stage. Before boarding the ferry I was chatting to Dougie, the harbour supervisor, who said to me, *'It must be frustrating being up against a brick wall all the time.'*

10:45 a.m. I have taken down a section of the shelving which was salvaged from the Rothesay Library's refurbishment. I have been up the road to Cowden's for a corned beef in a crispy roll, a bottle of water and a copy of the *Greenock Telegraph*. I am heading back across the watta.

Monday 20/08/2012

7:45 a.m. Jim, the roofer from Edinburgh, gave me a lift up the road along with Ian the IBMer and he was telling us that the Big Blue, which has been a massive industrial presence in Silicon Glen for almost 30 years, was shedding staff and relocating to Cairo.

9:25 a.m. Robert from Unit 18, who tells me that he is the inventor of a new fire escape ladder, has come by to collect some wooden chairs which he said he would sand and varnish.

Later: he and his workmate Kenneth are off down the hill to Morrisons for hot rolls and have invited me to join them.

10:25 a.m. Gerry and Taff from James Watt College have arrived with a load of more quality classroom furniture and textbooks. I was chatting to keen Aron, who tells me that he builds sets for stage plays; he is Robert the inventor's son. I told him that I would give his name to Jason the film maker. I am going to have a look through the delivery of textbooks from James Watt College; this lot of resources could be the basis for a teacher and student resource centre.

1:30 p.m. Jason, artist and film maker, has come by for a chat. I gave him Aron's phone number.

2:22 p.m. The sun is shining brightly. I have been unpacking the boxes of books from James Watt College: Biology; Chemistry; Biochemistry; Physics; Business Studies and English. All recent editions and virtually new. I am knackered, ready for a siesta, and ready to shove off.

I have to await the return of Gerry and Taff with more precious resources in the JWC van, so I might as well have a go at the inventory of this treasure trove of textbooks.

3 p.m. I am heading home.

4:24 p.m. Wemyss Bay Picr. I got the bus from Union Street, having walked down Brisbane Street from the post office where Gerry and Taff had dropped me off. I was about to leave Unit 29 when they appeared with more large tables.

Tuesday 21/08/2012

10:15 a.m. Unit 29. I got a taxi from the Holiday Inn where I had attended a meeting of the Greenock Chamber of Commerce. *Embrace the Space. A Digital Social Media Presentation.* I did not get off to a good start – as I was about to shake someone's hand I spilt my cup of coffee.

11 a.m. I received a marvellous delivery of educational resources, in mint condition, from the Spango Valley Glenburn School. I receive word that Michael from Glasgow, a chum from the early days, and Eric from Monrovia, Republic of Liberia, West Africa, who are from the Church Fellowship of Sandyford Henderson Memorial Church, Glasgow, are coming to view the educational resources in Unit 29 on 23 August at 10:30 a.m. This may be good news. I will have to wait and see.

1:50 p.m. It is time to leave. I have an appointment with the dentist on a beautiful afternoon.

Wednesday 22/08/2012

9:15 a.m. Home. I made contact with the very helpful Scottish Development International office, who are going to send me a list of Scottish firms operating in West Africa.

Thursday 23/08/2012

8:32 a.m. MV *Argyle* en route for Rothesay, Isle of Bute. I was aboard this vessel at 6:30 a.m. bound for Wemyss Bay. High ho, off to work I go. As I was walking up the pier I reached into my back pocket for my wallet. Oh no!

I searched my overflowing haversack. Could it be at home? No, because I had taken my ferry pension card out of it prior to

THE SHIPPING CLERK OPENS THE BOOK STORE

Unit 29, Lynedoch Industrial Estate, Greenock, Thursday 23/08/2012,
Top: The two Davids welcomed Eric Nyuma, Project Research Officer to the assistant minister of administration, Ministry of Finance, Monrovia, Republic of Liberia. Eric was on secondment to the School of Development Studies, University of Glasgow.
Bottom: Eric was made welcome by the RIG Arts team with whom we shared Unit 29. Thanks to Riverside Inverclyde Property Holdings Ltd., later that year SESF was to ship a 40' ocean freight container of curricular materials from Glenburn School and many other schools to a school in Paynesville, Republic of Liberia.

ticket purchase. There was nothing else for it but to retrace my steps. The stewards, John, Ian and Martin, were very helpful; John called the ticket office at my home port – yes, my wallet had been handed in, but Marion Hanschell had collected it and Marion was now on the 7 a.m. boat. I called her, thanks to mobile telephony: she would hand it in to the Wemyss Bay ticket office. *'Slow down, David!'* I can't move much slower. *'The steps and stops of a righteous man are ordered by the LORD. Amen.'* I kept my composure. I just unpicked the knots from that fankle and took the break in my stride.

9:40 a.m. Unit 29. I got a taxi up from Greenock town centre. The taxi driver told me that he once worked for an electronics facility in the unit occupied by Rainbow Cleaners Ltd and he said he knew Gary the forklift operator, who at that moment was delivering some pallets from the plant across the road.

11:35 a.m. The Book Store, No. 38 East Hamilton Street, with Michael and Eric, who tells me that he is a research and project officer in the office of the Assistant Minister Administration, Ministry of Finance, Monrovia, Republic of Liberia, West Africa, on secondment to the University of Glasgow School of Development Studies. Michael then drove us back up the hill to Unit 29 to view the palleted resources and what remained to be inventoried and boxed.

2:31 p.m. David has left with his parcel, which I had brought over with me this morning. I had introduced him to the visitors from Glasgow and the RIG Arts team. Later, Robert the inventor from Unit 18, before I knew it, was making arrangements of his own with Eric.

The sun is shining. I have made myself a coffee and I am about to list the priceless life sciences textbooks from James Watt College.

The Shipping Clerk Opens the Book Store

Friday 24/08/2012

9:40 a.m. Unit 29. I got a taxi up from the town centre and it's just me here at the moment. What next?

I call Eric at Grange Dock – do they have any 40-foot, seaworthy, ocean freight containers at Clydeport Ocean Terminal for sale? None for sale.

10:30 a.m. I have two visitors, business advisers Will and Alistair from Inverclyde Council Small Business. We spend time chatting, then David appears with bacon rolls and tea; he is now talking with them.

11:45 a.m. Gerry and Taff from James Watt College have brought some more tables and new executive swivel chairs.

2:45 p.m. Paul, practice team leader, the Action For Children charity, Scotland, has come by to ask for some tables. How many do you want?

4:42 p.m. I am waiting for Gerry and Taff, who said they would return. I told the James Watt College estates office that I would be here until 5 p.m. It is now raining. I am entirely on my own and it goes with the territory when you use your initiative and embark on a task that is way beyond your capability. *'It's on your own head,'* he said to me, all those years ago.

Saturday 25/08/2012

9:15 a.m. I called Freight Container Services (Scotland) Ltd, who tells me he has a high cube 40-foot at Duncan Adams Transport Ltd Grange Dock for sale: £2,200 plus VAT. I then called Tom Walker, the container surveyor, who will inspect it to see if it can be given a CSC seaworthy plate or not.

Monday 27/08/2012

12 noon Call Duncan Adams Transport Ltd to let them know that Tom will be there on Tuesday 28 August to inspect the container. I then call Knight Watson, freight forwarders, Grangemouth to see whether they can get the box to Monrovia, Republic of Liberia.

Monday 27/08/2012

8 a.m. Unit 29. Into the town for the early boat with the wind on my tail. I must make sure I don't lose my wallet this time. It is a blanket grey morning. I meet Joe, former pupil at the Port School, who tells me, '*I've got an apprenticeship to study engineering.*' '*That's great Joe, who with?*' I ask. '*Ferguson at Ardmaleish,*' he tells me.

7:10 a.m. Bus up to town centre. Smirry rain. I don my cycling jacket and its an up the hill effort along and down the road. I buy *The Herald*. The top gate is shut, so it is down Hope Street. I am ready to begin another week.

11:30 a.m. Andy and Aron from Unit 18 are around for a chat. Gerry and Taff deliver two new office desks. I have been listing teaching English as second language texts.

11:45 a.m. I was going to go up the road for something to eat, but it is raining heavily, so I will keep on working for the time being.

12:40 p.m. Still bucketing down, but I shall pack it in and head down the road. Enough is enough.

12:50 p.m. Before I leave the premises, Stephen, an associate of Paul from the Action For Children charity, assisted by helpers, brings over a 'new' table tennis table.

3:15 p.m. Home. I cycled through a strong wind and drizzle. The Hebridean Princess is tied up at Rothesay Pier. I make some telephone calls to Tom. *'We are on the motorway just now. Can you call me later. I will inspect the container tomorrow,'* he said. I call John the freight forwarder in Liverpool – no answer. I spoke to Knight Watson, then Gary and the London Mining Co Ltd.

4:38 p.m. That's me been on the phone all that time. Johanna has just brought me a mug of tea. I am now going to lie down.

Tuesday 28/08/2012

8:05 a.m. Unit 29. It is a clear-sky morning with a few puffy clouds brightened by sunshine.

I walked up the hill and here I am, going to inventory and box the remaining marvellous collection, the uplifted salvage donation, the just-in-time rescue of textbooks from James Watt College *(now rebranded as West College Scotland, Greenock Campus, as I type my script at 11:35 a.m. Tuesday, 8 February 2022).*

This morning, Tom Walker will be inspecting, checking over, a 40-foot high cube to be brought out from the Duncan Adams Transport Ltd stockpile of containers at their Grange Dock yard. I have started the moving out, removal process from Unit 29 and divesting the Surplus Educational Supplies Foundation of its own stockpile of educational resources. *(Little did I know then that it would take this Shipping Clerk another five years before he was able to dispose of those resources that were in storage at sites all over Scotland.)* Meanwhile what is Eric of Monrovia, Republic of Liberia, now a student at Glasgow University and a member of the Sandyford Henderson Memorial Church, going to do?

That's the sunshine outside. Get started

10 a.m. Gerry and Taff have delivered some more desks.

10:35 a.m. Paul from the charity Action For Children has brought

Saturday 01/09/2012

over a roll of printing paper, HP Bright White Inkjet Paper (36" x 150'/914 mm x 45.7 m.)

11:05 a.m. Jason came by to tell me that he had sports equipment from his last RIG Arts project. Thank you. All donations gratefully received.

11:30 a.m. Gerry and Taff back with more heavy office furniture.

11:45 a.m. The film crew came over when they saw me trying to move a heavy desk and they wanted to use the table tennis table. Fair exchange.

12:20 p.m. It's time to stroll. I have a dentist's appointment at 2:20 p.m.

Friday 31/08/2012

2:54 p.m. Home. I received a call from Frederick, in Edinburgh via Tanzania, who wishes to come and see what resources SESF has at Unit 12, West Shore Business Centre, Granton.

I call Clydeport Ocean Terminal, who tells me that they will waive the handling charges of any container that I arrange to ship from the Port of Greenock. Brilliant! I spoke to Craig at Clydeport Ocean Terminal, who then passed me onto Express Lines in Felixstowe, which has made my day. I call Express Lines. *'I am passing you on to someone on the second floor,'* he said. I speak to Julie who will get back to me next week.

Saturday 01/09/2012

9:50 a.m. Unit 29. I was slow in moving this morning. I awoke with pain behind my eyeballs and nausea. I did not leave the cottage until after 7 a.m. to get the eight o'clock boat. I chatted to John, the biker, who was telling me about his travels on the Continent. I got the slow bus via Gourock and then hoofed it up the hill in the misty drizzle. I stopped at the newsagent and then into Aulds. Cheery lassie. *'Can I have an Americano and a doughnut please.'* My treat.

What's ahead of me this morning? I am going to measure the height, length and breadth of the Jubilee Gardens Library shelving. Had I known a few years ago that this is what I would be doing with my time? Just as well I did not. Philip, design manager at Wilmot Dixon Construction Ltd, thinks that the Ealing Borough Council might like to have it back; will they give me anything for it now, considering the great expense I went to bring it up here when they were glad to get rid of it? I will have my treat before I begin the work.

12:25 p.m. I have made an attempt at measuring up the library furniture and the time has come to head for home.

Monday 03/09/2012

6:49 a.m. The MV *Bute* is chugging its way across the Firth of Clyde. I just managed to wake up in time. Sleeping fitfully. Getting out of bed so often to pee.

It is a grey muggy morning and I am on my way over to Edinburgh to meet Frederick from Tanzania, who had emailed me earlier to ask if I had any educational resources that SESF would donate to the Ngilla Community Secondary School. I told him that I did have some boxes of primary school resources that he was welcome to have. He told me that he had a friend with a container with some spare capacity that was being delivered to East Africa

1:39 p.m. *'This train is for Glasgow Queen Street,'* he said. I am leaving Waverley Station.

I bid Frederick au revoir. I had collected him by taxi on my

Tuesday 04/09/2012

arrival this morning from 13 Drummond Street, up the hill from here, and took him down to Unit 12, West Shore Business Centre. He will take some of the boxes of books away with him to be distributed to schools in Tanzania. He had had me on his mobile speaking to one of the ministers in his government. I left the key to Unit 12 with him. I introduced him to Iain the accountant and Bharam, Unit 5 Apfelsnapz Ltd, with whom he will leave the Unit 12 key when he has collected the boxes of books. We then walked up the road and over to the Telford College café, where I bought him a tuna fish sandwich and a hot chocolate, and managed to spill my cup of coffee all over the table and down his trousers. My hands begin to tremble at times unexpectedly – what does this portend?

Tuesday 04/09/2012

8 a.m. Unit 29. The sun is shining, hip, hip hooray. By force of will I have made it in here this morning. No prospects at the moment. I must complete the work before me. There are some more books to inventory and box. David said he would show up. Discuss with him what he wishes to do now that we, together, have basically prepared these educational resources, salvaged from the Inverclyde Council education system, for shipment.

10:25 a.m. I have inventoried the entire donation of textbooks from James Watt College and I have been up the road for a sandwich and an Americano from Auld the Baker. I stopped to speak to John the Chip Shop, who said *'If bizzness doesnae pick up, I'll huv tae quit. I'm 59, what do I dae?' I hope you get yer reward, before yuz get tae Heaven.'* I replied, 'There are dilemmas for us all, John.'

The film crew are standing around outside the Unit 29 SESF office window having a fag, waiting for Jason to show up.

10:40 a.m. The janitors from Glenburn School have delivered some boxes and a television.

11:10 a.m. Gerry and Taff have delivered two metal-legged drafting tables.

12:30 p.m. I have done all I can, it is time to head home.

Wednesday 05/09/2012

8:05 a.m. Home. I am working the telephone. I was speaking to John the freight forwarder in Liverpool, who tells me that the container must have been in plate for less than 10 years. I called Joe who said, *'Ah huv tae go tae mah wuk.'* I call Stewart at Pentalver Ltd in Southampton, who tells me 'All the boxes are going out to China and it is not a good time for you to be begging. Call me in October, we may have boxes available then.' I call Peter, editor of *SHD* magazine, who are going to run an article on SESF

Thursday 06/09/2012

5:45 p.m. Home. I have received an email from Osbert of the Presbyterian Church of Grenada to tell me that my 40-foot container shipment of educational resources to Samaritan Presbyterian School had been auctioned off by the Port Authority to a private school. This is a big blow. What can I do or say? Nothing.

I had to pick myself up off the floor when I got that news from the lovely people of the Caribbean Isle of Spices seashore. I spent all morning writing thank you letters to the Educational Institute for Scotland, Local Association secretaries, in East Ayrshire and East Dunbartonshire.

Monday 10/09/2012

11:45 a.m. No. 38 East Hamilton Street. I was dropped off by taxi. I got off the bus from Wemyss Bay and walked along to the cab rank and here I am.

12:40 p.m. The gas and smart meter man has left and I am going to walk up the road to Unit 29 in the Lynedoch Industrial Estate.

1:22 p.m. Unit 29. The water is still not on. As I was crossing the main road across from the big chapel, a van horn goes and it is Stephen and John, the removal gang. They gave me lift down the hill to Baker Street and I walked through cobbled Scott Street, crossed Dellingburn Street, up Hope Street and went in to see John the Fry Fayre Chippy, who gave me a poke of chips along with my bacon roll. There is enough water in the kettle for a coffee. I am going to chill and enjoy the purvey and then go around to all of the units and hand out John's Fine Fayre Fryer flyers.

3:25 p.m. David came by earlier. He had been to No. 38 East Hamilton Street and all the way to see if I was here. Good on him. I am heading home.

Thursday 13/09/2012

7:23 p.m. Home. Marion is doing *The Herald* crossword and Johanna has gone up the road to accompany Betty on the violin. I am about to go and have a shower, but before I do, I am going to pause for a moment to record some of the events of today.

I was out in time to catch the 9:30 a.m. ferry. While I was on the boat, Marion called to let me know that a 901 bus would go past Faulds Park Road and I could get off and walk up to Amazon and Company Ltd, to an awesome-sized warehouse.

I had arrived at reception earlier than the rest of the Greenock

Chamber of Commerce party, who were due to be given a tour of the Amazon distribution facility, and who ticked me off for handing out my SESF flyers. I met Andrew, general manager and chief executive of the Clydeport Ocean Terminal, who advised me not to approach Amazon for sponsorship and that any preferment would have to come from them. I got the chance, at the introduction session, to make myself known to my fellow members of the Greenock Chamber of Commerce; cue dismissive vibes to the tune of *'What was this nutter on about anyway?'* Finger munchies for lunch and I blagged a lift out of the complex from three youngsters from the Renfrewshire Chamber of Commerce, who dropped me off at 38 East Hamilton Street.

I couldn't find my keys, so it was a taxi from the ABC garage on McDougall Street up to Unit 29, a friendly welcome from Paul and Iain and back down the road in a taxi. I loaded the donation of hockey strips, sticks and trainers, and returned to Unit 29. £20. Hung onto keys. Another taxi – £20.

Friday 14/09/2012

2:05 p.m. MV *Bute*. I left home in the rain at 6:15 a.m. on this vessel for Wemyss Bay. Bus up to Greenock. I walked across to Tesco and put £20 on my mobile phone, and bought *The Herald* and a roll of Pritt Stick. I had to wait around until 8 a.m. for the café to open for a roll and fried egg and a cup of coffee. I met Craig, whose face was familiar, who joined me when he learned what I was doing in Greenock. He told me that he was a joiner to trade and that his dad had an engineering business in the Cappielow Industrial Estate, and he had always wanted to do some voluntary work in the Third World. I gave him one of the SESF flyers and copies of some SESF publicity from the Fourth Estate. I told him that he was welcome to get on the bus.

I had planned to meet David at Unit 29. I got a taxi up the hill and sorted through the pile of hockey gear, which had been donated many months ago; the strips need to be washed. I met David from the film crew, who said that he had borrowed some stuff for props. Later I met Jason, the producer and director of RIG Arts. I dropped in at Inverclyde Tool Hire Ltd to say *'Hi!'* to Paul.

11:30 a.m. I left Unit 29 and walked through the industrial estate up to Lynedoch Street and got a taxi for my appointment with dentist Alison, who is always welcoming and competent, and got the bus down to Wemyss Bay and here I am on top of chugging motors. My cup of soup has gone cold.

Wednesday 10/10/2012

12:16 p.m. It is a beautiful day. I am sitting outside at David Alexander's wee school desk, which was salvaged years ago from the Kilbarchan Primary School, listing a collection of engineering textbooks. I am calling the Republic of Liberia embassy in London. I wish to speak with the Minister Counsellor and Head of Chancery. *'She's in a meetin' she very busy.'* I was told to call again tomorrow.

Thursday 11/10/2012

2:46 p.m. Home. *'Call back in 10 minutes,'* she said. I am going to have a shower. I am wringing wet. I have returned from a good long walk from round the back and up and over Canada Hill and into the metropolis for messages and to collect a prescription from the pharmacist, and to have a bowl of soup, stale bread and butter and an Americano at the Victoria Hotel, which was acceptable.

3:12 p.m. She tells me to call again next week.

Tuesday 16/10/2012

2:05 p.m. Home. I have returned from Kilbarchan and am returning a call from Eric, who is in the Republic of Liberia and who tells me that I am to call him again after I have contacted their embassy in London.

Thursday 18/10/2012

2:24 p.m. Calling the Republic of Liberia embassy; they want a type written letter. She says she did not think that my focus was to get a container shipment of educational resources to the school in Paynesville. I thought Eric had sorted all of that.

2:48 p.m. I am waiting for a return call.

4:15 p.m. She wants me to call again after 13 November. I am the biggest mug on Blue Planet.
This morning I cycled into the town and stopped off at One2One Accountancy Services where I met Lesley the owner, who is encouraging and pro bono supportive of the Surplus Educational Supplies Foundation. Her colleague Donna photocopied my VAT returns and gave me an envelope for them. After a haircut from Wesley, I went along to the post office and sent VAT returns same-day delivery to Ross & Co accountants in Dunoon. I returned home to receive a helpful and supportive email from Gerry of the travel agents Just Grenada.

Wednesday 24/10/2012

10:05 a.m. Home. Grey and cool. Lethargic. Aching bones. *'David, you are not getting any younger.'* So what else is new? I did manage to cycle round the island yesterday and the day before – an all too familiar route, which gets a bit monotonous. I have to make the effort to find something in the passing scene: a buzzard flapping its wings over a wood; a flock of pigeons in flight; a submarine is sneaking past the Isle of Arran.

I am about to call Stuart at Pentalver Ltd in Southampton: will they sell me a 40-foot seaworthy container for less than £2,400? I am hesitant to call him as he called me a beggar the last time, and before that he did not care for my charm. He said that I *'laid it on thick with a trowel.'* What else have I got to work with but my winsome patter?

Here goes. I call their number. Tom answers with a friendly upfront tone of voice. I tell him what I need. 'I'll see what I can do for you. I might be able to pull some strings, you have got to do what you can,' he said.

11:06 a.m. That's Phil the Bosch washing machine engineer arrived and I've made him a coffee.

Monday 29/10/2012

2:07 p.m. I received a call earlier from helpful Gordon of Scottish Enterprise who has prepared a list of 200 companies in Scotland who manufacture and export. He is to send me the list and, when I have contacted them, he will send me some more. I am looking to establish an extra governmental entrepreneurial link to the Republic of Liberia.

I managed to make another circuit of the Isle of Bute this morning.

7:18 p.m. *'Who is calling me at this hour?'* It is Brian of the Fife Group, who tells me that they want me to remove, as soon as possible, the educational resources from the two 40-foot containers that they had bought from me, that I had parked at Babcock yard in Rosyth, and furthermore their warehouse in Dunfermline must be cleared of my stuff. The stress and pressure is back on my shoulders.

Tuesday 30/10/2012

9 a.m. Home. I am calling Eric in the Republic of Liberia. No answer.

2:08 p.m. David has ventured out on his new mountain bike.
   The educational resources from the Inveralmond Community High School, that I have had in storage in a Fife Group's Dunfermline warehouse for some time now, have to be uplifted as soon as possible. Where to? How?

2:14 p.m. I am calling around, working the telephone. Simon at Galt Transport Ltd said he would call me back.

2:45 p.m. *'We think what you are doing is honourable,'* he said. A little comment like that to 'Raleigh Spokes' (one of my school sobriquets) goes a long way to bolster self-esteem.

4:12 p.m. I call Amara Mining Ltd. Can Algernon and friends in Sierra Leone assist me in sourcing a beneficiary for educational resources from just one of the many schools that were destroyed during the recent civil war?

5:20 p.m. I am trying to call Eric once more.

Wednesday 31/10/2012

8:02 a.m. Home. I am down in the dumps, so climb out and give it another go. Call Eric, who tells me, *'Forget the embassy in London, they do not have your vision, okay?'*

8:15 a.m. I called AMC Engineering in Aberdeen and spoke to Doris, who has a sense of humour.

Friday 02/11/2012

8:34 a.m. I called Galt Transport Ltd to see if they could let me have a 40-foot container. *'I'll see if I can dig one up for you,'* said Alan. Call Cluff at Cluff Gold, Amara Mining Ltd. He is not in the office, but she will pass my message along. Spoke to Sam at Pentalver Ltd. *'I can't understand why they are going to make £1,000, when I have sold them one for half that'* was his comment when I told him that Freight Container Services (Scotland) Ltd wanted £2,400 plus VAT.

10:57 a.m. I have contacted Scottish Companies 192–200.

11:49 a.m. I have sent six email letters to the above.

12:10 p.m. I now have a migraine.

2:17 p.m. I accept, gratefully, the offer of plywood chairs from the Ardbeg Baptist Church, which they will deliver to Unit 29.

Thursday 01/11/2012

8:25 a.m. Home. I am returning a call to Sam. I called Allan Galt: *'I will see what I can drum up for you.'* I then called the Glenburn School, Tomorrow's People, and Clydeview Academy. I am to call Craig at Clydeport Ocean Terminal when I am ready to deliver the container for the Republic of Liberia.

3:15 p.m. I was speaking to George at CMA Delmas, who said *'Never give up!'*

Friday 02/11/2012

12:36 p.m. Home. I am waiting for R.F. Brown Ltd in Hamilton to call me back. This contact was given to me by Alan.

12:46 p.m. Call Tom the container inspector – before I could do that he has just called me! I give him the number of the container that I have just purchased, on spec, from Bobby Brown (AMZU8393485) and Tom, after the inspection of the box for seaworthiness, will hopefully make out a certificate. The dealer assured me that it was seaworthy.

To do for next week:
- Arrange for volunteers from James Watt College, RIG Arts, and the grown-up children from Action For Children Scotland, to load the container;
- Call the Glenburn School to see if their pupils can come up to Unit 29 to see their donation of educational resources being loaded for the Paynesville school, Monrovia in the Republic of Liberia West Africa;
- Notify Craig and team at Clydeport Ocean Terminal that the container will be on its way;
- Contact Chick and Gary at HAI Natural (Bri-Mac) to see if, yet again, they will be able to operate the forklift;
- Call Iain at Swordfish Signs Ltd to arrange for the SESF logo to be put on my container;
- Call Greenock telly news desk.

Monday 05/11/2012

1:35 p.m. Wemyss Bay ferry terminal waiting room.

The ferry is docking ever so slowly. It is a glorious, light-filled, early winter's day. On my arrival in Greenock this morning I walked up to Unit 29 and was chatting to Jason of RIG Arts, who was shifting some of the SESF furniture that I had loaned to their film crew. I told him he could leave it where it was for the time being. He is offering to be helpful – an attitude I appreciate. He told me that he may have some of his film crew available to load the container on Wednesday, 7 November, which is not likely since none of the lads and lassies who had been working with him for the past seven weeks could be bothered to show up and give a hand today to tidy up. I went over to Inverclyde Tool Hire Ltd to see Director Paul, who always gives me a welcome, and then went over to Robbert and Kenneth at my old Unit 18.

2:22 p.m. The MV *Argyle*. There is a slight ripple on the watta from the breeze. I am on deck and have scoffed some leek and celery soup and a pie. I met Jim the roofer coming over on the 10 a.m. boat, who gave me a lift up the road.

On arrival at Unit 29, as I opened the door, the burglar alarm went off. Not fazed, I changed into my boiler suit and thought I'd give Paul and Iain a look. As I was about to close the door, Chick from the incinerating plant next door came by and switched off the alarm for me. He told me that he had not seen me for a while. I told him that I had been hot-desking, trying to untangle myself from a huge stockpile of educational resources that had to be uplifted and stored at some other location. I told him I hoped to load a 40-foot high cube ocean freight container with the 16 pallets plus educational resources on Wednesday, 7 November. He said that he would be along with the HAI Natural Ltd team to load it. I am so grateful for his ilk and the many individuals who have assisted me in the SESF journey. I can't see too far ahead; I continue to travel hopefully.

This morning I called Eric in Monrovia, Republic of Liberia, West Africa and all he said was, '*I'm driving.*' I managed to inform him that a container had been purchased and would be loaded with all of the educational resources that he had seen on Thursday, 23 August with Michael from the Sandyford Henderson Memorial Church Fellowship. I asked him if he had got my emails – he did not answer. I still have my misgivings about this shipment, but we both have in common an association with the Sandyford Henderson Memorial Church in Glasgow, me from 1975 to 1990. '*I am part of the fellowship,*' he informed me; so was I, once upon a time. He has sent me some bona fides: a letter from his church fellowship in Liberia. I have had no response to my phone calls and emails to his Liberian government embassy in London.

I have had a prompt response from Tom Walker, container surveyor, with a CSC cargo worthy certificate for the 40-foot high cube ocean freight container that SESF/me has purchased from dealer R.F. Brown Ltd in Hamilton, and which will be uplifted by Galt Transport Ltd and brought to Unit 29 Greenock on Wednesday, 7 November. There will be no storage or handling charges of the container at Clydeport Ocean Terminal. I have never taken for granted the good will and practical support from Paul, Iain, Chick and HAI Natural Ltd. Onward and upward.

Tuesday 06/11/2012

10:55 a.m. Unit 29, Lynedoch Industrial Estate, Dellingburn Street. I have eaten a packet of Walkers cheese and onion crisps, and a dolphin friendly tuna mayo and cucumber sandwich from Aulds the Bakers' shop. I am still quaffing an Aulds Americano.

I got on the bus at Wemyss Bay and said, *'Wemyss Bay, please.'* I feel like an idiot. A cracked pot lets in the light – Chinese proverb. I get off at James Watt College Union Street bus stop and I walk up South Street. The design signage shop: friendly – he knows Joe and what I am after regarding a logo for my container.

I then walked along to Homebase to purchase hinges for The Bike Shed and nylon rope to tie the SESF banner to the container. I then walked to answer a just-in-time call from nature. I put money on my mobile and got a taxi from the rank to No. 38 East Hamilton Street. I am now detached from The Book Store at 38 East Hamilton Street and all the work and cost to upgrade the premises after feeling threatened by certain folk; there is no footfall. This venue has been a lost cause from the day I set foot in the premises. At the time I was just glad to get somewhere. I have nothing to be ashamed of.

Taxi driver Phil is helpful. He helped me take the SESF banner from off the mesh window guards. He then drove me back up the road to Unit 29. He told me that his son, who is a student at Inverclyde Academy, wants to be a doctor and loves reading, so he collected an armful of books for him; he is an ally. I went over to see Paul at Inverclyde Tool Hire Ltd and he showed me, the slow learner, yet again, how to use the grinder. I am now going to box up the hockey equipment.

12:45 p.m. The surveyor from Riverside Inverclyde Properties Ltd paid a visit while Archie the meter reader, who holidays in the Dominican Republic, was here. I have just boxed the gift of hockey sticks, strips and trainers, plus a new football goal net from Jason at RIG Arts. I am heading home.

Wednesday 07/11/2012

7:30 a.m. Unit 29. Stephen, our neighbour, was waiting at the Wemyss Bay car park as I came off the MV *Argyle*. *'Would you like a lift?'* he asked me. He dropped me off on Baker Street. I walked through cobbled Scotland Street on wet leaves. I opened up and called Galt Transport Ltd. *'Simon here.'* He told me that AMZU8393485 would be picked up from R.F. Brown Ltd in Hamilton and brought here.

9:30 a.m. Jason the RIG Arts producer and David the polymath have arrived with cameras.

10:15 a.m. Chick has come across from the incinerating plant to ask me what's happening; his presence here is a great encouragement to me. Apparently, when Morton FC was going down the tubes, he rallied the fans to roll up their sleeves and do all the work that needed to be done to keep the failing club viable.

Top: A container for Woburn Methodist School, Woburn, Grenada W.I, April 2016. This SESF container was loaded by volunteers in Greenock in 2014, and later reloaded and contents inventoried by students from West College Scotland, Paisley Campus in March 2016.
SESF became increasingly under pressure to salvage educational resources way beyond its capacity to do so, and, as a result, became a victim of its success.

Bottom: This shipment of educational resources to a Hurricane Ivan devastated school still in a state of refurbishment was made possible by a whole host of volunteers, and one company in particular, Sea Freight Agencies Lines of Miami Florida USA and it's chief executive and founder, Roland Malins-Smith.

Thursday 08/11/2012

11:26 a.m. Ben, the Galt Transport Ltd artic driver, has arrived with the SESF container.

2:30 p.m. Ben has just left with the container for Peel Ports Ltd, Clydeport Ocean Terminal. I managed to persuade a team of gardeners, just before they knocked off, to come and give me a hand. They did not tell me to beat it! I could not have loaded the container without their willing help. Jason also saved the day by acquiring a pallet lifter from InverStore Ltd, accompanied by Arran and his chum Simon, who also were a great help. Robert and his mate Kenneth ran me down to the ATM at the filling station at the bottom of Dellingburn Street to get some money: I gave each of the volunteers a token gift of £10. Chick, who drove the forklift, was the lynchpin who began the process of loading the 16 pallets.

2:55 p.m. It is time to head home.

Thursday 08/11/2012

9:29 a.m. Home. I called Eric, Monrovia, Republic of Liberia, West Africa. He was surprised that the consignee should contribute something to facilitate, in some way to defray the cost of, this shipment of aid for the Paynesville school's children, even if it was just to reassure me, the consignor, that the customs officials at their port in Monrovia were not going to extract payment from the Surplus Educational Supplies Foundation for this gift. Do they want everything on a plate? Could he agree to let me have the container back and we could call it quits? He assured me that I could keep the SESF container.

(As it turned out, his government reneged on this agreement and I never saw my container again, which had serious financial repercussions for me later.)

5:25 p.m. I was speaking to Eric again, who said he was going to approach the Sandyford Church Fellowship for assistance with the costs of shipment. This was not what I had anticipated, or wanted to happen. I called Galt Transport Ltd, whose tariff to bring the container to Unit 29 and two hours later deliver it to Clydeport Ocean Terminal was £400, which I paid there then. I did not expect a free lift from them: *'short accounts, long friends.'*

This morning was hectic. The container number was not the same on Tom Walker the container surveyor's certificate, which threw me off balance. I just had to pick myself off the floor and carry on in forward gear, cycling into Rothesay to get the twelve o'clock boat. I met a Scottish couple living in Brittany, who run a bed and breakfast establishment, who can't say anything bad about their experience of France; they sang the praises of their healthcare system. I got the bus up to Greenock, James Watt College bus stop, and walked round BEP Signs Ltd. Robert had not got around to looking into my logo/design for the container. I then walked up to Tesco and purchased thank you brews and biscuits for InverStore, for loan of their pallet truck, and for Inverclyde Tool Hire and then got a taxi from the rank up the road.

I met Jason and his dog in Unit 29. I collected the pallet truck and handed it over to the InverStore owner, Brian, who said I could borrow it again should I need it. I chatted with Iain and Paul at Inverclyde Tool Hire. I then set off down the road to the JWC bus stop. I just made the ferry.

Monday 12/11/2012

6:30 a.m. MV *Coruisk*. I just made it. I am facing another week. The ferry is heading slowly across the watta.

I stand and wait for the bus to Greenock and later walk up the steep Sir Michael Street, along to Roxburgh Street, buy *The Herald* from the Moroccan Imam, who now gives me a smile, then down to Lynedoch Industrial Estate, along Hope Street (the industrial estate will not have opened up yet), across to Dellingburn Street and over to Unit 29. I open up the office, take my shoes off and climb into a clean boiler suit; thank you Marion for washing it. I begin to tidy the stuff that's been left behind from the uplift on Wednesday, 7 November.

I run through this sequence of events in my mind as this slow ferry approaches Wemyss Bay.

7:45 a.m. Unit 29. I started to tidy up.

10:56 a.m. I am heading up through a dreich drizzle to Cowden's on Lynedoch Street for a piece: cheese and onion crisps, tuna fish sandwich and an Americano.

1:35 p.m. Robert the inventor and his sidekick Kenny have dropped by, and I stop what I am doing and make them welcome. I have managed to get the wooden shelving into place. It is time to head home.

Tuesday 13/11/2012

8:30 a.m. Home. To do:
- Call Grant Elliot, the freight forwarder at Allseas Global Logistics Ltd.
- Check with the *Greenock Telegraph* that their article on shipment to Liberia is in.
- Is the BEP Ltd signage ready?
- Prepare a file of SESF work for the Sandyford Fellowship.
- Call Galt Transport Ltd for recovery of VAT on delivery.
- List sale of containers for accountants Ross & Co.
- Post file/folder to Sandyford.
- Check SESF is paid £1,400 from the Fife Group for containers GATU4072944 and OCLU1354487, which had been in storage loaded with resources at Babcock Rosyth.

(I was reluctant to sell them, but I was now running into debt. I did not want to owe anyone any money. I also had to sell INBU4923875 to Tom the container dealer, who gave me a better deal for £1,200.)

9:46 a.m. I wrote a cheque to Allseas Global Logistics Ltd for £2,400 to ship the container to Monrovia, Republic of Liberia, West Africa and prepared a Word document list: myself as supplier/consignor, my address, description of the goods in the container, and total value of shipment for customs in Monrovia, Republic of Liberia (£300 far, far more than that sum).

3:05 p.m. Home. I am back from the town in the drizzle, under a blanket of thick grey cloud. I am heavy of heart for there was nothing else for it but to push through the morass, which was of my own creation.

The employees were very helpful at the Royal Bank of Scotland branch in Rothesay. I withdrew £1,400 from my account and transferred it into the SESF account – enough to cover the cheque to Allseas Global Logistics Ltd. I bought *The Herald* and decided against going into the Victoria Hotel for coffee, and I cycled back to home hearth to make my own cup of coffee.

Wednesday 14/11/2012

10:39 a.m. I got the MV *Argyle*. Bus to James Watt College. I walked across town, along Barehope Street and up Sir Michael Street, bought *The Herald*, and down Lyle Street. I had the cheek to ask the crisp honcho at Clyde Car Components Ltd on Lynedoch Street if they would like to put their logo on my container for a fee. I missed Robert. I am going to call him.

11 a.m. I called Alison at James Watt College to discuss with her and a group of the students their 'Education Into Enterprise for

Thursday 15/11/2012

Digital Promoters', which is a project to research through digital media the different methods of advertising the work of the Surplus Educational Supplies Foundation, to rework the SESF site on Facebook, and the different ways of promoting this social entrepreneurial 'business' via different social media, e.g. Twitter. The students' project will showcase what SESF has to offer and has achieved from 2005 to 2012. The lecturer said that she will speak to her class and has already cleared the project with the head of business studies.

2:35 p.m. I am back up to Unit 29 and I have been shifting the heavy bookcases from the Jubilee Gardens, Southall, Ealing Borough Council and it is a bit too much for me. I am going to give it a break.

5:36 p.m. Home. I barely made the 4 p.m. MV *Coruisk*; there was a message from Lorraine at James Watt College regarding electric cookers in the home economics classroom kitchen.

I don't know when, or how, to stop collecting stuff when I have no clear idea as to where it will be going, or the means to deliver it without getting further into debt.

Thursday 15/11/2012

7:55 a.m. I am leaving an empty house, our home, on the bike into Rothesay town. It is damp and dark. I put the Allscas Global Logistics Ltd cheque through the bank door, park the bike, buy a ticket, I am on the MV *Argyle*.

9:35 a.m. Unit 29. Break time. Corned beef in a crispy roll from Cowden's and an Americano from Aulds the Bakers.

12:15 p.m. Robert arrived, driven up here by Phil the taxi driver. Robert has brought his Leica digital camera to help me inventory the remaining stock of educational resources. Robert says he can sell them on eBay.

1:25 p.m. I am recovering from having stepped on the heavy furniture skateboard and cracked the side of my head. I am still in for the count, but how many more self-inflicted knocks like that on my head can I take?

I tell Robert that we are packing it in for today. I have a meeting with Lorraine at James Watt College Estates, who is going to show me the home economics equipment that SESF might be able to acquire, on the assumption that deserving beneficiaries will be found for it eventually.

3:20 p.m. I have another meeting with Alison and her HNC Business, Education into Enterprise Programme, students, in which I introduce myself and tell them what I hope to achieve through their help and commitment, and what they can expect to learn from working with the Surplus Educational Supplies Foundation. I will give them £7 per hour out of SESF funds; Alison will bring her class to Unit 29 on Monday, 19 November. I anticipate possibilities, providing they can step up to the challenge.

I have not sold anything on eBay or used that source to buy something online. It could be a means to generate funds; promote the redistribution of fit-for-purpose educational resources; encourage schools, colleges and universities across Scotland to begin making a serious attempt at the sustainable reuse of resources and reduce the carbon footprint; and link up with other organisations with a similar vision.

How can these students and their lecturer turn SESF from a 'dead duck' into a 'cash cow'?

Friday 16/11/2012

8.27 a.m. Home. I call Grant, freight forwarder with Allseas Global Logistics Ltd, who is not in the office. I called Freight Container Sales (Scotland) Ltd to find out the number of the container in the yard at Duncan Adams Transport Ltd; I try to find out from Eric if there is any information on the invoice at his end since customs requirements differ.

3:30 p.m. Home again. I was back out in the rain. I returned a call to Mary Terese, the ECO Coordinator at Glenburn School, who tells me that their janitors have left more resources up at Unit 29. Call Grant on Tuesday, 20 November.

Call the *Greenock Telegraph* journalist and SESF premier league supporter from early, to let him know when container AMZU39348545G1 will be leaving the Clydeport Ocean Terminal Greenock, and if it were possible could he be there, since I hoped some of the pupils at Glenburn School would be there to wish the shipment Bon Voyage: the container has a large quantity of their school's excess resources, which has become available as their school will be demolished and they are relocating to the new joint campus in Port Glasgow. I called Eric, who was surprised that there was a cost of £2,400 to me to ship the container.

I have no other option but to play ball with him.

10:15 p.m. I have put numbers to the containers that I have purchased, shipped and sold since 2006. It's time for bed.

Monday 19/11/2012

12:15 p.m. Unit 29. Alison and her Education into Enterprise class at James Watt College, HNC Business Studies, have just left. They came at 10 a.m. I have pitched to them and they have left with my dossier, SESF records and Ross & Co audited accounts. I laid on coffee for them from the caterer in the industrial estate.

It was hard to discern what these five students thought about what I had said. I cannot do any more for them if they are unwilling to accept the challenge, which requires a sustained effort and application of their 21st century digital literacy, iPhone, and social media skills that might make a difference in marketing this vast quantity of fit-for-purpose, surplus to requirements, resources that SESF has in stock.

Tuesday 20/11/2012

4:15 p.m. Home. I have been in bed all day. I have just surfaced. Migraine? What does that word mean for me? There is numbness in my left hand, usually, pain in the front of my head and the worst bit is when I am unable to string words together to make myself understood. I am also low in spirit. What's the point of it all?

A short while ago I received a message on the answering machine from Eric in the Republic of Liberia. He has received my SESF dossier; will I ever learn not to keep on expecting anything in return from the people I try to help? I will call him tomorrow after I have spoken to Grant at Allseas Global Logistics Ltd to confirm that it is all systems go, that the container will be on its way to the consignee in West Africa.

I have left two messages with Riverside Inverclyde Properties Ltd, my landlord at Unit 29. Can they offer me any more storage space after I have moved from Unit 29?

Wednesday 21/11/2012

10:30 a.m. Home. I have called the chief executive officer of Riverside Inverclyde Properties Ltd for the third time; I have left another message with his office and I await a reply.

Wednesday 21/11/2012

It is a brighter morning, the rain has gone and there is a slight breeze coming up the corridor and I am drinking coffee. Positive thoughts, once more, are beginning to surface in my brain. I give myself some advice to take positive life-affirming actions; nothing will happen without my input. I must remember to take courage and confidence in what I, along with helpful others, have achieved so far, and since I am surrounded by such a cloud of witnesses my actions in the here and now will have accomplished something worthwhile. It is my project, which I initiated and for which I must take full responsibility.

I called Liz the team leader at Tomorrow's People to let her and the team, which assisted way back in March to sort, inventory and box textbooks, know that the library books are now in a container on its way to Africa. I enquire after different members of that team and she tells me, *'That guy is no longer with us and some of them have jobs.'* I have just found, on a piece of scrap paper from a mathematics jotter, a note of their order for a tea break that I took their first morning in Unit 29, which was paid for by this frayed trousers philanthropist: Dean, a roll and slice with a tattie scone and a can o' Coke; Paul, chicken noodles with a buttered roll and can of Irn Bru; JP, curry noodles, buttered roll and a can of Dr Pepper; Craig, cheeseburger, Irn Bru and 10 fags (we'll skip the fags Craig); Pat, cheeseburger; Jordan, bacon and cheeseburger and a can o' Coke. So in all that's an order of purvey for which Cowden's did well out of me that morning, and so did Tomorrow's People.

I called the following: Head of Chancery, Sierra Leone High Commission; Grant, Allseas Global Logistics Ltd – I am to call again this afternoon, my cheque should have been cleared by then; Albert Henderson, chief executive, Education Services of Inverclyde Council, to let him know that the educational resources that were received by SESF over the past two years are on their way to a beneficiary in West Africa; and Yvonne at Delmas CMA, India Buildings, Liverpool, to confirm that the Maersk Altair can bring a cargo back in the SESF container AMZU8393485. What can the Republic of Liberia export to Scotland?

12:30 p.m. I am going to stop making a nuisance and boil an egg, and make some toast and a mug of tea. The sun is shining in at the end of the corridor, but I don't wish to move too far from the telephone.

2 p.m. I spoke with Simon at Galt Transport Ltd to make arrangements to have the container picked up from Clydeport Ocean Terminal and taken to Forth Ports at Grangemouth. I also spoke to Allan and Andrew in the office. I then called Forth Ports Grangemouth and I spoke with Murray, who was helpful and friendly, and who said, *'The container can be brought right in!'*

I called Clydeport Ocean Terminal and spoke with Hugh and Craig, who I have dealt with before, to let them know that Galt Transport Ltd will pick up the container, which I will meet at the port security gates at the Patrick Street entrance. They were, as usual, helpful, friendly and not a problem attitude. Grant has just told me that he has been in contact with Eric with details of shipping arrangements from Scotland. Great! Done and dusted.

Thursday 22/11/2012

2:25 p.m. Home. I was out early in the wind and rain: got soaked to the skin. I got the MV *Coruisk*, which finally made its way to Gourock.

I waited for a bus up the road to Greenock town centre and I went across to Tesco for fixings for the Clydeport Ocean Terminal bothy: tea, coffee and Tunnock's caramel wafers. I was met by Craig, who couldn't have been more helpful. Ben and the artic with trailer soon appeared at 8:30 a.m. There was some confusion with the container numbers, which was sorted by the Clydeport office team. Jamie took a digital of Ben and me holding up the SESF banner in front of the container.

Thursday 22/11/2012

I then walked back up Dalrymple Street and through the Oak Mall Shopping Centre, up Bank Street through the park, and around past the war memorial, which always puts my own petty picayune sacrifices into perspective, back into the Lynedoch Industrial Estate, and stopped off at Inverclyde Tool Hire Ltd to let Paul and Iain know that container AMZU8393485 was on its way to Monrovia Port, Republic of Liberia and I left the banner in the Unit 29 office. I got a taxi to Wemyss Bay in time to get the one o'clock ferry.

4:20 p.m. I called the freight forwarder at Allseas Global Logistics Ltd, who confirms that everything is in order. The schedule is as follows: from the Port of Grangemouth the container leaves aboard UNI Feeder Energiser 41F 26 November. Arrives Felixstowe 29 November, then is trans-shipped to the Maersk Altair 6 December. Arrives Port of Tangier 13 December. Trans-shipped (?) for Monrovia Port. Estimated time of arrival 21 December 2012.

That solves that problem. I humbly accept, verbally, what he has just told me and then get off my bed. No way do I wish to see the resources crushed without a struggle and I promptly send over 18 emails to Grangemouth Ward politicos to discuss the issue of wanton and unnecessary destruction of fit-for-purpose educational resources, and wait to see who replies.

4:45 p.m. Well, I sat here at the keyboard and posted emails to a number of Falkirk councillors.

The sun is shining. I am fighting upward.

Unit 12 West Shore Business Centre, Granton. Chief Executive clearing up Unit 12 in April 2017 prior to vacating premises.
The clean up after twelve years' graft. It was your problem, be it on your own head.

Appendix
Surplus Educational Supplies Foundation

Registered Scottish Charity SCO39331.
Company Registered in Scotland No. 337348

To transport unwanted educational supplies from Scotland to the Developing World.

CHARITABLE OBJECTIVES OF THE SURPLUS EDUCATIONAL SUPPLIES FOUNDATION:

1. To advance education through schools and educational establishments in disadvantaged communities in any part of the world and/or pupils/students attending any such educational establishments with classroom furniture, equipment, books, and/ or other resources; a school if necessary to improve the quality and/or scope of the educational services which are provided and the ability of pupils/students to benefit from such educational services.
2. To advance environmental protection and, in particular, protect the natural environment from further damage caused by the proliferation of landfill sites by the redistribution of classroom furniture and refurbishment of other fit-for-purpose, surplus to requirements, resources as referred in Objective1, which would otherwise be sent to landfill sites.

APPENDIX

Shipping Details

Recipient	Delivery Date	Container Ref/ Size/Cost to Funder (£)	Cargo/ Source	Funder Consignor	Shipping Service	Tonnage (Kg)	Total Cost (£)	Carrier	Consignee feedback
Grand Roy Government School, Grand Roy, St John's, Grenada, West Indies	01/07/2005	CLHU 2451793/ 20ft	Used educational goods/ Argyll & Bute (A&B) Council	Denholm Logistics/ A&B Council/ D Miles-Hanschell	Denholm Barr	3,470	2,255.38	East West Indies Line	Good
As above	09/12/2005	FSCU 337885/ 20ft	As above	D Miles-Hanschell	As above	3,560	1,971.00	As above	Good
Calliste Government School, Calliste, St George's, Grenada, West Indies	19/01/2007	ZCSU 8083681/ 40ft	Used educational supplies/ Fife Council	D Miles-Hanschell	Zim Integrated	4,500	1,190.22	CMA/ CGM	Poor
St Paul's Government School, St Paul's, Grenada, West Indies	03/09/2007	GSTU 895863/ 40ft/ 900.00	Used educational resources/ Stirling Council	D Miles-Hanschell	Zim Integrated/ SeaFreight Agencies	5,360	1,920.97	CMA/ CGM/ Sea Freight	Poor
Grenada Boys' Secondary School, Grenada, West Indies	13/07/2008	CRXU 410319/ 40ft/ 1,116.25	Charitable goods/ West Lothian Council	D Miles-Hanschell	W Knight Watson & Co Ltd/ SeaFreight Agencies	4,870	3,300.75	Unknown	Good
Christian African Relief Trust School, Ghana, West Africa	24/02/2009	MAEU 7412692/ 40ft/ 1,116.25	Assorted school furniture & equipment/ West Lothian Council	D Miles-Hanschell/ SESF	Container & contents gifted to charity	3,865	1,116.25	n/a	Good
Grenada Boys Secondary School, Grenada, West Indies	26/10/2009	MAEU 608565/ 40ft/ 528.7	Assorted school furniture & equipment	D Miles-Hanschell	Warrant Group Ltd	3,800	2,117.96	CMA/ CGM/ Sea Freight	Good

Shipping Details

Recipient	Delivery Date	Container Ref/ Size/Cost to Funder (£)	Cargo/ Source	Funder Consignor	Shipping Service	Tonnage (kg)	Total Cost (£)	Carrier	Consignee feedback
Bluefields Costa Caribena, Nicaragua, Central America	31/10/2009	Carrier-owned container	Children's library books/ Morningside Library Edinburgh	D Miles-Hanschell/ SESF	Warrant Group Ltd	500	225.00	CMA/ CGM	Good
Samaritan Presbyterian School, Grenada, West Indies	12/10/2011	TRIU 507942/ 40ft/ 1,116.25	Classroom contents/ Dunshalt Village Primary, Fife	D Miles-Hanschell/ SESF	W Knight Watson & Co Ltd	7,500	2,526.25	CMA/ CGM	N/A*
Research Project, Ministry of Finance, Republic of Liberia, West Africa	22/11/2012	AMZU 839348-5/ 40ft/ 2,580.00	Used school resources/ Inverclyde Council	D Miles-Hanschell/ SESF & donors	Allseas Global Logistics	15,870	5,280.00	Maersk	Fair
National Education Trust, Jamaica, West Indies	08/12/2014	ZCSU 830811-3/ 40ft/ 2,530.00	Used school books; used school furniture/ Inverclyde Council	D Miles-Hanschell/ SESF	Uni Express Ltd	16,580	3,578.73	Hapag-Lloyd	Fair
Woburn Methodist School, Grenada, West Indies	31/04/2016	TGHU 72302-5/ 40ft/ 2,340	Used school furniture/ Inverclyde Council	D Miles-Hanschell/ SESF/ Woburn School Committee	The Geest Line	5,840	2,940	The Geest Line	Excellent
Solidarite Ecole, Dame Marie, Republic of Haiti, West Indies	03/04/2017	TCRU 8229551/40ft/ 1,000.00	Used school furniture/ West Lothian Council	D Miles-Hanschell	Horizon International Cargo/ Crowley Inc	6,390	2,923	Hapag-Lloyd/ Crowley Inc	Poor

*I was informed later that my SESF container was seized on delivery, and the contents were sold at an auction.

APPENDIX

*Inveralmond Community High School Livingstone, 2009.
Clerk of Works and Shipping Clerk. " Your pro bono support and encouragement meant a lot.*

Charity Work in Detail

When I heard about the destruction of the Island of Grenada in the West Indies as a result of Hurricane Ivan on 7 September 2004, and later Hurricane Emily, I shared this news with my Primary 4/5 class at North Bute Primary School, Port Bannatyne, Isle of Bute as we were doing a project on the weather. They were eager to help and they began a small enterprise holding a bring-and-buy sale to raise money. With this they bought new books and primary school curricular materials. Their entrepreneurial spirit encouraged the rest of the school to follow their example and become involved. This activity also resulted in each pupil of the school filling A4 wallets with stationery, which resulted in five large cardboard boxes being air-freighted out to Grand Roy Government School, Grand Roy, Parish of St John, Grenada, West Indies on 16 June 2005.

However, I myself felt compelled to do something practical that would contribute to the relief and reconstruction of that devastated island's schools, since 90% of Grenada's schools were damaged, many beyond repair.

In Scotland the school closures (as a result of the falling birth rate and national government investment in new-build schemes), and the almost continuous – wasteful in my view – renewing of educational resources, by no means out of date, gave me the idea of recycling these surplus educational resources (textbooks, classroom furniture, IT equipment) wherever possible. This would extend the classroom usefulness of these resources, and perhaps might also help to re-equip and aid the recovery of Grenada's school system, and other schools in the developing world. I firmly believed that here was an opportunity where I could contribute to the reconstruction of at least one Grenadian school.

Over the next five years it was to become five schools in Grenada and eight, possibly more, schools by the time the SESF,

APPENDIX

Top: Classroom in Woburn Methodist School, St George, Grenada, West Indies 2016.
Bottom: Paynesville Community School, Monrovia, Republic of Liberia, West Africa 2012. 'To have, and to have not.'

myself, and corporate pro bono support made the most recent shipment in April 2017: Grand Roy Government School, 2005; Calliste Government School, 2007; St Paul's Government School, 2008; The Grenada Boys' Secondary School, 2009; Samaritan Presbyterian Primary School, 2011; Woburn Methodist School, Grenada, West Indies, March 2016; G-D's Glory Free Pentecostal Mission School, City of Faith, Paynesville, Republic of Liberia, November 2013; National Education Trust, Ministry of Education, Kingston, Jamaica, West Indies, November 2014; Solidarite Ecole, Dame Marie, South West Region, Republic of Haiti, West Indies, April 2017.

In 2004, Sterling Yacht Services Ltd, the Boatyard, Port Bannatyne, Isle of Bute, offered me space to store resources and in 2006 provided a crane to place a 40-foot container in position, which I had purchased on 24 April 2006, and to lift the container for inspection (all free of charge) until they bought my 20-foot storage reefer (see www.haitirelief.org.uk).

On 12 July 2006, I visited Grenada and had the opportunity to visit Grand Roy Government School at the invitation of the then Grenadian Government's Minister of Education and Human Development, the Honourable Claris Charles.

I established contact with the 32 Scottish Local Education Authorities as further sources of supply – six of which provided me with educational resources surplus to their requirements: Argyll and Bute Council (2005, 2014), Fife Council (2006–2008), Midlothian Council (2007), West Lothian Council (2008), West Dunbartonshire Council (2010), and Edinburgh City Council (2010).

On 2 December 2006, Fife Warehousing Company Ltd, Kirkcaldy, helped me to transport and store part of the donation of resources from two schools in Fife. John MacKirdy Haulage, Rothesay, collected pallet-loads of library books from Stirling District Libraries and boxes from Edinburgh Morningside library, and then in February 2011 over 450 boxes of books (adult and children's non-fiction and fiction) from the local library here in

APPENDIX

Volunteers from the Book Store, mark two, Units 8 and 10, Oak Mall Shopping Centre Greenock.
Volunteers were critical in the collection, inventory and boxing, paletting, shrink wrapping and loading of container shipments of educational resources for schools in the Republic of Liberia in 2012, Jamaica in 2014, and Grenada in 2016.

Rothesay, Isle of Bute. These firms gave their assistance without charge.

On 19 January 2007, my third ocean freight container of surplus educational resources from Fife's Department of Education, which I financed, left on its journey to Calliste Government School, Calliste, St George's, Grenada, W.I.

I became a member of The Edinburgh Chamber of Commerce on 11 June 2007, where I thought I might obtain commercial advice and make contact with business people who might have provided my project with assistance.

On 4 July 2007, I attended and successfully completed my first Speed Networking Marathon at The Hub, organised by the Edinburgh Chamber of Commerce, where I met and interacted with over 23 businesspeople, in particular, the marketing manager of Lofthus Signs Ltd and the general manager of Bishop's Move. Both of these firms subsequently were able to grant my charity pro bono assistance: in the first instance, preparing a large logo for one of my containers and for the signage done for the charity's move to Unit 12, West Shore Business Centre, Long Craig Rigg, Granton in March 2010, which I vacated in May 2017 after preparing a 40-foot container shipment to the Republic of Haiti. Bishop's Move assisted my charity with the loading of one of its 40-foot ocean freight containers with secondary school classroom furniture salvaged from St Andrew's High School Clydebank in July 2008.

I received media coverage (Grenada Broadcasting Network) for this social entrepreneurial project in Grenada when I visited the island for a second time in July 2007, and from the Scottish Press: *The Buteman*, *The Herald*, and *The Fife Free Press*.

I established contact with and visited St Paul's Government School in 2007, known as The Model School, in the parish of St George, Grenada, W.I. They received a 40-foot ocean freight container of educational resources which was awaiting shipment from Sterling Yacht Services Ltd's boatyard at Port Bannatyne and was

Appendix

The Book Store, Oakmall Shopping Centre, Greenock, Unit 8, January 2013. The Book Store had moved up more than a notch or two.

The Book Store became a regular hangout where all comers were made welcome and were crucial in its successful operation.

to be shipped from Grange Dock, Port of Grangemouth. Forth Ports waived all handling charges to Kingston, Jamaica and on to St George's, Grenada, in August and later three more. More 40-foot containers of educational resources in 2007, 2008, 2009, 2013, 2014 and 2017 were at my own expense. Peel Ports, Ocean Terminal, Greenock and Forth Ports, Grangemouth, provided pro bono assistance, and Malcolm Logistics, Linwood Container Terminal waived handling charges, along with Ioannis Kottoros of Noble Global Logistics (UK) Ltd and John Sas, HiCargo Ltd, Manchester, freight forwarders, doing all necessary paperwork pro bono. Thanks to them, acknowledging the input from these firms, which was crucial to the success of The Surplus Educational Supplies Foundation.

I made contact with one business in Grenada – Geo. F. Huggins & Co. (G'DA) Ltd – who contributed in part to the cost of the transport of the above shipment. Many companies have given their generous support to the work of this initiative. In particular see the article 'Call For Surplus School Supplies To be Donated' by Simon Bain, *The Herald,* Monday, 13 July 2009.

On 6 September 2007 the 40-foot container of educational resources was delivered to St Paul's Government School, St Paul's, Grenada, W.I.

The Surplus Educational Supplies Foundation was incorporated under the Companies Act 1985 as a private limited company No. 337348 on 6 February 2008.

On 23 February 2008 my charitable initiative, the Surplus Educational Supplies Foundation, received official charitable status from The Scottish Charity's Regulator and was entered on the Scottish Charity Register with the charity number SCO39331 and was dissolved in 2015.

A 40-foot container of educational resources was delivered to the Grenada Boys Secondary School (GBSS) on 16 September 2008. I financed this shipment from my own funds.

On 7 November 2009, one pallet (1 cubic metre, 1,000 kg,

APPENDIX

40 boxes) of educational books was delivered to the Oficina de Enlaces de la Costa Caribena, Centro Civico Camilo, Ortega, Managua, Ministerio de Educacion de Nicaragua, Meso America. I financed this shipment from my own funds, but the pro bono assistance of John G. Russell Transport Ltd, whose firm collected the boxes of books from the Elizafield Industrial Estate in Edinburgh and brought them to their transport depot in the container base, Coatbridge, prior to shipment was crucial.

A 40-foot container of educational resources was delivered to GBSS on 25 November 2009. I financed this shipment from my own funds.

On 1 April 2010 the Surplus Educational Supplies Foundation became the tenant of Unit 12, West Shore Business Centre, Long Craig Rigg, Granton, Edinburgh. It was leased from Waterfront Edinburgh Ltd, rent free, until 31 March 2017.

The Surplus Educational Supplies Foundation made arrangements with West Dunbartonshire Council, on 3 July 2010, to load one of the charity's 40-foot ocean freight containers with surplus primary school educational resources from Golden Hill Primary School, Goldenhill, Hardgate, Clydebank. Some of the resources collected that day were subsequently shipped to a school in Ghana, West Africa. This salvage could not have been accomplished without the pro bono and goodwill assistance of InterServe Projects Ltd, Birmingham and Galt Transport Ltd, Dumbarton.

On 13 September 2010 my charitable company was able to access the assistance of a team of five individuals from the Community Services Criminal Justice Department at the Muirhouse Social Work Centre, to work in Unit 12, the charity's industrial storage unit in Edinburgh. Over the previous three years the Surplus Educational Supplies Foundation also received vital help with the uplift and loading of containers from Community Services teams from their units in Glenrothes, Dunoon, Barrhead and Edinburgh. The leader of this charitable company worked alongside these teams in the loading of the containers whenever possible and sought the cooperation of these young people and explained why the assistance they gave was essential in achieving the charity's objectives. And again in the months of December 2016–April 2017 Payback Community Order Schemes teams helped load a shipment for the Republic of Haiti.

Around 11 May 2011 offers of large quantities of textbooks came in from the English, Science and Social Sciences departments of The Greenock Academy, The Gourock High School, Notre Dame High School and Port Glasgow High School (Inverclyde Council Education Department). Corporate support came from: Riverside Inverclyde Properties Ltd, ClydePort, Ocean Terminal (Peel Ports) Container Base; James Walker, Devol Engineering Ltd; National Semi Conductor (Texas Instruments); Morrison's Superstores, Greenock, and The Volunteer Centre, Inverclyde. They made the acceptance of this amazing offer educational resources possible.

On 19 November 2011 we delivered a 40-foot ocean freight container of educational resources, uplifted from four Scottish Primary schools, to the Samaritan Presbyterian Primary School Union, St Mark, Grenada, West Indies and donated US$1,000 to the school from the sale of that container for the purchase of new curricular materials.

We set up and ran a charity bookstore, 'THE BOOK STORE', Unit 8/ Unit 10 in The Oak Mall Shopping Centre, Hamilton Way, Greenock, from April 2012 to March 2014 and was loaned the use of two storage units (11 and 13) during that period, where books and educational resources were received from Inverclyde Council primary and secondary schools, and what was James Watt College. These were inventoried and boxed by teams of school leavers, who were provided with instruction, advice, and the minimum rate of pay, prior to the resources being loaded into three 40-foot ocean freight containers at Clydeport and which were subsequently shipped to schools in The Republic of Liberia, Jamaica, W.I. and Grenada, W.I.

APPENDIX

Pro Bono Assistance

The following is a list of those companies 2004–2017, that granted pro bono assistance with the logistics of delivering educational resources from Scotland to Grenada, Ghana, Nicaragua, and Tanzania:

Sterling Yacht Services Ltd, Port Bannatyne, Isle of Bute. Martin and John Stirling.

All of the individuals associated with this company made it possible for my charitable initiative to begin in 2004 and function successfully through their encouragement and practical support.

J&J Denholm Ltd, 18 Woodside Crescent, Glasgow. Jane Harris, Group Commercial Director. www.denholm-group.co.uk

Denholm Forwarding Ltd, Enterprise House, 168–170 Upminster Road, Essex.

This firm enabled my initiative to ship its first container of educational resources to Grenada, West Indies in 2005.

Freightliner Ltd, Container Base, Gartsherrie Road, Coatbridge. Fraser Russell, Account Manager, Kate Wall and team. www.freightliner.co.uk

Right from the beginning of my initiative this road and rail freight company provided vital advice and practical support for the successful operation of my social enterprise.

Fife Warehousing Co. Ltd, Frances Industrial Park, Wemyss Road, Dysart, Kirkcaldy. Brian Munro, Operations Manager and team. www.fifegroup.com

This firm were crucial in the removal and storage of educational resources prior to shipment from 2006.

Pro Bono Assistance

ZIM Integrated Shipping Services (Liverpool) Ltd, Suite 249, India Buildings, Water Street, Liverpool. Stephen Hopkins and team. www.zim.com

This firm continued to offer advice and practical help in the shipment of ocean freight containers by my charitable enterprise.

SeaFreight Agencies Lines, 2800NW 105th Avenue, Miami, Florida, USA. Mr Roland Malins-Smith CEO and team. www.seafreightagencies.com

Without the generous pro bono support from this firm, and the advice and encouragement from the chief executive, the delivery of five 40-foot ocean freight containers of educational resources to hurricane devastated schools from 2007 to 2017 would not have happened.

Duncan Adams Transport Ltd, Grange Dock, Grangemouth, Falkirk. Mr Duncan Adams, family and team.

This firm continued to play a vital role in the continuing success of my charitable initiative.

WH Malcolm Transport Ltd, The Malcolm Group, Brookfield House, 2 Burnbrae Drive, Linwood, Paisley. Mr Andrew Malcolm and team. www.malcolmgroup.co.uk

John G. Russell (Transport) Ltd, Container Base, Gartsherrie Road, Coatbridge. www.johngrussell.co.uk

The support from this firm was crucial in the storage and transport of educational resources.

Forth Ports PLC, Carron House, Central Dock Road, Grangemouth. Charles Hammond, Wilson Murray and team. www.forthports.co.uk/ports

Appendix

Clydeport Ocean Terminal Greenock, Container surveyor and Clydeport Operative complete inspection of an SESF container,
Colin Todd, Surveyor of ICS Intermodal Container Surveyors Ltd, gave of his expertise, encouragement and advice pro bono, to ensure that SESF containers were in shipworthy condition.

Pro Bono Assistance

Warrant Group Ltd, Warrant House, 157 Regent Road, Kirkdale, Liverpool. Patrick Kilfoyle and team. www.warrant-group.com

This freight forwarding company made it possible for my initiative to deliver, in 2009, 40 boxes of new library books to schools in the city of Bluefields, Costa Caribena, Nicaragua.

J&A Steel & Son Ltd, Steel House, 59 Lockfield Avenue, Enfield. Ian Steel. www.jasteelandson.co.uk

This company made it possible for my charitable enterprise to collect and store a large quantity of fit-for-purpose library shelving from the former Jubilee Gardens Library in Southall in 2008.

Willmot Dixon Construction Ltd, Willmot Dixon House, Park Street, Hitchin, Herts. Philip Turley and team.

This firm made it possible for the founder of SESF to purchase a 40-foot ISO ocean freight container and collect the entire shelving from the former Jubilee Gardens Library, Southall, Ealing Borough Council in 2008.

Galt Transport Ltd, Broad Meadow Industrial Estate, Dumbarton. Mr Allan Galt and team. www.galttransport.co.uk

This transport firm provided essential pro bono logistics support, enabling my initiative to move containers to different locations at short notice all over Scotland.

Carson Lifting & Transport Solutions Ltd, 5 Deerdykes Road, Westfield Industrial Estate, Cumbernauld, Glasgow. Mr John Morrison and team www.carsontransport.co.uk

This firm provided essential storage and logistics support to my company, as and when required.

Water Front Edinburgh Ltd, Madelvic House, Granton, Edinburgh. Nina McElroy, Estates Manager and team.

This firm made it possible for my social enterprise to acquire

Appendix

the use of an industrial unit for storage purposes. This assistance was crucial to the success of the Surplus Educational Supplies Foundation.

Clydeport Ltd, 16 Robertson Street, Glasgow; Greenock Ocean Terminal, Patrick Street, Greenock. Mr Andrew Hemphill and team. http://www.clydeport.co.uk

This firm continued to offer essential pro bono support by storing containers and educational resources temporarily prior to shipment.

Riverside Inverclyde (Property) Holdings Ltd, Suite G1, Clyde View, 22 Pottery Street, Greenock. Mr Bill Nicol, Chief Executive and team www.riversideinverclyde.com

This firm gave my initiative essential pro bono assistance by granting the Surplus Educational Supplies Foundation a temporary licence to occupy Unit 29 of the Lynedoch Industrial Estate, Dellingburn Road, Greenock.

James Walker Devol Engineering Ltd, 13 Clarence Street, Greenock. Mr Jerry Cannon, Shona Guthrie and teams.

This firm, at short notice, provided my enterprise with significant donations of packaging materials, which made it possible for the SESF to accept large donations of textbooks from Gourock High School and Greenock Academy.

National Semi Conductor (UK) Ltd, Earnhill Road, Larkfield Industrial Estate, Greenock. Jennifer Blackwood, Colin MacDonald and teams.

This firm offered essential storage of educational resources donated by Inverclyde Council secondary schools.

Greenock Telegraph, 2 Crawfurd Street, Greenock. David Goodwin Senior Reporter. www.greenocktelegraph.co.uk

This newspaper provided its readers with vital news about the current work of the Surplus Educational Supplies Foundation.

Inverclyde Council, Property Assets & Facilities Management, Cathcart House, 6 Cathcart Square. Mr Andrew M Gerrard and team

'We could not provide dedicated premises, however, we can probably find some space within a facility we use to store surplus resources.' This offer of pro bono support was crucial, as it made it possible for my initiative to collect and store, for a short time, educational resources from the Inverclyde Council's education system.

Morrison's Greenock, Rue End Street, management and staff.

This firm were very helpful to the work of my charitable enterprise by providing large quantities of packaging materials.

Administrative Help

The following companies assisted the Surplus Educational Supplies Foundation with administration, accounting, marketing, publicity, training advice, and practical help.

Burness Solicitors, 120 Bothwell Street, Glasgow. Stephen Phillips, his partner, and his team enabled the Surplus Educational Supplies Foundation initiative to become a credible legal entity.

One 2 One Accountancy Services, 10 Gallowgate, Rothesay. Lesley Paul and her efficient and helpful team recovered the VAT on all of the ocean freight containers that were purchased by SESF.

Ross & Company, Chartered Accountants, Windsor Buildings, 66 John Street, Dunoon. Mr Jim Ross and team were crucial from 2008–2016 in providing pro bono the accounts for SESF.

APPENDIX

Social Enterprise Academy, Thorn House, 5 Rose Street, Edinburgh. Neil McLean, Chief Executive.

Community Services Criminal Justice Department, Dunoon, Glenrothes, Edinburgh. Katherine McNiven, Dunoon Office.

Lofthus Signs Ltd, 14 New Mart Road, Corn Exchange. Gillian Anderson, Marketing, Business Development, Manager.

The Herald, Bearford House, 39 Hanover Street, Edinburgh. Business Editor, Mr Simon Bain.

The Buteman, 5 Victoria Street, Rothesay. Editor, Mr Craig Borland.

Fife Herald, George Inn, Pend, Crossgates, Cupar, Fife.

James Walker Devol Engineering Ltd, 13 Clarence Street, Greenock, Mr Gerry Cannon, factory, Ms Shona Guthrie, public relations.

ClydePort, Ocean Terminal Container Base, Patrick Street, Greenock. Mr Andrew Hemphill Chief Executive.

Just Grenada, Mr Gerry Copsey, The Barns, Woodlands End, Mells, Frome, Somerset.

Press Articles

Tanya Scoon, article, 'Surplus to help pupils in Grenada affected by hurricane', *The Fife Free Press, 1 December 2006.*

Leanna Maclarty, article, 'Hands – and a Few Container Loads –Across the Ocean: David Hanschell's plan to ship educational resources to Grenada could be the ultimate school recycling scheme', *Herald Society Education News Supplement*, 5 June 2007.

Liz Rougvie, article, 'Dunshalt Desks Grenada Bound', *Fife Herald*, 2 November 2007

Simon Bain, article, 'Call For Surplus School Supplies To be Donated', *The Herald*, 13 July 2009.

Liz Rougvie, article, 'Old School Equipment Bound For The Caribbean', *Fife Today*, 23 December 2009.

Paul John Coulter, article, 'School Books saved for kids in Africa', *Greenock Telegraph*, 11 August 2011.

APPENDIX